WHOLE-FACULTY STUDY GROUPS

2nd Edition

WHOLE-FACULTY STUDY GROUPS

Creating Student-Based Professional Development

2nd Edition

Carlene U. Murphy

Dale W. Lick

CORWIN PRESS, INC.
A Sage Publications Company
Thousand Oaks, California

T 50119

For information:

Corwin Press, Inc.
A Sage Publications Company
2455 Teller Road
Thousand Oaks, California 91320
E-mail: order@corwinpress.com

Sage Publications Ltd.
6 Bonhill Street
London EC2A 4PU
United Kingdom

Sage Publications India Pvt. Ltd.
M-32 Market
Greater Kailash I
New Delhi 110 048 India

Printed in the United States of America

Library of Congress Cataloging-in-Publication Data

Murphy, Carlene U.
 Whole-faculty study groups: Creating student-based professional development /
by Carlene U. Murphy and Dale W. Lick — 2nd ed.
  p. cm.
 ISBN 0-7619-7754-6 (cloth: acid-free paper) — ISBN 0-7619-7755-4 (pbk.:
acid-free paper)
  1. Teacher work groups—United States. 2. Teachers—In-service training—
United States. 3. School improvement programs—United States. 4. Academic
achievement—United States. I. Lick, Dale W. II. Title.
 LB1731 .M866 2000
 370′ .71′55—dc21   00-011783

This book is printed on acid-free paper.

01 02 03 04 05 06 07 7 6 5 4 3 2

Acquiring Editor:	Faye Zucker
Corwin Editorial Assistant:	Julia Parnell
Production Editor:	Diane S. Foster
Editorial Assistant:	Cindy Bear
Typesetter/Designer:	Lynn Miyata
Indexer:	Molly Hall
Cover Designer:	Michelle Lee

Contents

Tables and Figures

Foreword to the First Edition

Imagine a school that has committed itself to high levels of learning for all its students. The school has declared that it will educate all its students to meet national standards in the core academic areas. And the school recognizes that the knowledge and skills of its teachers will be its most important resource in meeting this lofty goal. Put another way, high levels of learning and performance on the part of all teachers will be the key to high levels of all learning and performance for all students.

The challenges faced by such a school are immense. As Carlene Murphy and Dale Lick point out in their preface to *Whole-Faculty Study Groups: A Powerful Way to Change Schools and Enhance Learning,* "like other organizations, schools are not naturally open or amenable to major change." What processes will perturb the status quo, create sustained commitment to innovative practices, and provide a means for learning that will enable teachers to plan the change effort and alter their day-to-day instructional practices?

Although no single professional learning process can measure up to that challenge, whole-faculty study groups are an essential element in the mix of strategies that can lead schools to high levels of learning for all students and staff members. Such groups involve the entire faculty in sustained, rigorous study of the innovations they will implement and in working through the problems that inevitably accompany such innovation.

The use of whole-faculty study groups is, the authors point out, "a holistic practical process of facilitating major schoolwide change and for enhancing student learning in the schools." These groups make it possible for teachers "to explicate, invent, and evaluate practices that have the potential to meet the needs of their students and the community their schools serve," Murphy and Lick write. "As teachers work together in these study group approaches, they alter their practices to provide new and innovative opportunities for their students to learn in challenging and productive new ways."

Consider the power of whole-faculty study groups in improving student learning. The faculty begins by committing itself to extended study by an overwhelming vote in favor of the study group process. The faculty gathers and analyzes data to determine the focus of its efforts. The teachers form groups that will meet weekly for about an hour to discuss research, consider alternatives for actions, and acquire instructional skills. Because everyone is involved in the study, the faculty develops a common vocabulary and strategies to address the student learning goals it has identified. Because of the meetings, barriers that isolate teachers are removed, and norms of collaboration, experimentation, and risk taking are nurtured. Whole-faculty study groups teach their participants through example that professional learning must be an ongoing, focused process if it is to affect student learning.

In such a school, the principal is a skillful leader who is a "keeper of the dream" and a holder of high expectations for students and staff. This person values continuous improvement and models this behavior by participating in a study group. Surrounding the school is an infrastructure of district support in the form of resources and visible district leadership and pressure in the form of high expectations and accountability for high levels of learning for all students.

If school reform efforts are to succeed, individuals who occupy various roles in the educational enterprise must be knowledgeable about the benefits and processes of whole-school study groups. Leading the list would be teachers, principals, and district leaders, such as superintendents, directors of staff development, and curriculum specialists. Education professors and consultants who work for educational agencies would also benefit from a deeper understanding of this process.

Carlene Murphy and Dale Lick bring a unique combination of experiences to this book. Murphy has distinguished herself as a national staff development leader and a consultant to numerous schools. She is familiar with both the practical day-to-day realities of school change and the theory and research that support those efforts, a special combination that makes this book a rare blend of theory and practice. Lick brings a background in organization development and leadership that rounds out the knowledge and skills required to transform schools and school systems. Together they have written a book filled with practical advice for those most closely involved with educational reform.

It is difficult to imagine a school seriously committed to high levels of learning for all students and staff members that does not use some form of whole-faculty study. *Whole-Faculty Study Groups* provides the theory, strategies, and examples that schools need to begin such a journey.

—DENNIS SPARKS
Executive Director,
National Staff Development Council

Foreword to the First Edition

This book is about a simple but powerful idea: people working in small groups to improve their professional performance. It's not a new idea; social psychologists have recognized the power of small groups for decades. But most organizations, especially schools, have not made effective use of that power.

We have committees, of course. Every educational institution at every level has them—with varying results. Teachers know that what appears to be a sensible device for getting things done can be fruitless and frustrating instead. And even when committees function well, their perspective is outward, not inward. Their focus is the task, not the growth of participants themselves.

The small-group process explained in this book is different. Members of whole-faculty study groups are concerned with what they themselves do and what they might do differently. If they find an idea appealing, they must decide how it applies to them and what they should do about it.

That can be threatening, but it can also be exhilarating. What could be more relevant to any professional than his or her own performance? And what responsible person wouldn't like to hear new ideas and learn new methods, if they can be freely discussed and evaluated?

The problem for many teachers is that they are already overwhelmed by the demands of their jobs, so they are unlikely to want to attend more meetings, no matter how apt. An eager few may voluntarily form study groups on their own. Most will need encouragement.

The authors understand this and offer sound advice on how to set up study groups that teachers will enjoy and support. They are supremely well-qualified to do so. Dale Lick, who has been president of three respected universities, is a scholar of organizational change, a researcher, and a consultant. Here, he teams with Carlene Murphy, who originated and managed an extensive program of faculty study groups when she was Director of Staff Development for the Richmond County, Georgia, Public Schools.

In recent years, Murphy has consulted with schools in numerous other districts, including Cobb County, Georgia, where principals report dramatic changes. Teachers, they say, are less likely to avoid important issues with small talk and more often discuss educational matters. One principal says teachers consider study groups the most important aspect of their school. "They'd do without me before they'd give up study groups," she jokes.

Teachers elsewhere may not be quite that enthusiastic, but many will find study groups satisfying because they are a refreshing antidote to the professional isolation that characterizes most schools. Observers bemoan the fact that teachers spend their days engaged with students and seldom interact with other adults. The study group format changes that, putting teachers in regular communication with a handful of colleagues. Researchers say this "professional community" is at the heart of successful school reform. Karen Seashore Louis and her coauthors Kruse and Marks (1996) write, "By collaborating on common objectives, sharing developmental activities and concerns, and reflecting together on the technical aspects of their teaching, teachers come to own in common the consequences of their joint work for students' intellectual progress" (p. 180).

A skeptic might ask why, if study groups are beneficial, so few schools have them. Part of the answer may be that recognizing the value of something is only the first step. To make it work, you need to know how. That is the contribution of this book. The authors provide detailed, practical advice that will help educators avoid missteps that could lead to misunderstandings and rejection. How large should the groups be? How often should they meet? Who decides what they will talk about? How can administrators keep informed and be responsive? What if most teachers are willing but a few are not? The authors answer these and other questions based on successful experience in schools large and small, urban and rural, elementary and secondary.

Educators seeking school improvement—especially principals and superintendents but also teachers, central office staff members, and others—will welcome this book because it outlines a process by which promising reforms can become realities. Whole-school study groups have value in themselves, contributing to faculty solidarity and a climate of professionalism. Beyond that, they are a vehicle for implementing the many other changes that must be made if schools are to meet the challenges of a new century.

—RON BRANDT
Former Assistant Executive Director of
the Association of Supervision and Curriculum Development
and Editor of the journal *Educational Leadership,* now retired.

Foreword to the Second Edition

The first edition of *Whole-Faculty Study Groups: A Powerful Way to Change Schools and Enhance Learning* is the basic text that ATLAS Communities uses to guide school teams PreK-12 in their implementation of whole-faculty study groups (WFSGs). ATLAS Communities, a nationwide network of schools dedicated to improving student learning, is a systemic school reform model requiring changes in beliefs, behaviors, and relationships within and among all stakeholders in the educational process. In ATLAS schools, teachers are challenged to develop professionally so that the work of teaching is theirs to own and shape. We have found that WFSGs are the cornerstone of professional development in a redesigned school and a powerful way to transform a school culture in the service of successful learning experiences for all students.

Gone are the days when professional development consisted solely of one-time workshops taught by outside experts. A crucial piece of the overall reform effort, WFSGs are one of the key launching activities for all ATLAS communities and help lay the foundation for successful whole-school transformation. WFSGs connect most directly with change in classroom practice by engaging the entire staff in the improvement process. The very existence of these groups assumes that the assets found in every classroom will be identified and shared as teachers regularly meet to learn from each other.

WFSGs in ATLAS schools keep their eyes on the prize—improving student achievement—by using student work as the basis for everything they do. Guided by the decision-making cycle (described in Chapter 6), faculty in ATLAS schools analyze data about their students' achievement to identify the content of their groups' study. In their weekly meetings, study group members look at student work as a means to reflect on their own practice so that they can begin to make the kinds of changes that will strengthen and deepen their teaching. Last, WFSGs in ATLAS schools chart their progress by once again looking at student work for evidence that will help answer the essential question, *What are students learning and achieving as a result of what teachers are learning and doing in study groups?*

Members of ATLAS communities are finding that, in addition to encouraging teachers' reflection on and strengthening of their classroom practice, WFSGs are having positive, dynamic effects on students. In the Strawberry Mansion cluster in Philadelphia, the Rhodes Middle School has used the rationale and strategies described in this book to establish student study groups focused on improving academic and social skills. Organized and supported by the Student Study Group Support Team, under the guidance of school faculty with the commitment of the cluster office, students are grouped in cooperative learning settings for the purpose of problem solving and strengthening critical thinking skills. Multidisciplinary projects, understanding and using rubrics, preparing for exhibitions (performances of understanding), and conflict resolution are examples of topics around which students are collaborating. An emphasis on student leadership is considered essential to the success of these groups, and leadership training for students is an important part of the process. Students become active participants in their own learning and hold their teachers accountable for maintaining a student-centered classroom that honors student voices.

ATLAS Communities challenges the conventional wisdom of education in that it envisions a PreK-12 pathway (feeder pattern) rather than isolated schools. Elementary, middle, and high school teachers work together to provide a coherent education program for each student. In this concept, WFSGs have been a key catalyst in creating the opportunity for teachers talking across grade levels and content areas to connect innovative, memorable learning experiences to state and local standards. In Everett, Washington, the pathway consists of an elementary, middle, high school, and alternative high school. Pathway study groups meet once every 3 weeks. With the commitment of building principals and support of the district office, schedules and union contracts were modified over $1\frac{1}{2}$ years so that everyone in the pathway had release time on the same day of the week. Each group had 4 to 6 teachers and at a minimum, two different levels (i.e., middle-high, or elementary-high) and some have all levels represented. Examples of the content of these groups include looking at how writing is taught across all grade levels, aligning the math and science curriculum with the Washington State standards, preparing students K-12 to publicly present and defend scholarly papers, understanding transitions and placement of students as they move from middle to high school, and developing integrated curriculum across grade and content areas around discipline-specific throughlines. Test scores have risen in reading, writing, and math across all the pathway schools; in some cases, scores have doubled over a 3-year period. Teachers report that these study groups are the most powerful professional development experiences in which they have participated.

We in ATLAS Communities know that the heart of teaching and learning rests with those close to the task, the teachers and students; the authority of those people is crucial. We value the authentic—teaching and assessment that is rooted in real intellectual activity. Real work engages the learner; the challenge for teachers is to place before students authentic ideas and situations that provoke in them further serious thought and, over time, the habit of such inquiry. The chances of this happening increase exponentially when teachers are given the time and space to engage in rigorous discourse about their practice and strengthen the professional behaviors that will result in more substantive student learning. In addition, ongoing support from the school principal, district office, and school board is a critical part of the equation for staff development that is collaborative and includes opportunities for practice and feedback. This second edition is a *must read* for all these audiences.

In this second edition, Carlene Murphy and Dale Lick have used their own strategies to integrate the implementation lessons learned from ATLAS and other reform models. What we can be sure of is that as more teachers join study groups, additional examples of practice will continue to clarify, reshape, and refine our collective work. In this book, you will find the best of the collective wisdom and practical strategies that will help thousands more teachers raise their levels of professionalism and refine their craft. Happily, the work continues.

—LINDA GERSTLE
Executive Director, ATLAS Communities

Preface

Whole-Faculty Study Groups: Creating Student-Based Professional Development is a new edition of our earlier one titled *Whole-Faculty Study Groups: A Powerful Way to Change Schools and Enhance Learning.* Although the two books are similar, many important modifications and significant additions have been included in this new edition.

The WFSG process has spread to school systems across the country, and the implementation and work of study groups has now become a daily occurrence in many schools. Because such work is continuous in these schools, the process and its refinement are constantly evolving. What one study group does has the potential for affecting others, not only in that school but also in other schools that use the WFSG process.

In addition, as Murphy travels from school to school around the country in her consulting role and Lick continues to research the theoretical basis for study groups, new ideas are generated that help to strengthen the WFSG process. These changes accumulate over time and lead to major adjustments that make the process even more effective.

In the 3 years since the first edition was written, over 100 schools have implemented the WFSG process. This number of schools translates into at least 1,500 individual study groups. From these and continuing groups, new insights into the WFSG approach have created a wealth of new material.

If the study group model were a "paper and pencil" design, it might stay in a fixed or rigid state. Because the model evolves from how teachers actually work together in schools, it is fluid, flowing, and readjusting itself. As leaders in schools chronicle the movement of study groups, we examine why some are high-performing groups and others struggle. What we learn is shared with continuing schools and those that are considering or just beginning the process. This new edition of our book is how we keep schools up to date with our findings on what is working best.

The major developments and insights we have found during the past 3 years are dealt with in greater depth in this new edition and include the following:

- The key sponsorship role of the principal

- The requirement that study groups must grapple with more substantive content

- How administrators can provide additional technical assistance to study groups

- The various developmental stages of study groups and how to deal with them

- Why institutionalization is critical for the sustainability of the study process

- Additional examples and illustrations of successful WFSG schools

- A detailed discussion of why the WFSG process, when properly applied, is so successful and helps move schools toward becoming learning organizations

Need and Purpose

Staff development, school reform, and the improvement of schools are not as simple as the general and educational rhetoric of the past decade would imply. Well-intentioned societal leaders and school personnel have talked about the necessity to change and improve, and schools and their personnel have attempted a wide variety of what appeared to be logical and progressive solutions. Unfortunately, most of these have failed or, at best, been only partially successful. This failure or limited success happened because change, even positively perceived change, is difficult to bring about in long-standing, well-established organizations. Like other organizations, schools are not naturally open or amenable to major change.

To successfully reform, improve, and transition schools to meet tomorrow's needs will require approaches and processes that are different than most attempted during the past decade. We must not only decide what changes or reforms are required, but we must also put in place meaningful staff development and significant transition processes to help negotiate the societal, organizational, cultural, and people barriers in and affecting schools.

One of the most successful and exciting new approaches to staff development, reform, and change in education today is that involving professional WFSGs. One of the two key elements in these efforts and unique to this book is "whole faculty" involvement, not just study groups but WFSGs, where all the faculty are committed to the effort, actively involved in it, and responsible for an important part of the total effort. Where WFSGs have been properly implemented, they have been unusually successful. The WFSG approach is a holistic, practical process for facilitating major staff development and schoolwide change and for enhancing student learning in the schools. This book presents a detailed discussion of WFSGs, their application, and the underlying change principles necessary for such study groups to be successful in the school environment.

The second key element is that WFSGs are a *student-based* approach to professional development, and they rest on this question: What do students need for us, the teachers, to do? Using this focus radically changes the tone and dynamics of professional development for teachers and brings it right to the heart of the matter.

Based on our work in leading and managing major change and our experiences in over 200 schools and 2,000 WFSGs in those schools, this book provides both the (a) *practical knowledge* required to implement and successfully use the WFSG approach in schools and (b) *theoretical foundation* to understand the key change elements involved and how these can be applied to facilitate staff development and schoolwide change, and enhance student learning. Furthermore, the book contains a generous collection of relevant and illustrative examples of real-world situations and a detailed, step-by-step practical methodology for the development of successful professional WFSGs in schools.

In particular, this book grew out of a wide array of real-world whole-faculty study group efforts and experiences, it encompasses the existing relevant literature on study groups, and it significantly expends this knowledge base through (a) new up-to-date information and refinements of processes, procedures, and approaches; (b) new experiences and applications from user schools across the country; and (c) the unique integration and use of practical and theoretical change knowledge concepts and change management approaches.

Who Should Read and Use This Book?

This book should be read and used by anyone who is interested in facilitating important staff development and change in schools and increasing student learning. A primary audience for the book should be the personnel in K-12 schools—all teachers, administrators, and staff.

For schools that choose to introduce the WFSG approach, all school personnel will be involved in their schoolwide effort. Consequently, in such schools, each faculty, administration, and staff member should have a copy, or many copies should be shared generously for school personnel, allowing full and convenient access across the school.

In addition, the book holds special potential for individual teachers and administrators and groups of teachers and administrators who are considering new options for seriously improving their schools.

Other important audiences for this book include

- Central office personnel in school systems, especially for consideration and possible implementation of study groups in their school system

- College of Education faculty in colleges and universities, for understanding this new and successful process for schoolwide change and enhanced student learning, as well as for possible use as a textbook or reference book in classes relating to teacher training and school enhancement

- Community college faculty and administrators for consideration of study groups and their application in their institutions for collegewide change and improving student learning

- School, community college, college, and university libraries

- Individuals and groups in national and international workshops on study groups and their application in education, from small seminars to large groups

- Individuals and groups in corporate, community, and governmental organizations involved with schools, education, and training

Knowledge Base of the Authors

Both authors have spent successful careers in education as teachers and administrators. The first author has an extensive background as a teacher and staff development director. During her 17 years as the administrator of a large school district's comprehensive staff development programs, the WFSG process was implemented in 10 of the district's schools. In 1993, she began working at the national level with faculties who wanted to initiate the WFSG process in their schools. She is past president of the National Staff Development Council; regarded as the national leader in the WFSG movement; recipient of several related state and national awards; creator of the Whole-Faculty Study Group Collaborative, a national organization for those interested in areas relating to WFSGs; and the most prominent national researcher, practitioner, and author on WFSGs (e.g., see typical publication examples in the bibliography). During her role as a private consultant who has narrowed her focus to schools implementing the WFSG process, her work has taken her to schools in urban, suburban, and rural areas; elementary, middle, high, and vocational schools; and, schools with as few as 10 teachers and as many as 250 teachers. Her association with ATLAS Communities, one of the seven design teams funded by the New American Schools Cooperation, has put her in the center of the nation's major national reform initiatives. The WFSG process, as it exists today, was developed by her and its name coined by her.

The second author has been a faculty member and educational administrator for 40 years, including faculty and administrative appointments at nine colleges and universities, with three college and university presidencies. Included in 40 national and international biographical listings, he is the author of four books; over 50 book chapters, professional articles, and proceedings; and 285 original newspaper articles. Over the years, his work and responsibilities have been directly and indirectly related to teacher preparation, school operation, and school improvement. More recently, he has been a researcher on the statewide school enhancement initiative "Florida Schoolyear 2000," served as a school consultant, and offered national and international educational workshops. In addition, he presently teaches and does research on educational and transformational leadership, leading and managing organizational change, new learning systems, and learning organizations, especially as related to education and schools. He is also formally trained and certified in Change Management (i.e., in the three certification areas: Change Knowledge, Trainer, and Consultant) and may be the only person in the country so certified to be working in the school improvement area and with WFSGs.

Organization and Contents

The book is organized so that its chapter contents logically build on each other, with each laying a foundation for those that follow. The contents include the key elements in the WFSG and change processes and their implementation along with a large number of real-world examples and illustrative cases. The book is written so that it can serve as a textbook, a detailed reference book, or a stand-alone guide for the effective initiation, comprehensive implementation, and successful completion of the WFSG approach to staff development and major improvements in schools.

Chapter 1 discusses the school reform environment and the potential of the WFSG approach, serving as a major change process to improve schools and student learning and enhance schools as learning organizations. Also, the history of the Whole-Faculty Study Group Model is recapped, including the initial players and programs, the national movement, the association with Atlas Communities, and the collaboration of the book's authors. Furthermore, this chapter summarizes fundamental faculty-student-school-teaching-research-support relationships and approaches and provides a helpful, reflective review of the key lessons learned.

The concept and nature of study groups, their strengths and perceived weaknesses, their purposes, and their ability to serve as vehicles for staff development and change and the creation of collaborative work cultures are described in Chapter 2. The principal functions of the WFSG approach are outlined and discussed, encompassing effective faculty development and the progressive transition of schools and their processes, such as curricular and instructional innovations, coherence of instructional practices and programs, identification of schoolwide needs, research on teaching and learning, and assessment of the impact of innovations on students and the workplace.

Chapter 3 sets the framework for the three components of the WFSG approach: context, process, and content. The four critical stages that study groups pass through—forming, grumbling, willingness, and consequence—are depicted.

Chapter 4 addresses the context for schools (i.e., the organization, the system, and the culture) in which study groups must function. Especially key among the context-related topics discussed are roles and responsibilities of school personnel, school district influence, and the change concepts of building commitment, developing effective leadership and sponsorship, dealing with human change and resistance, using the roles of change, understanding assimilation capacity, and modifying school-related cultures, as well as applying the important, overarching universal change principle.

The process for the WFSG approach, unfolded in Chapter 5, allows educators to acquire and develop the knowledge and skills necessary to increase student performance and improve schools. Toward these ends, 15 study group process guidelines are discussed, procedures are established for the creation of communication networks and strategies, and 23 study group "work time models" are provided.

The heart of the study group process, the content, detailed in Chapter 6, is what teachers study, what teachers investigate, and what teachers do to become more skillful in the classroom with students. This chapter discusses staff development content; academic knowledge, instructional strategies, instructional skills, management, and belief systems; and the central decision-making cycle involving data collection and analysis, student needs, prioritization of needs, organization around student needs, plan of action, implementation, and evaluation.

Chapter 7 discusses the difficult process of institutionalization of the study group process into the school and school system. In particular, it explains and illustrates how to maintain and continuously improve the innovative programs, materials, and behaviors of study groups and how to transform the culture to sustain them.

Effective study groups are effective teams. Teamwork is what differentiates an effective study group from a typical committee or other work group. Chapter 8 describes how to use the study group process to build effective teams and teamwork in schools. Discussed in this chapter are synergy and comentoring and the key elements of synergistic team building, including synergistic comentoring relationships, prerequisites of synergy, the synergy creation process, and a synergy checklist for diagnosing and correcting teamwork problems. The chapter also concludes with an analysis of why the study group process, when properly implemented, is so successful and a discussion of the 10 major success factors.

Chapter 9, the final chapter, highlights impressive results of the study group process in a representative sample of actual schools. These illustrations include a diverse mix of three elementary, two middle, and two high schools. The chapter closes with a discussion of how the study group process has the potential to help schools move toward becoming more like learning organizations.

In addition, the appendices contain important and helpful nuts-and-bolts information for the effective application of the WFSG approach, including examples of study group action plans, a set of study group logs, and artifacts from WFSG schools.

It is hoped that the material in this book will inspire you and help you understand and use WFSGs in your work to develop especially meaningful staff development, create more effective schools, and generate learning environments that significantly enhance student learning for the new century.

Acknowledgments

We acknowledge Joe Murphy for making all of the travel doable for Carlene, and her family for all they have done to accommodate the almost weekly trips she has made to WFSG schools over the past 4 years. To Carlene's grandchildren, a special word of thanks to Sarah and Joshua for helping with the copying and collating of the original manuscript and to Allison for staying out of the way. We recognize Angela Watkins at Kinko's in Augusta for doing the figures and forms in this book.

We acknowledge Marilyn Lick for her patience, understanding, and continuous support and encouragement of Dale and his work on the book.

We acknowledge all the faculties that have implemented and sustained Murphy's Whole-Faculty Study Groups for Student-Based Professional Development since 1987. We continue to marvel at the richness of learning at the original sites in Augusta, Georgia, with Bruce Joyce and Beverly Showers as our teachers. The sites that followed the Augusta schools taught us many lessons that greatly influenced and shaped the current work. These schools were in Americus, Decatur, Marietta, and Sandersville, Georgia; San Diego, California; Danville and Versailles, Kentucky; Lyons, Kansas; Round Rock, Texas; Greeley, Colorado; St. Charles Parish, Louisiana; and Maplewood, Minnesota.

We acknowledge ATLAS Communities, a national comprehensive school reform design, and the 91 public schools in 16 school districts that are currently implementing the design. We also acknowledge the founders of ATLAS Communities, Ted Sizer, Howard Gardner, James Comer, and Janet Whitla. We recognize the huge contribution the faculties of the ATLAS schools have made to the knowledge base of WFSGs since the relationship between Carlene Murphy and ATLAS was forged in Spring of 1997 when ATLAS included WFSGs as the cornerstone of its professional development component. We applaud the over 5,000 teachers in at least 850 study groups who have done stellar work and have exemplified the meaning of professionalism, student-based decision making, risk taking, perseverance, and unselfish giving. The faculties have given their energy, time, expertise, and heart in abundance. We especially acknowledge the professionals that support the schools at the ATLAS sites, the site developers, who have supported all of the study groups, taken the major role in assisting the work of study groups, and cared deeply about the work of the study groups. They have not only elevated the work of individual study groups but have elevated the thinking about all aspects of WFSGs. The courage of the individuals named in the following list gives us great hope for all the schools they touch and for all the schools that will learn from their example.

ATLAS Communities
55 Chapel Street
Newton, MA 02458-1060
1-800-225-4276

Linda Gerstle, Executive Director
Ron Walker, Associate Director

Core ATLAS Staff:
Brenda Artwell, Site Developer
Daniel Baron, Site Developer
Marcia Baynes, Site Developer
Penni Brooks, Site Developer
Tamela Brown, Site Developer
Karl Clauset, Site Developer
Stephanie Feger, Web Facilitator
Janet Hayakawa, Site Developer
Tricia Louis, Project Administrator
Kimberly Lucas, Site Developer
Patty Maxfield, Site Developer
Doris Perry, Site Director
Ron Rapp, Site Developer
Reggie Silberberg, Senior Administrative Assistant
Evangeline Stefanakis, Site Developer
Pat Turner, Site Developer
Jo Viviani, Site Developer
Sandra Wellens, Chief Operating Officer

And the faculties at ATLAS Communities' schools in
Au Sable, New York
Broward County, Florida
Cambridge, Massachusetts
Chicago, Illinois
Detroit, Michigan
Everett, Washington
Hamilton County, Florida
Highline, Washington
Memphis, Tennesee
New York City, New York
Philadelphia, Pennsylvania

Saint Paul, Minnesota
Seattle, Washington
Shoreline, Washington
Webster County, Georgia
Woodinville, Washington
Wyandanch, New York

About the Authors

Carlene U. Murphy began her 42nd consecutive year of work in public schools in September 2000. She was an elementary teacher for 15 years, coordinator of programs for the gifted for 5 years, and director of staff development for 15 years. From 1993 to the present, she has worked at the national level in public schools.

From 1957 to 1971, she taught fourth grade in Memphis, Tennessee. At the beginning of the 1971-1972 school year, she returned to her hometown, Augusta, Georgia, where she continued to teach until the spring of 1973, when she was appointed the coordinator of programs for the gifted for the 60-school district. At the time, the district did not have any formal programs for its gifted students. She was responsible for developing such programs for Grades 1 through 12. During that period of time, she started an organization for parents of gifted children and initiated organizational structures and curricula that continue today.

In 1977, new policies at the state level required school districts in Georgia to have a person designated as director of staff development, and Murphy was so named in the Richmond County (Augusta), Georgia, public school district. She often laughingly says that she became one when she didn't know what one was. These early years were learning years for her because staff development was not considered a field in education, and it was difficult to find information about effective staff development programs. In 1980, Carlene and her husband, Joe, attended their first of many annual conferences of the National Staff Development Council, when no more than 150 people were in attendance and the organization had less than 500 members. She likes to give these statistics as part of her story because today, with conference attendance over 4,000 and association membership approaching 10,000, the statistics put the field of staff development in perspective. She considers those early years of struggling with how to plan and deliver staff development services as the background for her current work. Without the struggle, the searching, the risk taking, and the experimenting, Murphy does not believe that she would have had the courage to embrace the work of Bruce Joyce and Beverly Showers in 1986. She states that her 3-year working relationship with Joyce and Showers in the Augusta schools was the greatest learning experience in her professional career, giving meaning to all her prior knowledge and experience.

The 15 years (1978-1993) as the Richmond County (Augusta, Georgia) School District's Director of Staff Development brought many accolades to the district and to Murphy. In 1991, Richmond County received the American Association of School Administrators' Award for Outstanding Achievement in Professional Development. The district also received Georgia's Outstanding Staff Development Program Award for two consecutive years. In 1992, she was awarded the National Staff Development Council's Contributions to Staff Development Award, one of the organization's highest honors. She was the first practitioner to receive that honor. Her personal service to the National Staff Development Council includes chairing the annual national conference in Atlanta in 1986 and serving as president in 1988 and on the Board of Trustees from 1984 to 1990.

After retiring from the Richmond County Schools in 1993, she worked through 1997 as a private consultant for the schools and districts that wanted to implement the WFSG process. This process, as it exists today, was not only developed by her, the name itself was coined by her. The work described in the book *Whole-Faculty Study Groups: A Powerful Way to Change Schools and Enhance Learning* and in this book began in the Richmond County, Georgia, School District in 1987 and continues today. She has written extensively about her work in *Educational Leadership* and *Journal of Staff Development*. A number of articles in these two widely read professional journals chart her work over the past 13 years with as many as 200 schools and well over 2,000 study groups.

Summer 1997, Murphy began her work with ATLAS Communities. She is a staff development specialist for ATLAS Communities and works with all ATLAS schools in the implementation of WFSGs. She also continues to work with schools that want to implement WFSGs that are not associated with any of the national school reform designs.

Dale W. Lick, is past president of Georgia Southern University, University of Maine, and Florida State University and presently University Professor and Associate Director of Learning Systems Institute at Florida State University. He teaches in the Department of Educational Leadership and works on educational and organizational projects involving transformational leadership, change creation (leading and managing change), learning organizations, distance and distributed learning, new learning systems, strategic planning, and visioning.

A mathematician by academic training, Lick previously held administrative and faculty positions at Port Huron Junior College, University of Tennessee, Drexel University, Russell Sage College, and Old Dominion University. He also served as a visiting research mathematician at Brookhaven National Laboratory, an adjunct professor of biomathematics at Temple University, and a scientific consultant to the United States Atomic Energy Commission.

Included in 40 national and international biographical listings, Lick is the author of over 50 professional books, articles, and proceedings and 285 original newspaper columns. His recent books are *Whole-Faculty Study Groups: A Powerful Way to Change Schools and Enhance Learning* (with Carlene Murphy) and *New Directions in Mentoring: Creating a Culture of Synergy* (coeditor with Carol Mullen). Other recent publications are "Mega-Level Strategic Planning: Beyond Conventional Wisdom" and "Change Creation: The Rest of the Planning Story" (both with Kaufman), two chapters in the book *Technology-Driven Planning: Principles to Practice;* and "Whole-Faculty Study Groups: Facilitating Mentoring for School-Wide Change," *Theory Into Practice,* Winter 2000.

Lick received both bachelor's and master's degrees from Michigan State University and a PhD degree from the University of California, Riverside. Furthermore, he holds all three levels of formal training and certification for Leading and Managing Organizational Change: Change Knowledge, Instructor/Trainer, and Consultation Skills, from the international change research and development organization, ODR, Inc., Atlanta, Georgia. He has completed formal programs on "The Seven Habits of Highly Effective People" (Stephen Covey) and "Learning Organizations" (Peter Senge).

For

Carlene and Joe's grandchildren

Allison Louise Wilson

Sarah Zemulaw Wilson

Joshua Gordon Brown

and

Dale and Marilyn's grandchildren

Ronald Wesley Lick, Jr.

Parker Addison Lick

Introduction 1

The past several years have helped us see more clearly than ever before that staff development, school reform, and the improvement of schools are complicated and challenging undertakings. As we discussed in the Preface, change, even positively perceived change, is difficult to bring about in long-standing, well-established organizations. Our schools are clearly among such organizations, and their cultures, the ones that have given us so much success and stability in the past, are deeply ensconced and rigid. Like all other such organizations, they are not naturally open or amenable to major change. Can we bring about meaningful reform and major change in our schools? The answer is "absolutely yes," and many such changes will be essential in the future! However, to do so will require approaches and processes that are different from most of those attempted during the past decade. We must not only decide what change or reform is required, but we must also put in place a significant transition process to help us negotiate the societal, organizational, cultural, and people barriers in and affecting the schools.

Major change in our schools, as is true in other types of organizations, requires active and effective sponsorship—support, encouragement, pressure, and accountability—from the leadership (e.g., boards, superintendents, principals, and directors). With strong sponsorship at each level in the school, teachers and other school personnel feel a greater sense of empowerment and, as a consequence, are more comfortable with change and more willing to seriously attempt new major projects and processes.

If genuine reform is to come from within our schools, then teachers and school personnel must be importantly and intimately involved. In particular, teachers must be perceived, treated, and held accountable as educational professionals. To treat them as such requires that teachers enjoy the latitude to invent local solutions and to discover and develop practices that embody central values and principles rather than to implement, adopt, or demonstrate practices thought to be universally effective (Little, 1993). One of the most exciting new approaches to staff development, reform, and change in education is Murphy's whole-faculty study groups (WFSGs) for student-based professional development. This approach to professional development has all teachers on a faculty actively involved in study groups addressing student needs. As we mentioned in the Preface, WFSGs are student based, and their foundation is the question, What do our students need us to do so that they can most effectively learn what they need to know? A properly implemented model encompasses the change characteristics discussed earlier as well as several others, including collaboration and synergy; comentoring; individual, team, and organizational resilience; elements of learning organizations; and culture modification.

WFSGs allow teachers the freedom and flexibility to explicate, invent, and evaluate practices that have the potential to meet the needs of their students and the community their schools serve. As teachers work together in study groups, they alter their practices to provide new and innovative opportunities for their students to learn in challenging and productive new ways.

Effective WFSGs are a complex mixture of many activities happening simultaneously. This model is a holistic, practical process for facilitating major schoolwide change and for enhancing learning outcomes in the schools. In particular, Murphy's WFSGs for student-based professional development in schools and for educators includes the following:

- Giving teachers in schools a structure for collaboration and school improvement

- Planning and learning together, testing ideas, and sharing and reflecting together

- Providing support for each other

- Reflecting on classroom practice

- Grappling with what broad principles of teaching and learning look like in practice

- Engaging in the pursuit of genuine questions, problems, and curiosities over a period of time and in ways that leave marks on perspectives, policies, and practices

- Constructing subject matter knowledge versus merely consuming it

- Immersing in sustained work with ideas, materials, and colleagues

- Experiencing the frustrations of dealing with "what is" while envisioning "what could be"

- Functioning not only as consumers of research but also as critics and producers of research

- Contributing to knowledge and practice

- Struggling with the fundamental questions of what teachers and students must learn and know

WFSGs: When and Where It All Began

In December 1986, Carlene Murphy, Joseph Murphy, Bruce Joyce, and Beverly Showers had their first conversation about how to increase student achievement through staff development in the Richmond County School District in Augusta, Georgia. Carlene Murphy was Director of Staff Development in the public school district, which comprised 60 schools, and Joseph Murphy was Dean of the School of Education at Augusta State University. Bruce Joyce and Beverly Showers, authors of a then newly published book titled *Increasing Student Achievement Through Staff Development,* were and still are nationally and internationally known scholars in the fields of staff development and models of teaching. This conversation led to a 3-year working relationship and an intense focus on

- The culture of the school and the process of innovation

- Ways teachers learn new teaching strategies

- Ways teachers transfer new skills into the classroom

One of the first decisions the foursome made was that their work would involve whole schools. They would not offer a staff development program at the district level where teachers from different schools would volunteer to enroll. The program, instead, would be offered to whole faculties, and every teacher in those schools would participate in all phases of the program. The program was voluntary for the school, but if at least 80% of the teachers voted to support the program, all teachers would be expected to participate. This understanding, whole-faculty participation, became in later years the central feature of what is today called the WFSG approach.

After the whole-school staff development program was described to Richmond County's school principals, Superintendent John Strelec invited principals to describe the program to their faculties and poll their teachers for the required 80% agreement to participate. Over a period of 5 years, 12 schools were a part of the whole-school improvement program. The content of the improvement program was several models of teaching (Joyce & Weil, 1999) or approaches to teaching designed to bring about particular kinds of learning and help students become more effective learners. The models selected were also models of learning that help students acquire information, ideas, skills, ways of thinking, and means of expressing themselves. The whole-school improvement effort was called the Models of Teaching (MOT) Program, which put the emphasis on the content or on what the teachers would be learning to do.

The skill development phase of Richmond County's program was two-pronged. One prong had the teachers attending training sessions in which they learned the theory that supported models they were learning, and they had many opportunities to see demonstrations and practice strategies with other teachers in a risk-free environment. In Summer 1987, the faculties of one middle school and two elementary schools met together for 2 weeks with Joyce and Showers to receive training in four models of teaching. During the school year, Joyce and Showers returned to the district six times and worked with each faculty in its school, continuing the training and demonstrating appropriate use of strategies.

The other prong of developing skill in using the models of teaching focused on redesigning the workplace. When school began in August 1987, every teacher at the participating schools was a member of a small group no larger than 6 that met weekly to design lessons together and practice teaching the lessons in the small groups. The teachers focused on classroom use of the four models of teaching that had been and continued to be the content of an ongoing training program. Study group members visited each other's classrooms and made videotapes of their teaching. By the end of the first year of implementation, all teachers in the three schools had reached the mechanical and routine levels of use (Hord, Rutherford, Huling-Austin, & Hall, 1987) of the teaching strategies. Student results over a period of time showed an increase in achievement and a decrease in disruptive behavior. (Joyce, Murphy, Showers, & Murphy, 1989; Murphy, 1991b, 1992, and 1995).

Because the name of the program, Models of Teaching, put focus on the content of the work, the study group structure put in place at schools was often overlooked by district and school leaders as being a critical component of the improvement process. Murphy states that it wasn't until Spring of the first year the program was implemented that she fully realized the impact study groups were having on the culture of the schools. She goes on to say that it was evident by mid-year, on walking into schools, that the schools were different. Teachers were talking to each other about instruction and saying "our students" instead of "my students." In random teacher interviews that Joyce and Showers were doing, teachers reported higher levels of satisfaction with the school, more respect for their colleagues, and better feelings about themselves as teachers. Even with all these indicators of a cultural shift, Murphy attributed the changes to teaching strategies that teachers were using in their classrooms. Murphy admits that her lack of experience in restructuring the workplace and in working with study groups caused her to initially miss the power of the weekly meetings. Because Joyce and Showers expected Murphy to keep a written record of her observations, impressions, and reflections, she came to understand that it was the study group process that was causing teachers to use strategies to the level that students benefited. One evening in Spring 1988, she was writing in her journal and reflecting over the work when "the light came on" and she yelled out loud "It's those study groups!" Without the work that occurred in study groups, the level of use of the models of teaching would not have been at the impact level, and cultural norms would not have shifted from teacher isolation to teacher collaboration. Even though Joyce and Showers had been very clear as to what the study group structure was intended to do, it took Murphy experiencing the process with the teachers for her to fully understand the power of the study groups. In the doing of the work, you cannot separate the content (MOT) from the process (study groups). If the program had not had powerful content, it would not have mattered what processes were used. It took a powerful process to push high levels of use of the models of teaching, otherwise models would not have been used in classrooms at the level that resulted in student benefits.

From 1987 to 1993, seven articles were published in professional journals and chapters in two books were written about the work in Richmond County. These publications are listed in the references and recommended reading list.

Going National With WFSGs

In January 1993, Carlene Murphy retired from the Richmond County Public Schools and began working with schools at the national level. Because Murphy's expertise was in staff development strategies or processes, she restricted her work to staff development systems. The models of teaching, the content of the work in Richmond County, were not her area of expertise. That expertise had come from Bruce Joyce and Beverly Showers. Because Murphy did not offer academic content or instructional strategies as part of her work with schools, she designed a process through which each school would identify its own staff development content. The procedure required a faculty to identify academic needs of its students and specify the content that would enable teachers to address the identified student needs. Murphy recognized that in most districts there were support personnel who had expertise in the different academic areas, such as reading, writing, mathematics, and science. University personnel, textbook representatives, and private consultants also provide services to schools in curriculum content and in effective teaching practices. After working with schools for several years and trying various procedures for identifying what study groups could do and how study groups could be organized, Murphy designed the decision-making cycle (DMC) described in Chapter 6.

In 1994, Murphy began a 3-year working relationship with San Diego (California) City Schools. Their work was challenging because it served as the bridge between how the work had been designed in Richmond County and how the work would have to be designed in places where the content of study groups was not predetermined. At the same time that Murphy's work was evolving in San Diego, it was also being shaped in schools in Americus, Marietta, Decatur, and Sandersville, Georgia; in Round Rock, Texas; in Greeley, Colorado; in Versailles and Danville, Kentucky; in Arbutus, Maryland; in Oakdale, Minnesota, and in Lyons, Kansas. The procedural guidelines given in Chapter 6 evolved from the work in all of these places. From 1993 through 1996, Murphy's work was constantly being adjusted to be more responsive to the context of different schools in different places.

It wasn't until 1994 that Murphy settled on calling the work she was doing "whole-faculty study groups." This title emerged as a result of the types of requests she was receiving. When school and district leaders began contacting Murphy about working with their school or district, it became apparent that callers and Murphy had different visions for study groups. The callers would tell Murphy that they wanted her help in forming study groups. Murphy would then ask, "A whole faculty?" Most often, the answer was "No. Any teacher who wants to be in a study group." Murphy's response was "My work is with whole schools, not setting up independent, stand-alone study groups." Over time, Murphy found it necessary to call her work "whole-faculty study groups" to distinguish it from other types of collegial arrangements. The first time this term appeared in a publication was in the Summer 1995 issue of *Journal of Staff Development*. The name of the article was "Whole-Faculty Study Groups: Doing the Seemingly Undoable."

The WFSG approach is not the same as the work that began in Augusta in 1986. Elements have been added to the original design and others deleted. Even so, the heart of the work resides in the genius of Bruce Joyce and Beverly Showers and the work that was done in Augusta. Since leaving the Augusta project in 1990, Joyce and Showers have not been involved with Murphy in her WFSG work. The full title given to the work as it is described in this book is Murphy's Whole-Faculty Study Groups for Student-Based Professional Development.

ATLAS Communities

In 1997, Murphy became associated with ATLAS Communities, one of the national comprehensive school reform designs. Starting with Murphy's involvement, the WFSG concept became the centerpiece of professional development in all ATLAS Communities' schools. The Murphy-ATLAS relationship greatly increased the number of schools implementing WFSGs and expanded its knowledge base. Through Spring 2000, 107 schools chose the ATLAS Communities design knowing that one nonnegotiable aspect of the design was that all faculty would be members of study groups. High schools, middle schools, and elementary schools in large urban areas, such as Memphis, Philadelphia, Seattle, and Detroit, are implementing WFSGs. High schools, middle schools, and elementary schools in small communities, such as Au

Sable, New York; Preston, Georgia; and Jasper, Florida, are finding that study groups in schools are making a difference in how teachers work together, and new practices are being used in the classrooms.

Authors' Collaboration

In Spring 1997, Dale Lick contacted Murphy after reading about the work in Augusta. Lick was intrigued with the idea that all faculty at a school were members of teams or small groups focusing on the goal of the organization, student achievement. Lick commented that the model was as close to a synergistic organizational development model as anything he had seen or heard in public schools. The two decided that Murphy's public school experience and Lick's organizational and change experience from his over 25 years of administrative work could be integrated. Lick would overlay his theoretical and practical knowledge of organizations and change and his experience in working with teams into Murphy's work. One major result of the Murphy and Lick collaboration was the book *Whole-Faculty Study Groups: A Powerful Way to Change Schools and Enhance Learning,* published in June 1998.

Lessons Learned

Since 1986, when the work began in Augusta, many lessons have been learned about the initiation, implementation, and institutionalization of WFSGs. Today, there is a national thrust for leaders of change to focus on whole-school change. More and more funding sources are requiring whole faculties to be involved in whatever is the improvement design. For those who are involved or considering a whole-school change model, Murphy's (1991b) article, "Lessons From a Journey Into Change," may be helpful. Four of the lessons in that article are as follows:

1. *Everyone at a school has to be involved.* Volunteerism most often supports individual development, not organization development. The whole school must focus on the goals of the school: that every student should have equal opportunities to learn in the best environment and under the best conditions. It is not an option for the whole school, meaning every teacher, to get better at meeting student needs: It is a must. The school has a choice of what design or model to use for whole-school improvement. Once the choice is made, everyone participates. It has not been Murphy's experience that a school can start with volunteers and have one or two or three or four study groups while teachers not in study group are sitting back and watching. In such a case, it is assumed that, over time, everyone will want to be in a study group. That assumption has not been validated. The distance between the "we" and the "them" just gets wider. The division grows. It is a cultural bomb. The nonvolunteers get more entrenched, even in the face of documented improvement in the classrooms of the teachers who are in study groups. It will actually be harder to get whole-school involvement when study group membership is at first optional. Once resisters are in a study group, there is a better than average chance that they will become committed. Left out, they will remain onlookers and, most likely, become saboteurs to the whole change effort.

2. *The principal is the most important factor to successful initiation, implementation, and continuation of WFSGs.* An example of a school (also see Chapter 10) that has had study groups in place for 5 years and continues to improve is a school whose principal, Barry Shelofsky, has been the leader every step of the way. He initiated the WFSG approach after attending a national institute where the model was presented. Shelofsky worked with a team of teachers from the school in designing an implementation plan and was key in getting 100% teacher agreement to begin. He shepherded, with a team of teachers, every step of the implementation plan. Shelofsky put on each year's calendar when the Instructional Council would meet. At midyear and at the end of each year, he and a team of teachers have planned appropriate celebrations. He and the team of teachers have integrated into the study group process major state and district curriculum initiatives. His school uses state test results as evidence that change is occurring. Shelofsky keeps the superintendent informed. He initiated a study group for principals and shares the action plan and logs from that study group with the teachers at his school. He has been doing this for 5 years and continues to do so at this writing. In a larger high school where this type of tending is not possible, principals often have publicly appointed an assistant principal to oversee the WFSG process and to do whatever is necessary and consistent with the implementation plan to maintain the process over time.

3. *Support and encouragement from district-level leaders are absolutely essential and play a key role in facilitating school change.* The superintendent and other top district leaders establish the climate that enables WFSGs or any whole-school change program to be successful. In every school, whether WFSGs have been successful or not successful over time has been directly attributable to the support and technical assistance provided by and through district leaders. Expectations for change must be clear and structural changes made to provide time for study groups to meet. The district usually determines what new district initiatives will be initiated and implemented each year that will affect every school in the district. The district also controls most budget considerations and determines what time schools begin and end each day and other scheduling concerns that affect the school year calendar. In most districts, schools are asked for input and can make requests and recommendations; however, the superintendent and board of education make final decisions about issues raised here. All of these issues affect what schools can do. Schools may have the resources to begin an initiative without district involvement, but it is unlikely that, over time, the school can maintain and continue the work without district involvement.

4. *Creating agreement to begin and maintaining commitment to continue are two different things that require two different approaches.* Initially, the leader is working for agreement from the faculty to just get started, to begin. The principal must verbally or through written materials describe the initiative with clarity and give examples of where the initiative has been successful. Schlechty (1993) states that in the beginning faculties may need the following:

- A concept development lesson: What is it?
- A demonstration lesson: Can it be done?
- A values clarification lesson: Should we do it?
- A skill development lesson: How do we do it?

In the beginning it is important that the principal takes responsibility for framing the work in such a way that the faculty is confident its principal knows what the change is and how it will affect them. With WFSGs, there is a clear, straightforward implementation plan. Chapters 5 and 6 tell initiators exactly what to do. WFSGs have a well-defined structure, a step-by-step implementation strategy. Giving examples of successful WFSG sites is one way to demonstrate that it can be done. It is during the early implementation stage, when teachers are in study groups, that they develop their own personal clarity as to the meaning of study groups. As the meaning becomes clearer, the commitment grows. We can't ask teachers to be committed to something in the beginning before they understand the meaning and implications of the change. We can only ask for their agreement to begin. With more knowledge and competency comes commitment. The better teachers start working in a small group, and the more they see positive changes in their classrooms, the more committed they become. To continue the WFSG approach over time takes an equal mixture of support and pressure that can enhance continuation or disrupt it. The initiation and first year of implementation is most often energizing. Continuing into the second and subsequent years is more difficult because as study groups are being continued, other initiatives are being introduced. These new curriculum and instructional initiatives often take attention and energy from the leaders who are also trying to provide support and pressure for the study groups. When WFSGs have been initiated, teachers are told that a study group is a vehicle for doing what teachers have to do. It is in the study groups that teachers work on the implementation of new curricular and instructional programs and materials. If principals and other school leaders don't use study groups as the place to work on new initiatives, such as standards, continuation becomes more and more difficult. Teachers will see that school and district leaders aren't using the study group structure for the declared purposes (see Chapter 2). Teachers will have been told one thing and will see that reality is another thing. Because that is a common perception among teachers, serious leaders are at a disadvantage. Teachers require continuous assurance that what they are learning to do, work together in small groups, is going to continue. Continuation takes great persistence. It takes constant tending. If the principal can't do it for whatever reason, then he or she should make sure that someone is publicly assigned that task. Some leaders are better at initiating and encouraging during the early stages of implementation. Those same leaders may find it difficult to keep providing support and pressure over time. With other principals, it is just the reverse. They have difficulty getting faculties to agree on an initiative, but once the decision is made, they are excellent at sustaining the initiative.

Summary: The Importance of History

The history of the WFSG approach is an important part of the work today in schools. It is important for those interested in doing what is described in the following chapters to know that the model has been through a long period of development. The evolution of procedures described in Chapters 5 and 6 are the result of the work of many faculties. The work in Augusta with Joyce and Showers is reflected in the functions of study groups described in Chapter 2 and in some of the procedural guidelines listed in Chapter 5. Stirred into the original Augusta mix is what Murphy has been learning and field-testing since 1993 when she began working at the national level.

Early in the Augusta work, Murphy met an internationally known leader in the field of educational change who was aware of the work in Augusta. That person said to Murphy that he would consider the Augusta work a success if the program were still in place in 5 years, which would have been the 1992-1993 school year. The political forces had begun to chip away at the program by the fifth year. When Murphy left the district in December 1992, it did not continue. Was the program then not successful? Did students benefit from the work from 1987 through 1992? The answer to the second question is a resounding yes. Are not the merits of any work measured in terms of effects of the program when it was in place? Again, the answer is yes. The hundreds of students that experienced increased academic success during the first, second, and third years, even if the fourth and fifth years did not happen, made the program a major success, especially for those students. One good year alone can make a program a success. In one year, students benefit. One special year is better than no such year.

No one can know what the future holds. There are no guarantees when any new work begins. Is that a reason for not beginning? No. We must have the will and skill to initiate and implement new programs, materials, and procedures that we believe, based on documented results, will benefit students and teachers and then sustain them as best as possible into the future.

2 Enabling Professional Development and Schoolwide Change

Organizing teachers into small groups or study groups to promote collegial interchange and action is not a new idea. Individuals have formed such study groups since at least Aristotle's time. The study group concept is an important approach to learning. Teachers who take courses or workshops together often form study groups. Across a school district, they may form a study group to dig deeper into new content areas. Or teachers may share a common interest or need, study for an exam together, discuss a book they have all read, research a problem, or pursue a project of common interest.

Although teachers working together in small groups or study groups is common, organizing the entire school faculty into study groups to bring about schoolwide improvement is unusual. *Whole-faculty study groups* is a term used when each faculty member at a given school is a member of a study group. In this context, a *study group* is a small number of individuals joining together to increase their capacities through new learning for the direct benefit of students. As the study group process grows in complexity, such groups may function in a way that enables members to actually implement new practices, change behaviors, and demonstrate new skills and knowledge in the classroom. These study groups develop not only a specific focus for their group but also an organizational focus for the school. In WFSG-approach schools, the faculty, through a consensus process, decides that the WFSG structure will enable every faculty member to collaboratively address student needs at the school and, therefore, each certificated staff member will be a member of a study group to support whole-school improvement. In these schools, study groups become part of a schoolwide design and are regular and legitimate entities of the school organization. The structure gives teachers the responsibility for designing their own professional development. The whole faculty has a voice in deciding if the WFSG structure becomes a part of a schoolwide design. However, no one tells a study group what to do. Each study group selects a student need the members want to address, and the members decide how they will go about addressing the need.

WFSGs: *Whole* Means *All*

By *whole faculty,* we mean all administrators, all classroom teachers, all resource teachers, all special area teachers, librarian, counselor, and anyone else holding pro-

10

fessional certification. Usually, administrators will form a study group of administrators within the school or will be in a study group with administrators across the district. Some of the schools that have teaching assistants will include the teaching assistants in the study groups with the professionally certificated personnel; however, most will have study groups with only teaching assistants in those study groups. In many schools, nonteaching personnel form study groups that focus on the role they have in supporting instruction. All study groups within the context of the WFSG approach follow the same procedural guidelines, meaning, for instance, that the groups have action plans and keep logs.

Making the school better for all students is a constant function of every study group in the school. It is the collective energy and synergy generated from the study groups that propel the school forward. In particular, a student does not excel as a middle school student because he or she had a great fourth-grade teacher. The more likely reason is because the student had outstanding learning opportunities as a kindergartener and first through fifth grader. Similarly, the middle school continues to excel because the student's teachers have an extensive repertoire and are masters of their content. The cumulative effect of good teaching over years of schooling produces a graduate that does well and can be expected to continue as a learner. When every teacher in a school is in a study group that targets effective teaching practices, an important range of schoolwide needs will be met. To focus on a schoolwide need, data and effectiveness of curricula must be examined from all grades. For example, the fourth grade is not singled out because it is the grade where the state tests are administered. If the standardized tests administered in the fourth grade indicate that reading comprehension is a problem, then that is a problem for all grades in the school.

In forming WFSGs, the faculty goes through a process of analyzing student and school data to identify student needs that study groups will address. When the needs are determined, groups form based on these needs. Each group then determines what its teachers will do when their group meets to address a specific student need. Often, this means examining what will enable teachers to effectively use new and refined instructional practices and materials in the classroom. Each group of teachers also decides how they will support each other and the use, at the impact level, of new practices and materials. As study groups implement new and more effective practices and materials, each classroom improves, resulting in improvement in the whole school.

The goal of WFSGs is to focus the entire school faculty on creating, implementing, and integrating effective teaching and learning practices into school programs that will result in an increase in student learning and a decrease in negative behaviors of students, as reflected in related, relevant data sources.

WFSGs bring individual needs and institutional needs together in an organizational setting. Teachers becomes more skillful, knowledgeable, and confident as their study groups progress and gain competence and as their students become more skillful, knowledgeable, and confident. The power in the WFSG process rests in the promise that teachers will become more knowledgeable and skillful at doing what will result in higher levels of student learning. Study groups that function simply to satisfy interests of group members often lack adequate content focus to boost the goal of the school. The primary goal of schools is to meet student needs; therefore, it is the collective energy and synergy from the study groups and the whole faculty that propels the effectiveness of the school forward.

To our knowledge, the documented effects of study groups on students and the learning environment are limited to situations involving WFSGs focusing on instruction. Schools that have successfully implemented the WFSG approach have many differences, such as those reflected in student age and level, location (e.g., rural vs. urban), the socioeconomic circumstances, and size. Even with the many demographic differences in schools, we have not seen that demographic factors make for significant differences in how the adults in the schools work together in study groups.

There is one factor that is constant in all WFSG schools: Faculties initially worry about the same things. They worry about when groups will meet. They worry about how groups will be organized. They worry about what groups will do. How they respond to these considerations is what makes each school different. It is not the size of the school, the grade levels in the school, or the types of students the school serves. The differences are reflected in the decisions that the faculty makes at each step on the DMC that is described in Chapter 7. The WFSG procedural guidelines are constant in all the schools that implement the model. The guidelines establish the structure. Within the framework of the guidelines, the teachers decide what study groups will do and how groups will be organized.

The whole-faculty study group process is not advised unless

- The whole faculty has an understanding of the process

- The whole faculty acknowledges that if at least 75% of their number endorses the process, that percentage obligates everyone

- The whole faculty participates in analyzing student data and identifying student needs that can be addressed through faculty study groups

WFSGs: The Guiding Question

There is one question that must be kept in front of the faculty at all times. There is one question that leaders ask over and over again. There is one question that should be on a large poster and placed where it can be seen at all times by the faculty. (One faculty taped such posters to the faculty restroom doors.) There is one question that sets WFSGs apart from other collegial arrangements. That one critical question is this: *What are students learning and achieving as a result of what teachers are learning and doing in study groups?*

WFSGs: The Guiding Principles

How we act and what we do is most often based on our principles. A principle is defined as a fundamental truth, a rule of conduct, integrity. Whole-Faculty Study Groups for Creating Student-Based Professional Development is based on five guiding principles:

- Students are first.
- Everyone participates.
- Leadership is shared.
- Responsibility is equal.
- The work is public.

The First Principle: Students Are First

Murphy's WFSG concept is an approach to staff development that does put the needs of students first. The theme "what do students need for us to do" runs throughout the book and throughout the WFSG process. Teachers in WFSG schools routinely examine student work collaboratively, listen to students, observe students in each others' classrooms, and pay attention to a wide variety of student data. The student voice is heard and is the factor that makes what teachers do in study groups authentic.

Major Strengths

The most obvious strength of WFSGs is the support and encouragement teachers give each other. The structure ensures that study group meetings become a routine for the school and for the individual teachers. With strong leadership from the principal (strong schoolwide sponsorship), study groups take on an additional sense of importance, and members are less likely to miss meetings of their study groups, especially if time is given for study groups to meet during the workday.

When professional study groups are part of a schoolwide design, the principal's support and pressure are positive forces for action and success. Pressure is typically perceived as a negative force or pain. However, change often occurs because some pressure or pain has built up to the point that it leads to action (Fullan & Steigelbauer, 1991).

The way the school is organized so that adults in the school can engage in serious and purposeful learning requires adjustments in scheduling activities. Providing time for study groups to meet weekly is a form of pressure. Allocating resources is a form of support. Fullan and Steigelbauer (1991) assert that it is increasingly clear that both pressure and support are necessary for successful change efforts that alter the fundamental ways an organization works. The WFSG approach fundamentally alters existing structures and roles. The principal, the primary and sustaining sponsor of school change, is the major source of the pressure and support that makes it possible for teachers to have the willingness and skill to establish and maintain collaborative work cultures. Study groups operating outside a schoolwide design seldom have the level of organizational sponsorship that connects teacher learning and student learning. In every school where WFSGs have become a routine feature of the workplace and where changes in teacher and student behaviors are evident, the principal, providing effective sponsorship, is the key factor.

A strength often overlooked in the study group approach is that all members are expected to be leaders and that the success of the study group is measured in terms of the collective energy, participation, and synergy of the whole group. Being a member of a study group becomes a norm of the workplace and its organizational culture; this helps the organization become a more effective learning organization—an organization continually enhancing its capacity to learn, create, and effectively act.

The question is not "Will you be a member of a study group?" Instead, the question is "Which study group will you join?" This understood and accepted attitude strengthens the norms of collegiality, collaboration (synergy), and continuous improvement.

Perceived Weaknesses

There is a perceived weakness in framing study groups within the context of the organization. The perception is that individuals have no choice and that the individual's interest or need is not considered or is secondary to the needs of the organization as a whole. However, this perception will be lessened if the decision-making cycle described in Chapter 6 is followed. A rationale for what individuals will do in study groups is established when all of the faculty participate in analyzing data, identifying and prioritizing student needs, and specifying what teachers will do to address those needs. Another perceived weakness is that individuals may be with other individuals that they do not know very well and with whom they feel they have little in common. However, once a study group gets started and becomes immersed in the content, individuals usually see their differences as a plus. Individuals soon discover that within the small groups, they are, in fact, in the driver's seat, making all decisions about how their group will function and what their group will do.

Getting Started

It is usually the principal who first receives information about WFSGs. The principal has the choice of whether or not to inform the school's faculty. If the principal chooses to inform the faculty and the faculty is receptive to the WFSG approach, the principal will use some mechanism to establish the level of agreement to begin. After faculty consideration and before voting on the implementation of WFSGs, it should be made very clear that if at least a given percentage, usually 75%, want to implement the model, that decision will obligate everyone.

If the vote indicates that WFSGs will meet the needs of the school, the principal identifies a team of teachers, called the *focus team* (Murphy, 1995), of which he or she will be a member, to learn and to decide exactly how to go about initiating and implementing WFSGs. There are several ways that this might be accomplished.

One approach is for the focus team to ask a consultant to work with them to help them

- ■ Understand the purpose and functions of WFSGs
- ■ Review the procedural guidelines that are discussed in Chapter 5
- ■ Experience the decision-making cycle described in Chapter 6
- ■ Develop a step-by-step plan for how the focus team will work with the whole faculty to implement the WFSG process

After the focus team leads the faculty through the DMC (decision-making cycle) and the study groups get started, the consultant should continue to support the faculty's implementation of the model in some form. This may be through visits to the school, meeting with representatives from each study group, responding to e-mail from the principal and faculty, or responding to action plans and logs by fax. The focus team continues to be cheerleaders for and supporters of the study group effort. At the end of the school year, the focus team reviews the DMC with the faculty to return the faculty to where it began. This prepares them for the beginning of the next school year.

The focus team usually has about 5 members, and, in most schools, there would not be a focus team member in every study group. Because focus team members choose what student need they would like to address, as do all teachers in the school, two focus team members could be in the same study group. Leadership in the study group is assumed by each member on a rotating basis, and all study group members are of equal status.

Another approach to initiating WFSGs would be to have one or more persons attend workshops at a regional or national level. Those attending would return to the school and help organize and report on the effort. Then, as discussed above, the school, too, would use the team approach to implementing the WFSG approach.

Still another approach to initiating and implementing the WFSG approach can be done after reading about how to implement the process, such as after reading this book. Whether implementation occurs as a result of reading this book or attending a workshop, it will take a major team effort to actually lead the whole faculty through the decision-making process and keep the process moving in the desired direction. A team composed of the principal and 4 or 5 teachers will need to carefully plan for every step of the DMC found in Chapter 6.

Roles and responsibilities of individuals and groups in the WFSG approach are defined and discussed in Chapter 4.

What WFSGs Are Not

Stand-Alones

An independent or stand-alone study group is one that does not depend on organizational support. It is a group of individuals that has a common interest and will consider itself a study group until, as individuals, they satisfy their need for the group. There are unlimited possibilities for professional study groups to function other than in an organizational setting. Study groups may form within or outside the context of a school or district. Study groups emerge as a result of individuals' interests or needs and are less structured. Independent or stand-alone study groups serve a very important role in the growth of individuals and should not be minimized.

The major strengths of an independent study group is that individuals are the initiators and no larger unit controls or directs the group. A group of teachers that decides that it has a common need and agrees to address that need may have more early successes than groups that are part of the WFSG design. Also, in study groups that are not part of a schoolwide design, individuals can choose who they want to include in the group. The options for study may be more varied because choices are generally not aligned with specific student needs. Meeting times are more flexible because the group is not tied to a school schedule. Teachers are often from different schools and may also be able to meet in the evenings or on weekends. Locations of meetings are more varied. Individuals frequently use their own resources and have wide latitude as to what they study and do.

A major weakness is that an independent study group is less likely to apply its study and results to the school or district setting. Other weaknesses of independent study groups include the following: They often do not keep to set routines, absenteeism is higher, intended results are less clear, motivation may be centered around "what the group can do for me," and a terminal point is more evident. Once the individuals satisfy personal needs, they usually stop attending study group meetings. Leadership often rests with the individual who brought the group together, and members tend to look to that person for making the arrangements and getting required materials. When a study group is initiated by an individual separate from an organization, there is usually less commitment to a larger body or greater purpose. In the long run, however, one cannot separate him- or herself from the workplace. The independent study group may function outside the school or district, but the effects of what is learned will most probably affect the organization in some way. We strongly encourage independent study groups to agree on a study group action plan and follow most of the guidelines in Chapter 5.

Committees

Study groups are vehicles for self-improvement for the benefit of the individual and the whole organization. It is not an appointed group with an assigned job or task. Committees have appointed or elected leaders who usually assume the major responsibility for the success of the committee. Study groups generally focus on professional development issues and not administrative issues. Committees are often larger than study groups, and an end point is assumed. Generally, committees come up with recommendations for someone else to implement. Study groups implement and try out the perceived solutions to a problem, collect information about the degrees of change, and share their information with the whole faculty.

A comparison highlighting the key characteristics of WFSGs, independent study groups, and committees is given in Table 2.1.

Traditional Meetings

Similar to the differences shown in Table 2.1 is the way study groups differ from the usual grade-level meetings in elementary schools, team meetings in middle schools, and department meetings in high schools. The following lists distinguish the differences.

Grade-level and departmental meetings generally

- Focus on managerial or logistical directives from the school, district, or state

- Have an agenda that is determined by directives from the school, district, or state

- Are leader driven by a grade chairperson or department chairperson

- Have a "talk to" format, meaning that the leader presents information and the participants primarily respond to topics generated by the leader

Study group meetings generally

- Are aimed at the professional development of the members

- Focus on "what I need to do and learn to change how I teach and what I teach"

- Have an action plan that is the group's agenda

- Are driven by member needs that are tied to student needs

- Rotate leaders, with the leader not being responsible for the content of the meeting or what the group will do

- Recognize all members as being equal in status and responsibility

Table 2.1 Comparison of WFSGs, Independent Study Groups, and Committees

	WFSGs	Independent or Stand-Alone Study Groups	Committees
Focus	Organizational	Individual (not part of a whole)	Administrative
Need	What's good for the whole school	What's good for me?	Predetermined purpose
Purpose	Classroom instructional improvement centered on needs of students	Individual's improvement centered on his or her interest or need	Centered on assigned task
Audience	All inclusive; whole faculty	Selective; based on choice of individual	Selective; based on others' appointment or assignment
Process or product	Ongoing	End point	End point
Size of group	3 to 6	3 or more	3 or more
Role of participant	Active	Active-passive	Passive-active
Expectations	Implementation of new instructional skills; changes in classroom behavior	Individual growth; increased personal knowledge	Recommendations made for others to implement
Leadership	Rotates among all members with shared responsibility for success	Tends to remain with person who initiates or volunteers	Leader appointed or elected who has primary responsibility for success

Vehicles for Change

We find that most major learning and behavioral-change projects attempted in the schools fail or are only partially successful. Why is this true? As we briefly discussed in Chapter 1, the simple answer is that major change efforts, especially those relating to the well-entrenched learning and behavioral processes, are extremely difficult to accomplish in the professional school culture that is rigidly tied to past education-related assumptions, beliefs, and behaviors, as we describe in Chapter 4. Study groups that function in ways we describe in the next section break rigid ties. Even under the best of circumstances, bringing about major change in the schools is hard and quite simply will require far more change management appreciation, understanding, and application than that used in the past.

On the other hand, the beauty of WFSGs is that the methods and processes implemented in a well-designed and properly coordinated effort provide an effective change management approach. The process itself is a management system for bringing about major school change and learning improvement. Change becomes manageable as study groups become units of change.

When WFSGs are initiated, teachers are told that a study group is a vehicle for doing what they have to do. With or without study groups, there are tasks that need to be done. If a school adopts new mathematics textbooks, teachers learn new materials and strategies in study groups. If the district adopts new mathematics standards, the standards are aligned with the curriculum and assessments designed in study groups. In schools where study groups are not in place, this work is done in isolation, by committees, or in extended grade-level or department meetings.

Functions or Purposes

WFSGs serve many functions or purposes, including the major ones in the following list and subsequently discussed in detail. Most often, these functions occur simultaneously.

- Developing a deeper understanding of academic content
- Supporting the implementation of curricular and instructional initiatives
- Integrating and giving coherence to a school's instructional programs and practices
- Targeting a schoolwide instructional need
- Studying the research on teaching and learning
- Monitoring the impact or effects of instructional initiatives on students
- Providing a time when teachers can examine student work together

Developing a Deeper Understanding of Academic Content

At ATLAS Communities' March 2000 Principals' Institute Murphy had a conversation with Howard Gardner, author of *Frames of Mind: The Theory of Multiple Intelligences,* Gardner stated that from his perspective, the reason for having teacher study groups is to discuss for understanding, to reconnect to ideas, to make greater use of the mind. Gardner went on to say that understanding is to take something new and apply it to something you already know. And he added that disciplinary understanding is why we have schools. As Murphy thought about this conversation, she searched for a definition of understanding that she thought would apply to teaching. In Blythe (1998), she found the following definition: "Understanding is a matter of being able to do a variety of thought-provoking things with a topic, such as explaining, finding evidence and examples, generalizing, applying, analogizing, and representing the topic in new ways" (p. 12). *Wow!* If teachers did these in study groups and with students so that students could do them, what remarkable outcomes would happen in schools. The most serious need that we see in schools is that many teachers do not have a deep understanding of what they teach. When this is true, teachers cannot expect students to understand what teachers teach. If students do not understand what they have been taught, they cannot be successful on assessments that require students to take their knowledge and use it in new ways. If teachers do not understand what they teach, they cannot design a variety of thought-provoking activities with a topic. In the WFSG approach, teachers select a student need and convert that need into a topic or an area of study. In study groups, teachers talk to each other to build their own and each other's understanding. They explain to one another what they know about a topic to deepen their understanding and look for new ways to apply what they know to enable them to explain it to their students in different ways. And they develop analogies of an idea or concept so they can help students develop analogies.

Reconnecting to ideas with colleagues is a luxury that teachers often have not had. To make greater use of the mind is a notion only Howard Gardner would put into words. As a fourth-grade teacher for 15 years, Murphy relates that during those years she frequently felt as if she could only think on the fourth-grade level. Teachers must be challenged in their thinking and to go beyond the obvious. Study groups help teachers "push the envelope," to stay on the cutting edge of their disciplines.

In Ted and Nancy Sizer's (1999) book, we gleaned an idea that fits this purpose for having study groups. Study group members tend to want to stay within their area of comfort and not to reach for the unknown. The Sizers challenge us to grapple, to do something that is harder for us. The opposite of grappling is boring. Substantive work challenges and excites teachers. Developing deeper understanding and grappling puts study groups in a context that accelerates learning for teachers and, as a result, accelerates learning for students.

Supporting the Implementation of Curricular and Instructional Innovations

The implementation of new learning is affected by the fact that our individual abilities to understand and use new curricular and instructional ideas frequently encountered in courses and workshops vary considerably, as do our personal assumption, values and beliefs, and experiences. By providing teachers of varying attitudes, understandings, knowledge, and skills with the opportunity for their support of each other, new learning will more likely be used in the workplace. Study groups create such opportunities, increasing the implementation of new practices learned in courses and workshops and the effectiveness of new curricula and educational materials.

For instance, teachers are trained to use new instructional strategies that are backed by a strong research base and apply to a wide variety of curriculum areas. Such strategies or models may include cooperative learning, inductive thinking and concept attainment, and mnemonics. These strategies are often categorized as higher-order thinking skills. The expectation is that all the teachers in a school are to reach high levels of appropriate use of these strategies in their classrooms. This is not likely to happen if the workplace is not designed to prepare teachers to support each other in the immediate and sustained use of the new practices. The leaders of such a training effort might ask study groups to

- Share lessons and materials already used so others could use the plans or materials and thus cut down on preparation time

- Observe each other trying the new strategies so as to learn from each other and to study student responses to the strategies

- Plan future applications of the strategies within their curriculum areas in an attempt to integrate new strategies with existing repertoires and instructional objectives

If teachers do not have a schoolwide, structured support system, teachers will often delay using the new practices. When they do use them and a lesson goes poorly, it will be an even longer time before they try again. If there is any fear or skepticism about the new procedure, delay gives anxiety time to develop, and practice will not ensue. Thus a major training effort fails to achieve its intended results.

However, if the school has a schoolwide design that encourages sharing successes and failures, there will be a high degree of comfort in practicing lessons together and doing joint work in preparing lessons. As a teacher's comfort level rises, so does the level of use with students and the assurance that new strategies and new materials will have a positive impact on the students in the school.

Integrating and Giving Coherence to a School's Instructional Practices and Programs

A charge given to study groups that has schoolwide benefits is for teachers to attempt to integrate new objectives, strategies, materials, and programs with those currently in existence. Schools and teachers are continually bombarded with innovations. At any point in time, teachers are confronted with questions concerning these issues (Guskey, 1990):

- If there will be ongoing, year-after-year technical assistance

- How the various innovations are similar and different

- How similarities can be used to positively influence different aspects of classroom application of the innovations

WFSGs serve as the vehicle for answering these questions and making sense out of past, current, and future instructional initiatives. They also serve as a vehicle through which instructional innovations are more coherent made by teachers who are expected to implement them. By exploring theoretical and research bases of various instructional models that routinely confront teachers, study groups can identify critical attributes to see how programs or practices are alike and how they differ, which would duplicate current efforts, and which would compromise or lessen the impact of current initiatives. This analysis would minimize or avoid the traditional layering of initiatives, bringing coherence to disjointed efforts, which happen all too often.

For example, various reading and writing programs, cooperative learning, and higher-order thinking skills are typically perceived as three separate strategies or programs, because they are usually introduced to teachers in three separate and distinct packages or by three different trainers. Frequently, it is left up to the teacher to try to figure out relationships and common attributes of the three strategies. A group of teachers that regularly meets over a period of time can synthesize the new information and innovations and together develop lessons that incorporate all three strategies.

Targeting an Identified Schoolwide Instructional Need

After the whole faculty analyzes information about the whole school and its students, the faculty will decide whether to

- Focus on several categories of student needs (e.g., reading, writing, and problem-solving skills)

■ Focus on one category and have the study groups address different aspects of that need

Targeting one schoolwide need would mean that if the repertoire of teachers is too limited, then expanding those repertoires would be the target of all study groups. If the school has just adopted new mathematics textbooks, all teachers may want to target the new mathematics curriculum. If the majority of the students in the school are scoring low on reading assessments, the faculty may decide that reading has to be addressed before anything else can be accomplished.

Faculties that focus on one category or area of student need will see whole-school results sooner. It is easier to track student changes when all teachers target one schoolwide need. However, targeting one category or area is more difficult in middle and high schools unless the area is a generic need that cuts across all content areas and grade levels. For example, in one middle school, all the study groups addressed problem-solving strategies. As first-year study groups are implemented, teachers seem to prefer to have several categories of student needs from which to choose. Having a choice is a big factor in getting the WFSG approach started. Usually, by the second year, teachers see the importance of considering a schoolwide target.

Studying Research on Teaching and Learning

An important aspect of the study group process is the reflection on research that describes effective teaching and effective schools, allowing the faculty to make wiser, research-based decisions. In WFSGs, teachers increase their contact, understanding, and application of new innovations from educational research in the United States and abroad, providing for better use of funds and an improved educational environment. Teaching is often perceived as being so personal to a particular teacher and classroom that the teacher does not feel that what happens with another class has any significance for him or her. This reality was made evident in the work in Augusta, where there was a commitment to increasing student achievement through the training of staffs in several models of teaching. At the beginning of the effort, teachers were given examples of successful efforts of schools in other states that used a similar approach to school improvement. The teachers responded, "That's California, not here." The next year, after successful implementation of the program in one middle school in the district, the success was shared with another middle school in the same district. The teachers responded, "That's East Middle School, not here." The school did decide, however, to join the school improvement program. The next year, after successful implementation in most of the classrooms in the new middle school, the success one teacher had in her classroom with her students was shared with another teacher in the same school. The teacher responded, "That's Mrs. Brown's classroom, not mine." It seems no matter how close to home examples of success are, the feeling that "my classroom and my students are different from anyone else's" is so pervasive that it is hard for many teachers to learn from what others have done or are doing. The personalization of teaching is one of the barriers broken when teachers meet routinely in study groups and share teaching practices. As teachers become more open and objective about teaching and learning practices, they feel and become less isolated. Contact with a broad base of relevant research encourages teachers to take more seriously what other districts are discovering about general improvement strategies and to be more actively involved in the collection and analysis of data that come from their own schools and classrooms.

Monitoring the Impact or Effects of Instructional Initiatives on Students

Study groups form according to a general category of student needs that the teachers want to address (e.g., technology). The student need was identified after reviewing general information about students. Once a group has formed and meets for the first time, the group will often want to look at more specific data or information to pinpoint the specific needs in the general category. The study group will list those specific needs on its action plan. This is the time for the teachers to look at student work to be clear on what the needs are. After the teachers have looked at all the information available to the group and have organized and interpreted the information, the group agrees on the instructional interventions or what the teacher will do to increase the students' proficiency in the area of need. For example, if students are not using technology for a variety of purposes, teachers plan lessons and deliberate opportunities for students to use technology in language arts, mathematics, science, music, and other content areas. Given such focused attention, teachers chart the students' use of technology when students are given choices as to how assignments may be completed. Teachers also chart student use of available software in a wide range of subject areas. Then, students are asked to respond to questionnaires that reveal their comfort and proficiency levels in using technology. At points along the way, teachers can track changes in student behavior. Taking action on a student need and monitoring the effects of that action is often referred to as action research. The collection and analysis of information over a period of time will tell teachers in the study group whether or not the intervention is having its intended result.

Providing a Time When Teachers Can Examine Student Work Together

Teachers rarely meet together to examine student work. Looking at student work in a study group gives teachers the opportunity to benefit from multiple perspectives. Because teachers routinely meet together, they are familiar with what each other is doing in the classroom. Looking at the student work from their classrooms is like looking through a special window. Through the student's work, they can see the teacher's work. Much of the student work that teachers bring to the study group is work they have jointly developed. The student work that teachers bring to a study group meeting is work that gives the group more information about student needs the group is addressing. If the study group is addressing mathematics, the student work would be in mathematics. Most often, study groups use a protocol for conversation around the work. There are a number of protocols that have been developed and field tested by the Coalition of Essential Schools, ATLAS Communities, and Annenberg Institute for School Reform. Once the study groups begin meeting, at least one person from each study group should be trained in how to look at student work using a protocol. It is recommended that teachers in a study group rotate the bringing of student work. For study groups that meet weekly, it is recommended that student work be brought to at least every other meeting. In Chapter 5, the eighth procedural or process guideline gives more details about looking at student work.

A Means to an End

When Murphy is contacted by a principal for assistance in getting the WFSG approach in place, she asks, "Why?" Often, the answer is "Because I think that study groups are an excellent approach to staff development." In this case, the principal is focusing on a "means." After more conversation, the principal usually understands that the "end," student learning, is the reason. One of the confusing problems we face in education is differentiating between means and ends. The WFSG approach is a means to an end: increased student learning.

In education, when someone asks about the success of our educational efforts, we often tell them about our teachers, our facilities, our libraries, our technology, and our curricula. However, what they were really asking about were the outcomes of our efforts, such as percentages of students graduating, levels of student accomplishment, and graduate preparation for college or work. The former (e.g., teachers, facilities, libraries, technology, and curricula) are means, the way to deliver ends, whereas the latter (e.g., graduation rates, academic accomplishments, and graduate preparation) are ends, the results, consequences, accomplishments, and payoffs of our efforts.

Means and ends are not the same! Means are the ways to deliver ends, including resources (time, money, students, teachers and administrators, Parent-Teacher Association, the community, technology, and facilities) and methods (teaching, collaborating, self-study, learning, thinking, planning, and developing).

Some typical means and ends are as follows:

	Means	Ends
Classrooms and laboratories	X	
Libraries	X	
Financial support	X	
Staff development	X	
Graduation		X
Board of education	X	
Teachers	X	
Study groups	X	
Graduate employment		X
Collaborative learning	X	
Strategic planning	X	
Shared governance	X	
Course grade		X
Technology	X	
Graduate competence		X
Policies	X	
Accountability	X	

The ends are the "what" to be accomplished, whereas the means are the "how" to accomplish the desired results.

Unfortunately, in education, we have a tendency to spend most of our resources on the means without first clearly determining the desired ends. If you don't have a target (a desired end), it's hard to find means that will help you hit it. If you want to enhance success, first clearly determine your desired results (ends), and then select your means based on the ends you wish to achieve.

Starting with means before identifying desired ends is backward and usually ineffective. One of the chief reasons for a lack of real success in educational reform over the past decade was that we spent most of our time and money on means without having well-defined goals that the means were to have successfully addressed. Test your own school's record: In your school's educational mission, decide what the means and ends are and observe how much attention has been given to the means.

Means help accomplish ends but are not ends in themselves! The definitions are as follows:

- End: A result, outcome, output, or product

- Means: The tools, methods, techniques, resources, or processes used to achieve an end

Kaufman, Herman, and Watters (1996) remind us that one of the six critical success factors in education is this: "Differentiate between ends and means" (p. 18)—focus on the "what" (the desired ends) before selecting the "how" (the means).

After the WFSG approach has been implemented, someone has to keep reminding the teachers why the study groups were initiated and implemented in the first place. The ends—student learning—have to be constantly put before the groups. When strong advocates of study groups want to organize study groups simply for the sake of having study groups, a disservice is done to WFSGs, the school, and the coerced faculty. Advocates need to understand and project to others that study groups are a means to an end and not an end in and of themselves. The desired end of study groups is positive change in student learning and the learning environment. When increased student success is the vision and guiding principle, individuals and study groups are motivated, work harder, and take responsibility for the successful implementation of the required processes and procedures.

WFSGs: Who Changes?

As study groups are created and implemented, individual members and the group find that for their efforts to be successful not only must students change but they, too, must actually change. For instance, teachers might change in how they approach and study issues; in deepening their knowledge in the academic content they teach; in their relations with others; in their basic assumptions, beliefs, and behaviors about students and the learning process; and in their implementation of new practices and processes.

It is also important that teachers see the relationship between their behaviors and the students' behaviors. Change in teachers' behaviors is the immediate target of study groups. As teachers work together in becoming more skillful in their practices and in the materials they use, the focus shifts to students as targets and their becoming more skillful. It is doubtful that students will become more skillful if teachers continue to use practices that are not causing students to change. Student change is measured by increased learning and by differences in how they behave.

For example, teachers become skillful at using mnemonics in teaching information that students should memorize. As teachers use this strategy, students will use the strategy as they confront new information that they must know, such as when preparing to take a test to get a driver's license. For the teacher, mnemonics is a teaching strategy; then, it becomes a learning strategy for the student. The general process is depicted in Figure 2.1.

Intended Results

The overarching goal of each school is student learning. Consequently, the fundamental end we seek with the introduction of any new means, such as study groups, is enhanced student learning.

As a result, WFSGs focus on whole-school improvement efforts that engage the staff in a study of how to help students learn more effectively. That is, the goal of study groups is to center the entire school faculty on implementing, integrating, and managing effective teaching and learning practices that will result in an increase in student learning and a decrease in negative behaviors of students.

WFSGs bring individual needs and school needs together in a collaborative setting. The purpose of schools is to create the conditions where young people can learn to their fullest capacity and potential. Therefore, the goal of all study groups at a school is to collectively meet that organizational goal.

Summary

Best practice is a term often heard in education today. We read about what are best practices for teachers to use with their students. In Zemelman, Daniels, and Hyde's (1993) *Best Practice: New Standards for Teaching and Learning in America's Schools,* on page 7, the authors list the underlying assumptions, principles, or theories that characterize integrated learning. Best practice is what we do in the classroom with students that exemplify those principles, assumptions, or theories.

In WFSGs, teachers are the students. The same principles that apply to elementary, middle, and high school students also apply to a 30- or 55-year-old student who is learning more about the art of teaching. As a professional development model, the WFSG presents an integrated learning experience for adult students; it is an approach to learning characterized by the following learning principles:

■ They are *student centered.* Teachers in a group determine what they must know and what they must do more skillfully to meet the needs of their students.

■ They give teachers the opportunity to *experiment.* In groups, teachers try new materials, new techniques, new strategies, and new technologies.

Figure 2.1. WFSGs' Impact on Student Performance

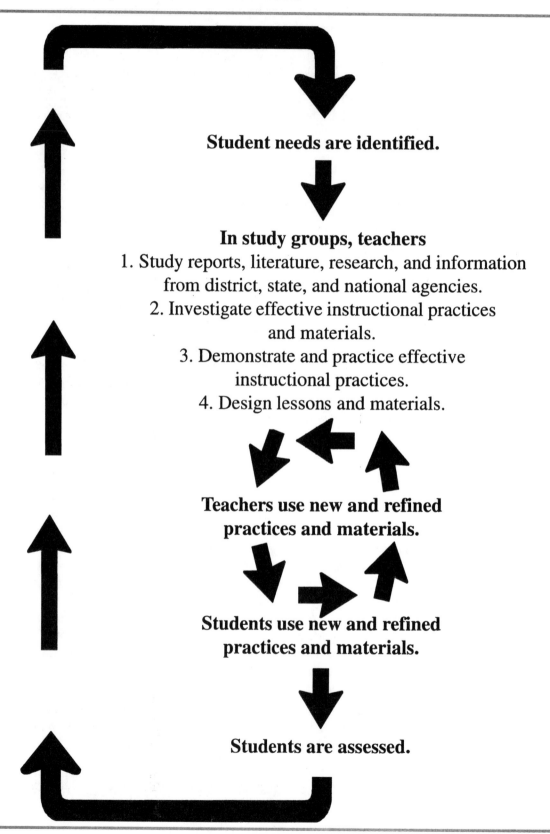

Student needs are identified.

In study groups, teachers
1. Study reports, literature, research, and information from district, state, and national agencies.
2. Investigate effective instructional practices and materials.
3. Demonstrate and practice effective instructional practices.
4. Design lessons and materials.

Teachers use new and refined practices and materials.

Students use new and refined practices and materials.

Students are assessed.

■ They inspire *reflection.* As teachers talk about their practices, they reflect on what works and does not work and why a critical element for change in practice is to occur and be sustained.

■ They provide *authentic* learning experiences. The teachers are not following an instructor's syllabus or set of objectives presented to them. Experiences are designed by the group and tied to the teachers' classrooms and students. Because the group is addressing its students' needs, the work of the group is real and meaningful.

■ They focus on the *whole.* The needs of the whole school, the whole class, the whole art of teaching are brought into focus. Isolation, once the norm, is broken. Not only has isolation from each other been a common work condition, but instructional programs and strategies have often been viewed separately.

■ They support *democratic* behavior. All faculty members have an opportunity to decide if having the teachers work together in small groups will benefit their students. All faculty members have a voice in what student needs will be addressed as well as the method that will be used to determine the membership of the study groups. And once the study groups are formed, each member of the group has a voice in determining exactly how the group will work and what the group will do.

■ They allow teachers to *construct* their own learning and their own meanings in what they read, hear, and see. The process validates a teacher's individuality and empowers a teacher to go beyond the boundaries that are usually set by others.

■ They give teachers the *motivation* to establish challenging and rigorous standards for themselves.

We are even more encouraged about the work in WFSG schools as we consider the six characteristics that Darling-Hammond and McLaughlin (1995) identified in effective professional development that involves teachers as both teachers and learners. We believe that all six characteristics are embedded in the WFSG approach as follows:

■ It must engage teachers in concrete tasks of teaching, assessment, observation, and reflection.

■ It must be grounded in inquiry, reflection, and experimentation that are participant driven.

■ It must be collaborative, involving a sharing of knowledge among educators, and focus on teachers' communities of practice rather than on individual teachers.

■ It must be connected to and derived from teachers' work with their students.

■ It must be sustained, ongoing, intensive, and supported by modeling, coaching, and the collective solving of specific problems of practice.

■ It must be connected to other aspects of school change.

This book will describe how these six characteristics are imbedded in the WFSG approach. We believe that WFSGs enable teachers to do what Darling-Hammond & McLaughlin (1995) endorse: "providing occasions for teachers to reflect critically on their practice and to fashion new knowledge and beliefs about content, pedagogy, and learners" (p. 595). Each subsequent chapter will describe one proven-in-practice approach for building collaborative cultures that respects and supports teachers as learners.

Key Components 3

Context, Process, and Content

Aframework for designing professional development has three major components. The components are *context, process,* and *content.* Each component requires thoughtful, deliberate action. Because each component has distinct characteristics, there are distinct actions that leaders should take when considering and making provisions for each component. These components are equally important and create a seamless whole. In the planning stages, each is given separate consideration, but in reality, the components are inseparable. The organizational framework for the National Staff Development Council's (2000) Standards for Staff Development is context-process-content.

The *context* addresses the organization, system, or culture in which the study groups exist. It is the organizational or cultural factors that facilitate or impede progress toward the organization's intended results. The context includes how the organization "feels" to the personnel, as well as the norms that govern their lives. It is often the informal structure of how things get done. The context will largely determine how psychologically safe individuals feel, how willing they are to take risks, what behaviors are rewarded and punished, and whether it is standard to work in isolation or with peers. The context of an organization is typically the first line of concern for sponsors or change agents.

Process refers to the "how" of staff development. It describes the means for the acquisition of new knowledge and skills. A process is a way of doing something. It is how change happens and continues to develop over a course of time. A process infers that there are steps or procedures that one goes through in the course of accomplishing a goal.

Content refers to the actual skills and knowledge educators want to possess or acquire through staff development or some other means. It is the substance of a process. For teachers, it is the history, the English, the science, the mathematics that they teach. It is also how to teach for understanding and what brain research tells us about how to meet the needs of students. We often refer to content knowledge or what one knows about a subject. When we read a book, the content is the text, what we learn. We could think of the content as the ingredients of a process, what is in the process, what the process holds. See Table 3.1 for a diagram showing the relationship between context, process, and content.

America Online (AOL) and Time-Warner merged. The two companies merged at a time and in a societal culture in which individuals and organizations had been depending more and more on the Internet for services, products and information. The

Table 3.1 A Framework for Designing Professional Development

Context: Organizational or cultural factors that facilitate or impede progress toward intended results, such as a shared vision and norms of continuous improvement and collegiality.

Process: How individuals, groups, and the whole will function, behave, or perform; procedures to be followed; means for the acquisition of new knowledge and skills.

Content: What individuals, groups, and the whole will study, learn, or become skillful in doing to achieve intended results; skills, attitudes, and knowledge to be acquired.

context was right for the merger to happen. On the day that the merger was announced, a reporter was heard to say that Time-Warner had the content to put into the infrastructure of AOL. Time-Warner had the content, and AOL had the process. In the same newscast, the reporter stated that AT&T was AOL's largest Internet competitor. However, now with the merger, AOL had Time-Warner's music, magazines, books, and news services to deliver to AOL customers. AOL had the process and the content in a context that would support the merger. AT&T has the process but less content in the same context or cultural conditions as AOL.

Let's try another image. A couple is going on a picnic. The weather is great. The park where the couple is going will be quiet and have adequate facilities. The weather is comfortable, and there will be others there that will make the surroundings interesting. The park is the context and creates the conditions for the picnic. The couple will take a basket containing their lunch. Because they plan to take utensils, sandwiches, and drinks, the basket will need to be solid enough to hold the weight of the contents. The basket represents the process or the means of getting the food from the kitchen to the table in the park. If the basket is weak with holes, part of the lunch is likely to fall through the holes and may not get to the table. The basket has to be strong enough to hold what the couple puts in it (see Figure 5.1 in Chapter 5). When they unpack the lunch, the basket's contents will be what the couple eats and uses. If the couple can't eat or use the contents, the contents are of no use. If it rains or the park becomes too noisy (the context), it will not matter whether the basket or food in the basket is adequate. The context will negate the process and the content.

The basket analogy in the foregoing scenario is compatible with what Susan Loucks-Horsley (1998b) wrote, "Teachers teach something (the content), and if that isn't a focus of their professional development, it's like crafting an elegant basket with nothing inside" (p. 7). It does not matter how the process looks, it has to hold content that has the power to change what teachers and students do and achieve.

Think about what you already know about the WFSG approach. The context is the school and conditions that exist at the school. The study groups represent a process for getting new strategies and materials into the classroom to benefit students. The new strategies and materials are the contents for the process. What the group does and learns in the process (in study groups) has to be of such substance that students will improve.

Following this chapter, we devote a chapter to each component. Chapter 4 focuses on context, Chapter 5 on process, and Chapter 6 on content. In this chapter, we briefly present each component of the WFSG approach and a discussion to help clarify differences in the components.

The Context for WFSGs

There is no one type of context that is an ideal precondition for WFSGs. WFSGs have been successful in different schools where the contexts are very dissimilar. One school that has successfully initiated and implemented WFSGs has a nurturing principal who is involved with all aspects of the study group work. Another school that has successfully initiated and implemented WFSGs has a principal that is aloof and has a "hands off" style. Schools can be successful coming into the WFSG process from quite different angles. The one thing that is constant, though, is the desire to increase student learning. This desire translates into a powerful and compelling contextual feature of the school.

We elaborate in Chapter 4 on contextual conditions that have to be considered when major change efforts are initiated. In this section, we briefly mention factors that seem to have the greatest impact on the context of a school.

District Influence: The district context or culture has a huge impact on the school. Schools can begin major initiatives without the involvement or direct support of the district. However it is hard, if not impossible, to continue those initiatives without the support of the district.

Nature and needs of students: What students are like at a school establishes the conditions for what needs to happen. It is for the students that the school exists.

Responsibilities of teachers: What teachers are expected to do has a great effect on how teachers feel about where they work. What are teachers expected to do that is directly tied to what they do in classrooms with students? What are teachers expected to do outside the classroom? Is professional development a responsibility?

Time for professional development: It is commonly believed that we find time for what is important. What are the indicators that professional development is important? Does the school see professional development for teachers and staff as an important school investment?

Resources: Some schools have more, some schools have fewer. Regardless of such circumstances, what resources are available for use in and outside classrooms?

Community support: Schools exist within communities, another context. A school community consists of parents, nonparents, businesses, community agencies, churches, and clubs. What are the levels of support from these groups, and what is the nature of that support?

History: All organizations have a history. Even new schools inherit a history from other local schools and their community. How many principals has the school had within the past 5 years? How long do teachers stay at the school? Does the school have a reputation of jumping on fads or being stuck in a rut?

Organizational culture: What are the norms relating to collaboration, continuous improvement, and experimentation?

Shared purpose: Do those at a school have a clear vision of what the school wants to become? What is perceived to be important?

Assessment of results: How important are data to the faculty? Is it the norm to ask questions and seek answers? Is the status of student learning clear to everyone?

Building capacity: Are all teachers themselves leaders, or are just a few considered smart enough to do what has to be done? What vehicles are available through which teachers can share leadership roles?

Organizational structures: How does the work get done? Are the critical relationships in place?

Equity: Are all students and adults respected and treated with dignity?

In great measure, the contextual conditions of a district and school determine what gets accomplished and what does not get done. These conditions create the school environment in which progress and change will potentially flourish or be inhibited.

District support structures exist in some of the districts that have implemented the WFSG approach to professional development and in all the districts where schools have chosen the ATLAS Communities national school reform design. Specific support structures are Principal Study Groups and Pathway Study Groups.

Principal Study Groups

Principal Study Groups are study groups that have principals as members. In some Principal Study Groups, other types of administrators may also be members, such as an assistant principal and a district-level administrator. These groups follow the same guidelines as do WFSGs (the guidelines are described in Chapter 5). The group size ranges from 3 to 6. In some large schools, there are enough administrators to form a group. Most often, members of Principal Study Groups are principals of several WFSG schools. In some districts, all principals may be members of Principal Study Groups.

In Augusta, 2 years after the MOT program was first implemented and study groups were active in seven schools, all administrators in the district, both school-based and district-based, were in study groups (Murphy, 1991a). Study groups had action plans, kept logs, rotated leaders, and had no more than six members. A deliberate strategy was used to ensure heterogeneous study groups, such as having an elementary principal, a middle school principal, a high school principal or assistant principal, and a district person together. When together in a study group, all are equal. The superintendent was a member of a group and was expected to be just another member. With 60 schools and a large district support staff, there were about 20 study groups. Groups were given a list of 15 book titles (multiple sets of those titles had been purchased), such as Fullan and Steigelbauer's (1991) *The New Meaning of Educational Change.* Each study group selected six books for members to read and discuss, and books were distributed on a rotating schedule. Roland Barth, from Harvard's Principals' Center, came to the district every 6 weeks during the school year and met with all members to reinforce key issues emerging on the national school restructuring and reform agendas. Study groups were expected to meet at least once every 2 weeks for 2 hours. Groups met at schools, restaurants for breakfast or lunch, and the staff development center. Barth suggested that when the principals were out of their schools for study group meetings that they put a sign on their doors that said "Out to Learn."

One of the components of the ATLAS Communities design is working with a pathway of schools in a district. A *pathway* is a PreK-through-12th-grade configuration of schools. Most often, a pathway is a feeder pattern, one or more elementary schools that feed into a middle school that feeds into a high school. The principals of the pathway schools are in a Principal Study Group. What principals decide to do may vary. They may address a common administrative issue, an issue particular to working with teachers, or the same student needs that teachers in schools are addressing. If WFSGs are addressing reading, principals will look at reading materials and examine strategies teachers are using. Principal groups have an action plan and keep logs. In schools where the WFSGs' logs are posted, there is a clipboard for the Principal Study Group. Teachers enjoy reading their principal's logs. Principal Study Groups are not considered as independent or stand-alone study groups because they are connected to common goals in schools where principals serve.

Pathway Study Groups

Pathway Study Groups are another organizational pattern for study groups. At all ATLAS Communities sites, *after* the WFSGs are in place at schools for one school year, Pathway Study Groups are formed. Again, the same WFSG guidelines apply. A Pathway Study Group would be composed of elementary, middle, and high school teachers. There is a system in each pathway for forming the groups. A Pathway Leadership Team identifies student needs from needs the schools are addressing. In Everett, Washington, Pathway Study Groups meet once a month. In their ATLAS pathway schools (one elementary school, one middle school, one high school, and one alternative high school), classes begin 1 hour later on Friday than on the other days. WFSGs meet on three of the Friday mornings. The pathway groups meet on the other Friday morning. Pathway Study Groups focus on the PreK-through-12th-grade continuum and the development of meaningful, instructionally focused conversation across the grade levels. The pathway groups support and enhance the work of the WFSGs.

The arrangements we have just described create an important part of the context in schools and districts that say to the community, learning is the top priority.

The Process for WFSGs

To recap, *process* refers to how individuals work together to acquire new knowledge and skills and usually involves a number of procedures or operations. Let's go back to the couple going to a picnic. The basket is the process and represents how the food gets to the park. The basket has to be strong enough to carry the contents, especially content that has substance. The WFSG basket is strong enough to hold strong content (see Figure 5.1) because of the 15 interwoven guidelines, the slats in the basket. These guidelines are discussed in detail in Chapter 5.

The Developmental Stages of Study Groups

The process or procedural guidelines alone will not determine how individuals will function within WFSGs. Leaders and others working with and in study groups must understand that study groups go through developmental stages just like all other types of groups. Study groups in a school will experience each stage to some degree. Some groups will stay in one stage longer than other groups.

We have given names to four growth stages that seem to fit study groups. The concept for developmental stages of teams or groups and the format we are using comes from the book *The One Minute Manager Builds High Performing Teams* (Blanchard, Carew, & Parisi-Carew, 2000). Others have used variations of Blanchard et al.'s stages to illustrate how groups develop. See Table 3.2 for variations on the names of the four stages.

Our four stages seem to fit study groups and are characteristics of how we have seen individuals function in study groups. We identify the stages this way:

Stage 1: Forming

Stage 2: Grumbling

Stage 3: Willingness

Stage 4: Consequence

Table 3.2 Synonyms for Names of Developmental Stages

Stages	Blanchard, Carew, and Parisi-Carew	Outward Bound	Author Unknown	Murphy and Lick
1	Orientation	Forming	Testing	Forming
2	Dissatisfaction	Storming	Infighting	Grumbling
3	Resolution	Norming	Getting Organized	Willingness
4	Production	Performing	Mature Closeness	Consequence

Stage 1: Forming

The forming stage for study groups actually begins when the faculty is first given information about the WFSG process and continues through the forming of the smaller groups. In the beginning, the whole faculty is considered "the group" and later, the six-member study group is "the group." The forming stage extends beyond the time when the individual study groups begin to meet.

During the forming stage, study group members may

- Feel eager to begin

- Have high expectations

- Feel some anxiety

- Have high levels of personal concern

- Need more information

- Wonder about expectations

- Depend on authority

- Feel dependent on what they have heard or read

- Prepare to participate

- Hesitate

- Be polite and guarded

- Fear differences

- Fear being a leader

During the forming stage, individuals need a lot of information. They must be able to express themselves and ask lots of clarifying questions. The principal and the focus team's members should be accessible and open to dissenting voices. Individuals may require one-on-one attention. Members' concerns focus on getting more information and details about what will be expected of them and the implications for them. Each individual is interested in substantive aspects of the process, such as the evidence initiators have indicating that student learning will improve. Group members will be uncertain about the effects of study groups and will see their school as different from any other school. They will want to know what is required of them, if the principal and district leaders are going to support study groups over time, and if teachers will have adequate resources for their groups. Participants want to understand how the process will affect them, how they will be part of the decision-making process, and what the potential conflicts may be with existing structures. In particular, their concerns will be about themselves, financial or status implications for self and colleagues, and time for study groups to meet. It is extremely important that school leadership present clear and reasonable options for teachers during this early stage.

The most critical aspect of this early stage is for the whole faculty to work together to make decisions about what study groups will do. Following the steps in the DMC (see Chapter 7) enables group members to feel a part of the effort. Teachers must know that their voices will be heard. When they experience the analysis of student data and see that what study groups do is grounded in student needs, they become more trusting of the process. Additional comfort comes when they realize that it is study group members who decide exactly what the group will do in relation to a student need.

As individuals move from the whole group to smaller study groups, many of the feelings of concern will be transferred to and expressed in their study group. Consequently, it is important that study groups are given clear and concise instructions as to what to do in their first two study group meetings. It is helpful for them to have materials with tangible information describing precisely what they are to do. During these first two meetings, groups establish group norms and leadership rotation schedules and begin developing the group's action plan. These expectations keep the focus of group members on tasks and not on themselves and each other.

Stage 2. Grumbling

It is usually during the grumbling stage that there is a dip in morale and commitment as the group comes to realize its tasks are harder than they initially expected. The old saying "It isn't real until it's real" is true. Fullan and Steigelbauer (1991) refer to this dip as the "implementation dip." In the context of study groups, this dip usually comes when the initial energy wanes and the group is faced with the logistical aspects of the process. During this stage, members actually see that no one outside their group is going to tell them what to do, and this reality becomes something to grumble about. A fly on the wall might hear "Why don't they just tell us what to do?"

During the grumbling stage, study group members may

- Feel dissatisfied with past decisions

- Experience a discrepancy between hopes and reality

- Feel frustrated

- Feel incompetent and confused

- React negatively toward the initiators of study groups

- Want permission to act

- ■ Want confirmation that what he or she is doing is right

- ■ Feel unsure about what will benefit everyone

- ■ Want to withdraw from the group

- ■ Feel that the group process is too hard

- ■ Feel impatient with other members

- ■ Compete for attention

- ■ Feel stuck

- ■ Focus their concerns on group management issues

- ■ Feel that the process is very mechanical

The grumbling stage is not an unproductive stage. It is a growing stage that groups go through on their way to being productive. This is usually when the seeds are sown for creativity and the valuing of differences. Concerns here are processes of group membership. They struggle with the best use of time, information, and resources. Issues related to efficiency, organization of the work, and roles and responsibilities are uppermost in their minds. It is in this stage that members focus on the short-term value of study groups and take little time for reflection. They tend to concentrate more on themselves and the mechanics of the process than on their students. The work of the group often feels disjointed and superficial during this second stage of group development. One might hear a teacher say "I could get more done in my room by myself."

Study groups require a lot of support and encouragement in this phase to move to the next stage. This is the stage when external support means the most. The principal and other support persons at the school and district level should respond to each study group's action plan. It is especially critical that the principal lets each group know that he or she is aware of what the group is doing. The principal can be encouraging by making suggestions to the group regarding how student needs have been expressed, actions the group plans to take, and resources that the group has identified. The log that each study group keeps should be responded to for at least the first three or four meetings. This is the point where the principal will have the greatest influence on the outcome of the study group work. The quicker the principal acknowledges what a group is doing, the quicker it will move into a more productive stage. What principals show by their actions to be important, teachers will generally take as important. Teachers should also know that district-level leaders are aware of each group's work and are ready to support it. Study groups in this stage often need a push for them to move to the next stage. When the logs are read, the principal will see a dominance of very passive verbs, such as *discussing* and *reviewing.* At this point, the principal should ask "And what action in the classroom will that lead you to?"

Helping study groups move through the forming and grumbling stages of group development require direct support and encouragement from the principal and district staff. Study groups receive both support and pressure from having permission to release students early 1 day a week for study groups to meet, from having a content specialist meet with the group once a month, and from the principal's attentiveness to action plans and study group logs. In this context, support and pressure are positive dynamics. Without high expectations, which is a form of pressure, resources are wasted. Without support, individuals become alienated from the process and from school leaders. Principals need the will and skill to guide and facilitate the movement of study groups into the final two stages.

Stage 3: Willingness

It is during this stage, the willingness stage, that group members become open to each other and willing to work cooperatively so the group can function successfully. Competition fades; collaboration increases. In this stage, there is a sense of expanding energy as the group pulls itself together to focus more clearly and effectively on intended results of the group's action plans.

During the willingness stage, study groups members may

- Resolve discrepancies between expectations and reality

- Decrease dissatisfaction

- Develop harmony, trust, support, and respect

- Develop self-esteem and confidence

- Be more open

- Share what is not working in their classrooms

- Visit each other's classrooms

- Give more feedback to each other

- Share responsibility and control

- Use common language

- Feel comfortable with sharing leadership

- Focus concerns on the impact of the group's work on students

During the willingness stage, group members begin to develop new and refined instructional strategies and materials, share interdependently with each other, and introduce new practices that have a positive impact on their students. When reviewing study group logs, the principal will see that there are a lot of overt activities. The section of the study group log titled "Discussions and activities focused on" will most likely use verbs such as *practiced, demonstrated, reflected, monitored, worked, experimented, taught,* and *interviewed.* Teachers are doing collaborative work, which means that they are taking joint responsibility for efforts in their classrooms and for their students' work. In particular, the "classroom application" section of their log is full, and student work is routinely brought to study group meetings. When study groups are at the willingness stage, there are high levels of synergy in groups and energy throughout the school. A cultural change is evidenced in both formal and informal conversations between principals and teachers, teachers and teachers, students and teachers, students and students, and parents and teachers. Study group members are focused more on the impact their work is having on students than they were in the earlier forming and grumbling stages.

Stage 4: Consequence

In the consequence stage, study group members have a high awareness of the consequences of the group's actions. Their concerns focus on the impact of their work on students. In the forming stage, initiators of the study group process tell teachers that forming study groups is a means to greater student success, whereas in the consequence stage, teachers fully understand through their study group experiences that this is indeed true.

During the consequence stage, study group members may

- Keep student work as the study group's centerpiece

- Feel strength from the group

- Participate fully

- Feel positive about the group's influence on each other and students

- Feel highly motivated to continue

- Seek more collaborative relationships in and out of school

- Focus concerns on coordination and cooperation with others

- Focus concerns on more intellectually rigorous work

- Not be satisfied with passive action but seek more direct and purposeful student interventions

- Combine efforts with colleagues to achieve a collective impact on students

- Feel empowered

- Feel strong sense of personal dignity

- Feel a high degree of commitment to all the students at the school

- Integrate study group work into other forms of professional development

- Have more positive views of students

In the consequence stage, teachers actualize the concept that students are the heart of professional development. Teachers in study groups focus on the impact that the work of the study group is having on students. They use words like "our students" instead "my students." At this stage, group members require many opportunities to share what their study group is learning and doing that is changing what their students are learning and achieving. Results of increased student learning must be shared! Data should be collected and charted when students are doing better on end-of-chapter tests, completing more assignments, and entering additional science fairs, as well as when fewer students are being referred to the office and more students are reading books for pleasure. Teachers should see the data and celebrate their successes. They need to see evidence that the collective power of their study group is making a difference with students. At the beginning of a new school year, it is also this knowledge and its acknowledgment that will change the question "Will we have study groups this year?" to "What student needs are we going to address this year?"

More Circular Than Linear

When group conditions change, the developmental stages are repeated to some degree and the stages become more circular than linear. Conditions change when a teacher takes a leave of absence in the middle of the year and is no longer a member of the group, when a teacher new to the school joins the group, when there is a major change in contextual conditions, when the group decides to rewrite the action plan and to select a new student need, and when new expectations are imposed on the group. Groups that have formed and are working at the willingness stage will find themselves having to reform, if only for a meeting or two. The second time around, grumbling will be at a minimum and will have less impact on the functioning of the group. Members will quickly recommit to each other with a renewed sense of willingness to move ahead and accomplish its goals.

Time in Each Stage

Typically, if study groups begin meeting by the middle of September and meet weekly, it will be November before most of the groups have cleared the grumbling stage. Few will reach the consequence stage by the end of the first year. When the second year begins, groups will return to the forming stage, even those study groups that do not change membership. If a study group does remain intact, the (re)forming stage will only last a meeting or two. If persons are in different study groups than they were the year before, the forming stage may continue into the fourth meeting. The grumbling stage is usually shorter for groups the second year because individuals have had a year of experience and they see that the study group initiative did not "go away." More study groups will reach the consequence stage the second year because all the teachers will be encouraged and motivated by the study groups that did reach that stage during the first year. When the third year begins, more groups, even those groups where membership changed, will move more quickly though the first two stages. During the third year of implementation, most of the groups will reach the willingness stage by the fourth meeting. The variable that has a great influence on the growth of study groups is what other initiatives the teachers are confronting, new and carryovers.

Within a school year, the factor that has the most influence on a study group's movement through the stages is how often it meets. Projections in the foregoing paragraph are for study groups that meet weekly or, at the very least, 90 minutes every other week. In schools where study groups meet only once a month, the groups will most likely remain in the forming and grumbling stages the entire school year because by May the group will only have met seven or, at the most, eight times. Study groups that meet weekly will have met seven times by the first of November.

From year to year, the factors that have the most influence on the start-up and continuation of study groups are contextual. The number of new initiatives that the school has adopted or changes in personnel and the level of ongoing district support have the potential to stop the process

The Content for WFSGs

The context and process components of WFSGs are often invisible. The context is the conditions of the workplace and the process is how individuals work together.

The descriptors of the context and process can be seen, but by virtue of the definitions, they are often without form. That is not true of content. Content can most often be seen, handled, and manipulated. It has form. It is a book, a video, an article, a lesson plan, a packaged program, an activity, or a strategy, and it can even be represented by a person. Content is what study groups do. High-performing study groups do intellectually rigorous work, meaning that the content is substantive enough to sustain and challenge the members as they strive for a deeper understanding of what they teach.

As we have stressed, teachers select the student needs they want to address. In Chapter 7, we describe how the faculty analyzes data to identify student needs. Each study group develops an action plan. In the action plan, teachers agree on the specific student needs they will address and what teachers will do when the study group meets to address the student needs listed in the plan. In this way, what teachers should do is preceded by what the students' needs are. Therefore, we can say that in study groups, teachers do what students need for them to do.

Answers to the five crucial questions listed in the following box will tell leaders of WFSGs what teachers should know and be able to do.

■ What do students need for teachers to do so that teachers will have a deeper understanding of what they teach?

■ What do students need for teachers to do so that teachers will be more skillful in how they teach?

■ What do students need for teachers to do so that teachers will challenge students to learn difficult and fundamental concepts?

■ What do students need for teachers to do so that teachers will give students skills to be deep thinkers and problem solvers?

■ What do students need for teachers to do so that teachers will be skillful facilitators in helping students develop attitudes toward being productive citizens of the world?

We expect readers to think that these questions are awkward, somewhat confusing, or even unreasonable. A colleague, after reading the questions, stated that the question should be simply "What do teachers need?" The response was "Why do teachers have the need in the first place? Why must teachers know anything?" Of course, the answer is "Because of the students." The foregoing questions are awkward because staff developers have not phrased questions in this way. When Murphy once spoke at a general session at a national conference, she read the questions to the audience. After the session was over, a gentleman who is head of the staff development division at a state department of education came up to Murphy. He said, "I have never thought of asking those questions. When you do, it really turns your whole thinking around. It reverses how we usually think." It does. This way of thinking is why Murphy uses the phrase "student-based professional development" in relation to WFSGs.

The source for determining what teachers need to know and be able to do is the students. Student work tells teachers what they must do. Results of various performance assessments tell teachers what they must know and be able to do with skill in the classroom. This is the content of WFSGs efforts.

Summary

What do we know about what teachers want to do in the context of school reform? In 1998, High Schools That Work (HSTW), a national network of high schools resulting from action by the Southern Regional Education Board (SREB) and State Vocational Education Consortium, surveyed teachers at the 1998 SREB HSTW sites. At those sites, 26,048 teachers returned the survey. A few of the responses are shared to illustrate context, process, and content issues:

- 43% of the respondents (11,200) said that they were not as familiar as they should be with the content and specific goals of courses taught by other teachers in their school.

- 58% said that they were not as familiar as they should be with the content and specific goals of courses taught in middle grades of schools that send students to their high school.

- 56% said that they wanted to plan interdisciplinary projects and units with other teachers.

- 57% wanted to be observed and receive feedback.

- 65% wanted to read professional literature.

- 77% wanted to work with other successful teachers.

- 76% (19,796) wanted to network with others.

- 48% (12,503) wanted to participate in study groups.

- 55% (14,326) wanted to be engaged in action research.

- 75% wanted a common planning time to work with a team of academic and vocational teachers to develop an integrated program of study.

The foregoing responses give us great hope. The leaders of HSTW are to be congratulated for asking the hard questions and for seeking this type of information. Teachers do want to work with other teachers. Teachers do want to know what other teachers are doing. Teachers do want to share with other teachers. And teachers want to learn more about teaching. It is the responsibility of district and school leaders to provide the structures and the time for teachers to work together.

Clarifying Roles, Responsibilities, and School Culture

Teachers' work is often assumed to occur almost exclusively within the confines of a single room. While the classroom is the dominant setting for teachers' daily professional life (Lortie, 1975), it is not the only context for their work (Kruse & Louis, 1994; McLaughlin, 1993; Siskin, 1994). The school's organization and faculty members and administrators who compose the school staff create a larger context that, at minimum, influences teachers' professional satisfaction. In addition, studies of the relationship of school context to teachers' work suggest that the inter-personal and structural conditions that characterize teachers' work will also affect the impact that they have on their students (Rosenholtz, 1989; Talbert & Perry, 1994).

—Louis, Marks, and Kruse (1996, p. 757)

Research Ties Collaborative Cultures to Student Learning

The University of Chicago's Center for School Improvement worked with a number of Chicago elementary schools over 3 years. Bryk, Rollow, and Pinnel (1996) reported that there is a need to restructure and renorm teachers' work so that a professional community emerges to sustain school improvement.

Professional community is also identified as important in a summary report titled *Successful School Restructuring* (Newmann & Wehlage, 1995). More than 1,500 schools throughout the United States were part of four large-scale studies: School Restructuring Study, National Educational Longitudinal Study of 1988, Study of Chicago School Reform, and Longitudinal Study of School Restructuring. Results of these studies were combined into summary findings. Newmann and Wehlage (1995) reported that "professional community not only boosted student achievement gains, it also helped to make the gains more equitable among socioeconomic groups" (p. 37).

Louis et al. (1996) reported on research based primarily on survey data collected from more than 900 teachers in 24 nationally selected restructuring elementary, middle, and high schools. The research had the assumption that how teachers interact when they are not in their classrooms may be critical to the future of school restructuring and its effects on students. Louis et al. found that a strong school-based professional community for teachers is associated with increased engagement and achievement for students. They also found five core characteristics of professional school communities:

- Teachers and administrators share basic norms and values about children, learning, and teaching.

- Reflective dialogue, rich and recurring talk about teaching practice and student learning, enlarges the teachers' world and helps them view teaching from one another's perspectives.

- Deprivatization of practice occurs when teachers practice their craft openly and problem-solve together.

- A collective focus on student learning drives decisions.

- Collaboration exists across grade-level groups.

The value of the WFSG concept and other designs that build collaborative cultures is well documented. Lucas (2000) found that the WFSG process had a positive impact on teachers' professional growth and on student learning in the schools in her study.

Sebring and Bryk (2000) reported that schools that are improving are characterized by cooperative work relations among all adults. They state that in schools where trust and cooperative adult efforts are strong, students report that they feel safe, sense that teachers care about them, and experience greater academic challenge. In contrast, in schools with flat or declining test scores, teachers are more likely to state that they do not trust one another, and both teachers and students report less satisfaction with their experiences.

Rosenholtz's (1989) research reports on an investigation of social organizational features in 78 elementary schools in eight school districts in Tennessee. Her investigation included school and classroom observation; interviews with teachers, principals, superintendents, board members, and parents; data collection from 1,213 teacher questionnaires; and the analysis of student achievement. Rosenholtz concluded that schools could be categorized as *moving* (i.e., learning-enriched environments) or *stuck* (i.e., learning-impoverished environments). The following comparison summarizes characteristics of the two categories:

Rosenholtz's Categories

Moving	*Stuck*
Learning was enriched for students and teachers.	Learning was impoverished for students and teachers.
Higher levels of student achievement were the norm.	Lower levels of student achievement were the norm.
Teachers worked together.	Teachers worked alone, rarely asking for help.
Teachers shared beliefs about on-the-job learning.	Isolation, self-reliance, and turf issues predominated.

Moving	*Stuck*
High consensus was shared on the definition of teaching.	Low consensus was shared on the definition of teaching.
Shared instructional goals occupied a place of high significance.	Inertia seemed to overcome teachers' adventurous impulses.
Teachers had a marked spirit of continuous improvement in which no teacher ever stops learning how to teach.	Teachers were less likely to trust, value, and legitimize sharing expertise, seeking advice, and giving help.
80% of the teachers responded that their learning is cumulative and that learning to teach is a lifelong pursuit.	17% expressed a sustained view of learning for themselves.

The studies by the federally funded Center for Research on the Context of Secondary School Teaching at Stanford University revealed that teachers' participation in a "professional community" had a powerful effect on how successfully they were able to adapt their instructional strategies to meet students' needs (Bradley, 1993). In one study described by Bradley, McLaughlin and Talbert conducted in-depth research in 16 high schools in seven school districts in California and Michigan. One case cited (that of Rothman) was of two high schools in the same California district. Both served roughly the same student population and lived under the same rules and regulations. The study found, however, that one school had high student failure and dropout rates, whereas the other had among the highest test scores in the state and sent 80% of its students to college. The difference was reflected in the professional characteristics of the schools. A summary follows of the factors associated with student achievement from the work of McLaughlin and Talbert (as cited in Bradley, 1993):

McLaughlin and Talbert's Comparisons

High Student Achievement	*Low Student Achievement*
High levels of collegiality	Low levels of collegiality
High levels of innovation	High norms of privacy (no sharing of resources or materials)
High levels of opportunity for adult learning	No support or opportunity for adult learning
Subject matter seen as dynamic	Subject matter seen as static (canons were not to be challenged)
Commitment to success for all students, publicly declared	Large number of students fail
High standards for all students	Low standards for students
High degree of commitment to the school as a whole	Low commitment to the school workplace
More positive views of students	More negative views of students

Louis et al. (1996) supported the work of Rosenholtz (1989) and McLaughlin and Talbert (as cited in Bradley, 1993), concluding that there are three benefits from promoting structural conditions and social and human resources that support school-based professional communities:

■ Teachers are empowered to work to improve student learning. Their "sense of affiliation with each other and with the school, and their sense of mutual support and individual responsibility for the effectiveness of instruction, is increased by collaborative work with peers" (Louis et al., 1996, p. 24).

■ Teachers' sense of personal dignity in their profession is increased. This sense of dignity relates directly to their sense of efficacy, their empowerment to affect student learning.

■ Teachers' collective responsibility increases. Their concern goes beyond the learning of children in their own classes and includes the progress made by students in the entire school. Whole-school improvement becomes the focus.

Saphier and King (1985) identified 12 norms of school culture that should be strong to create a healthy school culture. The norms were (a) collegiality; (b) experimentation; (c) high expectations; (d) trust and confidence; (e) tangible support; (f) reaching out to the knowledge base; (g) appreciation and recognition; (h) caring, celebration, and humor; (i) involvement in decision making; (j) protection of what's important; (k) traditions; and (1) honest, open communications. If these norms are strong, then improvements in instruction will be significant, continuous, and widespread, say Saphier and King. But if these norms are weak, then improvements will be infrequent, random, and slow. Of the 12 norms, Saphier points to 3—collegiality, experimentation, and reaching out to a knowledge base—that have the highest correlation with changing the school environment and improving student achievement. Saphier (as cited in Richardson, 1996), founder and executive director of Research for Better Teaching, stated that current data continue to support the 1985 Saphier and King study.

Saphier and Gower (1997) devoted a chapter to the conditions that build a professional development culture that incorporates optimal conditions for teacher learning. One of the conditions that open wide the gates for improving schools through professional development is for schools to have within them both collegial structures and personal support for reflection and for study of the knowledge base on teaching. We believe that WFSGs provide this condition as well as the other six conditions Saphier and Gower list.

Linda Darling-Hammond (as cited in Lewis, 1997) of Teachers College, Columbia University, has worked extensively with professional development in schools. In a September 1996 report to the National Commission on Teaching and America's Future, she and her colleagues recommended that new policies are required to accomplish the following:

■ Redesigning school structures to support teacher learning and collaboration around serious attention to practice

■ Rethinking schedules and staffing patterns to create blocks of time for teachers to plan and work together

- Making it possible for teachers to think in terms of shared problems, not "my classroom" or "my subject"

- Organizing the school into small, collaborative groups

Murphy's research (Murphy & Lick, 1998) validates the positive impact that high norms of collegiality have on student learning. In Chapter 9, several studies from WFSG schools are reported.

All of the research cited confirms our belief that when WFSGs are implemented properly and are sustained over time, the context of the school will reflect a strong professional community that contributes to student learning. The research leaves little doubt that effective schoolwide change and enhanced student learning require a structure or a process for greater collaboration among teachers. Furthermore, it is unlikely that the desired cultural norms described earlier will happen without a deliberate strategy. Knowing general educational research and acknowledging the validity of the research will not by itself change anything. Faculties must be given a framework and process for change that is flexible enough to give them the latitude necessary to transform the research into practice. The WFSG process is such a framework. It provides a structure that creates forward-moving, learning-enriched schools.

The purpose of this book is to give schools a practical, proven-in-practice strategy or step-by-step procedure for doing what researchers conclude that schools should do. The researchers cited, and many that we have not cited, clearly state that collaborative school cultures enhance student performance. What most do not do is to tell schools how to do what they say should be done. Chapters 5 and 6 tell schools how to implement a schoolwide structure that, if sustained over time, provides a process for a school to become a university for teachers where teachers are committed not only to student success but also to each other's success.

The remainder of this chapter describes the contextual conditions that support WFSGs.

Roles and Responsibilities in WFSGs

Everyone in the school must know and understand the roles that support WFSG work. Roles and responsibilities of individuals and groups within the WFSG structure are based on the following guiding principles:

- Students are first.

- Everyone participates.

- Leadership is shared.

- Responsibility is equal.

- The work is public.

Discussion follows of the roles and responsibilities of the principal, focus team, the instructional council (IC) representatives, study group leader, and individual study group members.

The Principal

The principal is the most important factor in the successful initiation, implementation, and continuation of WFSGs. Jackson Elementary School has had study groups in place for 5 years and continues to improve. Its principal, Barry Shelofsky, has been the leader every step of the way (also see the Developing a Collaborative Culture section in Chapter 9). He initiated the WFSG approach after attending a national institute where the model was presented. He worked with a team of teachers from the school in designing an implementation plan. He was key in getting overwhelming agreement to begin. With a team of teachers, he shepherded every step of the implementation plan. He scheduled the year's calendar for the IC to meet. At midyear and at the end of each year, he and a team of teachers planned success celebrations. He and the team of teachers helped integrate major state and district curriculum initiatives into the study group process. He has used state test results as evidence that change is occurring. He keeps the superintendent informed. He initiated a study group for principals and shared the action plan and logs from their study group with the teachers at his school. He has done this for 5 years and continues doing it today.

In particular, the principal establishes the conditions that make study groups possible. Sebring and Bryk (2000) reported that principals of improving schools in Chicago skillfully used a combination of support and pressure to promote teacher collaboration and that such principals created time for collaboration and allocated school resources to support it. To initiate WFSGs, one of the first conditions to be established is the set of options for when study groups will meet, and WFSGs require adjustments to the school calendar. Time is required at the beginning of the year for the focus team to work with the whole faculty. Time is required for the IC to meet. Time is required for study groups to share the work of the groups.

Also, WFSGs will change how principals work. WFSGs will not accomplish intended purposes, increases in student learning, if the principal does not establish the necessary conditions.

The principal

- Is the critical initial and sustaining sponsor and key advocate of WFSG

- Is an active participant in training and planning sessions

- Receives action plans and responds to them

- Receives the study group logs and responds to them

- Ensures that there is time for study groups to meet and guards that time

- Helps identify expertise, both internal and external, to support study group work

- Encourages and assists in making arrangements for teachers to observe students in classrooms working on assignments that focus on the student needs the study groups are addressing

- Establishes and maintains internal communication networks among study groups

- Puts the monthly meetings of the IC on the school calendar

- Is a participant at all IC meetings

- Receives the names of representatives who will attend an IC meeting and confirms logistics with all representatives (e.g., date, time, location, and what to bring)

- Works with the IC meeting facilitator prior to a meeting to ensure that the facilitator is well informed of the status of each study group

- Uses study groups as the primary units to implement the school's improvement plan

- Communicates to district leaders, parents, and the general community what study groups do

- Is assertive in providing technical assistance to a study group that loses its momentum or is not doing work that is likely to affect student learning in a positive manner

- Initiates procedures for study groups to assess progress of groups' work and uses assessment information to strengthen their work

- Charts the impact of study groups on student learning by always keeping student data in front of the faculty

The Focus Team

The focus team is made up of the principal and several teachers and is the unit that gets WFSGs started and assesses progress during and at the end of a school year. At the beginning and end of each school year, the focus team leads the whole faculty through the steps on the DMC to review data that provides direction at the beginning of a cycle and confirms progress at the end of a cycle. To begin the first year, the team needs special instruction or training. The first year may begin at any time from August through February. The special instruction occurs prior to the beginning of WFSGs. It can be received from a specialist in the WFSG approach, the team can be sent to a regional or national conference where the WFSG approach is featured, or a team can read this book and work through its various sections together. Any of these training avenues should result in an initiation plan, a step-by-step plan of what to do and who will be responsible for each activity in the plan. The end result of the focus team's work with the whole faculty when WFSGs are initiated is the identification of what study groups will do and the organization of study groups around identified student needs. Because of the specificity of the team's initial task, it is recommended that, regardless of the size of the school, the focus team be limited to from 4 to 8 members. Just as with study groups, the larger the size, the harder it is for members of the focus team to get together for additional planning sessions and assume equal responsibility for the tasks. There are no criteria for the selection of the team other than that members should represent a cross section of the grades at the school. Before accepting responsibility, prospective members should be given a written description of the team's responsibilities.

The focus team

- Is composed of the principal and a representative group of teachers from the WFSG process

- Attends local training, goes to a regional or national conference, or reads materials on how to design and lead the whole faculty through a workshop for faculty's understanding of WFSGs

- Leads the whole faculty in sessions to define WFSGs, review the research supporting them, develop understanding of their functions, and present the 15 guidelines for WFSGs

- Leads the whole faculty through the decision-making cycle at the beginning of the school year, resulting in the establishment of study groups and what they will do

- Leads the whole faculty through the DMC at the end of the school year, assessing student learning as a result of the study groups

- Decides which 3 of its members will be "standing" members of and rotating facilitators for the IC for one school year

- Is an advocate group for the WFSG process

- Initiates forms of communication to keep everyone informed about what all groups are doing

The Instructional Council

The IC is made up of representatives from each study group, and it meets every 4 to 6 weeks during the school year. The major functions of the IC and the focus team are different. The focus team leads the faculty through the DMC at the beginning and at the end of a school year. In the beginning, this gets study groups started, and at the end of the year, this assesses progress. The focus team requires special training. On the other hand, the IC oversees the total process, maintains WFSGs during the school year, and requires no special training for participation (refer to Resource D, minutes from the IC meetings at Jackson Elementary School). Three members from the focus team are standing members of the IC. These 3 individuals rotate serving as facilitators of the IC meetings. Other than these 3 individuals, persons attending the meeting will most likely be different each time the IC meets: Members of study groups rotate attendance at IC meetings. For instance, if there were 6 members of a study group, each member would attend every sixth meeting of the IC, meaning that most members will attend only one IC meeting per school year. Persons who attend the IC meeting are referred to as representatives, not members. Another section in this chapter gives more information about the IC.

IC representatives

- Represent each study group (one representative per study group)

- Rotate membership, except for the principal and 3 members of the focus team

- Meet once every 4 or 5 weeks (dates are on the school calendar), with the first meeting held immediately after the study groups have met twice

- Review action plans

- Share what each study group is doing, including successes and challenges

- Plan celebrations and whole-faculty sharing times

- Take at least 15 minutes of their next study group meeting to share information

- May take a study group meeting to teach their study group a protocol or lead their study group in learning more about a given topic

- Chart changes in student learning and keeps student data on the table

The facilitator of the IC

- Is one of the 3 members of the IC from the focus team

- Receives from the principal the names of study group representatives who will attend the meeting

- Establishes the agenda for the next meeting at the end of a meeting

- Confirms the agenda with the facilitator of the last meeting

- Starts and ends the meeting on time

- Reviews group norms at the beginning of a meeting

- Sees that someone takes meeting minutes and that these are distributed to the whole faculty

- Reminds all representatives of their responsibility to share information with their study group

The Study Group Leader

The leader of a study group requires no special training. The work of the group gives it direction. The focus of a study group is on the work of the group, not on that of any individual member. All members are equal in status and in responsibility for the work and success of their study group. Members of a study group rotate leadership by the week or after every 2 weeks.

The study group leader of a meeting

- Confirms logistics with study group members (e.g., date, time, location, and resources required)

- Checks the previous log to confirm the focus of the next meeting

- Reviews earlier logs to see if it is time to revisit the action plan and group norms and then takes the appropriate action

- Starts and ends the meeting on time

- Reminds members who stray from the focus of the meeting to refocus

- Sees that the study group log is completed and that members and the principal receive copies

- Shares any comments the principal or other individuals may have made on the log from the previous meeting

The Individual Study Group Member

The most important role in study groups is that of the individual member. If the study group is productive, it will be because every single member does his or her part. It will be because each member participates and is willing to give his or her colleagues what they require to be successful. The success of WFGSs rest of the shoulders of each individual member. WFGSs are only as successful as each member feels success. Each member of a study group has students for whom he or she is responsible. The critical end result of WFSGs is that each student learns more. This student focus requires that each teacher enables each of their students to learn more.

The individual study group member

- Respects norms established by the study group

- Takes a turn serving as leader, recognizing that leadership is a shared responsibility

- Takes a turn representing the study group at an IC meeting and shares with the study group what he or she learned

- Participates in the development of the study group action plan and commits to its actions

- Takes responsibility for his or her own learning and for seeking resources for the study group

- Takes responsibility for regularly bringing student work to the study group meeting

- Shares with the study group what he or she has done in the classroom as a result of the study group work

Table 4.1 charts the roles and responsibilities of all those involved in WFSGs.

The context of the school addresses the organization, system, or culture in which the study groups exist. The administration, the focus team, the IC, and individual study groups are units of the organization that support schoolwide change. How these units interact in a seamless and supportive way determines the success of WFSGs.

More About the Instructional Council

The IC establishes the conditions that make WFSGs a whole-school change model. Whatever such a group is called, it must exist and function as described in Figure 4.1. The name does not matter, but the purposes or functions of the group are critical for WFSGs to attain the intended results: that all students in the school achieve higher levels of learning. Every teacher is in a study group so that every student will learn and achieve more because of what teachers are learning and doing in study groups.

As previously described, the IC is an oversight group that has a representative from each study group and meets every 4 to 6 weeks to oversee the WFSG process and content. The first meeting should be held immediately after the second round of study group meetings (refer to Resource D, the minutes of an IC meeting at Maynard School). The purpose of the first IC meeting is to review all of the action plans. The action plan for each study group should be copied for the first meeting and each rep-

(text continues on p. 57)

Table 4.1 Roles and Responsibilities in the WFSG Process

The Principal

- Is the sponsor and key advocate

- Is an active participant in training and planning sessions

- Receives the action plans and responds to the plans

- Receives the study group logs and responds to the logs

- Ensures that there is time for study groups to meet and guards that time

- Helps identify expertise, both internal and external, to support study group work

- Assists in making arrangements for teachers to observe students in each other's classes

- Establishes and maintains internal communication networks among study groups

- Puts the monthly meetings of the IC on the school calendar and attends the meetings

- Receives the names of the representatives that will attend an IC meeting and confirms logistics with all the representatives (e.g., date, time, location, and what to bring)

- Uses the study groups as the primary units to implement the school's improvement plan

- Communicates to district leaders, parents, and the general community what study groups do

- Is assertive in providing technical assistance to a study group that loses its momentum or is not doing work that is likely to affect student learning in a positive manner

- Initiates procedures for the study groups assessing progress of the work of the groups and uses the assessment information to strengthen the work

- Charts impact of study groups on student learning by always keeping student data in front of the faculty

The Focus Team

- Is composed of the principal and a representative group of teachers

- Attends local training, goes to a regional or national conference, or reads materials for the purpose of learning how to design and to lead the whole faculty through a workshop to develop the faculty's understanding of the WFSG approach

- Leads the whole faculty in one or more sessions to define WFSG, review the research supporting WFSG, develop understanding of the functions of WFSG, and present the 15 WFSG guidelines

- Leads the whole faculty through the DMC at the beginning of the school year that results in establishing what study groups will do and in the establishment of study groups

- Leads the whole faculty through the DMC at the end of the school year to assess the status of student learning as a result of the study groups

- Selects 3 of its members to be standing members of the IC for 1 school year and to rotate serving as the facilitator of the IC

(continued)

Table 4.1 Continued

The Study Group Leader

- Rotates weekly, every 2 weeks, or monthly so that leadership is a shared responsibility among all study groups members

- Confirms logistics of meetings with study group members (e.g., date, time, location, and resources needed)

- Checks the log from the last meeting to confirm what the focus of the meeting will be

- Checks the logs to see if it is time to revisit the action plan and the group norms, then takes the appropriate action

- Starts and ends the meeting on time

- Reminds members that stray from the focus of the meeting to refocus

- Sees that the study group log is completed and that the members and the principal receive a copy

---

Individual Study Group Members

- Respect norms established by the study group

- Take turns serving as leader, recognizing that leadership is a shared responsibility

- Take turns representing the study group at an IC meeting and bring back to the study group what he or she learned

- Participates in the development of the study group action plan and commits to its actions

- Take responsibility for his or her own learning and for seeking resources for the study group

- Takes responsibility for regularly bringing student work to the study group meeting

- Brings back to the study group what he or she has done in the classroom as a result of the study group work

---

The Instructional Council

- Is composed of one person from each study group

- Rotates membership, except for the principal and 3 members of the focus team

- Meets once every 4 or 5 weeks (dates on school calendar)

- Focuses on what each study group is doing

- Is where successes and challenges are shared

- Plans celebrations and whole-faculty sharing times

- Is a two-way communication system

IC Representatives (continued)

- May need to take one full meeting to teach the study group a protocol or to lead the study group in learning more about a given topic

- Chart changes in student learning and keep student data on the table

Facilitator of the IC

- Is one of the 3 persons on the IC that are also members of the focus team

- Receives the names of the representatives that will attend the meeting

- At the end of the meeting establishes the agenda for the next meeting

- Confirms the agenda with the facilitator of the last meeting

- Starts and ends the meeting on time

- Reviews the group norms at the beginning of a meeting

- Sees that someone takes the minutes of the meeting and that the minutes are distributed to the whole faculty

- Reminds all the representatives of their responsibility to take information back to the study groups

District-Level Support Person

- Collects and distributes relevant information to the principal

- Assists the focus team, as needed

- Helps identify and make available district resources

- Attends faculty meetings and training sessions, as appropriate

- Is knowledgeable about the study group action plans

- Is an advocate for the school with the superintendent and board of education members

- Speaks for the school when district budgets are developed

- Supports need for time for study groups to meet with responsible parties

- Communicates what the school is doing with other district-level staff

Figure 4.1. WFSGs: The Network for Communication and Support

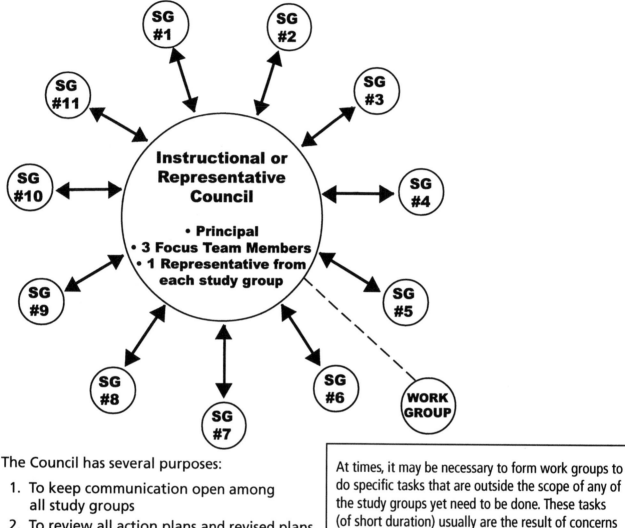

The Council has several purposes:

1. To keep communication open among all study groups
2. To review all action plans and revised plans
3. For study group representatives to share what the groups are doing

> At times, it may be necessary to form work groups to do specific tasks that are outside the scope of any of the study groups yet need to be done. These tasks (of short duration) usually are the result of concerns coming from individual study groups.

4. To hear problems groups are experiencing and to have joint participation in how those problems might be solved
5. To share successes and plan for dissemination of those successes
6. To determine how groups can share resources
7. To determine if the whole faculty requires common training
8. To coordinate events, speakers
9. To plan whole-faculty sharings and celebrations
10. To identify common instructional concerns
11. To set instructional goals
12. To set limits on instructional initiatives

The Council meets every 4 to 6 weeks, meeting the first time immediately after all groups have met twice.

resentative given a set of all the plans. At the study group meeting immediately following the first IC meeting, each representative should go over the action plan with his or her study group.

The group of representatives may be given any name, such as Representative Council, that does not conflict with the name of another group at the school. Because study groups are focused on what is taught and how it is taught, "instruction" has seemed an appropriate term to use. The primary purposes of the IC are for communication among the study groups and for delivering information to each study group. At times, that information will be presented in the format of specific skills all teachers must have to optimize the work of the study groups. Because the IC has a representative from each study group, it is the logical group to receive special instruction or training during the school year (refer to Resource D, minutes from the IC meeting at Webster County School). There are ongoing skills and information that each study group must have to continue to grow as a group and to attain intended results. There may be times during the school year when the representatives will need release time, an hour or as long as a day, to receive special instruction. For example, if a consultant is coming to the school to teach representatives how to use a protocol, the representatives will need time for this training. After such training, the representative will let the leader of the next study group meeting know that it will take one full study group meeting to share what was learned. The IC only has value if the representative of each study group shares what happened at the IC meeting at the next study group meeting.

Minutes are taken at IC meetings. Every teacher in the school should be given a copy of the minutes as soon as possible after the meeting. Minutes are somewhat like a newsletter, telling what study groups are doing. At some schools, one person assumes the responsibility for taking and distributing minutes. At other schools, the task is rotated. However, it is determined prior to the meeting who will be responsible, and that person comes prepared. Using a laptop computer for the task simplifies taking, printing, and distributing what happens at meetings.

If there are 6 study group members, each member would only attend one IC meeting a school year. A time limit is put on the length of the meeting. The IC usually meets for 1 hour after school. Some ICs meet while the study groups are meeting, when study groups all meet on the same day at the same time. In such cases, a member would only miss one study group meeting a year to attend an IC meeting.

Suggestions for Schools That Have More Than 20 Study Groups

The operation and functions of the IC in large schools and in small schools are the same. The only factor that may need modification is the number of study group representatives that attend the IC meetings.

One large high school had 47 study groups. Obviously, it would be difficult for 47 study group representatives to meet together and accomplish the IC's purposes. This school clustered the study groups, putting 3 study groups in each cluster, making 16 clusters. The 3 study groups in a cluster rotated sending a representative. That means that if the IC meets 6 times during the school year, each study group would only have 2 of its members going to an IC meeting that school year. In September, a schedule is established so everyone will know what the rotation is. The cluster study groups of 3 meet together for about 15 minutes during the study group meeting that immediately follows the IC meeting. If more time is needed, study groups in the cluster may meet together for the full hour. This would be the case when the representatives must teach study group members how to use a particular protocol or group technique.

When clustering is done, it makes sense to cluster study groups that are doing similar work. For example, technology study groups could be one cluster. Not only does the clustering facilitate communication, it also gives study groups addressing similar student needs the opportunity to share. In large schools, clustering provides a forum to accomplish a number of professional development needs, especially in the area of training. It is difficult to address any type of professional development need with over 100 teachers in a large room at one time. The high school that had 47 study groups had a faculty of over 250 teachers. The study group organization and the clustering system helped the school tailor its professional development needs.

District Influences

Major influences on the context of a school are the school district in which the school is located and the district leaders who are ultimately held responsible for the schools. Schools exist within the context of school districts. The school district is in fact the structural organization that typically shapes schools and schooling. It is the central board of education and district administrators that are ultimately responsible for what happens in schools. The district can be one of the most important sponsors of innovation in schools or a serious inhibitor of progress. The district level both constrains and facilitates. It provides a kind of supported enforcement. The culture of the district gives the underlying structure of meaning, and it permeates schools. It facilitates or constrains school administrators' and teachers' perceptions, interpretations, and behaviors. Schools want approval of district leaders and to be consistent and in compliance with district expectations. The district has influence that affects almost every major decision that school personnel make. Districts can reward, censure, or sanction. Often, that influence is invisible, not generally openly discussed. However, it is there. The district office can be a critical sponsor of change; it creates conditions for the process of change, establishes specific district goals, ensures accountability, and sets time lines. It is the district that initiates most of the instructional innovations that confront schools. The district usually sets priorities for budgets. How much money schools have for staff development, heavily influenced by district priorities, determines what schools can do. Districts determine whether consultants are used, what materials are purchased, whether teachers are paid for their involvement in staff development activities, and whether substitutes are obtained to release teachers for study or training.

Schools most often have building-level responsibility for implementation and staff flexibility to respond to their environment but not at the expense of district goals and priorities. It seems that the matter of school-district balance is not easily solvable. It represents an inherently complex dilemma between autonomy and accountability and variation and consistency.

The greatest problem faced by school districts and schools is not so much resistance to innovation but the fragmentation, overload, and incoherence resulting from the uncritical and uncoordinated acceptance of too many innovations (Fullan & Steigelbauer, 1991; also see the Assimilation Capacity section later in this chapter).

The key role of the district support staff is to help schools sort out and implement right choices for each school. Many good programs are diffused at the school level simply because schools are unclear as to the district-level priority of the program. A major function of WFSGs is to set school priorities and focus on implementing those priorities to the level that student effects are measurable. The school faculty is asked to identify instructional initiatives and bring coherence to what they and the school are trying to do.

Murphy's work as the administrator of a school district's staff development programs for 15 years gave her an insider's view of the operation of a school district with 60 schools within its jurisdiction. Within the context of WFSGs or any other school initiative, it is appropriate to examine how various district-level leaders respond to innovations that are in various stages of implementation in schools. A district-level leader is defined as a person with a title, such as superintendent, assistant superintendent, director, coordinator, and curriculum specialist. Such individuals are usually not assigned full-time to any particular school and work under the supervision of the superintendent, an assistant superintendent, or a department director. A conversation Murphy had with colleague Mike McMann in Shoreline, Washington, added validity to Murphy's own experiences. The two agreed that district-level leaders in the same district respond to an initiative in different ways, as do leaders in schools. The response may be to prevent, ignore, permit, acknowledge, expect, or empower. One leader may actually take action to prevent an initiative from happening. Another may simply ignore what is happening or about to happen. A leader with authority may permit an initiative to happen without actually encouraging the initiators or acknowledging work that the faculty has done. This last response makes school leaders uneasy and seems to be the most damaging, for example, in the first year of implementation. It is somewhat of a "wait and see" position, and just when the school requires the most visible support, key district support personnel, such as curriculum specialists, are unsure about priorities. As an initiative gets under way, the leader who permitted the work to begin may very quickly move to acknowledgment. For example, in Augusta, the superintendent, who permitted the MOT program work to begin, started many of the principals' meetings by having a principal of a MOT school share the good work his or her faculty was doing. This form of acknowledgment is very powerful.

Once an initiative does get under way, some leaders will ignore the work or try to prevent it from continuing. Some leaders who once ignored the work or may have even tried to prevent it from happening will come to acknowledge and expect the work to continue and to improve. Some leaders who once publicly acknowledged the work or expected the work to begin and continue may at some later time prevent it from continuing. Leaders may, in fact, change their positions or attitudes toward an innovation. Teachers in schools find these responses both confusing and disheartening. Teachers hear rumors one day that the work will continue, and the next day, they may hear that continuation is not supported. Teachers hear that one influential person feels one way and another influential person feels the opposite. This clatter in district offices has a significant influence on how principals and teachers feel and act in schools. It also affects the context of schooling. For a school initiative, such as WFSGs, to have the early momentum required to get groups moving and for teachers to be willing to spend the extra time and energy on collaborative work, acknowledgment from the district office is essential.

Figure 4.2, which shows leadership responses to initiates, does not represent a linear movement. A leader may initially respond to an initiative at one point, such as

Figure 4.2. Leadership Response to Initiatives

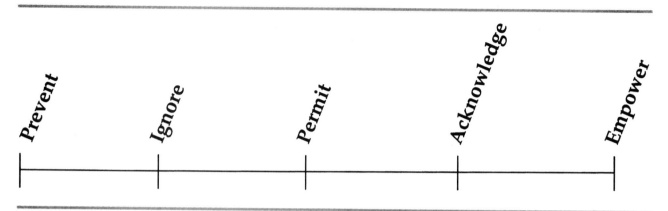

"expect," and over a period of time come to another, such as to "empower" the initiators or to "ignore" the initiative.

Schools that have been most successful in initiating and implementing WFSGs are those that are in districts that value schools as learning communities for the adults in their schools. Most of the initiators of the study group process are district leaders. Districts have used district funds to supplement school funds in efforts to support the study group process. Districts have recognized WFSG schools and asked their principals to speak at meetings for administrators. When districts stop showing signs of approval and support for what schools do, schools become discouraged, regardless of how well the process is going. Schools follow the lead of the district. As district interests shift, so will school interests (Murphy, 1991b).

We must take seriously the sponsorship role that districts play in change at the school level. We often forget that the district, not the schools, employs teachers and administrators. For the vast majority of teachers, districts are unquestionably important organizations. But most teachers, especially in large districts, only vaguely perceive districts. Districts are often perceived as unpredictable and hostile, the "they" who make ill-informed and unwelcome decisions. If positive change is desired in schools, then there must be as much concern given to the quality of district leadership and sponsorship as there is to the quality of schools.

Rosenholtz (1989) defined stuck and moving environments as learning-impoverished and learning-enriched environments for the adults and students. She found that stuck schools (learning-impoverished schools) were most often found in stuck districts; likewise, moving schools (learning-enriched schools) were most often found in moving districts. Rosenholtz went on to say that we must examine interorganizational relations, those conditions that drive schools to more or less efficient ends. She suggests that keys to unlocking sustained commitment and capacity for schools' continuous renewal are

■ How districts select principals and teachers

■ Whether districts offer them continuous opportunities for learning

■ Whether task autonomy is delegated to schools and thereafter monitored

These three areas can greatly facilitate the initiation and continuation of WFSGs. It is almost impossible for schools to redesign themselves without district sponsorship. The role of the district is critical. Individual schools can become highly innovative for short periods of time without the district, but they cannot stay innovative over time without district action to establish conditions for continuous and long-term improvement (Levine & Eubanks, 1989).

School Culture Is Central to Understanding the Context

Schools have evolved over a long period of time, and our general approaches to schooling have been in place for centuries. As a consequence, schools have well-established cultures, a part of the context for the study group environment (referred to in Chapter 3), that give them and their programs stability and govern how issues are addressed and what can happen in schools. However, school cultures are fairly rigid and make schools far less open to change than might be desirable when trying to introduce new concepts and practices for the enhancement of student learning and school improvement.

Among the best mechanisms for bringing about meaningful cultural change are professional WFSGs. When properly supported and applied, study groups have the potential to modify aspects of a school culture to allow for enough change so that educational processes and schools can be improved. Why is this so important? Because school cultures, like many others, are so difficult to productively and qualitatively change. Although not all cultural change is valuable, positive school change will come about only when the school's culture is changed appropriately.

School culture is not always visible to outsiders and even to many within it, but it is always there and always very powerful. School culture is the social and normative glue that holds together the educational and educationally related aspects of a school and creates the central features, structures, and approaches that characterize it (Birmbaum, 1988).

The culture is what sets one school distinctly apart from another; it is a school's self-concept, analogous to an individual's personality. The culture of a school, for example, establishes a unique set of ground rules, both stated and unstated, for how people in the school think and behave and for what they assume to be true.

The concept of school culture has generated many definitions and approaches to the subject. Because our interests in culture focus on its relationship to change (e.g., student learning enhancement and school improvement), we shall use a definition adapted from Connor (1993) that has been used extensively and successfully in organizational research and change efforts: *School culture* reflects the interrelationship of shared assumptions, beliefs, and behaviors that are acquired over time by members of a school.

Building Blocks of the Culture of a School

As stated, key building blocks of the culture of a school are the assumptions, beliefs, and behaviors of the school and its personnel. To change the culture of the school for its enhancement, we must change one or more of the assumptions, beliefs, or behaviors.

Assumptions in a school are the unconscious and therefore unquestioned perceptions concerning what is important and how people and things operate in and relating to the school—that is, the unconscious rationale for people continuing to use certain beliefs and behaviors. For example, teachers in schools often have the unconscious assumption that the lecture approach is a good way to teach, whereas research tells us that there may be more effective approaches.

Beliefs are the values and expectations that people hold to be true about themselves, others, their work, and the school. They provide a basis for what people in the school hold to be right or wrong, good or bad, and relevant or irrelevant about their school and its operation. Belief statements in schools, for instance, relate to such things as the vital role played by the personal interaction of the teachers and students, value of the grading system, importance of lesson plans, and the need for staff development.

Behaviors are the ways people conduct themselves on a day-to-day basis. They are perceptible actions that are based on values and expectations and are ideally aimed at carrying out the school's mission. Whereas assumptions and beliefs often reflect intentions that are difficult to discern, behaviors are observable and can be noted objectively. Behaviors of teachers, for example, might include such things as how they teach, prepare lesson plans, advise students, and use technology, whereas behaviors for administrators might include how they assess teaching, involve faculty in decision making, encourage innovation, and relate to other administrators.

Teachers in a WFSG school often have had unconscious assumptions about their self-esteem and professionalism. Their WFSG efforts helped them see themselves more like physicians and other professionals, changing their unconscious assumptions about their self-esteem and professional outlook dramatically. The change in these assumptions also brought about changes in the teachers' beliefs. Teachers now believed that they had professional training that they could be proud of; that they were as professional as physicians, lawyers, and other professionals; and that they could and should function more like professionals in their activities and responsibilities. As a result, the behavior of these teachers changed substantially, including displaying diplomas and certificates, taking more responsibility for colearning with colleagues, having greater confidence in themselves, and functioning more professionally and assertively with parents. These were important changes in the assumptions, beliefs, and behaviors of the teachers and the school and represented a positive, major shift in their culture.

School cultures can be realigned through a process called *cultural shift*. Such a cultural transformation requires realigning, in some measure, assumptions, beliefs, and behaviors to make them more consistent with the new directions of the school. No cultural shift can materialize without some modification of the assumptions, beliefs, or behaviors. One important strength of the study group process is that it has the capability to bring about a cultural shift and, through the shift, desirable changes in how a school functions. The following table illustrates a moving process and does not infer time. As study groups bring about cultural changes or cultural shift, student changes most often accompany the shift. The flow is more like a wave than a sequence.

| Study groups | ➠ | Cultural changes | ➠ | Student changes |

We outline study group processes in later chapters and show how these processes lead to important cultural shifts in schools.

Assimilation Capacity

One of the major problems in schools (and most other organizations as well) is that they have too many change efforts going on at any one time. This is a serious problem for the personnel of the school, the various groups that are functioning in the school, and the school itself.

People and schools have only so much capacity or resources to deal with change, their assimilation capacity. The assimilation capacity is different for different individuals; some individuals have little capacity to deal with change, whereas others may have substantial capacity. The same is true for groups and organizations, with some having limited assimilation capacity and others having much more.

When there is so much change that an individual's assimilation capacity is surpassed, then that individual's efforts are degraded and the individual performs below his or her normal levels of productivity and quality. In such a case, we say the individual is dysfunctional; that is, his or her actions or feelings divert resources away from meeting productivity and quality standards. Dysfunctional individuals can continue to perform, but they perform at lower levels of productivity and quality. In a similar way, groups and schools can be dysfunctional; this happens when their assimilation capacities are surpassed and they perform at lower than optimal productivity and quality levels.

Dysfunctional behavior in individuals ranges, for example, from low levels (poor communications, reduced risk taking, lower morale, and conflicts with fellow workers) to medium levels (lying, chronic tardiness, apathy, and interpersonal withdrawal) to high levels (covert undermining of the leadership, chronic depression, physical breakdown, and substance abuse). Simply put, if individuals, groups, or schools are asked to handle too much change in their total area of action, including work, home, family and friends, community, and beyond, they will become dysfunctional and cannot perform optimally. The students, school, family, and others all lose. When this is true for all or most of the personnel in a school, then the loss is major and serious. Often, this represents reality today in our schools and other organizations in society.

Typically, schools are filled with an excess number of low-priority to middle-priority projects that have some value or would be nice to have but will have little real effect on the productivity and quality of the school. In fact, these low- to middle-priority projects actually stand in the way of accomplishing the ongoing and other potentially high-priority efforts.

In particular, most faculties have exceeded their capacities to assimilate all the changes, and many faculties, as a whole, are dysfunctional. Such discoveries bring clarity to what must be done and give a sense of hope to teachers. Now that we understand these assimilation and dysfunction concerns better, what can we do about them? A five-step process for dealing with such concerns follows:

1. Leaders must become aware of the concepts of limited assimilation capacities and associated dysfunctions and their serious potential negative impact on the people and effectiveness of the school and its operations.

2. Before new projects involving major change are initiated, a thorough analysis of all existing projects should be undertaken and a list of them prepared.

3. Projects should be prioritized, ranging from low to high priority (imperatives).

4. All but the highest-priority projects should be considered for termination or reduction in scope.

5. A plan should be developed and implemented to eliminate or reduce in scope as many of the lower-priority projects as is practical, timely, and cost-effective.

Roles of Change in Schools

As schools attempt to build commitment for study group efforts that affect their people, processes, and outcomes, an understanding of the four *roles of change*—change sponsor, change agent, change target, and change advocate—is critical.

A *change sponsor* or *sponsor* is an individual or group who has the power to sanction or legitimize the change or efforts of the study group. In schools, depending on the specific change effort, a sponsor might be the school board, the superintendent, the principal, a department chair, or a combination of these individuals, because they typically are the ones who can sanction or legitimize study group efforts and change. Also, in a WFSG situation, where essentially the whole faculty has endorsed the study group initiative, the faculty itself becomes an important and potentially effective sponsor of the study group change process and results.

It is the sponsor's responsibility to decide which initiatives and changes will be authorized; communicate their decisions and priorities to the school and its personnel; and provide the appropriate encouragement, pressure, and support for study groups' efforts. Strong sponsors are key to the building of commitment for study group efforts and can create an environment in the school that enables their work to be effectively implemented and productive.

In school districts that seriously choose to participate in study groups, superintendents, principals, and the board of education sponsor the implementation of the study group process and legitimized it. This makes the study group process both important to the schools and legitimate for principals, teachers, and others to invest time and serious commitment in. Also, in educating parents and bringing them along with the effort, they too become direct or indirect supporters of the study group approach.

A *change agent* or *agent* is an individual or group who is responsible for implementing the desired change. Teachers and study groups often play the role of change agent, as do various administrators and supervisors. Agents' success depends on their preparation as change agents, their relations with others in the school, and their ability to diagnose problems, deal with the issues, plan solutions, and implement their plan effectively. Properly prepared study groups have the potential to be especially effective change agents in their schools.

A *change target* or *target* is an individual or group who must actually change. Targets are the people who must change if innovation is to be successful. In school improvement projects, targets typically are students, teachers, or administrators. For example, if the change calls for computer-assisted instruction, then students, as well as a number of teachers and administrators, would be targets and have to change by learning how to use computers in an instructional mode.

Like us, targets will be more responsive to our change efforts if we put things in their frame of reference and help them fully understand the desired change, why it is important, what is expected of them, and the impact of the change on them and the school. Fullan (1991) states that people must be able to attach their own personal meaning to the change experiences. The change agent, then, must be alert to how the meaning of change is communicated to the targets of the change. Figure 2.1 in Chapter 2 illustrates who is expected to change with the implementation of WFSGs.

A *change advocate* or *advocate* is an individual or group who desires a change but doesn't have the authority or power to sanction it. Frequently, faculty study groups, the principal, or nonschool persons or groups, such as parents, play the role of advocate when they want something new to happen but do not have the power to approve it. Advocates typically recommend actions to those with the authority to approve or further recommend. For instance, a community person may advocate for a special resolution to the school board, or a department may ask the principal for a special budget consideration, or a principal might recommend a certain policy to the superintendent for school board consideration. However, it should be noted that advocates are not sponsors or effective replacements for sponsors.

In different circumstances, an individual or group may play different change roles. Earlier, we described how study groups could play all four roles of change sponsor, agent, target, and advocate. In addition, various change projects might require an individual or group to serve in more than one change role. A typical example might be where a principal is a change agent to the superintendent but a sponsor to school teachers. The important thing to remember is to determine the role you are playing in the given situation and perform it well.

Effective Sponsorship of Change in Schools

All four change roles are necessary for the success of WFSGs. However, the roles of those in leadership positions are especially critical. Earlier, when listing the responsibilities of the principal, the first item was "the sponsor," and for district influence, the district is one of the most important sponsors. For major innovations to be successfully implemented in our schools, sponsors must demonstrate strong, decisive, and visible commitment to those efforts. Very simply, significant change will not occur without sufficient commitment and action by sponsors, such as those by a board of education, superintendents, and principals in the schools. Sponsors must show strong commitment to ensure that agents and targets are effective in their roles. Often, the difference between success and failure in school efforts comes down to the quality of the sponsorship!

In his excellent book on change, Conner (1993) outlines the characteristics of a good sponsor. What follows is an adaptation of these sponsorship characteristics to the school setting:

- Power: Power in the school to legitimize the change with targets

- Pain: A level of discomfort with some area of the school that makes change there attractive

- Vision: A clear understanding of what change must occur

- Resources: An understanding of the school resources (e.g., time, money, and people) necessary for successful implementation and the capacity (i.e., willingness and ability) to commit them

- ■ Long View: An in-depth understanding of the effect the change will have on the school

- ■ Sensitivity: The capacity to appreciate and empathize with the personal issues raised by the change

- ■ Scope: The capacity to understand fully the impact of the change

- ■ Public Role: The capacity to demonstrate the public support necessary to convey strong school commitment to the change

- ■ Private Role: The capacity to meet privately with key individuals or groups to convey strong personal support for the change

- ■ Consequence Management: The capacity to promptly reward those who facilitate the change or to express displeasure with those who inhibit it

- ■ Monitor: The capacity to ensure that monitoring procedures are established that will track both the progress and problems of the transition

- ■ Sacrifice: The commitment to pursue the transition, knowing that a price will most often accompany the change

- ■ Persistence: The capacity to demonstrate consistent support for the change and reject any short-term action that is inconsistent with the long-term change goals

The aforenamed criteria give a comprehensive set of characteristics by which to measure the sponsorship for WFSGs in a school or district. If most of these are met, there is a high probability for good sponsorship and support. However, if several of these are not satisfied, then there may be serious sponsorship problems; in such situations, leaders should work to improve sponsorship for the effort or replace the sponsors with stronger ones.

WFSGs and their schoolwide efforts represent major change in the school. As a result, they will require the same strong and effective sponsorship as that outlined. If a major study group initiative does not have a reasonably high level of sponsorship commitment or if such cannot be developed in an appropriate time frame, then the initiative has a high risk of failure.

What should be done if sponsorship is weak? When sponsors are not fully committed to the study group process, don't fully understand it, or are unable or unwilling to provide adequate support, there are only three options (Conner, 1993): Advocates must educate sponsors, find strong alternate sponsorship, or prepare to fail. Strong sponsorship is absolutely vital to the success of effective WFSGs and the change initiatives they hope to accomplish!

Human Change and Resistance in Schools

There is one certainty with change: Someone will resist. Why? Because resistance is natural and normal for people. Nonetheless, if there were one point we would like to communicate, it would be this: Don't let resisters stop necessary change. Too often, we let a small, loud percentage of a faculty rule the day. We should listen to concerns of others, try to understand, and take their concerns into consideration. Yet, at some point, we simply have to get started, include those resisting in study groups, and assume that in a small group with peers, the concerns can be worked out. Murphy often illustrates this point when she tells a story about a teacher in Augusta who initially was very reticent and vocal about her objection and opposition to the whole school improvement program, called MOT. The teacher did not want to be a member of a study group; however, like all teachers at the school, she was included in a study group. From August through October, she was cool to other members and somewhat reluctant to fully participate. By January, she was demonstrating strategies to her study group colleagues and bringing student work to show how well her students were responding. By April, she was being videotaped as an example of how to effectively use the strategies and study group meetings to fine-tune a lesson. Within 2 years, she was a member of Murphy's staff. Suppose she had been allowed to not participate? The gulf between this teacher and those teachers in study groups would have widened, and her constructive contributions would have been lost.

In their book chapter titled "The States of Growth of People in the Organizations," Joyce and Showers (1995) describe how individuals interact with the environment, drawing conclusions from 300 educators in 21 districts. They relate three prototypes that are useful in helping staff developers understand behaviors of individuals. One prototype is a "gourmet omnivore," those individuals, about 20% of the total, who will exploit and enrich whatever environment they find themselves in. The next prototype is a "passive consumer," those individuals, about 70%, whose degree of activity greatly depends on who they are with—amiable, though unenterprising. The third prototype is a "reticent consumer," those individuals, about 10%, that expend energy actually pushing away opportunities for growth. Joyce states, "The hard core reticent even rejects opportunities for involvement in decision making, regarding them as co-opting moves by basically malign forces" (p. 179). Knowing that about 70% of individuals in schools are passive consumers, we have a better sense for creating the WFSG environment. In particular, WFSGs stimulate these individuals and cause them to consume more than they would otherwise. This is the population on which we should focus. But what do we do? Too often, we see resisters and feel their rejection and use our precious energy trying to persuade them. We must understand that it isn't just our efforts that they don't want to do. They don't want to do anything, and they know exactly how to make enough noise so that leaders leave them alone. In WFSG schools, we simply include them. By including them, we have a chance to have an impact on their attitude and behaviors and to gain from their input and contributions. We must remember that resisters teach children, too.

Philip Schlechty (1993) writes that individuals play different roles in the restructuring process. The five types of roles that are activated are trailblazer, pioneer, settler, stay-at-home, and saboteur. The first three will go where they need to go and do what they need to do, just at different rates. The trailblazers are the first to go, not afraid to venture into the unknown; the pioneers follow, often cutting their own paths before the roads are clear; the settlers wait until they have assurances that roads are clear and some bridges have been built. The settlers go in large groups, believing that there is safety in numbers. This is the largest group, and as with any major movement, it is the settlers that will bring stability. These are the folks that once they understand and accept what is ahead of them, we know we can depend on them. The stay-at-homes won't keep the others from going, but they are simply happy with the way things are and want to stay put. However, once everyone else has gone, they don't want to be alone, and they will come lagging behind and grumbling along the way. The saboteurs don't want to move and, if possible, aren't going to let anyone else move either. They are lone rangers that are not afraid of taking risks, having many of the same qualities and needs as trailblazers. Schlechty says that the saboteurs were trailblazers in another life—translated into school change, trailblazers with past initiatives. Leaders are wise to keep the saboteurs in sight.

The foregoing two ways of thinking about individuals make for fun and interesting conversations, putting faces on each type of individual. However, we don't think one should take this discussion too literally because individuals change roles depending on the issue. Nevertheless, it is good to have some frame of reference when we are initiating and implementing major change efforts, such as WFSGs. When you work with an all-inclusive system, you have all types of individuals within the circle.

We also know that human beings have a strong need for control (Conner, 1993). This is especially true when it comes to change. When we have a sense of control over change and its circumstances, we typically feel comfortable. So the change we initiate, understand, and have a sense of control over is a change that we feel good about and are comfortable with.

There are actually two types of control we all seek: direct control, where we have the direct ability to request or actually dictate outcomes that usually occur, and indirect control, where we have the ability to at least anticipate the outcomes of a change. People usually have the highest level of comfort when they have a sense of direct control.

Indirect control results in less, but some, comfort with change. For example, if I am not in direct control of some change but understand it and know the implications of it, I then can anticipate what will occur. This, again, is indirect control, and I will feel less threatened by the change than if I had no sense of possible outcomes.

What all this means is that if leaders of an innovation want people to feel comfortable with a particular change, the leaders must do whatever is appropriate and necessary to give them a sense of control, either direct or indirect, for the change effort. If this can be done, leaders enhance the chances that people will be supportive of and helpful with the change.

However, if people aren't given some sense of control over the change by feeling able to directly dictate or influence its outcomes or at least anticipate its outcomes, they may feel threatened. As a result, they will do what comes naturally when people don't understand or appreciate what is going on; they will resist the change either openly and overtly or covertly. Human resistance to change is not an aberration or a reflection that something is wrong with someone. Instead, it is a natural reaction to change when one does not understand the change and its implications. Consequently, if you do not want people to do what is natural relative to change (i.e., resist it), then, very simply, you must make them feel comfortable with the change by helping them understand the change and its implications and giving them a sense of either direct or indirect control. The major change principle that describes how to do this is discussed in the next section.

Universal Change Principle for Schools

In this section, we describe a critical principle for dealing with and helping others deal with change. The principle establishes a contextual condition that prepares a faculty for a change. It gives an overarching approach for managing change and is applicable virtually everywhere. Because of its broad applicability, we call it the *universal change principle.*

For our discussion of change and the universal change principle, think of *learning* as gaining information, knowledge, or understanding for effective action relative to the change or the implications of the change under consideration.

Universal change principle: *Learning must precede change.*

That is, if people are to help bring about change, then they must be provided with the appropriate "learning" in advance so that they understand and appreciate the change and its implications. Providing the appropriate learning allows people to gain a reasonable sense of control with respect to the change.

Appropriate learning does not mean that change agents have an answer for every circumstance in the initiation and implementation stages of the innovation. In any complex change effort, such as WFSGs, there will be holes and blanks that cannot be filled in by any but the implementers. Appropriate learning would include knowing theoretical and practical underpinnings that support the proposition that the new process, practice, program, attitude, belief, or material would bring about the desired change in a specific school or with a particular group of students. Teachers should know what disagreements or conflicts may exist among researchers about the new practice. When the initiators or change agents confirm with teachers that there are few clear answers that fit every situation, teachers are more likely to see themselves as experts in their situation, given the latitude to find the answers for their students. Teachers with this attitude and who are part of a strong support system will be less likely to get frustrated and rebellious when the proposed change hits snags. The learning that precedes the change, then, includes a clarification of the meaning of the change and whatever information is required for the proposed implementers to agree to begin.

For example, a simple illustration of the universal change principle might be that of a driver who wants to make a turn ahead. He provides learning for those behind him by lighting his turn signal a few hundred feet before the turn. As a result, other drivers learn of the first driver's desired change and then have time to make their appropriate adjustments. In this case, learning preceded change for the success and safety of all.

A school example might involve a principal who wants the mathematics faculty to use a new approach for teaching basic mathematics. If that principal just announces one day that starting next semester the mathematics faculty will teach by the new method, probably most of the faculty will be unfamiliar with the new approach, not understand its value and implementation, not feel comfortable with this new change, and, as a consequence, resist rather than be helpful with what the principal desires to have happen.

However, suppose instead that the principal uses the universal change principle to guide the implementation of what he or she desires to have happen. Following this approach, the principal would first ask, "What learning must take place before this change can be successfully implemented?" In response, the principal would most likely involve the mathematics faculty in a series of discussions concerning what he or she is thinking about; why this is important to improving student learning, to the faculty and to the school; what the implications are for the students, faculty, and school; and how and when the new approach should be implemented. Doing all this doesn't guarantee that everyone will be in favor of the change and that all resistance will be averted. It does, though, ensure greater understanding of what's desired; why it's important; and what the implications are for the students, faculty, and school; and helps the faculty gain a sense of control for the project, making them feel much more comfortable with it and its implementation. As a result, the faculty are far more likely to help with the change rather than resist its implementation.

The proper application of the universal change principle does not guarantee that all resistance to change will be averted and that all desired changes can be accomplished. However, an appropriate application of the universal change principle does significantly enhance the likelihood of these desired things happening. The proper application of the universal change principle does take additional time and effort but generally pays off handsomely in terms of real accomplishment in the end.

The universal change principle and its applications are excellent examples of the concept of "slowing down to speed up," that is, taking a little longer initially to do the right things and then being able to speed up the process substantially later on as a result of the earlier foundation that was laid.

Notice that the universal change principle also says "No surprises!" If you want to bring about a desired change, don't surprise people with it. Their likelihood of reacting favorably to the change and assisting with it will be increased greatly if you take the time to provide people with a basis of understanding from which they can make the desired transition.

If L represents learning and C represents change, a nice way to symbolize the universal change principle is this:

$$L > C$$

and is read "Learning is greater than change."

Notice that this implies that if there is to be a lot of change, then there must be a lot of learning that takes place first. In fact, if the change is really major, then several iterations of learning may be required at several different times, depending on the change, circumstances, and people involved. For large school changes, this is what typically must happen: There must be several applications of the universal change principle at different times and with different groups of people. In fact, it is helpful, in advance of the announcement of a desired change effort, to develop a plan, based on the universal change principle, to provide the appropriate and necessary learning iterations to precede the desired change

Summary

In this chapter, we have presented in some detail several of the contextual conditions that support WFSG work. We do know that the context of school reform offers us the greatest challenge. *Where* change happens has to be the first consideration of those working with and in schools. We have to know where we are before we can get to where we want to go. Every school is unique. Every school, like every individual, has a personality of its own. Two schools just blocks away from one another, serving the same community, operating under the same policies and procedures, can be as different as night and day. We can't work in one school like we work in another school. Even though all WFSG schools follow the same 15 procedural guidelines, how those guidelines work within the context of a school makes the process different. The individuality of the people in schools, adults and students, make the difference. Even with WFSG guidelines and other consistent WFSG features, there is no cookie cutter solution. In the WFSG jar, each cookie is different. The contextual conditions make the difference.

Process 5

A Guiding Structure That Enables Teachers and Students

As previously stated, process refers to a particular method of doing something, generally involving a number of steps or operations. In the context of study groups, it relates to how members work together in a group to acquire new knowledge and skills. The WFSG model is a process through which teachers acquire and develop knowledge and skills in a collaborative setting. Intended results of the work are higher student achievement and performance.

Process Guidelines for WFSGs

The 15 process or procedural guidelines weave in and out of each other. The guidelines are interwoven so as to form a structure through which study groups work. Think of a basket, a basket with great utility. The guidelines are the wooden strips of equal strength and width in the basket. All the guidelines woven together form a basket or process strong enough to hold multicolored stones or substantive content. A guideline that is weakened would be like narrowing one of the wooden strips, causing holes to appear in the basket. A basket (the process) with holes might be too porous to hold the contents. To ignore or omit a guideline altogether would endanger the contents even more. At the beginning of Chapter 4, we used a scenario about a couple going on a picnic to illustrate context, process, and content. The strong basket represents a strong process, WFSGs, that can carry the weight of strong, substantive content (see Figure 5.1). There may be more attractive baskets. There may be baskets that are easier to manage. What has been fashioned for WFSGs is a basket that has great utility and can be used for a variety of purposes.

The guidelines that follow provide the process structure that is required for study groups to achieve their desired results. These process or procedural guidelines are the result of Murphy's work since 1986 with over 200 schools and at least 2,000 study groups in those schools. For schools that want results, it is strongly recommended that these guidelines not be altered. They form a framework that gives the process an effective operational structure. However, within that structure, there is great latitude for deciding what study groups will do and how they will be organized. When

Figure 5.1. Whole-Faculty Study Groups—Why They Work: Strong Process Holds Strong
Content

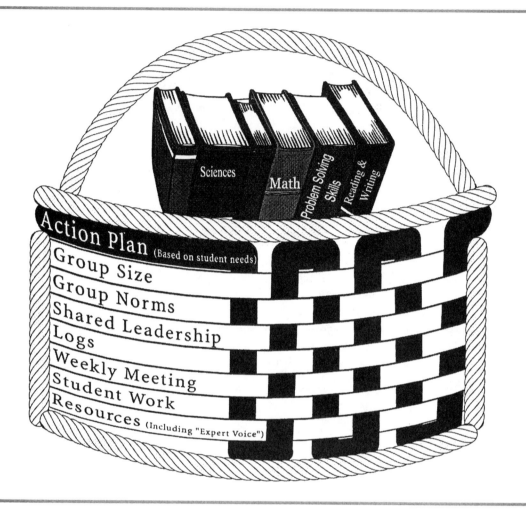

Murphy works with schools, the guidelines are nonnegotiable. What is completely
open, though, is what a group will do and how the group will go about doing it.

Here are the 15 procedural or process guidelines that all study groups follow in
WFSG schools; each is then discussed in detail.

1. Keep the size of the study group between 3 and 6 members.

2. Determine study group membership by who wants to address an identified student
   need.

3. Establish and keep a regular schedule, meeting weekly or every 2 weeks.

4. Establish group norms and routinely revisit the norms.

5. Establish a pattern of study group leadership, rotating among members.

6. Develop a study group action plan (SGAP) by the end of the second study group
   meeting.

7. Complete a study group log after each study group meeting.

8. Have a curriculum and instructional focus that requires members to routinely examine student work and to observe students in classrooms engaged in instructional tasks.

9. Make a comprehensive list of learning resources, both material and human.

10. Use multiple professional development strategies, such as training, to accomplish the study group's intended results.

11. Practice reflection by agreeing that each memeber will keep a reflective journal.

12. Recognize all study group members as equals.

13. Expect and plan for transitions.

14. Assess the progress of the study group according to the evidence specified on the action plan.

15. Establish a variety of communication networks and strategies.

1. Keep the size of the group between 3 and 6 members.

It is recommended that groups be no smaller than 3 and no larger than 6 members. The larger the study group, the more difficult it is to find common meeting times when all members can be present. In groups larger than 6, individuals can "hide" and not assume their share of the work. Because most study groups meet for only 1 hour, each of the 6 or fewer study group members have a chance to share. Also, the larger the study group, the more likely the group will splinter into two groups. With smaller study groups, each member will participate more and take greater responsibility. The size of groups affects how comfortable individuals feel about serving as leader. With groups of 6 or fewer, rotating leadership is comfortable. An individual does not feel the same sense of pressure with 5 other individuals as they would with 10. The intimacy of a smaller group generates such a supportive relationship that when leadership is rotated, an observer of the study group often cannot tell who the leader is.

2. Determine study group membership by who wants to address an identified student need.

It does not matter who is in a group. The student need that the group will address determines membership. Focus is on the work and not on personal connections of the individuals. The homogeneity or heterogeneity of the study group is not a critical element. Study group members may have similar responsibilities (e.g., first-grade teachers, mathematics teachers, or elementary principals) or unlike responsibilities (e.g., across grade level, across subject level, or across schools or districts). The composition of a study group is most often those who want to pursue or investigate a specific student need that has been identified through an analysis of student data. The content of the study, investigation, or training generally determines who will be a member of a study group. The focus is on adult-to-adult relationships in a learning situation. What grade or subject a teacher teaches is secondary to the adult relationship forged around teaching. For example, a study group focusing on technology could have teachers of kindergartners to 12th graders because the application of computer skills is generic.

Study groups actually form in a number of ways. If it has been decided by the faculty that all study groups at the school will address the same student need, any random system of assignment will work. Two examples follow.

At an elementary school where the faculty decided that all study groups would address a low math achievement, a random method was used. Because there were 52 teachers, 10 study groups were formed. The principal wrote each teacher's name on an index card and stacked the cards from the lowest grade level at the school to the highest. In front of the entire faculty, the principal dealt the cards, face down, into 10 stacks. She then picked up a stack, called out the names, and groups were formed. Each group then decided what aspect of mathematics the group would pursue.

At a large high school, the whole faculty decided that all study groups would focus on health needs of students, meaning that groups would investigate issues that would advance the physical, emotional, and social health of its students. The faculty further decided that study groups should span departments and grade levels. On a staff development day, all 152 faculty members went into the school cafeteria. On entering the room, each was given a name tag that was bordered in a color. All members of a department (e.g., social studies) had one color. After everyone was seated, a focus team member said,

> Now, it is time to form study groups. You will note that in the middle of each table is a sheet of paper divided into sixths. You may form your own study groups by putting your name tag in one of the six squares on the sheet of paper on a table. However, there can be only one color on each sheet. You have 5 minutes to form your groups.

As recorded on video, the faculty completed the task in under 5 minutes.

When the faculty decides that several student needs are to be addressed by study groups, a selection strategy will need to be devised. Two examples follow.

At an elementary school where the faculty had identified several different student needs that were to be addressed, the method of forming study groups was more deliberate. Each of the six needs was written on a piece of chart paper, and the chart papers were taped to the wall of the media center where the faculty was meeting. Each teacher was given a Post-it note and told to write his or her name on it. Then, teachers were asked to get up from their seats and put their Post-it notes on the chart paper that specified the student need that they wanted to address. It was immediately visible as to whether there was enough interest in all needs or whether several study groups should be formed to address one need. Because 12 teachers wanted to address reading comprehension, two groups were formed to examine the teaching of that skill. Within a very short period of time, teachers knew the membership of study groups and what would be the focus of each group.

In a middle school, after the whole faculty had agreed on student needs to be addressed, existing teams selected a need most relevant to that team. The team had a daily common planning period. During one planning period a week when the team met, it went into study group mode, meaning that administrative or managerial issues were put aside and the focus was on what and how teachers teach.

3. Establish and keep a regular schedule, meeting weekly or every 2 weeks.

It is strongly recommended that study groups meet weekly. At the first meeting, group members confirm when the study group will meet. The day and time for the meeting is written in their log from the first study group meeting. Weekly meetings, for about an hour, keep the momentum at a steady pace and give study group members ongoing learning and support systems. The study group should set dates and times of meetings for a given period of time. It is usually assumed that a group will stay together an entire school year and would establish a set schedule, such as every Tuesday from 3:00 to 4:00 p.m. or every other Tuesday from 3:00 to 5:00. Also, it is usually better to meet more frequently for shorter periods of time than infrequently for a longer block of time. More than 2 weeks between meetings is too long to sustain momentum and get regular feedback on classroom practice. An hour for a meeting is the minimum amount of time and seems adequate to accomplish the intent of a given meeting. Many schools have found creative ways to find time in the work day for teachers to be actively engaged as collaborative learners. An unexpected side effect of weekly meetings is less absenteeism than in less frequent meetings. It seems the bond created by frequency builds more commitment to the task of the group.

Meeting once a month works against the process. If a study group meets once a month for an hour, the total number of contact hours for the school year will be equal to 8 hours or about 1 day. If a study group meets twice a month, that will equal about 16 hours or about 2 days for the year. If a study group meets weekly, the total time the group will meet during the school year will be about 32 contact hours. Most college and staff development courses are 30 to 50 contact hours. Even weekly meetings will still not equal the time spent in a college course. When teachers first hear that the groups will stay together for a school year, they can usually be heard saying with astonishment, "A year?" An experienced leader of WFSGs will say, "Make that ___ hours" (whatever the total time will be).

The power of the WFSG approach is what teachers implement immediately after the meeting and the immediate feedback on classroom use at the next meeting. The "bouncing ball" or "back and forth" movement is less in biweekly meetings and practically nonexistent in monthly meetings.

At the end of this chapter, is a discussion of 23 ways that schools have found time for study groups to meet.

4. Establish group norms and routinely revisit the norms.

At the first study group meeting, members discuss and reach agreement on norms of behavior for the group. The norms are written in the log from the first meeting. Study group members should collectively agree on what is acceptable and unacceptable behavior in a study group meeting, such as the following:

- Begin and end on time
- Take responsibility for one's own learning

- Do what we agree to do

- Respect all

- Stay focused

- Implement what we learn

- No fault is to be given or taken

Norms set the basis for the operation of the group, help create its empowering synergy, and lead to the group's "learning team" success, as discussed in Chapter 9. Once norms are established and agreed on, members are encouraged to feel comfortable reminding each other when a norm is not being respected. Norms should be revisited frequently.

5. Establish a pattern of study group leadership that rotates among members.

Shared leadership is a principle of WFSGs. Members share leadership of a study group by rotating the role of leader. Members also share leadership by rotating who represents the study group at IC meetings. When the whole faculty learns how to follow a protocol for looking at student work or a protocol that has other functions, any one in a study group can facilitate the protocol. Leadership roles take practice, and the only way to get practice is to do leadership tasks. The principle of shared leadership is based on the belief that all teachers are leaders. The current norm is not expecting all teachers to be leaders.

At the first study group meeting, members should establish a schedule for the rotation of leadership. The schedule is written in the log from the first meeting. Each member serves as study group leader, on a rotating basis. The leadership rotation may occur weekly, biweekly, or monthly. Once a group forms around a student need, group members decide what the rotation will be. Leadership is shared to avoid having one member become more responsible than other members for the success of the group. All members are equally responsible for obtaining resources and keeping the group moving toward its intended results and desired ends. Individual members should look to themselves and each other for direction, not to a single person. This sense of joint responsibility for the work of the study group builds interdependence and synergy within the group (see synergistic relationships and prerequisites in Chapter 8). When every group member feels equally responsible for the success of the group, there is a higher level of commitment. There is no one leader to blame for the failure of the group to accomplish its goals; all must share the burden of any failure or joy of accomplishment. The most positive feature arising from the use of the rotation approach is the important assumption that anyone from the study group can represent the group at any point in time, expanding the effective capacity for leadership at the school. When a member takes a turn as leader, it is expected that this person will

- Confirm logistics with study group members (e.g., day, time, location, what to bring)

- Check the log from the last meeting to confirm what the focus of the next meeting will be

■ Check to see if it is time to revisit the action plan and the group norms

■ Start and end the meeting on time

■ Remind members that stray from the focus of the meeting to refocus

■ See that the study group log is completed and members and the principal receive a copy

■ Share any comments from the principal or other support persons that may have been made on the log from the last meeting

6. Develop a SGAP by the end of the second study group meeting.

Before study groups are formed, everyone writes a practice action plan in the session the focus team leads with the whole faculty. This is the session when the whole faculty experiences the DMC. At the end of this general session, each teacher is given the opportunity to select the general category of student need that he or she will choose when given a choice. Each teacher is then asked to write, with guidance, an action plan that the teacher feels will address the needs of his or her students. This practice gives all teachers an opportunity to learn how to write an action plan before they are expected to write one as part of a study group. When study groups are organized, each teacher will have a practice action plan to share with study group members. Often, ideas from the individual action plans form the basis for a single action plan for the study group.

By the end of the second study group meeting, each group's action plan is completed and given to the principal. It is important that a study group develop its own action plan. If there are 10 professional study groups in the school, then there should be 10 action plans. Student needs are identified by the whole faculty, but how a study group will go about its investigation is for that group to decide. The action plan sets the common goals for the study group. Every member is given a copy of the group's action plan. A study group's action plan should include the following:

■ The general category of student need

■ The essential question that will guide the study group throughout its work

■ The specific student needs to be addressed by the group (see Figure 6.2 in Chapter 6)

■ The actions the teachers will take when the study group meets (see Figure 6.4 in Chapter 6)

■ The resources the study group will use

■ The evidence of student learning, by specifying

   — Student performance goals

   — Data source

The part of the action plan that seems to be the most problematic is where the members state what they will do when the study group meets, not what their students are going to do. The members are to list the actions they will take when they sit around a table and work together. This portion of the plan serves as the study group's agenda for all its upcoming meetings. Teachers are most often either told what to do or tell others (e.g., students) what to do. We have found that it is difficult for teachers to focus on themselves and to be clear about what they are going to do when the study group meets.

The study groups should expect the principal and other appropriate leaders to give them feedback on their action plans. Typical feedback includes suggestions regarding resources and questions about the specific actions of the group. The action plan for each group is usually put on a clipboard, and clipboards are hung in a place where teachers frequently go. Plans are posted so that everyone will know what all study groups are doing. Teachers are encouraged to use Post-it notes to ask questions and give suggestions to other study groups.

The action plan should be revisited at regular intervals and adjusted to be consistent with current actions. A group may initially plan to go in one direction, then once into the study or training program, it sees a different avenue to follow. This takes on a higher level of importance when the group assesses its progress toward its intended results at the end of the school year. If the actions a group takes are not aligned with student needs, the assessment will indicate that the group missed its target. If intended results for students are not appropriate or adequate, the assessment will indicate that the group missed its target. Figure 5.2 maps out the action plan cycle.

7. Complete a study group log after each study group meeting.

A study group log, or log, is a brief, written summary of what happened at a specific meeting and, collectively, gives the group a history. The study group log should include the following information:

- Date, time, location, and leader of the meeting

- Group members present and absent

- What happened today? Brief summary of discussion and activities

- Classroom application: What are students learning and achieving as a result of what you are learning and doing?

- Was student work brought to the meeting? If so, who brought?

- What are you ready to share with other study groups?

- What concerns or questions do you have for school leaders?

- Next meeting (e.g., agenda items, work to prepare)

- Date, time, location, and leader of next meeting

After meetings, members are given a copy of the completed log. Each individual keeps a notebook of his or her study group work, including the action plan, the logs, and artifacts from meetings. Using the logs, a group can go back to past meetings and confirm why they decided to take a particular action. Members can see their progress in their relations with one another, their thinking, and their actions. After each meeting, a copy of the log is given to the principal and posted on the same clipboard that

Figure 5.2. Action Plan Cycle

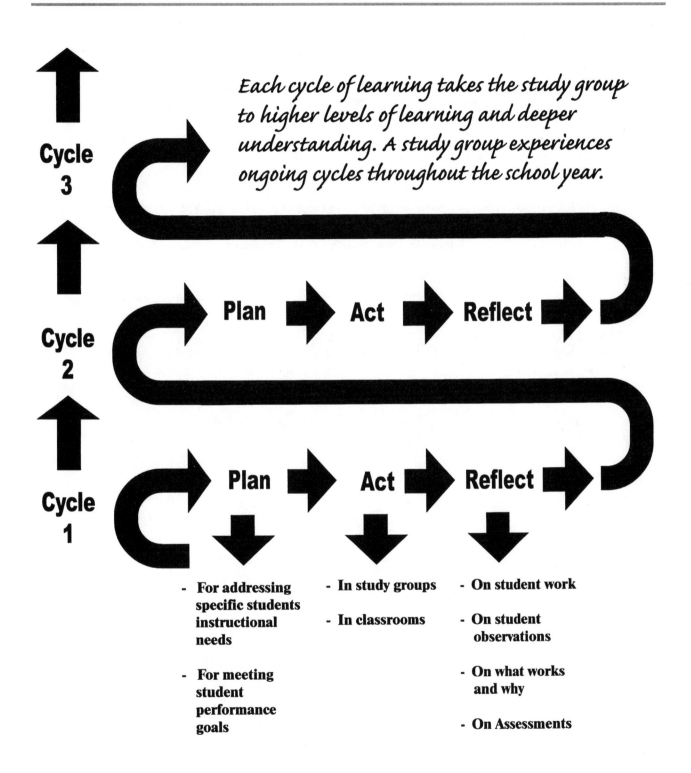

Cycle 3

Each cycle of learning takes the study group to higher levels of learning and deeper understanding. A study group experiences ongoing cycles throughout the school year.

Cycle 2

Plan ➡ Act ➡ Reflect ➡

Cycle 1

Plan ➡ Act ➡ Reflect ➡

- For addressing specific students instructional needs

- For meeting student performance goals

- In study groups

- In classrooms

- On student work

- On student observations

- On what works and why

- On Assessments

Table 5.1 Using Logs for Study Group Feedback

An elementary school has six study groups. After the fourth meeting of all six study groups, the principal asked Murphy to give each group feedback in response to what was written on the study group logs. Study groups did not see the feedback that other study groups received. Principals are expected to give some form of feedback to the study groups after each meeting or several meetings. A principal's feedback may not be as formal and detailed as the feedback Murphy gave; however, the feedback should indicate to the study groups that the principal is knowledgeable and interested in the work of the groups. For large schools, a principal would randomly select study groups and give feedback to a few after each round of meetings. Here are Murphy's comments to the study groups (SG):

SG #1: It seems that you are using several different Read Well resources. You stated several things that you want to do. In the next log, it should be clear what each of you has done with your students that is a direct result of the information you received from the resource persons who have shared with you.

SG #2: The item analysis of the mathematics section on the ITBS that you have done should pinpoint specific weaknesses. You might see if these correlate with other data. Each of you may want to select a weakness that you already know your students have and show how you are using specific materials and strategies to remedy those weaknesses. Act now while getting more information. The classroom application on the log should be more specific next time. One of you should bring math student work in an area of need that most of the students have.

SG #3: You seem to have a strong sense of direction. Activities #1-5 on the log were primarily planning. #6 on the log was the only item that had a direct tie to the classroom, and I wonder how much time was spent on #6 or was most of the time spent on #1-5. If all of you have a computer in your classrooms, all should bring student work generated on the computer.

---

has the group's action plan. It is expected that the principal or his or her designee will acknowledge in some way the group's work. This may be verbal feedback or it may be in the form of a Post-it note on the log of the last meeting and given to the leader of the next meeting. Table 5.1 gives an example of the feedback one principal gave study groups after the fourth time the groups met.

The log is not used in evaluations but as a tool for knowing what outside support may be helpful as well as to promptly address concerns that the group might be experiencing. Logs become part of the study group's portfolio or an individual teacher's portfolio if this is a direction the group wants to go in.

It is usually the third or fourth meeting when the "classroom applications" section of the log is completed. It takes about that long for the study group to get organized and to do the background work to support classroom use. The study group may collect classroom application information by taking the first 5 or 10 minutes of the meeting to go around the table and have each member share. Or the sharing can be

SG #4: Most of what you did seemed to be reviewing. Did each review have a purpose that will lead to classroom action? The classroom application section should reflect the problem-solving strategies each of you is using in your classrooms. One person should bring student work from a problem-solving activity.

SG #5: What in the video that the group watched can be translated into classroom practice? What was the purpose of watching the video? What was the key learning? When you watch a video, it should be for a clearly stated purpose, and I did not see that in the log. After viewing the video, I could not tell if your debriefing centered on classroom applications. Will anyone view the tape that you indicated you will watch prior to the next meeting? The leader of the next meeting may want to view the tape to make sure it is worth taking so much time out of the hour you meet. Sometimes, instead of watching a video during a meeting, each member watches it on their own before the meeting. The group would then use the meeting time to debrief the video and to design classroom work based on what the video suggests. Watching videos in two consecutive meetings is taking an undue amount of time from looking at student work that will tell the group what the students need.

SG #6: From the log, all of what you are doing seems to be focused on conditions beyond your classrooms. I see that you are spending all of your time developing schoolwide activities. At least part of the study group meeting should address what you are doing in your classrooms to develop respect for materials, respect between student and student, respect between teacher and student, and respect for content knowledge. What you are trying to do for teachers not in your group is important. However, it is more important now that you look within your classrooms to pinpoint strategies that work so you can then share what works with other teachers.

integrated into conversations throughout the meeting. Much of the learning about classroom practice comes from this sharing of what is and is not working in each other's classrooms. This generates concrete and precise "teacher talk" about teaching, a major function of study groups.

An individual's WFSG notebook contains

- The SGAP

- Logs from each meeting

- Articles the group reads

- Products from the group (e.g., rubrics)

8. Have a curriculum and instructional focus that require members to routinely examine student work and to observe students in classrooms engaged in instructional tasks.

The results of actions taken by study groups should be evidenced in the work students do. Collecting data from student work is the engine that drives the work of teachers in their study groups. Student needs that the faculty identifies in Step 2 of the DMC are needs that can be addressed through what and how teacher teach. Results of what and how teachers teach are mirrored in what students do. Students give back to us, in some way, what we have given them or led them to do or what they have discovered. It is this work that guides teacher work. Teacher action is grounded in student action that is grounded in teacher action. It is a cycle.

It is helpful if the study group uses a protocol for looking at student work. Protocols give teachers guidelines for conversation within a limited amount of time and create a structure for speaking, listening, and questioning. Coalition of Essential Schools, ATLAS Communities, and Annenberg Institute for School Reform have developed protocols for looking at student work.

Students use a variety of formats to show what they are learning and what they know and understand. Student work can be seen, read, heard, and felt in a number of ways. For study groups to look at student work, the work is usually brought to a study group meeting in a tangible format that members can handle, see, or hear, such as

- Written work on 8½ × 11 paper

- Worksheets

- A video of a class completing an assignment in the classroom

- A recording of an oral reading

- Computations in various oral and written formats

- Debates, recorded or videotaped

- Projects (e.g., manipulative science experiments, drafting, woodworking)

- Exhibits (e.g., posters, tri-boards, cutouts)

- Performances, recorded or videotaped

- Models, illustrations, diagrams, tables, and graphs

- Visual art work in all forms

- Skill development (e.g., physical education, videotaped)

- Computer-generated work

- Portfolios containing an assortment of work over time

For everyone in the study group to examine student work at the same time, the teacher bringing work on 8½ × 11 paper would need to bring multiple copies of one student's work or work from the same assignment from several different students. For large pieces of work, such as posters and models, the work would need to be positioned so that everyone in the group can see it. If the work is on video or on audio-cassette, the necessary equipment would need to be set up ahead of time.

Study group members routinely observe each other's students when lessons are taught that the group designed together or are lessons that address the student needs on the group's action plan. Through these observations, group members are collecting data that guide the work of the study group. During a study group meeting, members will determine which two will pair up during the following week. Because the teachers have been working together and know what the students should be doing, the observing teacher knows what skills the students will be developing. The observing teacher sits where he or she can see what students are doing and how they are responding to the instruction. The two teachers may have agreed that the two will move around the room looking at the individual work of students. As teachers spend time in each other's classrooms, teachers develop a greater sense of responsibility for each other's students, and the study group work becomes even more student based. After several such observations, a form of team teaching has occurred in a few situations. Teachers actually see the experiences as a help rather than a threat. When a teacher in a study group observes the students of another teacher in the study group, the two will need to be clear on what their focus will be. For example, if the study group is currently focused on a particular problem-solving strategy, the observations would occur during the time the strategy is being introduced or practiced. How the students responded and performed would be debriefed at the next study group meeting. The information or data from the observations would determine what the study group needs to do next.

The content of any professional development approach should have promise for positive effects on students. As outlined in Chapter 2, the functions of study groups are to (a) develop a deeper understanding of academic content, (b) support the implementation of curricular and instructional innovations, (c) integrate and give coherence to a school's instructional practices and programs, (d) target a schoolwide instructional need, (e) study the research on teaching and learning, (f) monitor the impact of instructional changes on students, and (g) provide a time when teachers can examine student work together. These seven functions require that members in groups do not get sidetracked by administrative issues or issues that have a low instructional impact. WFSGs take on the groups' content curriculum materials, instructional strategies, curriculum designs, use of technologies, standards, and assessment practices. The groups will use a variety of strategies to address the targeted student needs. For example, they may have an external person offer group training, and members may read books and articles, view videotapes, demonstrate strategies to each other, visit classrooms and schools, design materials, view and learn to use computer software, attend a workshop or conference together, and develop lessons that will be taught in classrooms.

Whatever the content, it must be complex and substantive enough to provide a practical vision, not just rhetoric or feelings. It is the content of the study group that will hold the members together while individuals are gaining trust and rapport with each other and developing skills for working together as a cohesive group. The content takes the focus off the individual. The content supplies a foundation for the process that will lead the group to joint, interdependent work. Through the content, colleagues can share responsibilities; support each other's initiatives; discover their unconscious assumptions; clarify their ideas, beliefs, and professional practices; and ground the group's commitment to serious, professional accomplishment.

9. Make a comprehensive list of learning resources, both material and human.

A study group designs its curriculum of study to include a comprehensive list of resources. Initially, groups should spend some time brainstorming learning resources that are easily accessible and those that are harder to obtain. Study groups need to hear an "expert voice," either in person, through the written word, or through video. This expert voice will lead the members of the group to deeper knowledge or higher levels of skill. Resource lists might include trainers, resource people, titles of books, professional journals, videos, audiotapes, computers and software, conferences, and other sources of relevant information. The most accessible sources for materials are the Internet and files of other teachers in the building. Principals often ask teachers in a building to share their files on specific topics or general areas of study to create an enhanced, central resource file for areas of study being pursued by the different groups. The Internet is a powerful resource that connects the school to teachers throughout the nation and the world.

Some schools have had a day proclaimed as Clean Out File Cabinets Day. If there are 10 study groups, 10 cardboard boxes are labeled and put in a central location. Anyone who has anything on the student need that a group is addressing puts materials in the appropriate box. If an item is to be returned to the original owner after a study group finishes with it, then the owner would write on the item "Please return to _____."

Other sources for materials are district offices, other schools, libraries, colleges and universities, businesses, and professional associations. Also included as learning resources are individuals who have special expertise, such as teachers, school administrators, district administrators and support staff, university professors, independent consultants, parents, and business and community leaders. The foregoing list of learning resources represents a valuable resource base for the learning that must precede the changes that teachers hope to bring about in their classrooms. A more detailed list of such resources is given in Chapter 6.

10. Use multiple professional development strategies, such as training, to accomplish the study group's intended results.

Murphy's WFSG approach to professional development can include most other professional development designs or strategies. Study groups conduct action research. Study groups invite persons to meet with the group to train members to use a particular skill, or the members go to a workshop together. Study groups can form any combination of twos for observing each other's students in classrooms. Study group members immerse themselves in mathematics, for example, to gain a deeper understanding of what they teach. Study group members develop curriculum and experiment with the curriculum in their classrooms. Study groups listen to students by interviewing them during study group meetings. Study groups videotape themselves and their students and share what they learn. Study groups are actively seeking new strategies to deepen their knowledge and develop skills.

Study group members are to be reminded that when we do not know how to do something, we can develop that skill by letting a person who is more knowledgeable in that skill area show us how. The more skillful individual may be in the study group, from elsewhere in the school, or from elsewhere altogether. When skill development is required, inviting a trainer or skilled practitioner to study group meetings to demonstrate effective practices may be necessary. Just reading about how to do something is usually not sufficient. Reading and discussing books and articles and studying relevant research are important because such efforts can affect attitudes, beliefs, and behaviors and can provide an expanded knowledge base for improving classroom practice. However, at some point, individuals must move from the abstract (from what is written, read, and discussed) to the concrete (to what one actually does).

Furthermore, to ensure skill development at a level that gives teachers the confidence to appropriately and effectively use the skill in the classroom, study group members will need to develop a plan that will include several training components. A plan for skill development would include (a) the theory that explains and supports the importance of the skill, (b) opportunities for participants to observe a number of demonstrations of the skill, and (c) opportunities to practice the skill to a reasonable competency level (Joyce & Showers, 1995). The study group provides a safe environment for teachers to practice skills, design lessons together using the skill, observe each other, and feel support in figuring out why some lessons go well and others do not. The value of ongoing technical training and support of effective classroom practices cannot be overemphasized.

There are other professional development strategies that will greatly facilitate the study group's need for increased knowledge and skill. Such strategies are listed and described later in this chapter.

11. Practice reflection by agreeing that each member will keep a reflective journal.

Definitions of *reflection* are "to give back an image; to think seriously on or upon; contemplation; a thoughtful idea." Reflection is an important aspect of learning. It is an important aspect of teaching. Study groups give teachers the opportunity for reflection—time and space to consider the impact of decisions, analyze data, and think carefully about next steps. Members of study groups are encouraged to keep personal journals of their reflections about their teaching and learning. Teachers encourage students to write to learn, summarize what they have learned, and make personal sense out of what they are learning. Teachers will benefit from doing the same. Writing what we are thinking helps us construct meaning for ourselves from our experiences. In a study group, not only are we thinking about ourselves, we think about group experiences. As an experience from the classroom is shared, members may write about how others perceive the experience and how they feel about those perceptions. Use of journals is up to the study group. From time to time, excerpts may be shared. Some study groups set aside time at every third or so meeting for deliberate and planned reflection. Killion (1999) expands on strategies for journaling. Serious journal writers keep their journals open during a meeting and from time to time make a quick note of key ideas.

Specific entries directly related to the work of the study group might include the following:

- Date, time, and location of the study group meeting

- Description of what happened

- Individual's analysis of what happened

- How what happened is connected to other experiences

- Interactions with other individuals that may have been especially helpful or bothersome

- Meeting's accomplishments

- What the group didn't get to

- What the group should do for the next meeting

- Individual's feelings about what he/she is learning

The journal reflects the individual's learning, reflections, and reactions. Expressions of frustration, joy, new insights, and references for the future are important parts of one's own reflections about the process and the content of the study.

12. Recognize all study group members as equals.

It is more productive if individuals do not feel intimidated, hesitant, or anxious about differences in job titles or certifications, experience, and degree levels among group members. No one is deferred to because of rank or other factors. Contributions from each member are encouraged and respected. *Comentoring* is a term we use to indicate that in the WFSG process, members of the group all mentor each other. The study group functions under the belief that all members have something valuable to contribute to the group (i.e., empowerment; see Chapter 8) and then provides an opportunity for all to fully share their ideas and experiences (i.e., participative involvement; see Chapter 8). This approach provides an environment for appreciative understanding, empowers its members, and enables the group to reach a higher level of synergy and meaningful productivity. It is the shared leadership and equal-status principle and a strong content focus that lessens the need to train groups in group dynamics. With a strong sense of individual responsibility and an action plan for accomplishing specific results, the focus is on what the group is doing and not on the characteristics of individuals. If the work of the group is substantive enough and tied to what teachers and students are doing in the classrooms, the related dynamics will hold the group together. As the individuals are progressing on the work of the group, they are developing trust and rapport with each other and learning how to work together cohesively within the context of their study. Thus comentoring becomes a routine activity, as illustrated by the frequency of observing in each other's classrooms. Through these observations, the teachers learn more about each other's students and can better address the needs of all the students in the members' classrooms. Without the element or condition of equality, comentoring isn't possible. Comentoring accepts that one study group member may be more skillful in one area than another, but such expertise does not put that person in a privileged position or status.

Equality within the context of the WFSG approach means that all members of a study group equally share the tasks of leadership. Each member of a study group serves as leader. Each member takes a turn at representing the study group at IC meetings. Each member learns to facilitate a protocol. The leadership function is shared in all aspects of the model. Recognizing all study group members as equals means equal in status, equal in responsibility, and equal in ability to lead.

13. Expect and plan for transitions.

The definition of *transition* is "passing from one condition, place, or phase to another." For study groups, a transition is when there is or is going to be a change in the current conditions. A transition is when the study group reaches closure on what the group intended to do, when a schoolwide need has to be addressed by all groups, or when there is a break in the school calendar. Transitions are times to *celebrate!*

A study group is expected to remain a group until the end of a school year. Changing group membership more often is disruptive to the group process, as each change in the composition of the group takes the group back through the stages of group development. A group may change its action plan at any time the group feels the plan is not meeting the needs of the students. If an action plan is developed in September and actions have been implemented to the group's satisfaction and the group wants to develop another plan in February, a transition occurs. The transition is not in group membership but in the content of the study. If the school receives information from the state or the district that an instructional issue has to be addressed immediately, such as alignment of new mathematics standards with the current mathematics curriculum, study groups are where the work should be done. In such a case, study groups would bring temporary closure to their action plans and transition to the new work. If it is the end of the school year, all groups should bring closure to their work. Even if the study group plans to stay together when the new school year begins and continue the work it is currently doing, it still must formally transition to the next year. For a study group that wants to stay together for another school year but feels it wants to tackle a different student need, a positive transition would be to celebrate its success for the year and then, at the beginning of the new year, return to the list of student needs. If current data confirm that student needs still exist, the group would reach consensus as to which of the student need categories (e.g., reading) it would now address.

At the end of a school year, study groups typically are given the choice of

- Staying together as a group and continuing present work
- Staying together as a group and addressing another student need
- Disbanding and forming new groups

If three study groups (15 people) out of nine study groups at the school want to disband, at the beginning of the next year, those 15 people will meet together. They would reconfigure themselves, forming new groups, and return to the schoolwide student data to determine what their new groups will do.

14. Assess the progress of study groups according to specific evidence.

When considering what and how to assess efforts of study groups, attention should be directed to

- Evidence specified on the study group's action plan

- Impact of study groups on students as documented in student work

- Impact of the study group on the school's culture (e.g., the school's underlying assumptions, beliefs, and behaviors, such as the school's norms of collegiality, faculty and staff learning, a change-adaptable environment, and continuous improvement)

- Effectiveness of the study group process, especially how each study group functions

Assessment questions should be referenced to the SGAP and to the student performance goals written on the plan. More general questions are

- Were the specific student needs listed on the action plan fully or partially met? To what degree?

- What current data indicate improvement?

- Did teachers accomplish each action listed on the action plan? To what degree?

- What teaching behaviors changed? What is the evidence?

- Which of the resources were most helpful? Why?

When all study groups at a school address the same student needs, schoolwide improvement should be the expectation. If study groups address different student needs, one cluster of classrooms may see results in one instructional area, whereas another cluster may observe results in a different area. Refer to Resource A for examples of formats used in assessing progress of study groups.

15. Establish a variety of communication networks and strategies.

Communication among study groups helps create the context for whole school change. Establishing lines of communication among study groups and with other groups is a critical element to the WFSG approach. An integral part of WFSGs is that every faculty member will be in a study group and that everyone (the whole) will know what all groups are doing and learning; so effective communication enhances the chances that everyone will receive benefit from others' work.

As discussed in Chapter 4, the IC includes a representative from each study group. The representatives meet together every 4 to 6 weeks to share the work of study groups. Resource D contains examples of minutes from IC meetings.

It is important to include on agendas for grade-level, department, and team meetings what study groups are doing. When a majority of the study groups at a school have heterogeneous (across grade levels, departments, teams) membership, grade-level and department meetings are opportunities for communication. For example, if only one fourth-grade teacher is in a particular study group that is addressing listening skills, that teacher could share a listening rubric that his or her study group developed with her fourth-grade colleagues . The other fourth-grade teachers could then give their colleague feedback and that feedback could be shared with the original study group. This creates a powerful feedback and input cycle for all study groups. Teachers do not have to wait for a whole-faculty sharing time to benefit from what all study groups are doing.

Some schools publish a faculty newsletter that has a brief description of what each study group is doing. In some schools, a study group may decide to do a newsletter about its work or about an idea that has excited the group.

In most schools, there is a whole-faculty sharing time at least twice a year: mid-year and the end of the school year. Celebrations are so important. These are special times for leaders to let teachers know that they appreciate and recognize the work that study groups are doing. Celebrations are special communication times for groups to have fun and do creative things to excite others about the status of learning at the school.

Schools also should communicate with the board of education, district leaders, parents, students, and the general public about what study groups are doing.

Students, too, must be told what is taking place in study groups. Teachers are encouraged to tell students that a particular strategy or activity used in classrooms with students is a strategy they learned in their study group. This type of sharing has great influence on students and on parents when students repeat this information at home. It is important that students see teachers as learners and that they understand that learning is a lifelong process.

Here are some additional communication strategies:

- Have SGAPs and study group logs posted in a public place. One clipboard for each study group is usually hung in the office area. Each study group puts its action plan on a clipboard and after each meeting, the group's log is added.

- Encourage "showcase" times. When a study group gets really excited about a strategy that gets results in its classrooms, the group will send all the teachers an invitation to "come to the media center at 3:00 on Tuesday to see what is working in our classrooms!"

- Use newsletters aimed at specific groups (e.g., faculty and parents). In school newsletters that go to parents, have one corner reserved for "Study Group News."

- Create brochures. One study group that was investigating motivational strategies for reading did a trifold brochure on blue paper that listed ways to motivate students to read and distributed it to all the faculty.

- Develop videos. One technology study group did a video showing students using the digital camera, scanner, and computer for writing and designing their own books.

- Hold exhibits or seminars. Before a PTA meeting, one school had each study group assigned to a classroom so that parents could visit study groups to learn more about what they were doing.

- Designate a bulletin board in a public place in the school to display study group work.

A checklist to assist with the assessment of success in implementing the 15 procedural guidelines is given in Resource A.

Another Aspect of the Process: Strategies Study Groups Use

Remember that WFSGs are a professional development strategy, an approach that was designed to be the centerpiece for a school's professional development program. Most professional development designs or strategies can be achieved through the WFSG approach. To understand this, picture a food processor, a large glass blender with rotor blades in the middle (see Figure 5.3). The large glass blender represents WFSGs' 15 process or procedural guidelines. There is a basic recipe that can be followed time after time, with cooks getting bored with the results. Or from time to time, different ingredients can be added to vary the outcome or results. Using the WFSG approach, the different ingredients are other professional development strategies, such as action research, case studies, sharing observations of students, co-mentoring, curriculum development, immersion, journaling, listening to students, portfolios, shadowing students, tuning protocols, training, and synergy. The rotor blades are the study group members. The processor is powered by student needs. When the study group members blend a variety of ingredients or strategies into the basic recipe, the results are creativity, major change, and powerful new learning experiences for teachers and students.

Multiple strategies and designs make study group time more active, engaging, and student centered. These strategies, when blended into the work of a study group, greatly enrich the process. The following are brief descriptions of professional development strategies that are easily incorporated into WFSGs.

Examining Student Work

This strategy has already been discussed and emphasized as an integral part of the study group process. Study groups are strongly encouraged to make this one action that is written in all action plans. A study group would examine student work that reflects what the study group is addressing. This gives the group direct guidance as to what it should do more or less of to affect the student need the group is addressing. Student work constitutes the evidence that student work is improving (or not) and also gives data for a group's action research design. It is recommended that study groups use protocols for looking at student work that have been developed by the such organizations as Coalition of Essential Schools, ATLAS Communities, and Annenberg Institute for School Reform.

Sharing Observations of Students

As you now know, the work of WFSGs is shaped by what students need for the teachers to do. (Remember the five questions near the end of Chapter 3?) There are several sources for identifying student needs. One is to look at student data. Another is to listen to students. Another is to look at student work. Another is to listen to their teachers. And another is to observe them. The most current and probably the most reliable information is gleaned from looking at the students' work and observing the students. Study group members observe each other's students during instruction. Teachers in the same study group can pair themselves in any way at any time.

Figure 5.3. Whole-Faculty Study Groups: A Recipe for Teacher and Student Learning

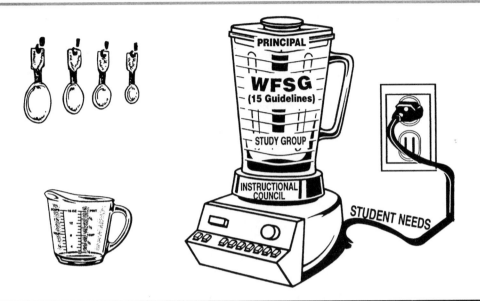

RECIPE

Before beginning preparations, have information about those you are serving.

Equipment needed: processor with large, see-through blender; strong lid; solid base; power cord; 3 to 6 rotor blades

In large blender, put the following ingredients:
- 1 action plan
- Instructional materials
- Instructional strategies
- District/state standards
- Curriculum framework (sequence of learning)
- Academic knowledge.

Mix for 1 hour once a week.

Stir in student work.

Add according to taste:
- Training (on-site or away)
- Discussing books and articles members read
- Sharing observations of students working in members' classes
- Demonstrating to each other strategies that work
- Viewing or discussing videotapes members take of themselves teaching
- Examining the research on best practices
- Interviewing students to hear what they think about current classroom practices
- Digging deeper into academic knowledge

Imagine the following situation. During several study group meetings, the group members develops concept attainment lessons. In the study group meetings, they practice the lessons. They then inform each other as to when they will be teaching the lessons during the coming week. The teachers pair up and work out a schedule for observing in each other's classrooms. When observing, teachers *focus on how students are responding* to the lesson. During the next study group meeting, teachers debrief the observed lessons and share how students responded. The data are used in the next round of lesson development.

It has been Murphy's experience that teachers learn most about what works and what does not work when using a new strategy when another teacher observes their students' responses and reports on those responses. Conversations and work prior to the observations and those after the observations are all part of the comentoring process explained in the next section. Teachers in the same study group should observe each others' students at least once a month as an ongoing data-collecting strategy. Such observations should be standard procedure among and between study group members. Usually, study group members establish norms for student observations. Prior to the first student observations, the norms are written in the log. Examples of such norms are as follows:

- Focus is on student behavior.
- Focus is on the student needs the study group is addressing.
- Pairs can be any combination of group members.
- Pairs inform each other of the student behaviors on which they want data collected.
- Data are used for the ongoing work of the study group.

Comentoring

Comentoring occurs when members of a study group all mentor each other. This happens when the teachers are in the study group meetings, when they talk one-on-one between meetings, and when they are in each other's classrooms. The 12th WFSG procedural guideline states, "Recognize all study group members as equals." This means that regardless of years of experience and level of certification, all teachers have information and skill to share. When one teacher in a study group has recently attended training in a particular teaching strategy, that teacher will be the one to demonstrate the strategy to other study group members either during the study group meeting or in the classroom with students. If another teacher in the study group has had the opportunity to become more immersed in a new mathematics program, that teacher would demonstrate the new knowledge either in the study group meeting or in the classroom with students. Spending time in each other's classrooms is a natural outgrowth of the WFSG process. In a study group, teachers coach and comentor one another, plan together, teach lessons to each other, and demonstrate effective practices to each other. "The Coaching of Teaching" (Joyce & Showers, 1982) introduced to the field of staff development the notion that teachers could work with each other much like coaches work with their players. Since then, many coaching systems have been introduced to teachers. Many such systems have been so formalized and structured that the original concept that Joyce and Showers (1982) envisioned has been compromised. In many schools, the word *coaching* is an automatic turn-off for teachers. *Peer observation* is another term that carries baggage from prior experiences. Many evaluation systems have a peer observation component, and the term has a negative ring to teachers. It has been our experience that using these two terms creates teacher tension and resistance. Any system that becomes too formalized will be met with some form of resistance. In comentoring relationships within study groups, the members determine when and how to use each other's classrooms as learning laboratories. Chapter 8 provides more information about comentoring.

Listening to Students

Listening to students in another strategy for hearing the student voice and for making student-based decisions. Study groups are encouraged to invite a student to attend a portion of a study group meeting from time to time. Study groups members would decide prior to interviewing a student what the group wants to gain from the interview. One middle school study group addressing mathematics asked a high school student to attend a study group meeting. The members asked the student what experiences he had in middle school that best prepared him for high school mathematics. An elementary school study group addressing student needs in the area of writing invited a first grader to attend a study group meeting and asked her what she most liked about writing. Such information is used by a study group to shape its work.

Shadowing Students

Teachers can learn from a student's routine. One or more teachers in a study group could shadow middle or high school students to learn from the students' routines. If a study group is targeting writing, a teacher would watch for the opportunities students have to write in the different disciplines during a school day. A study group in a high school that was addressing higher-order thinking skills decided to have one teacher in the group shadow one student for a day, to have another teacher shadow another student for a day the next week, and another teacher to shadow still another student the subsequent week. Each teacher kept a record of all opportunities students had to use problem-solving skills and how students responded to each opportunity. This data collection technique gave the study group its most valuable input. The study group compiled and analyzed the information, and during a sharing session, it seriously applied the data. It is this type of real-world data that the faculty should gather, understand, and use. Teachers learn from watching students, not just their own students but students in different contexts than a teacher's own classroom. This is the place to remind teachers that not only do teachers learn from watching students, students learn what is important from watching the routines and behaviors of teachers (Sizer & Sizer, 1999).

Videotaping

All teachers in a study group have access to blank videotape. Suppose a study group is addressing a student need in reading, and the group has examined a number of materials and strategies. Over the period of a week, each teacher does the following: videotapes the students as he or she is teaching a reading lesson in a content area, views the tape in privacy and lists several things he or she liked about what was done and several things that he or she would change, and erases the tape. At the next study group meeting, each shares what he or she wrote about the lesson taped. In 3 or 4 weeks, the group repeats the process, and over time, the cycle is repeated several times. At some point, after one of the cycles, teachers may want the study group to view the tape. After the group views the tape, the teacher will share his or her reflections on the lesson and how the students responded. It works especially well if the teacher brings student work that was done during the taping or as a result of the lesson that was taped. When this type of taping is done, a tripod is usually placed in the front of the room facing the students. Often, when a teacher is teaching, so much thought is going into the content of the lesson that he or she often misses how the students are responding. Watching the students or particular students at the completion of the lesson and in privacy often yields surprising results.

Action Research

Action research is a disciplined inquiry. The study group collects data to identify a student need. It identifies and selects a student need (a problem). The study group determines what the student performance goals are. The study group investigates alternatives to solve the problem (decrease the need). The study group selects interventions. It implements those interventions in classrooms. Members track the effects of the interventions on students. At the end of a school year, the group determines if the student performance goals were attained. Monitoring effects of new teaching practices and materials is a basic function or purpose of study groups.

Case-Based Learning

Case-based learning involves using carefully chosen, real-world examples of teaching (Barnett, 1999) and learning. A study group focusing on student mathematics needs, for example, can select cases from a source such as the Mathematics Case Methods Project and discuss a case that all can read. The case, selected from a book of field-tested cases written by teachers, describes a classroom experience that had an unexpected outcome or ran into difficulty. The author of the case uses dialogue and student work to describe how the instruction was planned and what actually happened. The teachers in the study group try the same instructional strategy or material and see if they have the same or different results.

Curriculum Development

A study group may decide that one area of the current science curriculum needs to be updated or developed. The group members use their own experiences, input from textbook manufacturers, discipline frameworks, standards, and information from peers (Glasglow, 1997). How the study group will develop the curriculum has one more aspect. At every step in the development process, after the group decides what should be included, members try the material and strategies in their classrooms. It is only after trials and reflections on the trials that a product is ready to be shared with other science teachers.

Immersion

Students should be taught by teachers who have a deep knowledge of what they teach. Loucks-Horsley (1998a) states, for instance, that the need for more challenging mathematics for students means that their teachers will also have to learn more challenging mathematics content and how to teach it. *Immerse* means to plunge into, as if into a liquid; to absorb deeply; engross. This is precisely what teachers of mathematics, science, literature, history, art, music, or anything else must do to be effective teachers. If students are not performing at higher levels on mathematics, science, or other content area tests, could it be because the teachers do not know and understand the content to the degree that they should?

Journaling

One procedural guideline for WFSGs is that teachers keep a personal reflective journal of their work in the study group. That journal would not only include their actual experiences in the group but also include their reflections on activities and relationships. It would even include what happens in their classrooms as a result of group meetings. In their journals, they would include other professional development experiences as well. Journals provide teachers with an opportunity to analyze their own practices, record their perceptions, voice their joys and fears, and reconstruct experiences. It is a permanent record. From time to time, teachers in a study group may share parts of their journals. Time should be allocated at designated meetings for this purpose.

Portfolios

In a study group, teachers may choose to keep individual portfolios or a group portfolio of their work. In one elementary school, teachers in a technology study group constructed a portfolio of their work and displayed it at the end of the school year at a PTA meeting. The following school year, a new technology study group used the portfolio to give them ideas for how they might build on the lessons learned from the preceding year's technology study group.

Protocols

A protocol gives structure and purpose to an activity. A protocol is a purposeful and thoughtful way to have conversations in study groups. Coalition of Essential Schools, ATLAS Communities, and Annenberg Institute for School Reform have developed and field-tested a variety of protocols for a number of different purposes. After study groups have completed their action plans, two study groups may be paired and a tuning protocol used to fine-tune the two plans. At any point during the school year, study groups can be paired and fine tune each other's work. Protocols may be used for looking at student work, teacher work, data, process or procedural guidelines, and text discussions. The Final Word is an effective protocol for debriefing an article or another assigned reading.

Training

If the focus of a study group is to learn how to use new skills in the classroom, one or more study group members will require training. The study group may invite a skilled person to meet with the study group routinely over time or it may go to a workshop or take a course together or have one person represent the group in a workshop or course. One study group wanted to become more skillful in using mathematics and science manipulatives. One person in the group enrolled in a course. After each class, that person worked with the study group using the manipulatives, related materials, and techniques learned in class. Not only did this help other members, it also gave the person enrolled in the class an opportunity to practice the new skills.

The teachers had an agreement that they would use the strategy in their classrooms during the week after they had been introduced to the new materials and techniques.

"Stuck" Study Groups

Study groups that lose momentum or whose members talk of boredom are what we call "stuck" study groups. One of the first interventions on the part of school leaders would be to analyze the study group logs to determine what strategies the study group is using to accomplish its work.

Chapter 7 provides guidance for providing technical assistance to study groups.

Finding Time for Study Groups to Meet

Finding time for study groups to meet is the number one issue for faculties considering WFSGs and those that have adopted WFSGs. It is the one common obstacle schools face in the study group process. We want to say with conviction: *There is time in the school day for teachers to collaborate, if the administration and faculty are willing to change other things!* Schools have been most creative in how they have found time to make the WFSG process work in their schools, as the following 22 approaches demonstrate.

1. Release students early 1 day a week. Many schools exceed the minimum number of instructional minutes required by the state. For such schools, releasing students early 1 day a week would not require changing the dismissal time the other 4 days. For schools that do not exceed the minimum instructional minutes, adding minutes to one or more of the other 4 days would be necessary.

2. Have a "late start" day once a week when students report to school 1 hour later on that morning. This gives the teachers 1 hour for study groups to meet.

3. Have a "late start" day once a week that begins only 30 minutes later than the other 4 days. The teachers report 30 minutes earlier, and the two half-hour blocks are put together for 1 hour of study group time.

4. Use teaching assistants to release teachers for study group meetings. A team of five teaching assistants can release five teachers the first hour of the school day for them to have their study group meeting. For the last hour of the day, the team of teaching assistants could cover the classrooms of another five teachers. Each day, two study groups could meet. For schools that have 10 or fewer study groups, this plan has worked.

5. Use teams of parents or business partners to release teachers for the hour their study groups meet.

6. Pair teachers. Teachers from one study group take students from teachers in another study group for the first or last 30 minutes of one day. The next day, the process is reversed. Because teachers arrive at least 30 minutes before students arrive

and stay 30 minutes after students leave, a 1-hour block is created for study group meetings at the end of a day or at the beginning of a day. In combined classes, students have individual study, reading, and journal writing time; students work one-on-one with each other; clubs meet; and other types of student planned activities are initiated.

7. Identify a team of five substitutes that spends a day every other week at the school. On that day, the team releases five teachers at 9:00 a.m. to meet as a study group and continues to do this each hour of the day. The team of substitutes moves from class to class. As many as six study groups meet on that one day. For schools that have more than 6 study groups, the team of substitute teachers returns for part of another day. On the weeks that the substitute teachers do not provide released time, study groups meet for 1 hour after school.

8. Limit faculty meetings to one afternoon a month (e.g., the second Wednesday). On the other three Wednesdays of the month, study groups meet. Some districts expect teachers to reserve one afternoon a week for faculty or other types of meetings.

9. Use part or all of a daily team planning period once a week. On 1 day a week, the planning period is labeled "study group time." During that hour, teachers meet in their study groups.

10. Permit teachers to use WFSGs to earn compensatory time for their after-school study groups. The 1-hour weekly study group meetings total what 2 full days of staff development time would equal. Therefore, on 2 days designed as staff development days on the school calendar, teachers do not report to school.

11. Dismiss students 2 hours early one day a month and have each study group submit a plan to the principal for another 2 hours during each month.

12. Dismiss students 2 hours early on one Wednesday a month. On another Wednesday of the month, teachers meet after school in study groups. On the other two Wednesdays, the principal chairs a faculty meeting.

13. Design an assembly model to give teachers time to collaborate during the school day. This option also provides enrichment opportunities for students. Special assemblies are scheduled every other week at the school. The assemblies are part of a cultural arts enrichment program that is funded by the school's PTA or the school's adopters. Various art groups, such as a theater group, the opera, the symphony, a ballet group, storytellers, dancers, musical groups, drama clubs, and other performing groups present programs to the students. On assembly day, there are two assembly periods that are 90 minutes in length. Half of the classes in the school are scheduled for each assembly. Each period consists of two 45-minute performances that occur concurrently. Half of the students scheduled for an assembly period go to one of the 45-minute performances and the other half goes to the other performance; then, they switch. This creates a 90-minute block of time for the teachers, who attend study group meetings during the time their students are in the assembly. Administrators, paraprofessionals, and parents stay with the students during the two assembly

periods. Classroom teachers have the responsibility of delivering and settling the students in the designated area (e.g., cafeteria or gym) and getting students when the two performances are over. Students know that teachers are meeting in study groups while they are in assemblies. When students return to their rooms, they share with the teacher what they have learned. Likewise, teachers share with students what they learned in study group meetings. The principal has reported that on assembly day parents show up who are not scheduled to assist and ask "May I help?" On alternating weeks, when assemblies are not scheduled, study groups meet for an hour after school.

14. Do an analysis of the number of instructional minutes in a regular school day. If it is determined that the school is banking time in terms of instructional minutes, specify the number of minutes. For example, a high school exceeds the minimum number of minutes per day for instruction by 5 minutes daily. To have time in the school day for study groups to meet, take the accumulated 5 minutes and combine it with the time from a staff development day. This means that the school had 26 days on which it could begin classes 45 minutes later. On 1 day a week, study groups meet from 7:30 a.m. to 8:15 a.m., with classes starting at 8:20 a.m. and all periods shortened. On the other 4 days, classes begin at 7:30 a.m. Students know that on study group day, the bell schedule is not the same as on the other 4 days.

15. Take the holistic approach to when all study groups would meet. All times allocated on district and school calendars for staff development and staff meetings are viewed as one big block of time; this includes full days, half days, and after-school time. Instead of focusing on the exact weekly clock hours study groups meet, focus on tasks that must be completed over a period of time. For example, after looking at several data bases, one faculty made the decision that all 8 study groups would focus on reading instruction. Another understanding was that groups would cover the same material in the same block of time, but how they did it was up to each group. Blocks of time to cover the predetermined content were established. For instance, through a whole-faculty consensus process, it was decided that from December 11 to February 12, study groups would cover teaching vocabulary with context clues, word identification and phonics, and comprehension questioning. The groups would look at the calendar and see all segments of time as a whole and decide how they would organize that amount of time to cover the research and shared practice on the predetermined content.

16. Allow teachers to select for themselves when their study group will meet once a week. At one school where this was done, not only did groups meet at different times, they met on different days. Several study groups met early in the morning; others met during lunchtime or during planning periods; still others met after school; and one met in the evening. Teachers accounted for their professional development time, and on designated staff development days, teachers were not expected to attend meetings.

17. Redesign a modified day plan that may have been in place prior to the initiation of the study group process. At one school, the modified day, Monday, was formed by having the school start 5 minutes early and end 5 minutes later on Tuesday through Friday, making the student's day 8:40 a.m. to 3:25 p.m. 4 days a week. On Mondays, the students left at 1:45 p.m., and the teachers left at 4:25. Prior to study

groups, teachers spent that block of time doing individual teacher preparation, meeting in committees, and participating in faculty meetings. Now 1 hour of that block of time was earmarked for study groups to meet.

18. Reconfigure a modified day. One district had 1 day per week that was modified so that students were dismissed 2 hours earlier than on the other 4 days. Generally, this time was for individual teacher preparation time, faculty meetings, and district meetings. When five elementary schools elected to initiate the study group process, those schools reconfigured the modified day. Four faculties decided to use 1 hour of the 2-hour time block for study groups. The faculty at the fifth decided that study groups would meet every other week for 1½ hours. On study group day after study group meetings, the whole staff met together for half an hour to report on the progress of each group.

19. Schedule weekly common planning periods for teachers in the same study group.

20. Enlist college students who are willing to spend 1 day a week at the school. For example, college students participating in Eco Watch, an outward-bound environmental leadership program, are expected to do classroom and schoolwide environmental activities with elementary students. This frees teachers to meet in study groups. The college students keep a record of the hours they spend in school, and at the end of the school year, the hours are converted into dollars for college tuition.

21. Make allowances for the time teachers spend after school in their study groups. If teachers are expected to stay 45 minutes after students are dismissed and a group of teachers in a study group stays an hour and a half beyond dismissal time, those teachers will be allowed to leave earlier than the 45 minutes on the other days of the week. A version of this idea would be for schools, where teachers, by contract, are expected to stay 45 minutes after students are dismissed, to shorten the 45 minutes to 30 minutes on 4 days, carving out an hour for all study groups at the end of 1 day a week.

22. Release teachers from their teaching duties for an hour and a half each week. The students would remain at school, being dismissed at their regular times. Professionals from area universities, health care facilities, community agencies, businesses, and city and county governmental agencies consider how volunteers can provide instruction in foreign languages, physical education, athletics, nutrition, civics, drama, music, art, environmental education, and other areas for the students during that hour and a half. Students could be grouped differently than in the regular classes, forming larger and smaller classes across grade levels. PTAs consider budgeting funds for this purpose where funds are required.

All of the preceding strategies for finding time for teachers to collaborate require that the time allocated be spent in serious and purposeful work, increasing the teachers' relevant knowledge and skills. Because it might be perceived by the public that time is being taken from students, strategies must be put in place to inform internal and external publics about how students directly benefit from time allocated to this form of teacher development. However, communication must be continuous and effective. As time passes, information regarding student gains will encourage the community to continue to support the idea that student development is directly linked to teacher development. Teachers should tell their students what they do and learn in their study groups on a regular basis. Right after a study group meets is a good learning opportunity for students. Teachers can often say "Today, we are going to do something that I learned in my study group this week." From this information, many students go home and tell their parents; they then see the connection, and the idea of how students benefit when time is allocated for teacher learning is no longer an abstract concept. If information about study groups and their effectiveness is meaningfully presented, parents and other groups can become strong advocates for this form of teacher development and school improvement.

One outcome of the study group structure is the realization that professional development is inclusive of various models that interact with each other to make a more dynamic whole. At the beginning of the study group process, faculties have generally seen study groups separate from professional development days. They saw study groups and professional development days as separate from specific whole-faculty training events at schools. And they were likely to see all of the earlier mentioned as separate from attending conferences and doing independent activities. By the end of Year 1, faculties were more able to see and develop professional development plans that had various staff development strategies or models feeding each other. In these schools, what teachers did in study groups to become skillful in the classroom enabled them to see more clearly the need for a more integrated and holistic approach to professional development. When this concept becomes reality in a school, time becomes less of a problem. Teachers see, as a unified effort, different time frames as one large block for continuous learning.

Faculties and principals have made heroic efforts to find the time required for professional development to routinely occur within the school day. Major efforts to find time for study groups to meet take energy away from the learning process. To achieve success for all students, districts and states must shoulder the responsibility for making meaningful professional development for teachers a seamless part of the daily work life of school personnel (i.e., make learning become the norm). Setting aside days in the school calendar as staff development days does not lighten the load or eliminate the pressure that teachers feel toward further developing and fine-tuning what and how they teach. For effective schools, development and increased learning is an everyday task and takes time and commitment.

Summary

Schools with evidence that the WFSG approach has had positive effects on student achievement and on the culture of the school followed the 15 procedural guidelines presented in this chapter. When faculties ask Murphy if it is acceptable to alter a guideline (e.g., not meet weekly or have more than 6 in a group), her standard answer is "That is your choice. If you alter the guidelines, you can't expect to get the results that schools have gotten that followed the guidelines." The 15 guidelines evolved over a period of at least 14 years and are the result of many revisions. From 1993 through the writing of this book, the guidelines were reexamined and revised at the end of each school year and after reflecting on the work in progress in very different schools.

Content **6**

Identifying Student Needs and Making Professional Development Decisions

Content refers to the actual skills, attitudes, understandings, and knowledge that educators possess or acquire to achieve intended results. In schools, content is the disciplines (subject areas) that are taught and how they are taught.

The Heart of WFSGs

The heart of the study group process is what teachers do to develop understanding of what they teach, what teachers do to become more knowledgeable of what they teach, what teachers investigate, and what teachers do to become more skillful in the classroom with students. That "what" is the content of study groups, and without appropriate content, the process is empty. Without intellectually rigorous work, the process is boring and can be a waste of time. It is substantive teacher work that requires teachers to immerse themselves in searching for deeper understandings of what they teach that creates high-performing, motivated study groups.

The process, by itself, has little power to change what teachers actually do with students. Change in what students know and do is the end result of WFSGs. If students are to become more knowledgeable and skillful, then teachers must have control of the academic content they teach and have an expansive repertoire of instructional strategies to deliver that content to students. Teachers increase their teaching repertoires so that students will increase their learning repertoires.

The need to continuously examine and expand the tools of teaching is directly aligned with the constancy of change in the work life and workplace of teaching. Each new set of students, each new expansion of knowledge, each new set of circumstances, each new set of curriculum guidelines and materials, and each new set of regulations and expectations creates the need for teachers to examine what and how they teach.

The Content of Study

Murphy has found that of the three components or elements of a professional development design—context, process, content—for study groups, content is the most problematic. Teachers have no difficulty deciding what students should know. Teachers design curriculum for other teachers to use with students. In curriculum guides that are developed by teachers, they specify objectives, select materials, and design activities for students. However, when it comes to designing curriculum for themselves, it is like hitting a brick wall. When it comes to specifying what they should know, what they need do to gain new knowledge and skill, and the content of their learning, content becomes somewhat of a mystery. In relation to the study group process, content includes two considerations: one, what teachers will study when the group meets to become more knowledgeable and skillful, and two, strategies the group will use to master the new knowledge and skills.

In a recent conversation with a consultant for WFSGs, the consultant said, "It is so difficult to get teachers to understand the importance of the content of teacher work." This is so puzzling because teachers know how important the content of student work is. Teachers in study groups need to determine what will be the teacher work just as they determine what will be the student work. Teachers teach mathematics content, social studies content, science content, and reading and writing content. And everyday, teachers make decisions about what strategies or activities they will use in teaching content. What to learn and how to learn it are the two aspects of study group content.

The other puzzling aspect of teachers having difficulty identifying substantive and engaging content stems from what teachers say.

Teachers Say	We Say
We have too much to do.	Pool resources and strengths to reduce the time it takes to individually develop lessons.
Too many new programs. Don't have time to figure out how to use these materials.	Select the new writing program and take the time to immerse yourselves in how to use the materials to increase writing scores.
The study group is a waste of time.	Who decided that you would do what you are doing?
There's no time to align new math standards with math curriculum.	Do that in your study group.
No time to prepare to implement what we were trained to do.	In a study group, work with teachers who attended same training and practice new strategies together.
We don't know enough about what we are trying to do.	Ask the principal to locate a specialist in that area to work with you.
My study group is boring.	How would you respond to a student in your class who said that?

In Augusta, where the WFSG work had its beginning, the content was predetermined. As described in Chapter 1, the content (what study groups would do) was part of the school improvement package. The package included being in a study group that focused on implementing in classrooms several models of teaching. Faculties that voted to implement the improvement program were told before they voted that the content would be several models of teaching and that the process for learning teaching strategies would be to organize the entire faculty into study groups. Once the improvement program began, there were pockets of resistance. Some teachers resisted the process, being in a study group. Some teachers resisted the content, the models of teaching. Some teachers resisted the process and the content. A visitor to the school could hear a teacher say, "I am so frustrated with this new program." The visitor would ask, "Oh, you don't like the models of teaching?" To which the teacher would say, "The models are great! I don't like meeting in those groups every week." That same visitor would see another teacher, and the teacher would say, "This new program is really difficult." The visitor would ask, "Oh, you don't like weekly study group meetings?" To which the teacher would say, "I love meeting with my colleagues each week; the models of teaching are just too hard." The one thing visitors did hear from all teachers was that students were learning more. This acknowledgment confirms that centralized or district sponsored initiatives can be very effective and beneficial to students.

When Murphy began working in other districts, it was assumed that the content, what teachers do in study groups, would not be the source of teachers' grumbling. If teachers selected the content, Murphy wondered, would the process seem more democratic? Would the study group work would seem more relevant? Would there be more buy-in? Would the process not seem so "top down"? Would teachers not feel so coerced? Generally, Murphy has found that initially there is a higher sense of teacher satisfaction when teachers choose the student needs that groups will address. However, that satisfaction does not continue if teachers do not see changes in student learning. Most often, grumbling persists. The source of the grumbling is the outward frustration of teachers realizing that the content they chose is not having the desired impact or what they chose to do is not useful. Self-selection does not necessarily mean that the end result of the work of study groups will be higher levels of student learning. If faculties do not have all the data for the choices that students require for the faculty to make and if faculties do not have leaders who will speak for students, faculties may make choices that, over time, will create dissatisfaction and will not result in changes in their behavior or in changes in student behavior. Still, even when teachers are shown evidence that student learning increased in places where district leaders used districtwide data to determine what study groups in schools would do, they are clear that they do not want to be told what they are to do in their study groups. There are study groups in WFSG schools that have difficulty connecting teacher learning to student learning. Once this is evident in the action plan and in the first few logs from a study group, the principal or other support person must intervene. Chapter 8 in this book tells leaders how to intervene. The intervening person should be one who

- Knows the context

- Has examined relevant data

- Knows the status of student learning

- Knows the instructional initiatives that are currently operational at the school

- Knows what resources are available, both human and material

- Knows the skill level of teachers in specific content areas

The people who usually have this knowledge are the principal and one or more district leaders. That person would meet with the study group, examine student needs the group is targeting, and determine what resources are available to get the group moving. Study groups experience the greatest content success if someone in the district has expertise to help study groups as they confront new knowledge and the need for new skills. When someone accessible to the study group can provide resources to the group and can meet with it on some regular basis, the study group is much less likely to go astray. If there is no one in the district who can supply that service, then the school should secure the services of a content specialist. The key to the success in Augusta was the content expertise that consultants brought to study groups.

What some teachers have found helpful when trying to get a handle on the content of their work is to equate the study group work to a college course. Teachers usually select college courses or they are expected to take courses because of the course's content. Let's draw some parallels. The SGAP is the course syllabus. The study group logs are the notes for each class meeting. The notebook that every study group member keeps has the action plan and logs in it along with the artifacts from each meeting (e.g., articles and lesson plans the group develops). Artifacts would be the same as course handouts. The work between study group meetings would be the homework or the practicum side of the course. In a college course on reading, what would be the content? What would teachers enrolled in the course learn? What would materials be that teachers would use and read? What materials would teachers enrolled in the course be expected to develop as part of the course work? What instructional strategies would the course instructor use? Answers to these questions tell us about the content of the course. In some districts, if a study group is addressing reading, the study group members can apply for course credit and, on examination of what the group did, receive credit for a reading course equivalent to a college course.

Once student needs are identified and groups are formed, a study group designs its own work just like a college instructor designs a college course, except the study group's design will be more practical. The course that study group members design is tailor-made for the study group. The work that the study group plans for itself is the content of the study group's work. What teachers work on and what strategies the group uses to do that work is the study group's content. We are not going to list here all the choices teachers have in terms of a study group's curriculum of study. If the study group's general category of student need is mathematics, the content of the group's work could be the district's mathematics standards. If the general category is writing, the content of the group's work could be a new writing program that the district is initiating. Generic content for either of those two areas of work could be the latest brain research or the use of technology. Whatever the study group selects, its content should be aligned with student needs. Teachers must do what will enable their students to become more knowledgeable and skillful. The study group's action plan will indicate student needs and what teachers will do when the group meets to address student needs. Again, what teachers will do and how teachers will go about doing it is the study group's curriculum of study, the content.

Resources to Support the Content

The following resources may help teachers become more concrete about what a study group will do and strategies the group will use to do its work.

1. *Student work:* The work of students is a group's most valuable resource.

2. *Teachers' manuals:* This is one of the most underused resources that teachers have. Manuals that go with textbooks have a wealth of information about how to teach the content. Bringing teachers' manuals to study group meetings to explore how basic skills are introduced at each grade level is valid work. Supplementary materials that accompany the text also should be examined.

3. *Student textbooks:* Because developing vocabulary is one student need often addressed, study groups frequently examine textbooks in one content area (e.g., mathematics). This examination usually leads teachers to be more consistent with the vocabulary they use when teaching. Even though publishers have published vocabulary lists, actually manipulating student texts would give teachers a greater feel for what students experience. In heterogeneous study groups, some teachers have not looked at student texts at other grade levels. Some upper-grade teachers that teach one subject area have not reviewed student texts in other subject areas.

4. *People* (real live): Persons from district offices, other schools within a district, teachers within the school, regional service agencies, universities and colleges, technical schools and centers, state departments, textbook representatives, independent consultants, other school districts, and local businesses and community agencies could be rich sources of information. Once the study group matches itself with a resource person, it is suggested that the individual work with the group on some sort of routine basis, for example, once a month.

5. *Books:* Sources might include textbooks from courses previously taken (e.g., reading courses), college bookstores, publishers' lists, and materials from professional organizations, such as Association for Supervision and Curriculum Development (ASCD) and National Staff Development Council. A book will give a study group more structure. A cycle for using a book could be to read a chapter or section of the book, discuss and reflect on the reading (one meeting), try ideas in a classroom, share results of actions in classrooms and demonstrate lessons taught (one or two meetings), reflect on outcomes and examine student work (one meeting), and go on to the next chapter and repeat the process. The cycle (plan, act, reflect) for one reading could take up to four study group meetings.

6. *Articles:* School libraries usually subscribe to periodicals, such as *The Reading Teacher, The Journal of Reading, The Journal of Educational Research, Educational Leadership,* and others. If an article is to be used to generate ideas for actual classroom trials, it should be copied for everyone in the group. The plan-act-reflect cycle described in Item 5 should be considered. The Final Word protocol is also a good way to debrief readings.

7. *The Internet:* There is unlimited information from this resource.

8. *Computer software:* Computer programs in all content areas and reference materials that go beyond anything we could have imagined a few years ago are available and abundant.

9. *Public television:* Many state departments of education and universities have courses and other professional opportunities offered via television.

10. *Workshops and conferences:* One person from the study group may attend workshops and conferences and bring the information to the study group.

11. *Commercial sources:* In many states and communities, businesses and agencies have materials that stress the importance of reading, writing, mathematics, and other content areas. In Georgia, the Georgia Power Company, Pizza Hut, Atlanta Braves, and Six Flags Over Georgia have materials teachers can order.

12. *Students:* A student invited to attend the first 5 or 10 minutes of a study group meeting could, in an interview format, give study group members valuable information about instructional practices. The study group would decide what they want to ask prior to inviting the student. Students at any grade level, including kindergarten, can provide helpful and interesting information to a study group.

13. *Program materials:* Most instructional programs that schools adopt have an array of materials in print, video, and audio formats. These programs also have individuals who are trained in the use of program strategies that should be available to study groups.

14. *District and state sources:* State departments and school districts have materials specifically developed to help teachers implement frameworks, standards, and curriculums endorsed by local units.

The resources just listed will give the content substance. It is what teachers have in their hands when they walk into a study group meeting that gives the meeting substance. It is what is on the table around which the teachers sit that gives the meeting substance. When even one teacher in a study group walks into a study group meeting empty-handed and when there is nothing on the table with which a person can work, an observer knows the study group is floundering, at least for one member.

No one outside the study group can make the work of the group meaningful. That is a task for its members. When study group members say that study group meetings are a waste of time, the person hearing the statement should say "And who determines what the group will do?" There is so much work to do in schools. The study group is a place to do that work with colleagues, not in isolation, as has been the case in the past for many teachers. The content of the work of study groups is the work teachers have to do to prepare to help their students learn more.

We repeat ourselves: Without content that will change behaviors of teachers and behaviors of students, the WFSG process has little power to change anything. The power of collaborative relationships is in

- What teachers study
- What teachers investigate
- What teaching strategies teachers add to their repertoires
- What materials teachers add to their resource bank

- What teachers do to become more skillful in their classrooms

- What strategies group members will use when the study group meets to accomplish its intended results

The following sections describe how faculties decide what instructional student needs the study groups will address. Each study group decides the content of the group's work to address the student needs it has selected. Resource A has a content checklist that may be helpful for study groups to use.

Early Decisions

The first decision that is made by the whole faculty is whether or not the WFSG approach is to be put in place at the school. Once that decision is made, it is expected that all faculty members will participate in a study group. Second, it must be decided who will lead the whole faculty through an inquiry process to determine how groups will be organized and what groups will do. Most often, this is done by a team from the school, called the focus team.

A major decision comes when the focus team decides what data will be examined to determine student needs. Data must be collected and organized for the faculty to use in making decisions about what study groups will do and how study groups will be organized. What student data and general information about students the faculty will review is the most important decision that leaders of WFSGs will make. All future decisions will be shaped by what data the faculty analyzes. If data that the faculty reviews won't lead it to target those student needs that are the most serious instructional needs, the whole process will be in danger of not accomplishing intended results. If, for example, the most serious need students have is in the area of reading, and the faculty does not have data to validate that need, the faculty may miss its opportunity to address that need.

When the whole faculty works together during these early stages of decision making, teachers feel empowered and begin to see that they do have a say in what is going to happen. Teachers begin to feel a part of the effort and, as a result, feel less coerced during the implementation stage. It is during the initiation stage, when everyone is involved in the decision making, that individuals see the process for what it is intended to do. Those who may not have been in favor of the process when the faculty took a vote on whether or not it was to be put in place at the school are most often brought more willingly into the process when their voice is heard in this developmental phase. Some teachers will still continue to feel that the process is contrived collegiality until, in their study groups, they experience total control over what they do and how they go about doing it.

Parameters for Identifying Student Needs

Districts and schools make the decision to use Murphy's WFSGs for one primary reason: to increase student learning. Therefore, it has proved helpful to specify the types of student needs that become the focus of the work of WFSGs. Student needs that do not fall within these parameters would be assigned to a committee, department chairs or grade-level chairs, department or grade-level site council, an administrative team, or any other appropriate organizational structure. Just because a student need is deemed not appropriate for a study group does not mean that the need is not valid. It simply means that there is a better way to address the need. No student need should be ignored and not addressed.

To keep teachers' work focused on instruction, there are three parameters that faculties are given to provide direction in what types of student needs are addressed in WFSGs. These three parameters are as follows:

- Student need is evident in the work that students produce. Teachers can look at student work for evidence of the impact of the study group work on student learning.

- Student need can be addressed through how and what teachers teach.

- Student need is an enabling need, meaning it is one that enables students to be academically successful, such as the need to comprehend what they read, express themselves orally and through their writing, compute, and understand science concepts. An enabling need could also be classified as a "terminal" need, meaning that at some point, the need will no longer exist as it did or at the level it existed because teachers intervened and took corrective action. Teachers have direct control or influence on terminating the need. This is unlike a perennial need, meaning a student need that is always there, such as the need to attend school, feel good about self, cooperate, be respectful, behave, and have their parents involved. Perennial needs are best addressed through an enabling need. For example, as study group members are addressing mathematics, they will also be targeting ethical issues. As study group members learn to appropriately use a range of teaching strategies that actively involve students, discipline will improve. Study groups will have a primary focus that will be an enabling or terminal student need. At the same time, study groups could have several perennial student needs that weave in and out of what all groups do.

The Decision-Making Cycle

The DMC (Murphy, 1999), shown in Figure 6.1 and described in the remainder of this chapter, outlines a series of steps. Its steps have been successfully followed in schools that are very different from one another. Differences are reflected in school size, grades, demographics, locations, and leadership styles of the principals.

This decision-making cycle is recommended for making decisions regarding how study groups will be organized and what study groups will do. Individuals who lead the whole faculty through the steps of the cycle must carefully think through each step. Even though those leading the decision-making process may have firm opinions as to what study groups should do, they should maintain open minds, keep their opinions to themselves, and be totally free in letting the faculty find its own way. It is critical that the whole faculty participates in Steps 1 through 4 of the cycle. Every faculty member should have a voice in how groups are organized and what groups will be doing. Open participation now will diminish problems after study groups begin their work. Teachers own the process and should feel that ownership.

Figure 6.1. The Decision-Making Cycle for Schoolwide Change Through Whole-Faculty Study Groups

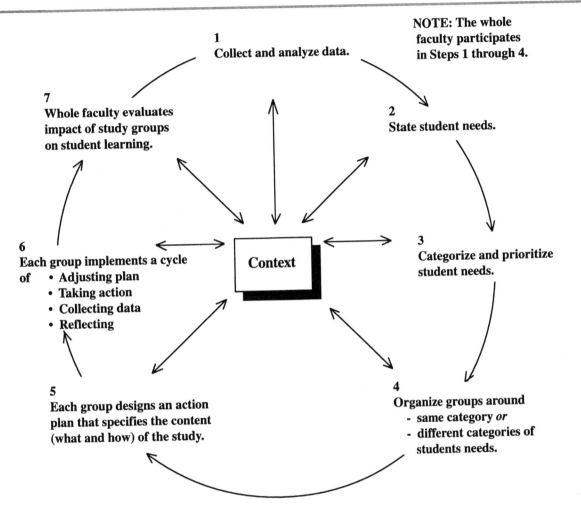

1
Collect and analyze data.

NOTE: The whole faculty participates in Steps 1 through 4.

7
Whole faculty evaluates impact of study groups on student learning.

2
State student needs.

Context

6
Each group implements a cycle
of • Adjusting plan
 • Taking action
 • Collecting data
 • Reflecting

3
Categorize and prioritize student needs.

5
Each group designs an action plan that specifies the content (what and how) of the study.

4
Organize groups around
 - same category *or*
 - different categories of students needs.

The overarching contextual question asked at each step...

"Is this school's uniqueness considered?"

The decision-making cycle is a seven-step, cyclic decision-making model that will lead the faculty to what their study groups will do and how they will be formed.

Step 1: Data Analysis

Collect and organize a range of data describing the status of student learning for the faculty to review. The focus team is usually assigned this task. The faculty as a whole analyzes the data. If faculties use 2 or 3 consecutive years of data from several sources, they will have a more accurate picture of the level of learning. High schools should also consider data from elementary and middle schools that feed into the high school. Similarly, elementary and middle schools should consider data from the high schools their students attend. *Remember: Study groups will address student needs.* Student needs are identified from the data that the faculty reviews. Gathering the data that the faculty will review is the most important decision that the focus team will make. What study groups will do and how they will be organized will depend on what comes out of the data that the faculty analyzes. Data might include several of the following:

- Standardized test results over a span of several years: The faculty will need the item analysis of all the subcategories tested, subject area subscores, or any other reporting system the test maker uses to show how students did in specific areas tested. For example, the faculty should not only see the score for reading but also for reading comprehension, vocabulary, and work attack skills. One school in Massachusetts used the Iowa Test of Basic Skills for Grade 3, the Massachusetts Comprehensive Assessment System for Grade 4, and the California Achievement Test for Grade 5.

- Performance of students on the district's content standards

- Early Literacy Assessment or other tests that indicate how successful students are in preschool, kindergarten, and first-grade classes

- Oral reading assessments

- Informal reading inventories

- Exit exams from high school courses

- Criterion-referenced tests

- Writing assessments

- Journals, authentic writing samples

- Student portfolios that contain at least 1 year of work in one content area

- Checklists from textbook companies (e.g., reading series often have end-of-book tests)

- Performance assessments

- Results of open-ended response questions

- Results of tests given by Title I and other special testing programs

- Results of tests similar to New York State's Regents Examination, analyzed by subject area

- The number of graduates from high schools that the elementary and middle school students attend, categorized by types of diploma

- Cumulative grade point averages by subject area and grade for a random sample of students

- An analysis of why students quit school

- The number of students that enroll in postsecondary education

- The number of students that go to college and graduate
- An analysis of why students are referred for disciplinary action
- An analysis of why students are absent
- An analysis of the education levels of parents
- Distribution of student grades by subject and grade levels
- The numbers of students placed in advanced placement courses and in remedial or lower-level courses
- An analysis of why students are referred to special education and how many referrals are placed in special programs
- Promotion and retention rates by grades and subjects
- Samples of student and teacher portfolios
- Analysis of types of employment opportunities for which students qualify who do not enroll in postsecondary education
- Responses to questionnaires and interviews
- An analysis of circulation reports from the school library
- Level of participation in science and social studies fairs
- An analysis of students enrolled in debate, academic bowls, and other activities that are subject area related
- Student interviews
- Reports from accrediting agencies or other groups that rate the schools
- An analysis of the access students have to computers and the Internet
- An analysis of why teachers leave the school

After the study groups are formed, they will want to return to some of the data used with the whole faculty. On the SGAPs, study group members are required to be more specific about student needs than may have been done in the whole-faculty session. This would be the appropriate time for study groups to look at student work to either validate student needs or give the group more information about student needs.

Step 2: State Student Needs

From the data, generate a list of student needs. Included in Resource A is a form that Murphy uses, titled "Stating Specific Student Needs," for individual teachers to list the student needs they see evidenced in the data. When stating student needs, teachers will need to be reminded of the parameters discussed earlier. Can the need be evidenced in student work? Can the need be addressed through how and what teachers teach? Examples might include the following student needs (numbers do not indicate priority):

1. Improve and enlarge vocabulary in all content areas

2. Meet mathematics standards

3. Use correct grammar, punctuation, and spelling in all areas of the curriculum.

4. Communicate their thinking of mathematical processes (oral and written)

5. Develop skills for project-based learning

6. Be taught by teachers who have a deep understanding of the content they teach

7. Be more successful in solving word problems

8. Write and speak for an audience or for a purpose

9. Use the five-step process in writing persuasive and expository pieces

10. Increase reading comprehension

11. Know how to proofread and edit work

12. Incorporate technology in gathering, understanding, and evaluating information

After individuals have listed students needs they see evidenced in the data, a recorder at each table records the needs identified, making a chart that represents the table group.

The focus team has at least four strategies for leading the faculty through Steps 1 through 4 of the DMC. Resource E contains explicit examples of each strategy: descriptive stories about how each strategy has worked in the real world of schools. Regardless of which strategy the focus team selects, someone on the faculty should use a laptop computer to enter all the needs listed on all the charts.

Table 6.1 gives some examples of how to express student needs. Notice that the first word in each phrase is a verb.

Step 3: Categorize and Prioritize Student Needs

When student needs are categorized or classified, several usually cluster around a subject or skill area, such as mathematics. This task is similar to separating dirty clothes in piles for washing. We put all types of towels in one pile. When we categorize the long, brainstormed list of student needs, we put all types of student reading needs in one pile. Some student needs, like the dirty clothes, can be put in any or in more than one category.

On completion of Step 2, we may have a random listing of 30 or more student needs. That list is important and, later, we will directly use this long list of specific needs. However, at this point, we need to group or categorize the list so it is more manageable. We will ask teachers to review the list(s) and to put similar or like needs together. The system suggested for grouping needs is to use the number in front of a need as a simple way to identify it and put it in a group. After numbers of like needs have been written down in one group, give the group or category a name. Resource E gives specific examples of how the categorizing can be done.

At this point, all student needs have been placed in one or more categories, and all categories have a name. Now, it is time to prioritize the categories. If the faculty feels that until the students are better readers in all content areas, nothing else is going to get better, then reading would be the first priority. When asked to prioritize, some faculties will indicate that they do not want to prioritize categories because they feel that all categories are important and they want to leave all categories as choices for study groups. In such cases, don't prioritize.

Table 6.1 Some Examples of How to Express Student Needs

Data indicate that students need to

- Improve and enlarge vocabulary in all content areas

- Meet mathematics standards (substitute any content area)

- Use correct grammar, punctuation, and spelling in all areas of the curriculum

- Demonstrate improved self-esteem by taking more responsibility for the quality of assignments

- Use higher-order thinking skills to solve problems

- Communicate mastered content through a variety of performance assessments

- Have the ability to read and comprehend the textbook in all curriculum areas

- Demonstrate ability to gather and synthesize significant information

- Communicate their thinking of mathematical processes (oral and written).

- Be engaged in quality, research-based learning experiences

- Develop skills for project-based learning

- Be taught by teachers who have a deep understanding of the content they teach

- Develop listening skills to promote understanding and appreciation for what is presented auditorally.

- Be more successful at solving word problems

- Know how to proofread and edit work

- Incorporate technology in gathering, understanding, and evaluating information.

- Increase computation skills

- Understand figurative language

- Integrate and apply math and science knowledge in real-life experiences

- Draw pictures, diagrams, and tables to aid in solving problems and visualizing solutions

- Demonstrate ability to distinguish between significant and insignificant oral and written information when taking notes

- Write and speak with clarity for audience or purpose

- Know how teachers expect them to show what they have learned

- Have multiple opportunities to demonstrate achievement of standards

- Know how to evaluate their own work

- Have opportunities to apply what they know to real-life experiences

- Complete projects that have multiple requirements

Using the 12 student needs listed in Step 2, categories and priorities might look like this:

Number of Student Needs	Category Name	Priority
3, 4, 5, 6, 8, 9, 11, 12	Writing	2
1, 6, 8, 10, 11, 12	Reading	3
1, 4, 5, 6, 7, 12	Problem Solving	4
1, 2, 4, 5, 6, 7, 8, 12, 11, 12	Mathematics	1

There are readers who are thinking "I would not have categorized needs in this way nor would I have given categories those names." There is no right or wrong way to do this step. How a faculty does the categorizing and prioritizing is contextual, meaning each school will have a different perspective on what student needs mean.

Step 4: Organize the Study Groups

Decide whether the whole faculty, all of the study groups, will address one category or several categories: Once the categories and priorities are established, the faculty is asked if their first priority is such a high priority that the category must be addressed by all study groups before any other category is addressed.

If the answer is "Yes, we all need to address mathematics," for instance, then all study groups address mathematics, and it does not matter who is in what group. If all the study groups will be meeting at the same time, and time of meetings is not a consideration, a random assignment could be used, such as putting names on index cards and dealing the cards into stacks. If there are 50 teachers on the faculty, that would equate to 10 study groups with 5 teachers in each group. Another strategy would be for the faculty to break down the mathematics category into more specific needs; then groups could form around those specific student mathematics needs.

If the faculty says "No, we do not want to have only one choice, we want to have several categories from which to choose." Then a method for making choices must be put in place. The faculty would decide if the choice will be two categories, three categories, or all the categories. Each study group would form around the category of its individual choice. Those teachers who want to address mathematics would go to a classroom and form study group(s). If 14 teachers want to address mathematics, that could be three study groups. If 17 teachers want to address reading, that could be four groups. If 11 teachers want to address problem solving, they would probably group according to the type of problem solving each is interested in pursuing.

Figure 6.2 illustrates Steps 2 through 5. In Step 2, we identified specific needs. In Step 3, we put specific needs in general categories. In Step 4, general categories will be choices that teachers have for what study groups will do. In Step 5, we will go back to specific needs listed in Step 2. In Step 5, each study group will develop a SGAP, and in it, the study group will indicate specific student needs in the general category that the group will address (see Table 6.1). If the teachers who want to address writing have formed a study group, that group would go back to the eight specific writing needs to determine exactly what writing needs the group will address and then list them in its action plan. The study group, for example, may only want to

Figure 6.2. Specific to General to Specific

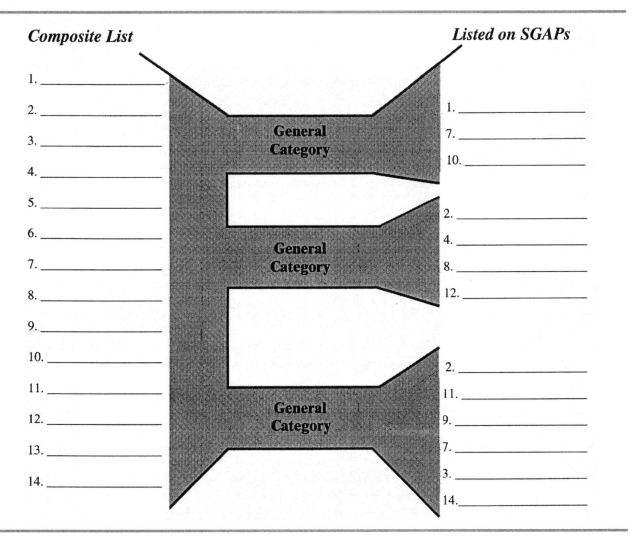

Composite List   *Listed on SGAPs*

1. _____

2. _____   1. _____

3. _____   **General**   7. _____
                            Category
4. _____   10. _____

5. _____

6. _____   2. _____

7. _____   **General**   4. _____
                            Category
8. _____   8. _____

9. _____   12. _____

10. _____

11. _____   2. _____

12. _____   **General**   11. _____
                            Category
13. _____   9. _____

14. _____   7. _____

                                                    3. _____

                                                    14. _____

address two of the eight. The study group may feel, after more thought, that some important needs were not on the list of specific needs initially generated by the whole faculty. The study group may add student needs in their action plan that were not on the brainstormed list. Before doing so, the study group should validate the need by looking at more data and student work.

Step 5: Develop a Study Group Action Plan

Create a SGAP. The plan is analogous to a course syllabus, except learners develop the syllabus instead of a college instructor. Each study group will take the first two study group meetings to develop its SGAP. Teachers in each study group used the broad categories of student needs as the basis for forming their study groups. To do its action plan, each group will need to go back to the list of specific student needs (Step 3) that formed the category of choice. Teachers that chose the mathematics category, for example, would now decide which specific mathematics needs the group wants to address. Study groups may want to do a more in-depth investigation into the specific student needs in the category of their choice. A study group may want to review information that the whole faculty may not have had access to. This would be the time for student work to become part of the data collection and review. Teachers in study groups would bring examples of student work that validate or indicate specific difficulties students are having.

The SGAP has six parts:

1. The general category of student needs, such as mathematics

2. The essential question that guides the work of the group

3. The specific student needs within the category that the group will address (see Table 6.1)

4. The actions the teachers will take *when the study group meets* to address specific student needs (see Figure 6.4)

5. The resources the group will use in its work, including the names of individuals, print material, audiovisual materials, conferences individuals may attend, and workshops or courses in which individuals may enroll

6. The evidence of student learning, by specifying

   — Student performance goals

   — Data source

In Step 3, we described how the list of specific student needs is grouped into general categories and how the general category the group will address is determined. An essential question is one that will guide the work of the group. If a group will address the general category of reading, the guiding or essential question would be one that defines what the group will do to solve or reduce a problem the students are having learning to read at a higher level. The question is written at the top of the action plan. A few examples follow of general categories and related essential questions:

■ Measurement: How can we teach students to develop measurement skills in all content areas?

■ Reading: How can we teach students to comprehend what they read?

■ Communication: What do students need to know to communicate effectively?

■ Problem solving: How can we help students effectively use problem-solving skills and strategies? Or, how can we teach students to communicate their reasoning for arriving at a solution to a given problem?

■ Writing: How can we help students become better writers?

The part of the action plan that usually gives study groups the most difficulty is the top right quadrant of the action plan. In this space, the study group indicates what members will do when the study group meets—not what members are going to do

Table 6.2 Examples of What Teachers Do When Study Groups Meet

In study groups, teachers will

- Design and teach to each other lessons that integrate different curriculums

- Examine student work routinely using a protocol

- Identify common performance indicators that ensure that assessment of student achievement is consistent across teachers and grade levels

- Share and demonstrate how lessons are related to district and state academic standards

- Debrief professional articles that members read by using The Final Word protocol

- Have a skillful person attend meetings to train or guide study group members

- Compile and document evidence of student success

- Share and demonstrate how we provide for students to inform us that they can relate _____ standards to what they learn

- Plan what we have recently been trained to do for classroom implementation

- Demonstrate lessons to be taught or that have been taught in classrooms

- Practice and critique teaching strategies used with a specific lesson

- Reflect on new knowledge, new experiences, and student responses

(continued)

when they return to their classrooms, not what their students will do, but what study group members will do. For example, when the study group meets, teachers will

- Examine student work using a protocol

- Compile a list of techniques to help students evaluate their own work and share the results of our trials with these techniques

- Debrief articles we read, select ideas from the articles that we can try in our classrooms, and share our trials.

By the end of the second study group meeting, the action plan is usually complete. Those groups that want to look at additional data may extend the planning work into the third meeting. The completed action plan is given to the principal. Study groups should expect feedback on the plan from the principal. The action plan should be updated at regular intervals. If after a period of time, a study group feels that the group has done what it stated it would do on the action plan, the study group should do another action plan. The group would either stay with the same category or could go on to a different category.

Table 6.1 provides a list of how to write student needs. Table 6.2 provides a list of examples for what teachers do when study groups meet. Resource A contains a checklist for writing an action plan.

Table 6.2 Continued

- Identify, discuss, and practice strategies that help develop reading skills, such as vocabulary skills and skills to decode words

- Compile a list of techniques we can use to help students evaluate their own work

- Identify, discuss, and practice strategies for reading in the content areas, such as using context clues

- Evaluate assessment techniques used in the classrooms

- Investigate ways to increase the joy of reading

- View (alone or together) videos of ourselves teaching and share with members changes you will make in the lesson that was taped

- Discuss case studies that have been selected from field-tested cases describing a teaching experience that had an unexpected outcome or ran into difficulty

- Develop skill and plan for routine use of various forms of technology

- Investigate various diagnostic resources and techniques for testing reading comprehension and strategies for remediating deficiencies

- Identify different types of word problems and strategies for solving the different types

- Design a math dictionary or develop a strategy for students to design one

- Examine a variety of sample tests to determine skills necessary for success

- Examine, develop, and critique use of rubrics

- Invite students to attend meetings from time to time to listen to students' points of view

- Observe each other teaching a lesson we developed together, preconferencing and postconferencing in our study group

- Share observations of students working on assignments that focus on the student needs the study group is addressing

- Monitor the effects of our instructional interventions by charting student progress after we decide what data will need to be collected

- Share the information gleaned from shadowing a student

- Correlate reading standards to our current classroom practices

- Use student performance data to revise lessons collaboratively planned

- Design activities that are aligned with _____ standards

- Bring ungraded student work to exchange and grade to compare scoring consistency

- Plan multiple opportunities for students to demonstrate achievement of standards

- Gain a deeper knowledge of _____ (any academic content area)

- Design a unit of study using the Teaching for Understanding framework

Step 6: Implement the Study Group Action Plan

Now, when it meets, the study group does what it committed to do in its action plan. On the action plan, teachers listed what the group would do when the group meets. If the plan states that the group will "assess and discuss reading levels," that is what they should do. If the plan also states that the group will "develop and teach to each other innovative lessons that incorporate different learning styles," that is what they should do. The list of actions the group will take when it meets is actually the foundation for a year's agenda for study group meetings.

Study group logs should indicate a bouncing-ball effect. In the study group, members prepare to use a new strategy and either use new materials or old materials in a different way. Members use the strategy and materials in their classrooms. Members also share what happened in their classrooms and reflect on the experiences. They adjust strategies and materials based on what they learn from each other. Members then use their strategies or materials with their students. In the study group, they share and reflect. Furthermore, members plan lessons together and actually teach lessons within the group to get feedback. Again, members use these lessons in their classrooms. In addition, they visit each other's classrooms and observe how students respond to these strategies and materials. Members monitor effects of teaching strategies and materials on students by collecting information about student performance and participation. The SGAP is updated every 4 to 6 weeks to reflect new directions that the study group will take. Figure 6.3 illustrates the three sources of information that study groups interweave in their work together: cycle of planning, doing, and reflecting. When a principal or other support person reads the logs, he or she should be able to see the cycle occurring over and over and over, a bouncing-ball effect.

Step 7: Assess the Impact of the Work on Students

Assess the impact of the study group work on student learning. Effects of the work of study groups on students may be monitored in multiple ways, including informal ones. Looking at student work is the best way to tell if the study group work is making a difference. Grades teachers give to student work reflect student learning. Comparing how students did on a unit when teachers did not use a specific strategy and on a unit when they did will give an indication of the impact on students. A study group decides how it will assess progress when the group does the action plan. Resource A consists of a collection of forms that may be used for assessing the progress of study groups.

The Cycle Continues

At the end of a school year, all study groups go to Step 7 in the DMC. At the beginning of a school year, all study groups return to Step 1, and it does not matter if study groups are continuing from the year before or if they have reconfigured. All study groups return to the data for guidance as to what study groups form and what they will do.

Figure 6.3. WFSGs Hear Voices

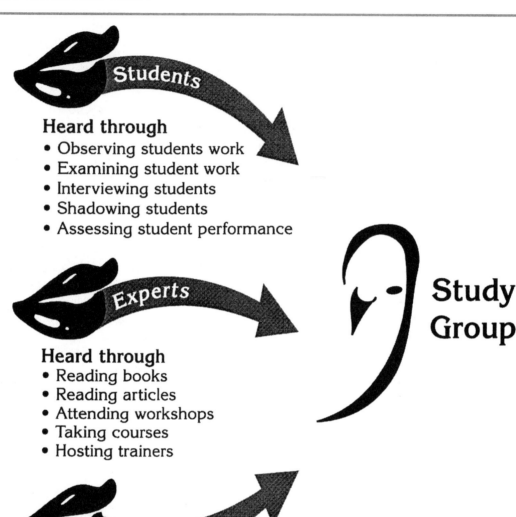

Heard through
- Observing students work
- Examining student work
- Interviewing students
- Shadowing students
- Assessing student performance

Heard through
- Reading books
- Reading articles
- Attending workshops
- Taking courses
- Hosting trainers

Heard through
- Sharing experiences
- Sharing knowledge
- Sharing work
- Sharing student information

A Script for Leading the Faculty Through the Decision-Making Cycle

Resource E contains a script for how the focus team may want to lead the faculty through the DMC. The script elaborates on how to establish conditions for doing each step with the faculty.

The School Improvement Plan

Most schools have a plan that the district expects the school to have that is called the school improvement plan or a similar name. The first year that WFSGs are implemented, the faculty may want to use the improvement plan to accomplish Steps 1 and 2 of the DMC. At the end of the first year of implementing WFSGs, study groups actually, at least in part, determine what will be in the school's improvement plan. Most of what will be in the school improvement plan is a combination of all of the SGAPs, remembering that all the SGAPs are based on student needs, which is what the improvement plan targets. As we have already said, there are student and school needs that may not be appropriate for study groups to address. Needs that are not specific to how teacher teach and what teachers teach would be assigned to other school structures.

An Individual's Professional Development Plan

A study group's action plan is, in large part, the individual's professional development plan for each member of the study group. The work that the study group does often contains what the individuals need to do to help accomplish expectations of the district. Most districts require that all teachers and administrators have individual plans of professional development. Figure 6.4 illustrates how the study groups, the school improvement plan, and individual plans for professional development all work together.

A Summary of the Importance of Data-Based Decisions

As we've stated, increased student learning is the goal of WFSGs. Therefore, use of data regarding the level of students' achievements before the study is begun, during the study, and after the study is completed is essential.

Using Data to Select the Student Needs That Will Be Targeted for Study

As the study group process is initiated, the entire faculty is involved in a review of student data and other information, such as school improvement plans and district-wide initiatives, which can provide a basis for faculty study. Prior to the involvement of the entire faculty, the focus team or some other subgroup of the faculty should collect and organize data and other information in a format that will facilitate the faculty's review. The purpose of the review is to determine general categories of student needs, such as reading, technology, composition, and mathematics, by comparing the level of student achievement evidenced in the data with the level of achievement desired (e.g., comparing "what is" with "what should be").

Figure 6.4. Whole-Faculty Study Groups Support Plans for Improvement

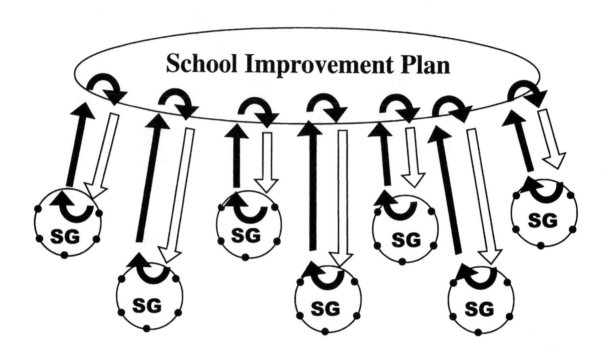

 The school improvement plan gives direction to study groups.

 Study groups give direction to the school improvement plan. The study group action plans are the instructional improvement component of the school improvement plan.

 Individuals in each study group use the study group action plan as the major component of the individual professional development plans.

Using Data to Identify Specific Student Needs

Once general categories are determined, study groups are organized to address specific student needs within them. At this point, study group members should become more focused in their efforts. They should reexamine data and other information pertinent to their specific area of study. This more detailed examination should include an analysis of those standardized test results that are directly related to the topic chosen for study, review of student work related to that topic, and information provided by other faculty members regarding student strengths and weaknesses in that area.

Standardized tests fall into two general classifications: norm referenced and criterion referenced. Norm-referenced tests are those that allow educators to compare a student or group of students to national or regional averages. The results are often reported in terms of grade equivalents, percentiles, stanines, normal curve equivalents, or other statistical interpretations. Criterion-referenced tests are designed to measure whether or not a student or a group of students has mastered specific learning objectives of the curriculum. These results are often reported as either pass or fail for each objective for each student. They are also summarized for each class as a percentage of students passing for each objective tested. Study groups may wish to obtain the advice of a specialist in the area of tests and measurement to assist in the interpretation of standardized test results.

In addition to standardized tests, the study group should examine student portfolios from previous years, students' current class work, results of teacher-made tests, and any other information that can be used to diagnose student needs.

Analyzing data in order to begin appropriately is an important task for the study group; however, the group must not let this identification of student needs take more than the time allocated for two meetings. Student needs that are identified after the study has begun can be added, and those found to be inappropriate to the study can be removed at any time.

Using Data to Assess Progress

Student data should continue to be used during the year's study group work. As teachers implement ideas that result from the study group's work, the effect on students should be shared within the study group. This sharing (e.g., receiving suggestions and encouragement from other study group members) can be in terms of student test results, teacher observations, examples of students' work, and other types of formative evaluations that will assist the teacher.

If members of a study group decide to use a method or strategy that is new to them, then they may find it helpful to observe in each other's classrooms to determine the effect that the new procedure is having on students. A videotape of students experiencing the teacher's use of the new strategy would also provide data for the study group.

Using Data to Evaluate the Study Group's Work

At the completion of the year, there is to be an evaluation of the study group process and products resulting from the group's work. Although both process and product evaluations should be conducted by members of the study group, some form of external review is also desirable. This review might be a report to the entire faculty describing difficulties and successes of the study group process as well outcomes for teachers and students.

When conducting the process evaluation, the study group should review process guidelines to determine the degree to which each guideline was followed and whether or not more attention should be paid to one or more of the guidelines in the future. A review of the study group's action plan and logs should be a major part of process evaluation. After the review, group members should be given an opportunity to respond by making evaluative comments regarding their study and its effect on them and their students.

The product evaluation should include products of teachers and students. The teacher products include materials made or used by teachers with students as a result of study group activity. Lessons that came as a result of study group discussions, teaching methods developed or practiced in the study group, and videotapes of a study group member using methods or materials discussed by the group are all teacher data that can be used to evaluate the study group. Samples of student work gathered over time to show student growth are the primary means of evaluation of a study group's effects on student learning.

Once again, the purpose of WFSGs is to increase student learning. The use of student data in planning, implementing, and evaluating the entire study group process can make a powerful contribution to the success of WFSGs.

Maintaining Professional Development and Ongoing Commitment

7

It is well known in the field of professional development that more is understood about initiating and implementing change than about maintaining or continuing the change. We are good at initiating. We have also become better at implementing new initiatives. Often, though, maintaining what we start is problematic. Administrative and support personnel in schools and in school districts spend most of their time, energy, and budgets initiating new programs, obtaining new materials, and training teachers to implement such programs and materials. The missing link is the institutionalization of innovative programs, materials, and behaviors and the transformed culture to sustain them. It takes not only strong initial support, encouragement, strong sponsorship, and success but also comparable ongoing support, encouragement, strong sponsorship, and success, over time, for creative strategies and behaviors to become routine and sustained long term, that is, institutionalized. In this chapter, the focus is on providing support to study groups during the implementation phase and on into the institutionalization and maintenance of WFSGs.

Reviewing the First Two Stages

The Initiation Phase

The initiation phase for WFSGs usually gets started the year prior to seriously beginning the WFSG process. As we've mentioned, this phase includes gathering information, contacting and contracting with consultants, purchasing materials, meeting with teachers, getting approval from district leaders, budgeting funds, gathering pertinent data, articulating intended results, and deciding to begin. The primary source of support during this phase is the principal and an expert source within or outside of the school.

The Implementation Phase

To recap, the implementation phase usually begins with some form of instruction or training in the procedures of WFSGs. Most schools, after the decision has been made to begin, have a team of 5 to 10 teachers, along with the principal, who take the lead in getting the process started: the focus team. After reading about or receiving the necessary information, the team develops a two-part plan. The first part addresses the need for the whole faculty to develop a deep understanding of the study group process. The second part is the plan to be used by the team in leading the whole faculty through the decision-making cycle. The implementation of the plan results in the whole faculty making the decision to immerse the school in the WFSG process and then making decisions about what study groups will do and how they will be organized. When this work has been done, the study groups are ready to get started.

The Institutionalization Phase

Institutionalization comes about when practices that were once new are integrated into and become an important part of the fabric of school and teacher structures and routines. This phase is also called *maintenance, continuation, incorporation,* or *routinization* and refers to whether the change gets built in as an ongoing part of the system or whether it disappears by way of a decision to discard it or through attrition (either it is killed or dies from neglect). Successful institutionalization requires continued support, encouragement, strong sponsorship, and recognition. How long institutionalizaton takes is unclear. Contextual factors are most often what determine whether a practice is continued and maintained or not.

One of the most puzzling aspects of continuation is that success does not guarantee that an initiative will be continued. Not only is success not a guarantee for continuation, success can actually create political foes that will kill the initiative. Leaders of initiatives in school districts assume that if success can be validated through student results, support for the initiative will grow. Because of the organization pattern of many school districts, however, what makes one department look good may in fact make another department look less than good. What we are suggesting here is that power relationships or power struggles are part of the context of districts and schools. Seymour Sarason (1990) wrote, "Schools will remain intractable to desired reform as long as we avoid confronting their existing power relationships" (p. 5). And Sarason continues, "Changing power relationships consistent with the goals of the changes is, to indulge understatement, no simple affair. History, tradition, overlearned attitudes, and unrealistic time perspectives ensure turmoil" (p. 64). We mention this only because we do not want initiators and implementers of WFSGs to feel personal defeat if WFSGs do not continue in schools. Continuation is often due to factors over which they have no control. The worth of a program or practice may not be great enough for organizational support to continue. It is hard for schools to continue an initiative without the ongoing support of district leaders. Likewise, it is hard for teachers to continue an initiative without the ongoing support of the principal, especially structural changes, such as WFSGs. Even with documented student benefits, lack of perceived support within the organization may simply be too great to overcome. As we have said, initiators of major change often feel that they failed when, after several years, a successful initiative is not continued at the organizational level. However, if any type of student benefits are evident, even after 1 year, we believe the effort had success and should be celebrated.

Using WFSGs as an example, one school had the study group model in place for 4 years and student benefits were evident. A new principal to the school discontinued the early release for students that had provided the time for study groups to meet. The new principal indicated that it would be up to individual study groups and teachers if they met and when they met. Some study groups continued, others did not. Without ongoing, broad-based pressure and support for WFSGs, and with new initiatives sponsored by the new principal getting the attention, the powerful study group routine was unfortunately broken.

Does that discredit or cancel out benefits to students and staff when the study groups were in place? No. It just means that students and staff benefited from the work of study groups during the 4 years the study group process was in place and that those benefits will enhance the future work of those students and teachers. Initiators of change should be joyful in the work of the day and be encouraged by its benefits. While working toward institutionalization, we should not lose sight of the now.

Someone once said, "Today is all we have." Therefore, sponsors of change, whether it is whole-school change or individual change, have to do what is in the best interests of students today and build for tomorrow. What may or may not happen tomorrow can't keep us from doing the work and progressing today. We hope that once WFSGs are initiated and implemented that the structure and practices will become and remain centerpieces for future professional development at the school. In some schools where we work today, the reality is that after our direct involvement ends, the faculty may revert to former practices. What may or may not happen tomorrow cannot diminish the importance of the work for today's students and teachers and the importance of its impact on their later lives.

Maintenance

Maintenance means the support, encouragement, and recognition given to an initiative to keep it going. Maintenance tasks do not end. If leaders of a school or district want a structure and practice to continue, then they must continue to provide the pressure, support, and strong sponsorship for continuation. This is truer for a process or structural change, such as WFSGs, than for instructional materials and strategies. An individual teacher may continue to use a specific book or strategy when the visible support for using that book or strategy is not longer obvious. One reason is that using the book or strategy is an individual task that can be done as an individual action. On the other hand, changes that are more procedural and structural and require the involvement of others can't be continued alone and in isolation.

One important aspect of maintenance leadership is to put in place conditions, processes, and techniques that keep individuals implementing new procedures and materials and programs energized. Study groups are more likely to feel bored or dissatisfied with the study group process if the group is engaged in passive work and does not vary what it does. If group members spend meeting after meeting discussing concerns, gathering information, researching materials, and only telling stories about what is happening in their classrooms, they will eventually lose interest. Such groups experience information overload and burnout. For such struggling groups, leaders must gently push the group out of the collecting and discussing routine toward more active strategies. Typically, the more varied, supported, and progressive the strategies, the less likely the group will become dissatisfied with its work. Remember that Chapter 5 included a discussion of 14 effective strategies that any study group can use to give it an increased sense of movement and enthusiasm.

Unpacking the WFSG Bundle

The person most central to maintenance issues is the principal. He or she is the primary sponsor and provider of support, encouragement, and pressure. What makes maintenance issues so complex in the WFSG approach is that it is a bundle of innovations. An innovation in this context is anything that is new to an individual. New materials, new practices, new skills, new procedures, and new policies are just a few of the types of innovations that teachers confront. Confronting only one type, such as new materials, can be daunting. However, with WFSGs, the confrontation is with a collection of new things, like picking up a bushel basket of fruit instead of reaching for one apple. The WFSG bushel basket has in it

- Having the whole faculty participate

- Adhering to the 15 procedural guidelines

- Learning new content

- Implementing new strategies in the classroom

- Reflecting on teaching practices with colleagues

- Monitoring student effects

- Looking at student work in a group setting

- Adjusting to new time requirements or different uses of time

- Understanding and accepting cultural shifts

- Being part of synergistic groups

This WFSG bushel basket or bundle of innovations can be unpacked into smaller baskets or components of professional development (see Chapter 3). It is easier to diagnose why a study group is not being productive by examining each of these components. If our car stops running, the mechanic doesn't stand back and look at the whole car in hopes of spotting the problem. Instead, the mechanic looks at the major parts of the car, such as the engine. To sustain WFSGs, to diagnose why a group is not moving and to provide technical assistance, we begin by asking three questions that focus on the major elements of WFSGs:

- Is it the context?

- Is it the process?

- Is it the content?

Returning to the car analogy: Is it the engine? Is it the transmission? Is it the electrical system? Just as the engine has individual parts, so does the context of schools. Just like the transmission, the process has parts, parts that we call guidelines. The electrical system of a car runs throughout all the systems and can cause disconnections at many points, much like study group content can cause members to become disconnected to the process. Support persons and individual study group members need to understand that often the answer to why a study group is not productive is not obvious. We have to dig deeper, take apart the engine, unpack the WFSG bundle.

In the following sections, we take each component of WFSGs and uncover what support persons need to consider.

Context Issues

Conditions at a school that may be hindering WFSGs might be better understood by school leaders asking the right questions, such as the following:

- What norms of the workplace are interfering with a group's work (e.g., isolation vs. collaboration, risk taking vs. staying with what is safe)?

- Do teachers perceive the principal as a strong sponsor for the study groups, the "cheerleader" and one who will go the extra mile with the district administration to get what the faculty requires to be successful?

- Do teachers feel administrative interference (e.g., taking time from the study groups, assigning study groups unrelated tasks)?

- Is the principal knowledgeable about what groups are doing?

- Did the whole faculty participate in Steps 1 through 4 of the decision-making cycle?

- Has the IC met so that representatives from each study group can share study groups' work and identify common problems?

- Is there clarity among the faculty in terms of people's roles?

- Are those roles respected (e.g., a grade chairperson who just wants to be an equal participant in a study group)?

- In a large school, has the principal delegated the day-to-day, routine school-wide leadership role of the study group process to another staff member (e.g., the assistant principal)?

- With delegation, has authority to act been given?

- Has delegation been done in some public way with the faculty?

- Are group meeting times interfering with the productiveness of study groups?

- What is the understanding with the faculty regarding persons outside the school reviewing and making comments on the action plans and logs?

- Are study group action plans and logs posted in a public place?

- Do teachers feel comfortable responding to logs from other study groups?

- Is the work of the study groups considered private work or public work?

- If some teachers are not attending meetings of their groups, how is the problem being addressed?

- Have faculty sharing times been held and scheduled for the remainder of the year?

- Is there a schedule for IC meetings?

- Is there visible support from the district office for WFSGs?

- Has the superintendent recognized in some way what the study groups are doing?

Process Issues

Understanding about how group members are interacting can be gained from reading study groups' logs and from observing a study group. To get a study group moving toward its intended goals, it may only take doing what a question prompts the principal to do.

- Is the group too small or too large?

- Do individuals have a common commitment to student needs listed in the action plan?

- What strategies is the group using to do its work?

- Has the group established group norms?

- Are norms being revisited and revised as needed?

- Do individuals recognize and address those norms that are causing conflict within the group?

- Is leadership being rotated?

- Do group members understand the role of the leader?

- Do group members accept the notion of shared responsibility and equality of members?

- Does the study group have an agreed-on procedure for keeping group members focused on the meetings agenda?

- Are the things that group members should do for or to bring to the next meeting noted in their logs?

- Does a study group take the last few minutes of a meeting to establish what the agenda will be at the next meeting?

- Are all members of a study group given a copy of the log within 24 hours of the meeting?

Content Issues

Understanding whether the content is substantive enough to hold the group together can be gained from reading the group's action plan and logs, observing in classrooms and the IC meetings, and observing the study group. Most schools have access to content area specialists through the school district, departments of education, universities, and textbook companies, as well as independent consultants. The most common reasons study groups feel "stuck" are content related. The value of the study group process depends on the relevance and substance of what the group is studying, investigating, and becoming more skillful at doing and what is happening differently in classrooms. The content is the glue that pulls and holds the group together. To get a study group moving toward its intended results, it may only take doing what a question prompts the principal to do.

- Once the study group was formed, did the group go deeper into student data to be clear about the student needs the group will address?

- What specific actions did the group agree to take when the action plan was written?

- What actions have been taken?

- Is student work giving the group its direction?

- What materials do members bring to the study group meeting?

- Are the resources (human and material) substantive enough to give rigor to the study?

- What evidence of impact is the study group collecting?

- What strategies is the study group using to get its work done (e.g., action research, visiting each other's classrooms, using protocols)?

- Does the content require that members be trained in specific techniques or strategies to increase the level of appropriate use of strategies in their classrooms?

- If the focus of the group's work is teaching practices, models, or strategies, are members practicing and seeing demonstrations of those behaviors in their study group meetings?

- If the focus of the group's work is the academic content that teachers teach, are content specialists being used? Could the study group benefit from using a book (e.g., reading in the content areas) to organize and guide its work? Some groups need the concreteness of a book to guide the study.

- Are members actually doing joint work, meaning are they working together to produce products (e.g., integrated units) or materials for which all will take responsibility?

The Eight-Step Technical-Assistance Plan

Just as Rosenholtz (1989) described moving, moderately stuck, and stuck groups in her work on organizational groups, we also have moving, moderately stuck, and stuck study groups. When study groups get stuck or seem to be at an impasse, it may be due to context, process, or content issues. When a study group loses its momentum, we often refer to the study group as being stuck. Study groups can lose their momentum in any stage of development. A study group may be in the consequence stage and for some reason lose its focus. The discussion that follows covers in detail both the reasons why study groups may get caught in the various stages and what leaders can do.

The eight-step technical-assistance plan outlined on the following pages is more detailed and overly specific than such plans need to be. However, it is presented in this way so that individuals may pick and choose what is relevant in very diverse situations. We cannot imagine a situation when a technical-assistance provider would go through every step and ask themselves every question. Most likely, there will be only one question or one suggestion within a step that will give the support person the direction needed. Intervention strategies should be followed as soon as there is any evidence that a study group is floundering.

Any study group that seems to have lost its momentum, regardless of the stage of development in which it is perceived to be, requires some type of facilitation or assistance. The assistance may be as simple as asking study group members clarifying questions, such as "How do you plan to test the instructional strategies you are identifying as effective?" Persons available to provide such assistance are the principal, an assistant principal, a district-level support person, an external consultant, and anyone within or outside the school that is familiar with the process and content of study groups. Most technical-assistance suggestions given here are framed as if the principal is the chief giver of support and pressure. Technical-assistance suggestions are also presented as if there is a logical sequence of events. However, every suggestion has to be judged for appropriateness in terms of its context and circumstances. Steps may be short-circuited at any point. The principal and other support persons could jump any step or begin the support process at any point, again depending on the circumstances. Often, one question will prompt the support giver as to what he or she should do. It is recommended that the principal and other appropriate persons read all suggestions early in the initiation stage. Just becoming aware of behaviors that may cause study groups to lose momentum will prevent some problems from happening. When problems do occur, the principal can pick and choose suggestions that fit the situation. Sometimes, asking this simple question is all a principal needs to do: "What is your problem?" To ask that question, a principal has to know what the study group has been and is doing. The following steps and questions within steps cover the bulk of the problems a study group might have.

Step 1

Study group members recognize that they are not being productive. Individuals feel frustrated and confused. Members are saying to each other and colleagues not in the group that study group meetings are a waste of time and nothing is being accomplished. Study group members may even be using the word "stuck" if they have heard the word in relation to the work of groups. If this is not being said directly to the principal, it will surely get to him or her secondhand. In most situations, at least one member of the group will ask for intervention or help from someone. What we don't want to happen is for a group to remain in a nonproductive stage for as long as two or three meetings. An intervention should occur as soon as there are indicators that help is required.

To reduce chances that study groups will get stuck early in the process, the IC should meet before the third round of study group meetings. The representative from each study group will learn from other representatives' sharing. All groups will feel a little shaky, so just seeing that this is a normal state of affairs for this stage of the process will build confidence. A helpful piece of content for this first IC meeting is information about developmental stages of groups. At the IC meeting, what the representative from each group shares will have meaning for every other group. When one representative says that the group is struggling with how to keep its focus, others will say they, too, are having similar problems. And they will begin to give each other advice. A person will often see someone else's problem clearer than his or her own. As a result, as they give suggestions to others, they will see the need for their groups to do something similar.

Step 2

The principal recognizes that a study group is a stuck or low-performing group. This will most likely happen through

- Comments from a member of the study group
- Comments from a visitor (e.g., content specialist to the study group)
- Reviewing the action plans; reviewing study group logs
- Personal observation
- Comments made at the IC meeting
- Observations or comments from a focus team member

It would be helpful at this point for the principal to review the descriptors of study groups at the forming and grumbling stages. In the grumbling stage, a study group will express levels of dissatisfaction. Often, to move on to the next stage, members only require additional assurance of support and confirmation that the group is on the right track. It will not be necessary to do all that is described in the following steps. The following steps are for study groups that require more direction.

Step 3

The principal reflects on his or her role and observations to this point. Talking with an internal or external support person often helps. Thinking about answers to the following questions will bring some clarity to what should be done next. Sometimes, all it takes to get a group moving is for the principal or another person to see what has not been done and to make the group aware of the oversight.

- What indicators does the principal have that the group is struggling?
- Is the study group addressing a need that can be evidenced in student work?
- Are the student needs being addressed too ambiguous?
- What has the principal done to provide support?
- What type of feedback did the principal give the study group when its action plan was completed and reviewed?
- What type of feedback has the principal given the study group through its logs?

- What does the principal think the group should be doing or have done by now?

- When the principal observes in classrooms, can behaviors be noted that directly relate to what the study group is doing?

- Has the study group requested resources?

- Has anyone external to the school been invited to attend a study group meeting?

- Is there an individual in the group that the principal feels is the root of the problem?

- Does the principal feel the problem is process related (e.g., how the group is interacting)?

- Are process guidelines being followed?

Step 4

The most appropriate person should intervene. Appropriateness depends on the perceived reason why the study group is stuck. Is the problem contextual, process related, or content specific? The person who intervenes may be the principal or another internal support person or a support person external to the school. In the following list are conditions that would determine whether it should be the principal or another person.

The principal intervenes *if*

- The principal has not given the study group feedback on the group's action plan.
  - Intervention: Do it now.

- The IC has not met.
  - Intervention: Call a meeting.

- The principal has not responded to concerns or recommendations expressed in logs.
  - Intervention: Do it now.

- The principal has questions about the level of work reflected in logs and has not yet communicated those questions to the group.
  - Intervention: Do it now.

- The logs reflect that the study group does not have adequate resources.
  - Intervention: Ask questions now.

- There is one person in the study group that is obviously disrupting the work of the group.
  - Intervention: Talk to that person or observe the study group.

- One or more persons are routinely absent or late.
  - Intervention: Talk to the individuals to determine the root of the problem and make expectations clear.

- Leadership is not being rotated.
  - Intervention: Remind the group that this is nonnegotiable.

- The study group is not revisiting or following its norms.
  - Intervention: Remind the group.

- The study group could use a process observer.
  - Intervention: Serve in that capacity or invite a person who has that skill.

- The group does not see how what they are doing will affect the whole.
  - Intervention: Review with that study group its action plan in relation to the total school effort.

The principal invites a content specialist or a district-level support person to intervene *if*

- The stuckness is primarily due to the content in the study.

- There are questions about the scope and sequence of the reading curriculum or if there are new reading materials that group members have not mastered.

- There are similar questions for another curriculum area.

- There is not enough expertise in the group for individuals to help each other with required skills.

- There are questions about how to get access to resources that textbook companies and other suppliers or venders offer.

- Teachers want to know about or visit teachers in other schools that are using strategies and materials with success that the study group is investigating.

- The teachers in the study group require specialized training.

If the person who is to intervene is external to the school, that person should be well informed about the study group process.

Step 5

If a person external to the school is the intervener, that person should

- Review the study group's action plan for the answers to the questions that follow.

- Make a copy of and note on the action plan about what should be seen during observations.

- Look to see how specific student needs are stated.

- Look to see how specific the actions are that the group will take when the group meets.
  - Do actions have promise for affecting stated student needs?
  - Is looking at student work a routine activity of the group?

- — How is the study group getting its work done (e.g., action research, using protocols, demonstrating teaching practices)?

- — What would you expect members to bring to the study group meeting to get the work done?

- — What additional resources are available to the group?

■ Try imagery. With eyes closed, try to imagine a group doing what this group has stated that it wants to do. Compare it with what the group is doing.

■ Review all of the study group's logs for answers to the following questions:

■ Is the work of the group consistent with your imagery? If not, what is the inconsistency?

- — Has the group established group norms?

- — Does the group revisit its norms?

- — Can you tell what the group will do at the next meeting from what is written in the log?

- — Does the work appear to be more passive than active?

- — Can you tell what materials individuals are bringing to meetings?

- — Does one name appear more often than the others in the group when you look at what is discussed?

- — Is leadership being rotated?

- — Are members often absent or tardy?

The external support person shares his or her observations from reviewing the group's action plan and logs and then discusses the appropriateness of someone observing the study group. The observation would be to note interactions among members and the substance of the work. If it were deemed appropriate, the principal would tell members of the study group the following things:

■ Who will observe

■ When the visit will occur

■ Why the visit will occur

■ That the observer will visit the study group twice, if possible

■ That the first visit is only to observe the group work

■ That the second visit is to share with the group what was observed and to have study group members reflect on observations

■ Not to expect to engage the observer in a dialogue during the first observation

It is preferable for the observer to attend two consecutive study group meetings. However, that may not be possible. If not, the person would establish a day and times when he or she can meet with the study group. The second meeting may be later on the same day as the observation. The study group should be given feedback as soon as possible.

Step 6

After the study group knows what to expect when the principal or other support person observes a study group meeting, the observer attends the designated study group meeting. The observer reminds the group that it should continue its work as planned and do exactly what it would do if he or she were not there. The observer sits with the group, not outside the group. Body language and facial expression should indicate a willingness to learn from the group, as opposed to a stance that indicates that this is a critique or evaluation. In other words, the person is to observe as if there as a learner, not someone looking for something wrong. If the observer is asked a direct question, a response might be "That's a point that we might consider when I share my observations with you." The observer should not get drawn into the discussion! The observer should not noticeably be writing or looking down at a tablet. He or she should keep his or her eyes on the group. Instead of writing complete sentences, the observer should have a code of short words or symbols that can be interpreted later. It may also be helpful to draw a table and as individuals arrive, indicate their place at the table. As the discussion begins, arrows can be used to indicate the flow of the discussion. The observer should watch for such things as

- The time when all members are present

- What individuals bring with them to the meeting

- How the meeting begins

- How focused each member is

- What strategies the group uses in doing its work

- How this meeting is connected to the last meeting

- Interactions among group members (e.g., synergy)

- What part of the action plan members appear to be doing

- How students are brought into conversations

At the end of the meeting, the observer might ask each member to write on a piece of paper (no name) a list of adjectives that would describe the study group's meeting. The observer could ask any other type of reflective question that would give the observer insight into the functioning of the group. Collecting the papers, the observer confirms with the group when he or she will meet with the group to share his or her observation.

After the meeting, the observer should stay where the observation occurred if the study group members leave the room. Or if not possible, the observer should go to a quiet place in the school where there is privacy to complete notes, writing the impressions in more detail. This would be the time to write recommendations. A good way to sharpen the observer's thinking is to write five verbs that describe the group's actions and five adjectives that describe the group. The observer's final conclusions should indicate whether the root of the dysfunction is more context, process, or content related.

If the observer is not the principal, the observer shares his or her observations and conclusions with the principal.

Step 7

The observer meets with the study group to share his or her observations. The observer describes what he or she saw in the observation, action plan, and logs, stating what "I saw" or "I did not see." Staying away from judgmental statements, appropriate statements might be similar to the following:

- I saw that at 3:00, only one person was present, at 3:05 four members were present, and at 3:10 all members were present.

- I did not see in the log of the meeting that preceded the one I observed what you would do at the meeting I observed; and I did not see in your other logs that you routinely indicate what is to happen next.

- In your action plan, I saw that you stated that you intend to (read actions). I could not tell which of these actions you were implementing when I observed you.

- I did not see any evidence that you routinely look at student work.

- I saw that only one member brought anything to the meeting.

- I did not see in your logs that you have revisited the group's norms.

- I saw that two members did not say anything during the meeting.

- I did not see that the work of students was discussed or shared.

- In your action plan, I saw a list of resources. In the logs, I do not see evidence that those resources are being used.

- I saw that _____ did most of the talking when I observed.

The observer reads responses to the reflective question. The observer invites members to respond to the observations. Integrating responses from members, recommendations might be similar to the following:

- Revise the action plan to make it consistent with what you currently feel you should do to meet student needs you have identified.

- Review roles: leader's role and individual member's role.

- Revisit group norms.

- Agree to only those norms that you are willing to support.

- I recommend that (name) meet with you and share a protocol for looking at student work.

- I recommend that (name) provide you with several books that will give your work direction and will describe strategies to try with your students.

- I will share with you information about several workshops and conferences that you may want to consider attending.

Step 8

If the observer was not the principal, he or she should share the outcome of the meeting with the principal. If the recommendations require contacting a person to be used as a resource, it should be decided who will make the contact. If recommendations require obtaining a book or other material for the study group, decide who will do that. The study group should know what is expected to happen next. Whatever needs to be done, confirm who is to do what and communicate the result of the actions with the study group.

As we have already said, it will be a rare occurrence for all eight of the steps to be carried out. These steps are offered to provide principals and support persons with a technical-assistance plan from which they can choose appropriate actions. It is the principal's judgment as to the appropriateness of each step and subset of a step. Appropriateness is contextual and circumstantial.

More Reasons Why Study Groups Become Stuck

We have discussed reasons why some study groups become immobilized or stop moving, that their members become disillusioned and disgruntled. In addition to the reasons already outlined, consider the following:

■ To meet a particular student need, the content focus of the study group may require training both at the beginning of the study and continuing over a period of time.

■ If a group wants to use the cooperative learning strategy in the classroom, reading about the strategy will not be sufficient. Teachers should see demonstrations in several curricular areas and have the opportunity to practice the strategy both within the study group and with their students. The teachers should share lessons and materials, observe each other using the new strategy, and plan future applications together.

■ Sometimes, a group focuses on what others in the school should do. The group will come up with guidelines or procedures for others to follow. The focus is not on "how I need to change," but "how you need to change."

■ In another situation, a group may get bogged down with doing surveys or inventories primarily for the benefit of the rest of the faculty. After awhile, the work gets burdensome. Study groups should target student needs, not teacher needs. If members are not doing what they should do for their own learning and development, the group is off track.

■ If the student need is a problem that can be solved administratively, then a study group should not undertake it. For example, a common set of problems that study groups tackle is discipline, attendance, and tardiness. A study group focusing on discipline, for example, often becomes a forum for formulating new rules, policies, and procedures for students to follow and not a meaningful investigation into underlying causes of disruptive behavior and different instructional approaches to minimizing those behaviors.

■ Sometimes, the underlying cause of a student need is not being confronted. For example, if the reason why students are disruptive is because the teachers' instructional strategies are inadequate or not appropriate, new rules are not going to improve the situation. Not facing basic issues will keep the study group from moving ahead.

Summary

Maintenance concerns often make initiators of change wish they had never started. One of the best pieces of advice Bruce Joyce gave Carlene Murphy in the early days of the work in Augusta was "Smile. Be kind. Don't stop." That pretty much sums up what maintenance is all about. It is the hardest work for staff developers and leaders. Teachers often complain because leaders keep introducing new programs, materials, and practices. Leaders will hear teachers say, "Why do we keep changing things? Let's just stay with what we have." When you stick with an initiative, you will hear "How much longer do we have to do this?" Trying to stick with an initiative that works will often bring with that "stick-with-it-ness" problems of another sort, such as boredom and anxiety with the realization that what everyone thought would go away is actually here to stay. Maintenance work is often not fun work for leaders because they get bored, too. They get bored with saying the same things over and over and with fighting the same battles. Initiating change has a certain level of excitement to it, like going to a place you have never been. Sometimes, though, getting somewhere is more fun than being there. Many leaders are more competent at initiating and implementing change than at maintaining and institutionalizing changes they have started. If this is the case, then the leader who initiated the change has to identify someone to help maintain it.

Creating commitment and maintaining it are two different things; each requires different approaches. At the beginning of an initiative, you can generate commitment by vocalizing obvious needs. To maintain that commitment, you must not let anyone forget why you started the program in the first place—you can't let them let go. We know that people who are well informed about effects of the initiative hold it in higher esteem than those who either don't have the information or who don't pay attention to it.

In school districts, it is often people outside the school who are the greatest threats to a school's ability to continue. Budget ramifications and political factors that have nothing to do with merits of the initiative will often be the death of highly effective programs, materials, and practices. Leaders who read Murphy's (1991b) article "Lessons From a Journey Into Change" may better understand that changing the workplace of teachers means changing the workplace of principals and district administrators, too.

Supporting Synergistic Groups and Teams 8

Effective study groups are effective teams! No study group will be effective if it does not have real teamwork. Teamwork is what differentiates an effective study group from a typical committee or other work group. The following is an insightful story of four people named Everybody, Somebody, Anybody, and Nobody, which very nicely helps us understand what teamwork and team building are not.

> There was an important job to be done and Everybody was sure that Somebody would do it. Anybody could have done it, but Nobody did it. Somebody got angry about that because it was Everybody's job. Everybody thought Anybody could do it, but Nobody realized Everybody wouldn't do it. It ended up that Everybody blamed Somebody when Nobody did what Anybody could have done.

On the positive side, the great automobile industry leader, Henry Ford, gives us a sense of the meaning of teamwork: "Coming together is a beginning; keeping together is progress; and working together is success."

A group of friends went down the Colorado River in an inflatable raft. After 2 days, as Pat Riley (1994) describes in *The Winner Within*, "the river became a great equalizer. People accustomed to being pampered and indulged had become a team, working together to cope with the unpredictable twists and turns of the river" (pp. 56-57).

The twists and turns that study groups encounter are as real and personally as scary as those in the raging river. Consequently, study groups cannot make it as just a collection of individuals but, instead, can work together cooperatively and have tremendous success as an effective team.

Teamwork is the ability of people to work together in a genuinely cooperative manner (i.e., interdependently) toward a common vision. Teamwork means joint work and joint responsibility. Teamwork is a vehicle that allows common people to attain uncommon results.

Good examples of teamwork are California's giant Sebring trees. Their roots are barely below the surface of the ground. The Sebring grow in groves, and their roots intertwine. When strong winds blow, the intertwining (i.e., interdependent) roots of the Sebring help hold them all up.

Another impressive illustration of teamwork happened in the 1980 Winter Olympic Games at Lake Placid, New York. Rather than just trying to find the top players, the coach of the United States ice hockey team selected individuals who could function in a team setting and respond effectively under pressure.

The U.S. team began ranked seventh in a field of eight. But when the closing seconds ticked away, the final score read USA 4 and USSR 3. Maybe the U.S.A. team didn't have the best players on the ice, but it did have the best team! It was a synergistic team, collectively striving for a common vision, interdependently playing and empowering each other, and functioning as the best Olympic ice hockey team in the world.

True teamwork is called *synergy;* it occurs when the teamwork of a group allows it to get the maximum results from the available resources. Effective study groups are synergistic, self-directed, learning teams.

In the remaining sections of this chapter, we describe and discuss the specifics and details of this type of teamwork, including its prerequisites, the process for attaining it, and its development in study groups.

Synergistic Relationships

In a group or team, relationships are established that make the group more productive or less so. If a group collectively is less productive than the sum of what the individuals would produce, we say we have a *self-destructive relationship* in the group. This, unfortunately, happens frequently and comes about in a group because of such things as poor communication or miscommunication, lack of trust, blaming, defensiveness, self-centeredness, backbiting, and internal competition.

In groups with self-destructive relationships, the group uses up so much energy in nonproductive ways that it has little additional energy to be creative and to generate new ideas and more effective processes. No doubt, you have seen groups composed of bright, capable individuals that couldn't seem to accomplish much of anything, and it made you wonder, how could such a strong group of individuals be so ineffective? Unfortunately, the individuals were most capable, but the relationship in the group was self-destructive, keeping the group from effectively using the many talents of the group.

Typically, self-destructive groups or teams are self-defeating and negative in a school setting, making it even harder to accomplish school goals. These are the groups that generally function at the level of the lowest common denominator of the group and accomplish less than if the members worked alone. Peter Senge (1990), in his book *The Fifth Discipline,* describes destructive teams in what he calls the "myth of teamwork": "Most teams operate below the level of the lowest IQ in the group. The result is skilled incompetence, in which people in groups grow incredibly efficient at keeping themselves from learning" (pp. 9-10).

Another type of relationship exists in a group or team when the group produces the same as would be produced by the members individually. In this case, we say we have a *static relationship* in the group. Static relationships exist because of some of the same types of negative, nonproductive features described earlier for self-destructive groups. Static relationships produce enough energy to get by but nothing extra for doing new and creative things beyond what the individual group members could have produced. In static-relationship situations, hopes are generated for groups and teams, but little is gained by having people working together.

A third type of relationship in a group, the desired one, is the *synergistic relationship*. In a synergistic relationship, the members of a group or team work together to produce a total result that is greater than the sum of the efforts of the individual members. Saying it another way, the synergy of a group or team is the combined cooperative action in the group or team that generates additional energy beyond that consumed by the group and produces a total outcome beyond what could be obtained by the individual members. In a truly synergistic group, people energize and inspire each other, and the diversity of ideas and openness to them provide the basis for new creative ideas and approaches.

The power of synergy or synergistic relationships is nicely illustrated by the following physical example. If you take a piece of wood 2 inches by 4 inches and 8 feet long and place it on blocks at the ends of the 2 by 4, the 2 by 4 will hold 100 pounds of weight before it breaks. If, however, you take two 8-foot 2 by 4s and glue them together, the pair will hold a staggering 800 pounds! Why? The glue bonds the two boards together, creating a synergistic relationship between them, so that when the fibers in one board run in different directions to those of the other, one gives strength at the places where the other might be weak. This significantly enhances the total strength or weight capacity of the combination. The expected or intuitive increase in strength in this situation would have been twofold; instead, the synergy or synergistic relationship in this situation gave an eightfold increase in strength.

In the hockey team example of the previous section, the coach said that he didn't necessarily have the best players but he did have the best Olympic hockey team that year. Why? Because they functioned as a synergistic team. They were striving together for a common vision, playing in an interdependent manner (genuinely cooperative), and significantly empowering each other for the collective best of the team. As a result, they functioned that year as the best Olympic hockey team in the world. Another good real-world example of synergy is that found in a healthy marriage. In a healthy marriage, the spouses develop a caring support system in which they genuinely and openly cooperate with each other and provide creative sharing, assistance, and encouragement toward the couple's common goals.

Communication is an important part of effective, synergistic teams. In his book *The Seven Habits of Highly Effective People,* Covey (1990) says about communicating synergistically, "You are simply opening your mind and heart and expressions to new possibilities, new alternatives, new options." And he adds about synergistic groups, "you begin with the belief that the parties involved will gain more insight, and that the excitement of that mutual learning and insight will create a momentum toward more and more insights, learning, and growth" (p. 264).

The characteristics that Covey describes are among the critical factors for turning groups or teams into effective, synergistic groups or teams. But what exactly are the vital prerequisites for synergistic groups, and how do we generate them? In the next two sections, we discuss the four prerequisites for synergistic groups and teams and a four-step process for developing them.

Synergy Prerequisites

Just how important is synergy in our work with study groups? Daryl Conner (1993), one of the world's top experts in change and effectively dealing with change, says that synergy is the "soul of a successful change project" (p. 188). Our efforts with study groups are aimed at change projects that, ultimately, will help enhance student learning and improve our schools. So synergy and synergistic study groups will be critical to our success; they will be key vehicles to increasing both quality and productivity in our schools.

In one high school involved in the study group process, the focus team discussed the important nature of synergy in their work, as follows:

> The logistics of how the focus team conducted their work was secondary to the synergy that was created by the joint work of the team. The team felt that they had the power to influence the future of their school and conditions of its students. Five interdependent Focus Team members became many interdependent individuals in the study groups. The momentum generated by their collaborative efforts made the mountain easier to climb. (Murphy & Lick, p. 91)

And in another school, a study group said about its synergy,

> Most important, the rapport that grew from becoming more open about our beliefs and classroom practices increased our willingness to try new methods and to share how those strategies worked for our students. For the first time, we openly shared lessons that were not effective and jointly worked on ways to make the lessons more powerful. (Murphy & Lick, p. 86)

When we talk about the *capacity* of a group to do something, we find that we must take into consideration two factors, the group's *willingness* and its *ability*. To be effective, a group must both be willing and have ability. If either of these factors is missing, then the group has a lesser capacity. The same is true when we consider the potential capacity for synergy. That is, for a group to be synergistic, it must be willing to do what is required to bring about synergy, and it must also have the ability to do so. Most groups fail to be synergistic because they really are not willing to do what is required, or they do not have the ability or circumstances for them to be synergistic, or both.

In his more than 20 years of research and experience with change, Conner (1993) found that the key fundamentals for the development of synergy in a group were (a) willingness, arising from the sharing of common goals and interdependence (i.e., mutual dependence and genuine cooperation), and (b) ability, growing from member and group empowerment and participative involvement.

As we've discussed, the four prerequisites for synergistic study groups are

Willingness	*Ability*
1. Common goals	3. Empowerment
2. Interdependence	4. Participative involvement

As we have seen from the examples of this chapter, synergistic relationships are both powerful and productive. However, most groups don't function synergistically; they don't understand the fundamentals of synergy or don't apply them very well. Why? Because developing and maintaining synergy in a group, though vitally important, is not an easy task.

One of the key things to remember when working with people and trying to develop synergistic relationships is insightfully expressed in the following quotation by Covey (1990):

> People are very tender, very sensitive inside. I don't believe age or experience makes much difference. Inside, even within the most toughened and calloused exteriors, are the tender feelings and emotions of the heart. That's why in relationships, the little things are the big things. (pp. 192-193)

Willingness: Common Goals and Interdependence

The first step in creating a synergistic group is the development of a common goal or common goals for the group. This gives a clear-cut focus for the group and can be an inspiring incentive to keep the group on track. Unfortunately, most groups don't initially take the time and make the effort to clarify or create the common goals that the group is working together to accomplish.

A common goal for a study group, for example, in the context of enhancing student learning and improving the effectiveness of their school, might be to understand a new learning process and successfully implement it in their school or to do research on a new student evaluation system, understand the new system, and successfully integrate it into the learning processes of their school.

Willingness to seek, create, and continue to focus on a common goal or goals for a group is critical to the full success of the group. The same can be said for the group's willingness to function interdependently—that is, for the members of the group to operate in a genuinely cooperative and mutually dependent fashion.

People in a group do not have to agree on everything to have a synergy. In fact, having differing ideas and bringing diverse information, opinions, and approaches to the group are part of the building blocks for successful synergistic groups. However, to be synergistic and effective, groups must agree on and focus on common goals and must function interdependently.

For example, consider two soldiers in a foxhole in a battle. Their common goal is survival. One has the ammunition and the other has the machine gun. They are genuinely dependent on each other, one to provide the ammunition and the other to fire the gun. It doesn't matter whether they like each other or care about the same things in the other parts of their lives. What matters now is that they clearly know what their common goal is (survival) and that they work interdependently (feeding the ammunition into the gun and effectively firing the gun). This kind of willingness, a clearly defined common goal and effective interdependence, we refer to as *foxhole mentality*.

A foxhole mentality is when people who have different backgrounds and viewpoints accept that they have the same intent and are willing to genuinely cooperate. For study groups to be effective, they must develop a foxhole-type mentality, where diverse members are willing to set and accept common goals and to work in a genuinely cooperative and mutually dependent manner with each other. They must determine that their differences are less important than their need to work together.

Often, foxhole mentalities, having common goals and functioning interdependently, happen as the consequence of special opportunities that would not be realized without synergistic teamwork. The key for successful study groups is either to exploit naturally formed foxholes (e.g., groups that spontaneously and sincerely come together around a common intent and openly and freely work together as a team) or build new foxholes that have the potential for successful teamwork.

When study group members feel that they are in a foxhole situation with each member working with them and that success depends on working together, then synergy can occur. If those in the study group have a feeling that they are the ones "carrying the ammunition" or "firing the gun," it boosts their sense of self-worth and team worth. They feel that the study group "needs me," I "need the study group," and we "must work together" to accomplish our important goals. Such relationships motivate team members to be willing to do what is required for having a synergistic and successful study group.

Ability: Empowerment and Participative Involvement

Common goals and interdependence motivate and are necessary for people to work together synergistically, but more than these are required for teams to be fully effective and synergistic. For study groups to operate at or near their maximum effectiveness, their members must feel empowered, and they must participate completely in the activities and work of the study group. That is, empowerment and participative involvement are key abilities that study group members must have to function synergistically with other team members and increase team synergy.

Empowerment is not the same as delegation. Someone may give you the authority to take responsibility for or make the final decision in a particular matter. That is not empowerment but delegation. Empowerment is quite different. You have a sense of empowerment or are empowered when you believe that you have something valuable to contribute to the situation and that what you offer might have a bearing on the outcome. In other words, the circumstances are such that you feel you have something of value to contribute, and what you contribute may affect the decisions being considered.

With empowered study group members, each person is more willing to share their part of the diversity of the group, increasing the potential for new and possibly valuable information, knowledge, and ideas to be added to the work of the group.

In a study group, if members feel comfortable saying what they feel about each matter under consideration, they are empowered by the group and circumstances and can be important contributors to the success of the study group. Study groups have their best chance for success when their members feel empowered and want to openly and fully express their views and ideas throughout the work of the study group.

However, empowering study group members is not always an easy task. The circumstances of the study group and how other members of the study group behave are critical. For members to feel empowered, they must be willing to overcome their inhibitions and feel a sense of personal security that others will respect what they say, not judge them, and will consider their input seriously.

Feeling a sense of empowerment is necessary for an ability to function synergistically, but it is not enough by itself. You must not only be empowered but also must have the opportunity to share your knowledge and ideas. Members of a study group have *participative involvement* when they are encouraged and free to openly and fully share their skills, knowledge, and ideas in the study group.

Participative involvement is both a philosophy and a method of operating study groups. Philosophically, participative involvement focuses on the belief that all study group members have a genuine interest in the success of the study group and each member has something valuable to contribute. Participative involvement is also a method for managing human resources, whereby circumstances are created so that study group members are respected and their contributions are encouraged, valued, and used. Like empowerment, participative involvement does not come easily. It requires conscious concern and deliberate action for how the study group will operate. The leader and the members of the study group must understand the concept and importance of participative involvement and then together, collectively and individually, work toward its becoming a reality for the operation of their study group. To do so will mean that strong egos and aggressive personalities must be kept in check and that the normal competitive interplay among study group members gives way to an open and balanced approach in the discussion and consideration of matters before the study group. Everyone must have and feel comfortable with their opportunity for full participation in the business of the study group.

The ability of a study group to operate synergistically requires both member empowerment and participative involvement. This approach offers potential for substantially increasing the effectiveness of the study group and involves members freely and fully sharing knowledge and ideas and functioning as an entity, a team, to learn together, plan initiatives, make decisions, solve problems, and evaluate results. When study groups operate synergistically in this fashion, the productivity and quality of their efforts are increased significantly.

Synergy Process

As we've said, the prerequisites for synergistic study groups are the willingness to establish common goals for the group's initiative and develop a genuine interdependence among its members and the ability to create circumstances that provide empowerment for members. This can give them a sense of importance and free them to participate and offer participative involvement so that they interact openly and fully in the work of the study group.

Now that we know and understand the fundamental prerequisites for synergistic study groups, what is the process for creating these prerequisites and synergistic study groups?

To answer this question, we turn once again to the master of change dynamics, Daryl Conner (1993). His research and writings tell us that an effective four-step process for building synergy in study groups is

1. Interaction

2. Appreciative understanding

3. Integration

4. Implementation

Interaction

The dictionary (*Webster's,* 1986) defines *interaction* as "action on one another or reciprocal action or effect." The first step in the process says that if study groups are to be synergistic, they must be interacting, that is, they must have members acting on one another or reciprocating.

Most of us have been in groups where some of the members don't say anything. Clearly, in this situation, those individuals are not interacting. As a result, the group will have a difficult time being as effective as it might have been because those non-interacting individuals are not helping to enrich the group's mix of knowledge and ideas. In fact, they are often a deficit to the group because they are filling positions that more contributing, interacting persons might have taken. By the same token, those who interact too much (e.g., members monopolizing the discussions) also have the potential for diminishing the study group's effectiveness.

The three elements of interaction that reduce related group problems (e.g., misunderstandings, alienation, and confusion) and enhances group potential are (a) effective communication, (b) active listening, and (c) creating trust.

In the development and operation of synergistic study groups, effective communication among members is essential. Effective communication means direct communication in a well-understood language, covering relevant and thoughtful material, and reflecting a undistorted sense of what the communicator believes.

In most groups, the typical approach of members is the competitive one, where each person is an advocate for certain ideas, makes that case at each opportunity, and listens with an ear attuned to information for countering contrary ideas rather than trying to see the merits in others' ideas. Such approaches are usually destructive and seriously hamper the prospects for study group synergy.

Instead, study group members must become active listeners. Active listening means that a study group member will eliminate, as best as possible, one's competitive aggressiveness and listen intently to understand, appreciate, and search for value and application in the communications of others.

To be synergistic, study group members don't have to be friends or even like each other, but they must generate relationships among themselves that *create trust and credibility.* Trust is fundamental to the development of synergy in a study group.

If the members of a study group communicate effectively with one another and listen actively to their colleagues, over time, the relationship that develops has the potential to be one of trust and credibility. People begin to let down their guard with each other and allow themselves to become vulnerable within the group. When this level of trust occurs, the group has an opportunity for genuine sharing and use of the valuable diversity that each person in the group brings to the discussions.

Appreciative Understanding

As we work to develop synergy in our study group, we find that meaningful interaction (i.e., effective communication, active listening, and trust) is a necessary element of synergy but is not sufficient to guarantee it. Something more is generally required. In the earlier section on synergistic prerequisites, we presented a Covey (1990) quotation that reminded us that "people are very tender, very sensitive inside. That's why in relationships, the little things are the big things." One of the keys to help people deal with these sensitivities is the operational concept of appreciative understanding.

Appreciative understanding is the capacity to value and use diversity. For the members of a study group to achieve appreciative understanding, each must understand why others see things differently than they do and work to appreciate the differences.

Covey (1990) reminds us that we cannot achieve win-win ends with win-lose or lose-win means. If we want to have the team success of synergy, win-win ends, in our study group, then we must have genuinely effective means, win-win means, in our group relationships.

The four methods for building appreciative understanding (i.e., win-win means and relationships) are to (a) create an open climate, (b) delay negative judgment, (c) empathize with others, and (d) value diversity.

The effective communication, active listening, and trust generated by genuine interaction by members of a study group lay a foundation for appreciative understanding to develop. In particular, even with the inevitable differences of opinion and perspectives of members, conflicts, and possible misunderstandings, members realize that all of this is fundamental to surfacing important issues, understanding different frames of reference, seeing things in a new light, and generating the basic building blocks for new and potentially better solutions.

An *open climate* in an environment is where study group members allow and encourage constructive discussion, conflict, and differences to take place, fostering win-win relationships and helping its members understand relevant issues and gain new insights. By creating an open climate, study group members learn to appreciate conflict and differences and use them to broaden their basis of understanding toward the development of potentially more valuable answers and solutions.

Have you ever been in a group discussion where someone offers a thought that seems silly or out-and-out stupid, and yet from that idea comes a cascade of ideas that leads to new insight and a better solution for the original problem? If, on the other hand, someone had intervened earlier in that sequence of ideas and said something like "That's a dumb idea," then that discussion would have no doubt been cut short, the innovative cascade of new ideas would not have taken place, and the better solution might very well have never been discovered. Events comparable to this latter situation happen all the time, creating win-lose relationships and effectively inhibiting real synergy in the group.

Most new and creative ideas or perspectives come from sensitive people and are extremely vulnerable to attacks by others. At the same time, they frequently are the ideas and perspectives that have the highest potential for leading to innovative solutions and productive synergy. Consequently, study groups function best and have the greatest potential for synergy when team members have the discipline to *delay forming negative judgments* about the ideas and perspectives of other members.

The dictionary (*Webster's,* 1986) defines *empathy* as "the projection of one's own personality into the personality of another in order to understand him better" or "ability to share in another's emotions or feelings." When we empathize with other study group members, we are allowing ourselves the opportunity of knowing what the others are experiencing and feeling and being emotionally sensitive to these.

Although showing empathy to other team members' ideas and perspectives does not necessarily mean agreeing with them, it does provide a good position from which to understand others' ideas and perspectives, why they feel about them as they do, and how their ideas might fit into the overall discussion and possibly become part of the desired solution. When study group members empathize with other members of their team, they increase the group's chances of generating greater team synergy and building meaningful solutions.

Whether we want to admit it or not, we are all sensitive about our ideas and perspectives, especially those that are personal to us. As a result, we tend to hold them back and only slowly let them come out as we test the water to see how others will respond to them. Yet these ideas and perspectives in a study group are the very diversity that gives the group its unique strength.

By genuinely *valuing diversity* in a study group, members are showing their respect for each other and their ideas and perspectives, increasing trust, enhancing cohesiveness, and searching for the most appropriate input and building blocks. In such situations, study group members are committed to finding positive aspects in the input of others, each member is motivated to freely and fully share their diversity, and the team and each member have an improved basis for generating synergy and the best solutions.

Integration

Synergistic interaction (i.e., effective communication, active listening, and creating trust) and appreciative understanding (i.e., having an open climate, being nonjudgmental, showing empathy, and valuing diversity) provide a strong foundation for effective study group teams. With these effective relationships and mechanisms in place, a study group is in an excellent position to take on the difficult task of integration: considering all input from the group, evaluating its value and usability, and synergistically pulling together the appropriate ideas and perspectives to generate the best available solution or outcome. Experience has shown that the effectiveness of the integration process is often enhanced by tolerating ambiguity and being persistent, flexible, creative, and selective (Conner, 1993).

Many of the problems facing study groups will be extremely complex and will lead to ambiguous information, ideas, perspectives, and circumstances. Like most people, study group members have a tendency to seek quick, easy solutions. Frequently, this approach proves to be nonproductive or leads down a path to a less valuable result. Consequently, study groups must shift from the more typical quick-fix approaches to problem solving and be more persistent with the ambiguity of the input and circumstances as they bring together and flexibly, creatively, and selectively integrate their relevant ideas and perspectives and move synergistically toward the best available solutions.

Implementation

The first three steps of the process to generate synergy—interaction, appreciative understanding, and integration—provide the study group with its desired outcome. Thus, the remaining step in the synergy process is to implement and manage the various parts of the desired outcome effectively in the school. The four key elements of successful implementation are to (a) strategize, (b) monitor and reinforce, (c) remain team focused, and (d) update.

To increase the likelihood that the study group outcomes will be implemented and managed effectively, the group must strategize, creating a plan for the implementation that sets its direction, manages the resources, determines priorities, and ensures that the various implementation steps are compatible. Once a strategy and plan have been developed and the implementation process begun, it is critical that the process be monitored and reinforced to ensure that appropriate behavior and progress are sustained.

In the implementation process, there will be potential for some members of the study group and others involved in the implementation to move ahead more rapidly than their colleagues. Doing this has the potential for getting people out of step with each other and reducing the synergy of the total effort. Consequently, it is important and valuable to remain team focused, respecting the team's common goals and interdependence and continuing to function as a unified, integrated work team.

Circumstances and environments may very well change during the implementation process. When this happens, there often should be an updating of the study groups implementation and action plan. Teams have a tendency to fall in love with their plans and become resistant to their change. However, the implementation process is most effective when an action plan is continuously and appropriately updated.

Synergy Development

Creating strong, effective study groups means doing those things necessary to build synergistic teams. Developing synergistic teams requires a substantial commitment and effort, but the cost for not operating in this manner is high, and the potential for producing meaningful results is reduced dramatically. The synergistic process is an extremely powerful approach for increasing the effectiveness, productivity, and quality of the work of study group teams.

As you attempt to apply the concepts, principles, and approaches discussed in this chapter to create synergistic study groups, it will be beneficial to stop from time to time and monitor how your efforts are going. The Synergy Checklist that follows should be helpful in identifying which elements of the synergy development process are working well and which ones require improving.

Synergy Checklist

The following eight question sets provide a practical checklist for assessing the effectiveness of a group and identifying how to make the group more synergistic:

1. *Common goals:* Has your study group discussed, agreed on, and written a clearly and precisely stated goal or goals for its work?

2. *Interdependence:* Has the discussion, interaction, and sharing of your study group been interdependent (i.e., mutually dependent and genuinely cooperative)?

3. *Empowerment:* Do members of your study group feel a sense of empowerment? That is, does each member feel that what he or she has to offer is important and valuable and may have an effect on the outcome of decisions?

4. *Participative involvement:* Do the members of your study group feel that they can and do openly and freely participate in the discussions and activities of the study group?

5. *Interaction:* Do the members of your study group, individually and collectively, interact effectively? That is, do they communicate effectively and actively listen to each other, and has a sense of trust and credibility been created in the group?

6. *Appreciative understanding:* Do the members of your study group show appreciative understanding of each other and each other's ideas? That is, does the group have an open climate and value diversity, and does each member delay judgment and empathize with the ideas of the others?

7. *Integration:* As those in your study group work to consider all input, evaluate its value and usability, and pull it together to generate the best decision or outcome, do they show persistence in their deliberations and tolerate its ambiguity, and are they flexible, creative, and selective as they consider the issues and transition toward their final result?

8. *Implementation:* Once your study group arrives at the desired outcome to be completed, are the members effectively initiating and managing the implementation process for a successful conclusion? That is, did your study group create a plan for the implementation that sets its direction, manages the resources, determines priorities, and ensures that the various steps are completed; that ensures that appropriate behavior and progress are sustained; that remains team, not individual, focused; and that continuously and appropriately updates the action plan for the implementation?

Comentoring Groups

A comentoring group is one in which members of the group all mentor each other. In effective comentoring groups, each member acts as a sponsor, advocate, guide—or teaches, advises, trusts, critiques, and supports others to express, pursue, and finalize goals (Vanzant, 1980), as well as, in general, being competent, supportive, sharing, unexploitive, positive, and involved (Cronan-Hillix, Gensheimer, Cronan-Hillix, Cronan-Hillix, & Davidson, 1986). Ideally, in a comentoring situation, "each member of a group offers support and encouragement to everyone else which expands individual and group understanding, improving the group's effectiveness and productivity" (Mullen & Lick, 1999). A comentoring group, for example, might be a study group that explores a learning area together and whose members assist one another in increasing each other's capacity for understanding.

Synergy and comentoring can be meaningfully combined in study groups, as synergistic comentoring, to generate unusually effective and productive teamwork. This is illustrated in a study group of six high school science teachers, where one physics teacher wrote,

Our group's foremost benefit was that I got to know the teachers in my department much better than I had in 7 previous years. We grew to understand each other's priorities and view of science and education, invented new labs, researched and designed a new curriculum in marine science, worked together to calibrate old equipment, learned of treasure we could borrow from each other's hoards, and laughed a lot at ourselves, each other, and our big city high school. The meetings were our responsibility—ours to make productive or frustrating, enlightening or confounding. It left us with the lingering, seductive taste of "freedom." (Murphy & Lick, 1998, pp. 87-88)

Multiple Levels of Synergistic Comentoring

In the WFSG process, a synergistic comentoring group functions on several significant levels to enhance its total effectiveness and productivity, as described in detail in the article, "Whole-Faculty Study Groups: Facilitating Mentoring for School-Wide Change" (Lick, 2000).

When those in a school decide to approve the study group process, that establishes a collective sponsorship base, a serious buy-in, for leaders and teachers to become potential synergistic comentoring support groups for the process. This, in turn, gives the school and its leadership overt commitment for their faculty's total involvement in such efforts. When the faculty accepts the study group process (hopefully, with at least a 70%-80% approval), this commits every teacher to the process, to faculty-led, fundamental change in the school and being an active member of a study group. This in turn creates a powerful "whole-faculty-change" sponsorship for the change process. This then provides the basis of support for the faculty becoming a synergistic comentoring team of the whole, agreeing to share overarching common goals for their school, function interdependently, empower each other, and actively participate in the change activities of the process. This creates a driving force toward progressive, schoolwide change.

As we've outlined, early in the process the principal typically appoints a leadership group of teachers, a focus team, that along with the principal, initiates the study group process, generates a step-by-step plan for the faculty to implement the process, and coordinates and monitors the overall effort. The focus team also meets regularly with study group representatives to assist them with their expectations, activities, concerns, resources, and results. This initial approach alone gives three potential levels for synergistic comentoring: the focus team and the principal, the focus team itself, and the focus team and representatives of individual study groups. In particular, these opportunities provide for the creation of synergistic comentoring to increase communication, interdependence, and empowerment for those involved and, indirectly, the study groups. In addition, they cultivate circumstances for sustaining sponsorship of the study group process and for promoting transitioning change agent activities.

However, key synergistic comentoring opportunities come in the study groups themselves. The unique strength of study groups comes from their functioning as self-directed, synergistic comentoring teams, setting common goals, working interdependently, empowering one another, and, in a balanced fashion, openly sharing their ideas and perspectives. In these colearning, action research, synergistic, comentoring groups, the basis for meaningful change is built and the intellectual and emotional commitment for progressive classroom and school transformation is generated.

Further levels of involvement come from students, parents, and the community. Students desire to help and are receptive to new approaches and materials from their teachers. Students also can be active participants in synergistic comentoring processes with teachers, classmates, and others. The same kinds of synergistic comentoring possibilities exist for parents and the community, with respect to school activities and reforms.

Moreover, a vertically structured synergistic and comentoring arrangement, involving the community, parents, students, and study groups through the top leadership, seems to accompany growing synergistic comentoring relationships among these various levels. This parallel advancement further strengthens team building, sponsorship, advocacy, support, and commitment to significant change in school culture, programs, and materials, leading to enhanced student learning and school improvement.

Success Factors

The study group process, centered around multilevel synergistic comentoring, is, in fact, a massive change management process. It is one of the most practical and effective approaches we have seen in our research and studies. In particular, the study group process dramatically increases the following:

1. *Focus on imperative changes,* as determined by school personnel

2. *Change sponsorship effectiveness,* project and schoolwide

3. *Preparation of change agents,* including the principal, faculty, and others

4. *Commitment of targets and the reduction of resistance*

5. *Positive advocacy,* including that of the school board, superintendent, principal, faculty, students, parents, and others from the general community

6. *Individual, group, and school resilience,* enhancing stakeholders' change adaptability

7. *Knowledge of change and change principles* for stakeholders

8. *Organized processes for transition,* including integrated, cocreative learning experiences that are teacher and student centered, experimental and research oriented, reflective, supportive, and inspiring

9. *Group synergy, comentoring, and learning team development,* setting new school operational and relationship norms for action research and improving learning systems

10. *School and educational culture modification,* allowing a critical reexamination of basic assumptions, beliefs, and behaviors and required learning system and practices (Lick, 2000; Mullen & Lick, 1999)

The WFSG process, through the listed 10 elements for leading and managing change, generates collective and inspiring vision and creates a high level of synergy and comentoring, allowing substantive learning, change, and continuous improvement to become the norm in the school workplace and school culture.

Learning From the Experiences
of Seven Schools

For effective staff development, meaningful school reform, and real school transformations, schools must not only determine what changes and reforms are required but must also implement an intentional, well-designed transition process to deal with societal, organizational, cultural, and interpersonal barriers affecting schools. Schools must find ways to transition individuals and groups from old to new paradigms and related processes and circumstances from the previous to the required ones. Furthermore, teachers, administrators, and other key stakeholders must be broadly and intimately involved in the process.

Where properly implemented, the WFSG process has been unusually successful in facilitating schoolwide change and enhancing student learning (e.g., Joyce et al., 1989; Murphy, 1991b, 1992, 1995). The driving force in the study group process is its self-directed, synergistic comentoring teams (see Lick, 1998, 2000). Such teams creatively (a) produce learning communities and set common goals, support member interdependence, empower participants, and foster active participation; (b) plan and learn together; (c) engage broad principles of education that modify perspectives, policies, and practices; (d) construct subject matter knowledge; (e) immerse everyone in sustained work with ideas, materials, and colleagues; (f) cultivate action researchers, producing, evaluating, and applying relevant research; and (g) struggle with fundamental questions of what teachers and students must learn, know, and apply (Murphy & Lick, 1998, p. 2).

Once again, the focusing question for study groups is what are students learning and achieving as a result of what teachers are learning and doing in study groups? And with that vision, "study groups are motivated, work harder, and take responsibility for the successful implementation of required processes and procedures" (Murphy & Lick, 1998, p. 18).

In this final chapter, we discuss the WFSG process in a representative sample of actual schools and highlight results from their study group efforts. These illustrations include a diverse mix of three elementary schools, two middle schools, and two high schools. We close the chapter with a brief discussion of how the study group process has the potential to help schools move toward becoming more like learning organizations.

As we write this final chapter featuring seven schools that have implemented Murphy's Whole-Faculty Study Groups for Student-Based Professional Development, Murphy remembers a speech Ron Edmonds gave at the 1980 Annual Conference of the National Staff Development Council in Detroit. Paraphrasing what she remembers, he asked, "How many effective schools would you need to see to be persuaded? . . . If you have seen one (and don't believe), then you have reasons of your own for preferring (not to believe)." We are often asked the "how many" question. How many high schools? How many schools in inner cities? How many schools where most of the students speak English as a second language? How many schools ___? We often wonder how many is enough to be enough. Murphy shares that in a meeting in Dallas she was asked, "How many schools have you worked in that have a student population that is 100% African American?" She responded, "How many would satisfy you?"

The WFSG Question Most Often Asked

Will WFSGs increase student achievement? This is the question asked most often of us. The answer is this: It depends on what the study groups do.

This question becomes Murphy's dilemma as she works in schools and is asked "What research do you have that indicates that study groups increase student achievement?" In the Augusta schools where she was a district-level leader, she had joint control over the design for training (the process), the content of the study groups, and the data collection procedures. As a longtime member of the staff of the district, she understood the contextual conditions that affected the work of the schools. As an external consultant in the WFSG process, she has had no control over what study groups do (the content), what data collection instruments and procedures will be used in the districts and schools where she works, or the contextual elements that affect success. She is an independent consultant without a research unit. Therefore, Murphy can only report what she sees in the schools, what she reads in the reports from the schools, and what she is told by teachers and other school and district leaders.

What has been stated in other sections of this book needs to be repeated here. Simply having study groups in place at a school will not increase student achievement. It is what teachers do in the study groups and in their classrooms that will increase student achievement. Study groups are a means through which teachers work together on how to make academic content more meaningful to students so as to increase the students' understanding of what they are taught. There is no simple "yes" answer that Murphy can give to the question, Will study groups increase student achievement? Her answer would have to begin with, "It depends on . . ."

Increases in student achievement can rarely be attributed to one factor. In schools, there are so many factors or variables constantly interacting and changing moment by moment. In any one school year, teachers are using new and refined materials, adhering to new standards, using new teaching strategies, talking more to each other, involving parents to a greater degree, attending district-level training sessions, benefiting from more resources and allocations of money, using more technology, having an increase in personnel, being given more technical assistance through the adoption of National Comprehensive School Reform designs, benefiting from repairs to the physical facilities, being led by new school or district leaders, and so on. How can any one of these factors be singled out as the reason test scores went up or went down? WFSGs tend to pull many of these factors together so that the environment is more cohesive and initiatives made more seamless.

The schools are reliable sources of information and reports from testing, and state agencies tell what students are accomplishing in terms of state and local standards. The seven schools described in this chapter used a variety of data sources to determine whether school and student needs were being met.

ATLAS Communities

Descriptions of successes in ATLAS Communities' schools are not included in this chapter. Outstanding successes are documented. Standardized test scores have shown steady gains. These test results can be attained by calling ATLAS Communities at 1-800-225-4276. The data are not included because, in addition to having WFSGs as one element of the ATLAS framework, there are four other elements that in combination with WFSGs lead to demonstrable improvements in student achievement and performance. Because this book is not the appropriate place to elaborate on the other four elements or components, readers are encouraged to contact ATLAS headquarters to request materials describing ATLAS Communities' national comprehensive school reform design. The over 100 ATLAS schools in 13 states have greatly contributed to the evolution of WFSGs, and the successes that students and teachers are experiencing are attributable to many factors.

Enhancing Student Learning:
East Middle School—Impressive Success

In East Middle School, the desired ends were an increase in student achievement and a decrease in negative student behavior. The means to those ends was a staff development effort involving WFSGs that included the following:

■ Administrators and teachers attended a 2-week training program during the first summer of the initiative, focusing on several models of teaching.

■ Administrators and teachers learned the theory, observed demonstrations, and practiced four key models of teaching: concept attainment, inductive thinking, mnemonics, and cooperative learning.

■ Administrators expected teachers to use the models or strategies frequently and appropriately throughout the school year.

■ Teachers met weekly for about an hour in study groups of 5 or 6 to jointly plan and practice lessons using the models.

■ Teachers made videotapes of their teaching on a regular basis.

■ Administrators and teachers attended similar training programs for the next two summers and continued to meet in study groups during the school years.

■ Virtually all teachers learned to use the teaching models and strategies to a mechanical level of competence, and some reached higher levels of skill by the conclusion of the first year.

Models and strategies of teaching were new to almost all teachers and students, requiring substantial amounts of new learning. Administrators scheduled time for study groups to meet, teachers practiced strategies in the classrooms, and teachers taught the students how to use teaching strategies as learning strategies. Some study groups were comfortable planning and sharing, whereas others were anxious. New teachers hired during the first 3 years had to be integrated into the process. The degree of change that occurred was dramatic, including the following:

- Only 34% of the students reached promotion standards the year before whole-school improvement efforts began. That percentage rose to 72% following the first year of implementation and 94% after the second year.

- At the conclusion of the first year of implementation, the percentage of "promotions by exception" dropped from 33% to 13%, and the percentage of students retained dropped from 33% to 15%.

- Eighth graders taking the state's Eighth Grade Basic Skills Writing Test (BSWT) scored the lowest (11th) in the district the year study groups were initiated; students who were sixth graders that year went on to score third in the district when they were eighth graders.

- Out-of-school suspensions were reduced from 343 the year prior to the training and study group implementation to 124 during the first year of implementation.

- The Iowa Test of Basic Skills (ITBS) battery in social studies was administered to sixth graders at the conclusion of the first year of the initiative and again 2 years later when these same students were eighth graders. Their rate of growth was 6 months more than their past rate would have predicted.

During the first year of implementation of the staff development program described earlier, all other factors at the school stayed the same as they were during the year prior to the initiative. There were no changes in the administration, facilities, or curriculum; no increase in instructional funds; and no additional personnel. The only interventions were the study group design and the training in the models and strategies of teaching.

When teachers in East Middle School were organized into study groups to help them learn new teaching models and strategies, their students' achievements and behavior improved remarkably (Joyce & Calhoun, 1996). The school developed an improvement program based on principles derived from research, including the following:

- Modification of the culture of the school and processes of innovation

- The ways that teachers learn new instructional models and strategies

- How teachers transfer new skills to the classroom

- Creation of more of a learning organization environment in the school

- A restructured workplace by organizing teachers into collegial study groups, providing regular training on teaching, and inducing faculties to set goals for school improvements and strive to achieve them

A Major Concern

At East Middle School, the positive changes in student achievement were well documented over a period of 4 years, and those changes were directly linked to a major staff development initiative. This initiative included the WFSG design and an intensive training program aimed at enabling teachers to be masters of several models of teaching. The seamless integration of these two components had proved to be successful in changing teacher and student behaviors. Because the intensity of such an effort also brought personal and professional discomfort to school and district leaders, support was not sustained (see Chapter 8 for a discussion of sustaining study group efforts, including continuance, maintenance, and institutionalization). The politics of schooling was evident. Within 5 years of the start of the staff development initiative, school and district leaders began to focus their attention and resources on other initiatives. Teachers saw a gradual disintegration of encouragement and support. They saw that school and district leaders were not displaying the same level of sponsorship and advocacy that had initially been evident. Without strong sponsorship and support, individuals returned to old habits and former practices. Some continued, but apart from the whole. Without constant tending by internal and external sponsors and advocates, what was once perceived as important was no longer perceived as important. Over time, the administrative team changed at the school level, and new initiatives were introduced that took the energy and attention of the staff. Teachers transferred to other schools. The administrative team at the district level changed, and the attention and resources that had been given to the staff development initiative at East Middle School were diverted to other programs. However, the school did not lose all the ground it had gained. Fewer of the students who were served during the years of the initiative dropped out of school, and many of these students became leaders in the high schools they attended.

A Vehicle for Change: Sarah Cobb Elementary School

The 1999-2000 school year was the seventh that Sarah Cobb Elementary School has had its whole faculty in study groups. Study groups are no larger than 6 members and still meet weekly to focus on instruction. The principal states that the question is no longer asked as to whether or not there will be study groups. Study groups are now a routine. The last time the question was raised in an IC meeting, the response from the principal was, "Until someone comes up with something better that will achieve the same outcomes." And that has not happened!

Sarah Cobb Elementary School draws its 692 third, fourth, and fifth grade students from a small rural community. Over 50% of the children are on the Aid to Families with Dependent Children list. All students are eligible for free or reduced-cost lunch. Only one third of the students reside in traditional, two-parent homes.

At the beginning of the 1990-1991 school year, the school had undergone a major change. This was 2 years before schoolwide study groups were implemented. The school, which had housed Grades 5 and 6 for 15 years, became a third grade through fifth grade school. Two thirds of the faculty were new to the school, and the faculty was led by a new leadership team consisting of a principal and two assistant principals. Year 1 (1991-1992) was a time for blending the two faculties and assessing student needs. In Year 2 (1992-1993), the faculty focused on examining student achievement and the effects of the school's curriculum and its delivery. One recommendation resulting from an examination of the school's needs was that teachers required more support in the implementation of the many initiatives that were aimed at student success. In Fall of the third year (1993-1994), after the school's new grade structure was initiated, WFSGs became the design to provide teachers a structured support system.

The results of the WFSG design after 1 year (1993-1994) were as follows:

■ Teachers examined strategies and materials that had been the content of staff development programs, practiced and used strategies and materials with each other and in their classrooms, and reported classroom results to each other.

■ Teachers petitioned the State Board of Education to approve a waiver to allow early release of students 1 day per week for teacher study. The waiver was approved and implemented in January of the first year.

■ Discipline referrals declined.

■ The number of books read independently by student increased, as did media center circulation.

The results at the end of the second year (1994-1995) were the following:

■ Teachers designed and implemented a back-to-the-basics plan called "Immersion in Basic Skills."

■ All teachers committed to and began participation in a 2-year, site-based training program that included immersion in the theory and practice of three key teaching strategies: concept attainment, inductive thinking, and mnemonics. Study groups were the vehicle for practicing and demonstrating these strategies and discussing their effects on students.

■ Iowa Test of Basic Skills (ITBS) results indicated growth for every grade and in every area tested.

■ Discipline referrals continued to decline.

■ The number of books read independently by students increased dramatically.

■ Surveys indicated a high level of teacher satisfaction.

The results for the third year (1995-1996) of the WFSG design were these:

■ All of the earlier results continued.

■ Chapter 1/Title I students posted significant National Curve Equivalent gains in all areas, with substantial growth recorded in reading and mathematics problem solving.

In the fourth year (1996-1997), there was an interesting development. The staff decided that after 3 years they had the study group process down pat. Therefore, they chose to make some changes to the design and content. The administration and teachers felt that they could ease off on the expectations. The decision was to use one action plan for all study groups, not require that logs be turned in, and allow groups to simply read books that were of interest to members. In other words, study groups turned into book discussion groups. At the end of the school year, data indicated that discipline problems increased, the number of books checked out from the school library decreased, and standardized test scores dropped. When the assistant principal called Murphy to inform her of the outcome, he said, "I have bad news and good news. The bad news is our scores dropped. The good news is that teachers know that it is because they lost their focus."

The next school year (1997-1998), the faculty returned to the guidelines that were followed for the first 3 years. Logs were given to the principal, and the faculty used student data to determine what study groups should do. A big push was made in Language Arts. Study groups returned to developing lessons together and reflecting on and adjusting those lessons in study groups. Even though the faculty did not have any formal training in how to look at student work collaboratively, student work was brought to study group meetings.

In July 1998, a report to the Georgia State Department of Education stated,

> Our data on student performance indicates a dip at all grade levels on the ITBS in the Spring 1997. This Spring 1998 ITBS indicates a slight rise at all levels. Most important for the purpose of evaluating Sarah Cobb is the fact that in the fifth grade where results for students at the school for three years continue to be significantly higher than fifth grade scores in 1994 when they began early release for study groups.

On surveys in Spring 1998, 97% of parents, teachers, and students responded "yes" that teachers expect all students to do their best, and 96% of parents gave the school a high rating.

In Spring 1999, scores continued to show a slight rise and hold the ground gained. It is believed that at the end of the 1999-2000 school year, this trend will have continued in spite of the rise in the number of students enrolled in special programs and the number of students receiving services from state agencies.

Learning Teams: Elder Middle School

The 1999-2000 school year was the eighth for Elder Middle School to have all of its teachers as members of study groups. Before the school implemented WFSGs in Fall 1992, teachers worked in teams, as they still do. However, one team planning period per week has been designated study group time, when the configuration of who meets together may vary from who attends a team meeting on the other 4 days. Even when the individuals are the same, the dialogue is different. As one teacher wrote,

> A majority of our team meetings were centered around business that needed to be conducted, such as break duty schedules, student schedule changes, discipline problems, parent contacts, record keeping, and resource sharing. Before we started the study group time, most of the teachers in our team didn't read much from professional journals. To be honest, unless the teachers were taking a course that had required reading, they did very little reading to keep up-to-date in current educational issues. Study group time helped us stay abreast of current issues and the latest research findings, so everyone

began to read more. Most importantly, the rapport that grew from becoming more open about our beliefs and classroom practices increased our willingness to try new methods and to share how those strategies worked with our students. For the first time, we openly shared lessons that were not effective and jointly worked on ways to make them more powerful.

The longer the teams experienced the study group mind-set (of learning teams) one period per week, the other planning periods became more like the study group time. As study groups became the norm at Elder Middle School, dialogues in the faculty lounge, in faculty meetings, and in department meetings were also noticeably different. Teachers talked about instruction. When the school was designated for the third time as one of Georgia's Schools of Excellence, interviews with teachers reflected the attitude that "we are a community of learners." The cumulative effect of this dynamic was also validated in student data.

Elder Middle School has remained steadfast in its commitment to study groups (i.e., learning teams). A collaborative mind-set abounded, and 8 years later, teacher talk continued to focus on teaching and learning.

After completing a needs assessment in Spring 1998, it was determined that the instructional focus for the following year would be on student achievement in written communication. The state writing scores for the school were not meeting the state average of 208. This was a considerable goal, as Elder's scores had never met this average. Two consultants, Terri Jenkins and Lynn Baber, worked with the whole faculty for 5 days in Summer 1998, and they continued meeting with study groups monthly, focusing on the teaching of writing throughout the 1998-1999 school year. Jenkins and Baber continued to model and demonstrate these practices, and teachers worked collaboratively to plan their lessons. The consultants spent time each month working in classrooms with students, providing teachers with opportunities to observe in the native environment the methodologies that they were being asked to use.

In Spring 1999, state writing tests were taken, and scores were returned to the school in May. For the first time in the history of Elder Middle School, it not only met but exceeded the state average in writing. The school average had risen from 198 in 1998 to 216 in 1999. Overall improvements in all areas were reported, and only 4% of the student body remained at risk according to state criteria, even though many students received Special Education services. Once again, in a search for excellence, the study groups provided the springboard for whole-school staff development and large gains in student achievement.

Cultural Change: Skyview Elementary School

A teacher at Skyview Elementary School eagerly shared her reactions to being in a study group. The second grade teacher said that she felt more like a professional than she had at any point during her 10 years of teaching. She was more confident, felt better about herself, felt she had contributed to the learning of her colleagues, felt proud to be a colearner with colleagues that shared new practices, and felt confirmed that her craft was based on a field of knowledge.

The teacher went on to give two examples of her improved self-esteem. She hung her diplomas and other professional certificates on her classroom walls for parents and students to see. She asked, "Physicians, lawyers, and other professionals do this, why not teachers? Why shouldn't parents and students see that teachers do have impressive credentials that verify that they have high levels of training?"

Another outcome of her positive feelings about herself came in the form of being more confident with parents. She said that she is now more assertive with parents in stating her evaluation of a student's work or behavior and what action she felt needed to be taken. Again, using medical doctors as a reference point, she said,

> Physicians tell us what their diagnosis is and what we need to do to get better. And we don't usually argue or second-guess the doctor's opinion. Now, I speak with more professional confidence when I talk with a parent.

This teacher had certainly changed some of her personal and professional assumptions, beliefs, and behaviors.

As other teachers at Skyview mirrored this teacher's feelings and actions, the change in the culture was felt and even observable upon entering the building.

Building Commitment: Sweetwater High School

Sweetwater High School is a large urban school with 110 certificated instructional staff members. The school serves a low socioeconomic-status community. It is a year-round school using block schedules to meet the diverse needs of its students. In May 1993, by an 89% approval vote, the staff elected to participate in the WFSG process. In December 1993, 15 heterogeneous study groups of 4 to 6 educators were formed; they met for 1 hour each week within the professional duty day to study, reflect, and develop strategies that would strengthen their curriculum and instruction.

The 1-hour study group period once a week provided the environment to build a strong, collaborative work culture that enhanced the school's capacity to change. Groups considered genuine questions (e.g., What will the practice models look like in my classroom? How will portfolio assessment benefit my students and assist in evaluating my instructional program?). This left a mark on Sweetwater teachers' perspectives and created a climate for change in policy and practice.

The diversity of the study groups was substantial; for example, one study group, addressing the self-esteem of high school students, was made up of teachers from physical education, fine arts, mathematics, and social sciences and a counselor.

The focus team was composed of seven teachers and two administrators who attended the initial and follow-up training. The team distributed a monthly newsletter, called *FOCUS,* which shared what the study groups were doing. At the beginning of the year, the team established a calendar of study group events for the coming year. Once a month, the team dispersed and met with assigned study groups, to serve as liaisons. The goal of the liaison was to promote communication among study groups and problem-solve areas of concern. The team also served on the school's IC, which met once a quarter and was made up of the leader of each of the study groups. Since leadership rotated among study group members, the one attending the council meeting was the one who was the leader the week the council met. In this way, the composition of the council was very fluid and always changing. The focus team also planned schoolwide activities, such as the celebration of the 4-year anniversary of study groups at Sweetwater High.

To assess the effectiveness of each year's study groups, a survey was distributed to all staff members during the last staff development day of the school calendar. The survey included questions to be answered by study groups as teams as well as in-depth individual assessments. Feedback from both strands of the survey was used to further strengthen the tie between teacher learning and student learning. The focus team summarized the information and shared the results with the faculty. Future decisions about how study groups would function and what they would do was based on this survey information and student data.

All of the energy emanating from the study groups produced dramatic improvements in student achievement. In 1992-1993, Sweetwater ranked eighth out of nine schools in the high school district in grade point average (GPA) and second in failure rate. Through sustained study group engagement, these rankings were changed. In 1994-1995, Sweetwater's cumulative GPA was second highest in the district, and course failure rates dropped 40% overall and 62% for students identified as limited English proficient. In April 1996, Sweetwater High School was notified by the Superintendent of Public Instruction in California that it had been selected as one of the state's 1996 Distinguished High Schools.

Sweetwater High School continued to improve in all areas for which data have been traditionally collected. During the 1997-1998 school year, the school received commendations on all areas assessed by the Western Association of Colleges and Schools, when it applied for accreditation.

During Summer 1998, the principal was assigned to another high school within the same district. A number of staff followed the principal, including the teacher who had assumed most of the coordinating responsibilities for WFSGs. Murphy has not continued her contact with Sweetwater. As far as she knows, it did not continue WFSGs as we have outlined the process in this book.

We do want to emphasize key points made in the summary of Chapter 2 and in the Institutionalization section of Chapter 8. Our desire is that once WFSGs begin at a school, the structure will continue in place at that school. Whether it does or not, does not diminish results of WFSGs when they were in place. Many factors contribute to continuation. Most often, the principal is a key factor. WFSGs require changes that affect schedules and organizational structures within the school. The principal, in large part, controls these types of decisions. A change in the principalship is most often the reason why WFSGs are not continued.

Staff Development as the Element of Change: Destrehan High School

The coordinator of staff development, Stephen Keyes, at Destrehan High School asked us the question, Would the best ACT scores in the school's history and rising Grade Exit Examination and standardized test scores interest you? His response was that "such improved scores are facts at Destrehan, and are due, at least to some degree, to the evolving WFSG staff development process." For example, from 1996-1997 to 1998-1999, the average Grade Exit Examination scores in the five key areas, Language Arts, Mathematics, Science, Social Studies, and Writing, increased by 2.4 points.

The WFSG process evolution began in the mid-1990s. In those days, most of the staff development came from the district office and was received with a cacophony of complaints. The research-based topics that were chosen by the district office were educationally sound; however, they were not implemented at an acceptable rate in the classroom. The fact was that even though good strategies had been taught to teachers, there was little time built into the school year for reflection and dialogue among teachers, and implementation was sporadic at best.

After years of such top-down staff development, the district decided to allow schools to choose topics for staff development. This decision has been met with a great deal of validation. In Destrehan High School, some 3 years later, not every teacher is using every research-based strategy that he or she has been taught, but nearly all are using some strategies. Comparatively speaking, there is much more effective implementation in the school today. The school's staff development plan, with the support of the principal and sustaining sponsorship and leadership of the staff development coordinator, has nudged the school toward the admirable and desirable goal of becoming a learning community. The school is a learning community in that teachers, administrators, counselors, librarians, paraprofessionals, secretaries, and others are all involved in learning what they should know to more effectively meet the needs of their students.

Between 1997 and 2000, the school's staff development has evolved from choices of topics for professional growth, to faculty study groups after school, to WFSGs that meet every other Wednesday during the first $2\frac{1}{2}$ hours of the school day. Students come in late on those days, but class time is given back to them on days when the rest of the district's schools are having staff development days.

For the study group time period, the whole faculty is divided into groups of 3 to 6 members. The groups are not assigned. Group members choose staff development groups and their work goals. The study revolves around meeting one of the three school improvement goals by meeting the needs of their students. Each group studies, implements, and evaluates the success of its implementation by looking at student work. Staff development at the school is not only job embedded but also specifically used to meet the needs of students. Note that these are the two integral elements in the national standards for effective staff development created by the National Staff Development Council and endorsed by the Board of Elementary and Secondary Education.

A 1-day random sampling of feelings and comments by staff members gives a good sense of the direction that staff development is taking at Destrehan High School:

- Innovative and worthwhile—Charles, teacher, 22 years

- Helpful and useful—Jemi, teacher, 8 years

- Laissez les bons temps roulet—C. J., counselor, 18 years

- I see more research-based strategies than ever before.—Linda, administrator, 30 years

- More teachers willing to try ideas because they come from other teachers—Chuck, teacher, 30 years

- Ongoing, diverse, up-to-date—Mary, teacher, 5 years

- Individualized—Jenny, teacher, 14 years

- Outstanding: It gives teachers options, attempts to meet every teacher's needs, and is directed by an outstanding staff development coordinator. Best in all my years of teaching—Glen, teacher, 35 years

- Advocates personal and professional growth—Nina, teacher, 3 years

- Allows teachers to meet students' needs by its openness—Kelly, teacher, 7 years (2 months at Destrehan)

- Outstanding, excellent. I have learned more about teaching in my 4 years at Destrehan than in the rest of my 12 years—Joey, teacher, 12 years

- I have learned more from my school's staff development about practical teaching strategies than in most of my university methods courses—James, teacher, 4 years

- It has freed teachers to use strategies in the classroom that have a purpose, and it makes learning fun. It has empowered teachers and given them permission to really teach—Debra, teacher, 25 years

- Accommodating, personalized—Stephanie, teacher, 10 years

- Personalized, dynamic, motivating—Rob, teacher, 4 years

- The number of required hours in the parish is excessive. I like the idea of study groups—Anonymous, 5 years

- Our staff development days give us time to be professionals. We actually have the time and resources to develop the research-based strategies which aid us in meeting our students' growing needs!!—Cherie, teacher, 5 years

- It gives us time to dialogue with our colleagues rather than just those in our discipline—Karin, teacher, 4 years

- Teachers can work together—Eric, teacher, 3 years

The staff development coordinator at Destrehan High School insightfully challenges our schools and us when he inquires, "If you were to ask every faculty member that passes your door or that you see in the hall tomorrow to describe staff development in your school or district, what would your results be?"

The scores at Destrehan High School are improving. Teachers do feel differently about staff development. Staff development is based on student needs and is job embedded. And as their staff development coordinator says, "The future looks brighter because, thank goodness, the WFSG process evolution continues."

Developing a Collaborative Culture: Jackson Elementary School

In his summative report on the WFSG process, Jackson Elementary School's principal, Barry Shelofsky (1999), related that implementing study groups "helped our school develop a collaborative culture." He goes on, in that report, to describe the beginning of study groups in his school:

After attending a workshop entitled *WFSGs: A Fail-Safe Design for School Improvement* presented by Carlene Murphy, a nationally recognized expert in the study group process, I knew that I had come across a school improvement process that had the capacity to foster staff collegiality and enhance student achievement.

In May 1995, Jackson's School Improvement Planning Team and the school staff displayed 100% support for initiating the study group process the following year. The developments at Jackson provide a real story about how one person, the principal, can begin and sustain an initiative in his school through his own personal influence and leadership style. The information and data in the balance of this section comes from Principal Shelofsky's (1999) report and personal communications with him.

Jackson is the only school in its district to have adopted the WFSG process. Although those in his district have not inhibited the study group effort in his school, he has received no extra resources or support from the district. The principal summarizes his motivation and need for the WFSG process as follows:

> I chose to implement study groups with the Jackson staff because of a strong belief that professional development is best accomplished at a grassroots level—by teachers. In the past, I felt that all too often teachers were asked to attend 1-day or 2-day workshops and then to implement a program, strategy, or activity with their students. The problem, as I've seen time and time again, was that there was very little or no support provided to the practitioners as they began the implementation process. As a result, the rationale for WFSGs at Jackson became: Successful schools are distinguishable from unsuccessful ones by the frequency and extent to which teachers and administrators learn together, plan together, test ideas together, reflect together, discuss practice, grapple together with the fundamental questions of what teachers and students need to know and do, and engage together in the pursuit of instructional strategies and programs that will develop students to their fullest capacity.

Overarching Goals and Process Flow

The overarching goals at Jackson Elementary School have been the following:

■ To improve student achievement through strengthening instructional skills of teachers and administrators by marshaling the collective power, energy, and knowledge of the whole faculty

■ To build strong collaborative work cultures that develop long-term capacity for change and create a synergistic environment

■ To develop school cultures that build site-level capacity for professional improvements as a way of life in schools

■ To develop a school-level process that will support teachers in their implementation of curriculum and instruction

The essence of the flow of the study group process in Jackson Elementary School during 5 years (1995-2000), as described by the principal, is as follows:

> Since December 1995, we have striven to be more collegial in our efforts to increase student performance. Our dialogue in study groups has been, for the most part, very professional in scope. This has enabled study group members to become interdependent. For example, during the 1999-2000 school year,

third and fourth grade teachers are responsible for assessing children in reading and writing through the Colorado Student Assessment Program (CSAP) tests. In order to increase student performance in these areas, teachers engaged in thoughtful and purposeful study group sessions designed to develop a strategic plan that would make students more aware of the test's format, vocabulary, and structure. It is exciting to see classroom teachers—Title I specialists, special education teachers, teachers on special assignment, and others—work together to create such a comprehensive test preparation package while remaining focused on our schoolwide efforts in writing. When the tests were given to students, there were not many surprises that stymied our students.

Another example of teachers becoming team oriented is seen in our first grade study group. As our school's focus is on literacy, and in particular writing, the first grade teachers put together a wide-ranging, chronological-based calendar of events that built off of our school's scope and sequence of writing activities. This project, created in study groups, provides the basis for teaching writing to all first grade students.

Fifth grade and special education teachers have brought their study groups together to discuss and implement ways to modify and accommodate needs of special education students in the area of writing. While this has been going on for a short period of time, the teachers feel positive about their work thus far. I feel that this is an example of teachers empowering themselves to make positive changes in the best interest of students.

Preschool and kindergarten teachers working together in study groups is key to our future success. At this level students formally begin to experience reading, writing, listening, and speaking lessons. It is vital that these teachers implement our writing scope/sequence so that the curriculum can spiral from grade to grade. These connections are crucial if we are to increase student performance.

Synergistic Comentoring Relationships

A high level of synergy and comentoring are especially notable in the Jackson study groups. When asked to "list reasons, both professional and personal, that make their study groups work," teachers said such things as the following:

- Our group is genuinely cooperative and wants to continue for the rest of the year.

- We have created a positive atmosphere wherein members can openly and freely participate in discussions.

- We enjoy sharing information about connections we have made with students.

- We all have and value a sense of humor.

- We appreciate and respect each other's ideas and experiences as educators.

- We feel we have a no-nonsense approach and will use this to achieve practical and immediate results in our classrooms.

- The diversity of the group's teaching assignments

- Our willingness to participate and try new things in our classrooms

- The focus on kids' success

- We enjoy each other and respect each one's gifts and talents.

- Our willingness to be change adaptable

- Our sharing of ideas, disagreeing with respect, and building off of one another

- Classroom application that make study groups more valuable, relevant, and meaningful

- Our group has remained focused during each of our meetings.

- The climate of our interactions has been open and relaxed and has allowed each member to voice her opinions freely. This is the result of the groups' norms to which we agreed to early on and have continued to honor.

- Our group had a foxhole mentality because of the trust, interdependence, support, and sharing amongst members.

- Our group remained persistent and positive and challenged by our tasks.

- Bonds formed within the group assisted us with problems that existed outside the group.

- Our ideas were valued and each of us was seen as an expert in our own area.

In January 1999, 39 staff members at Jackson completed the Synergy Checklist (see Chapter 9) to measure the level of synergistic relationships in the study groups. A 10-point Likert-type scale was applied to the eight sets of questions in the Synergy Checklist (i.e., common goals, interdependence, empowerment, participative involvement, interaction, appreciative understanding, integration, and implementation). The means of results ranged from 8.17 to 9.06, with standard deviations ranging from 1.06 to 1.31. These results provide strong evidence of a high level of synergistic relationships in the study groups. The strongest attributes included "appreciative understanding" and "participative involvement," which means that study group members felt a strong sense of oneness to participate, freedom to discuss ideas, and that their ideas were respected in a climate of diversity and validation. "Interdependence" and "interaction" were also highly rated, suggesting that group members felt genuine cooperation and a mutual responsibility for the group. Furthermore, group communication was effective with active listening and a sense of trust and credibility in the group. The study groups seemed to catch the true essence of synergy when they related it to snowflakes, as follows:

> *Snowflakes are such fragile things!*
> *But look at their enormous power when they stick together!*

Parent-Community Satisfaction

Parents and the community-at-large continue to support Jackson's commitment and performance. This is evidenced in the results from their Spring 1999 Parents Survey (74% response of 347 families, given in percentages):

Statement	Agree	Disagree	No Opinion
1. Staff prepares my child for the next grade.	94.3	1.2	4.5
2. Teachers challenge students to develop to their fullest.	93.2	1.6	5.6
3. I am pleased with my child's achievement in mathematics.	95.5	6.4	4.8
4. I am pleased with my child's achievement in writing.	83.8	7.7	8.5
5. I am pleased with my child's achievement in reading.	83.9	7.2	8.8
6. My child has a strong sense of belonging at Jackson.	85.1	5.6	9.2
7. Jackson is a safe school for my child.	87.9	3.2	8.8
8. Students are recognized for displaying pride, respect, and responsibility.	84.9	3.6	10.4
9. My child is treated fairly at Jackson.	85.9	2.8	8.0
10. Staff helps me understand how to support my child's learning.	89.2	2.8	6.1
11. Staff provides my child with materials and resources to learn.	91.1	1.6	7.3

Writing, Reading, and Mathematics Assessments

All fifth grade writing, reading, and mathematics composite assessments increased during the study period, 1996-1997 to 1998-1999, with percentage increases indicated:

Area	Percentage Increase
Writing (District Six Writing Assessment)	
Content (1997-1998 to 1998-1999 due to calibration change to align with CSAP)	10
Mechanics, Grammar, Punctuation, and Spelling	8
Reading (Michigan Educational Assessment Program)	
Narrative Selection	2
Information Selection	9
Mathematics (Michigan Educational Assessment Program)	7

Referrals to the Principal

With Jackson's implementation of the WFSG process, including high expectations for learning for all students, the referrals to the principal have decreased, as indicated below.

	1996–1997	*1998–1999*
Referrals to the principal	123	76
Male	111	73
Female	12	3

Conclusion

The above information and data help show the progress that can be made with effective school leadership and implementation commitment and strong sponsorship of the WFSG process. As Jackson Elementary School focused the study group process in the current year on writing and reading performance, the principal gave a sense of his expectations:

> I believe that this year so far has been very positive in terms of the study group process. The synergy and comentoring within study groups coupled with our solid focus on improving the writing/reading performance of all students has been gratifying. I see this weekly as I review reflection logs which show that what's been discussed in study groups is being applied in classrooms with students. Hopefully, we will see the fruits of our labor when the Colorado Student Assessment Program-4 Writing results are made public late this coming summer.

Schools Becoming Learning Organizations

As shown in the foregoing examples, the professional WFSG process has the potential for transforming schools and bringing about major change efforts for enhancing student achievement and school improvement. The soul (i.e., vital and essential part, Guralnik, 1986) of this massive, structured, schoolwide, faculty-directed change process is multilevel synergistic comentoring (see Chapter 9). Through this innovative approach, learning becomes an investment, and the norm, common goals, and expectations are set, compelling sponsorship for change is communicated and accepted, and creative synergy is enacted, enriching and enhancing everyone's efforts. Centering on multilevel synergistic comentoring, the study group process becomes a meaningful and effective change process. It examines school and learning needs and underlying assumptions, beliefs, and behaviors and helps transition them to new sets of school and learning patterns and approaches and a fundamentally modified culture. In the final analysis, through the study group process, the school and its stakeholders are change catalysts for their school becoming more like a learning organization (Lick, 2000).

A *learning organization* is one in which the organization itself is committed to individual growth, learning, and creativity as a path to institutional growth. In such an organization, systems are in place to capture, share, and institutionalize the insights of individuals and teams. The institution, as a whole, [builds off of past failures and successes and] gets smarter [and more effective] as a result of the shared learning of its members. (Graff, 1996, p. 5)

Learning organizations leader Senge (1990) reminds us that "the organizations that will truly excel in the future will be the organizations that discover how to tap people's commitment and capacity to learn at all levels of the organization" (p. 4). The WFSG process provides a process for a school to become more like a learning organization where people continually expand their capacity to create the results they desire, where new and expansive patterns of thinking are nurtured, where collective aspiration is set free, and where people are continually learning how to learn together (Lick, 2000).

It is our hope that in this book faculties will find a way to make the struggles of public schooling less lonesome. The isolation that teachers often feel is unbearable to many, so they leave the profession. Through this book, if teachers learn how very willing teachers are to give to each other whatever will make all their students more powerful learners, we will have accomplished our purpose.

Resource A

Forms

Forms

- Study Group Action Plan
- Study Group Log
- Checklist for Data Sources
- Stating Specific Student Needs After Analyzing Data
- Checklist for Writing a Study Group Action Plan
- Checklist for the First Three Study Group Meetings
- Checklist for Implementation of Process Guidelines
- Checklist for Substantive Content

Forms for Assessing Progress

- What Has Changed as a Result of Your Study Group Work?
- Status Check: Do We See Eye-to-Eye?
- Using the Study Group Action Plan
- Reflection on the Process and Examination of the Inquiry

Study Group Action Plan

School _____ Study Group # _____ Date _____

Group Members _____

What is the general category of student needs the group will address?

_____ Reading _____ Writing _____ Math _____ Other: _____

Essential Question *(Example: How can we teach students to comprehend what they read?)*:

We **PLAN** according to data indicating that **students need to**   ➤   We **ACT** on the students' needs by agreeing that **when the study group meets** we will ➤

We **REFLECT** on the results of our actions and on our use of the **following resources.**   ➤   We **ASSESS** our work according to evidence that **student learning has increased and understanding has deepened.**

STUDENT PERFORMANCE GOALS	DATA SOURCE:

We **REFLECT** on intermediate measures and ongoing assessments that inform us as to how the students are progressing toward the above performance goals. These measures are described on the back or on separate paper.

STUDY GROUP LOG

School _____ Log# _____ Date _____

Group Name or # _____ Today's Leader _____

Members Present _____

Members Absent _____

What happened today? Brief summary of discussion and activities. Keep artifacts in notebook.

Classroom Application: What are students learning and achieving as a result of what you are learning and doing?

Did you examine student work today? _____ Who brought? _____

General comments, such as: what you are ready to share, IC/Reps meeting.	What concerns or questions do you have for leaders or what do you want them to know?

Checklist for Data Sources

What data will be used by the whole faculty to make the initial decisions (DMC) about study group choices?

What data will a study group use to get more information about the student needs in the general category they chose? These student needs are to be listed on the SGAP.

What data will a study group use to identify the student performance goals? These goals are to be stated on the SGAP.

■ Standardized test results: The faculty will need the item analysis of all the subcategories tested, or subject area subscores, or any other reporting system the test maker uses to show how students did in specific areas tested. For example, the faculty should not only see the score for "reading" but also for reading comprehension, vocabulary, and work attack skills. One school in Massachusetts used the Iowa Test of Basic Skills for Grade 3, the California Achievement Test for Grade 5, and the Massachusetts Comprehensive Assessment system for Grade 4.

■ Performance of students on the district's content standards

■ Early Literacy Assessment or other tests that indicate how successful students are in preschool, kindergarten, and first grade classes

■ Oral reading assessments

■ Informal reading inventories

■ Exit exams from high school courses

■ Criterion-referenced tests

■ Writing assessments

■ Journals, authentic writing samples

■ Student portfolios that contain at least 1 year of work in one content area

■ Checklists from textbook companies (e.g., reading series often have end-of-book tests)

■ Performance assessments

■ Results of open-ended response questions

■ Results of tests given by Title I and other special testing programs

■ Results of tests similar to New York State's Regents Examination, analyzed by subject area

■ Number of graduates from high schools that the elementary and middle school students attend, categorized by types of diploma

■ Cumulative grade point averages by subject area and grade for a random sample of students

- An analysis of *why* students quit school
- Number of students that enroll in postsecondary education
- Number of students that go to college and graduate
- An analysis of *why* students are referred for disciplinary action
- An analysis of *why* students are absent
- An analysis of the education levels of parents
- Distribution of student grades by subject and grade levels
- Numbers of students placed in advanced-placement courses and in remedial or lower-level courses
- An analysis of *why* students are referred to special education and how many referrals are placed in special programs
- Promotion and retention rates by grades and subjects
- Samples of student and teacher portfolios
- Analysis of types of employment opportunities for which students qualify who don't enroll in postsecondary education
- Responses to questionnaires and interviews
- An analysis of circulation reports from the school library
- Level of participation in science and social studies fairs
- Analysis of students enrolled in debate, academic bowls, and other activities that are subject-area related
- Student interviews
- Reports from accrediting agencies or other groups that rate the schools
- An analysis of the access students have to computers and the Internet
- An analysis of *why* teachers leave the school
- Other:

Stating Specific Student Needs After Analyzing Data

Step 2 on the Decision-Making Cycle

The team has looked at all the data or the data each person was assigned to review. Now, each team member is to write in the space at the bottom of this form the specific student needs evidenced in the data. In the left column, write the specific needs; in the right column, the data that documents the needs. Be as specific as you can; don't state broad, general needs. After this has been done, each person will use their list during the brainstorming exercise when the needs are condensed into one list.

A broad, general need would be, Students need to be better readers.

A specific need would be, Students need to know how to use context clues.

Students Need To (the first word should be a verb)	**Evidence of Need Is Documented In**

After listing the student needs, use the top of the "Checklist for Writing a Study Group Action Plan" to see if you can say "yes" to each of the items.

Checklist for Writing a
Study Group Action Plan

When completing the space on the action plan that is titled **"Data indicate that students need to,"** be sure that each need meets *all* the following requirements:

_____ The need is evidenced in student work. This means that study group members can routinely bring student work to study group meetings and examine the work to determine if students are improving.

_____ The need can be addressed through how teachers teach (instruction).

_____ The need can be addressed through what teachers teach (the curriculum).

_____ Teachers have direct control or influence on eliminating or terminating the need.

When completing the space on the action plan titled "Therefore, in this study, group teachers will," be sure each action listed in that space meets *all* the following requirements. Each action should

_____ Begin with an action word that tells what actions teachers will take when they work together in the group: For example, the following verbs describe what teachers do in study groups:

Investigate	Explore	Search
Demonstrate	Examine	Develop
Practice	Use	Research
Critique	Design	Make
Plan	Construct	Read

_____ Give the reader a visual image of what the study group members will be doing when they sit around a table to work together

_____ Not describe what the teachers will do in their classrooms with their students or what the students will do

_____ Be aligned with the student needs, meaning that all of the actions the study group takes will address the student needs written in the left column on the action plan.

Checklist for the First Three Study Group Meetings

First Meeting

1. Attend to logistics:

- ☐ Choose a group leader for this meeting.

- ☐ Choose a group member to record today's decisions and activities on the log.

- ☐ List the projected dates for each study group meeting.

- ☐ Decide on the beginning and ending times for each meeting.

- ☐ Count the approximate number of hours the group will be meeting until the end of the school year.

- ☐ Decide where the group will meet.

- ☐ Decide on the schedule for the leadership rotation.

- ☐ Decide on the schedule for the rotation of recorder.

2. Decide on group norms:

- ☐ Decide on operating procedures, standards of behavior, or norms for the group. Consider including norms for

  - ■ Consensus

  - ■ No fault

  - ■ Collaboration

  - ■ Responsibility for the work

- ☐ Confirm that the norms are written on the log, the group understands that the norms will be routinely revisited, and the norms may be revised at any time to accommodate the needs of all the members.

3. Begin developing a study group action plan:

- ☐ Review together the action plan form, making sure that everyone understands what is to be written at the top of the plan and in each of the quadrants.

- ☐ If, in the whole-faculty decision-making meeting, each individual wrote an action plan, share the plan each member wrote.

- ☐ Confirm the general category of student needs the group will address.

- ☐ Discuss what the essential question is that will guide the work of the group.

- ☐ Revisit the specific student needs that the faculty identified in the general category the group is addressing.

☐ Decide if there are other specific needs in this category that the faculty did not identify.

☐ Decide if the data the faculty reviewed should be revisited and if the group should review additional data, and if so, what data.

4. Decide what needs to be done at the next meeting:

☐ Establish what needs to be done to finish the action plan at the next meeting, such as

■ Bring data to review

■ Bring a list of ideas for what the group will do when it meets

■ Bring ideas for resources

☐ Confirm the leader, the recorder, the date, the time, and the location of the next meeting.

☐ Confirm that the leader of today's meeting will make copies of the log for all members, the principal, and the clipboard.

Second Meeting

1. Attend to logistics:

☐ Acknowledge the leader and the recorder.

☐ Confirm that the norms will facilitate the work of the group.

☐ Acknowledge and discuss any feedback on the log from the first meeting.

☐ Share reflections and thoughts about the first meeting.

2. Continue developing the study group action plan:

☐ Discuss and review student needs, looking at any data members brought.

☐ Decide on the specific student needs that the group will address in its work. Recorder lists the student needs on the plan.

☐ Share actions that members feel would be appropriate for the group to do when the study group meets.

☐ Decide on the actions to list on the plan. Recorder lists the actions.

☐ Share the resources that members feel would benefit the group's work.

☐ Decide on which resources to list on the plan. Recorder lists resources.

☐ Discuss which of the sources of data the group used to identify the student needs should be used at the end of the group's work to determine the progress students have made.

☐ Decide on the student performance goals for recorder to write on the plan

(continued)

Checklist *(continued)*

3. Take action:

☐ Decide which of the actions listed on the plan will be the first action the group will take.

☐ Decide what each member will need to bring to the next meeting and what each member will need to do prior to the meeting to ensure a productive third meeting, remembering that each member is responsible for the work of the group and the level of productivity.

4. Bring closure to meeting:

☐ Confirm the leader, the recorder, the date, the time, and the location of the next meeting.

☐ Confirm that today's leader will make copies of the action plan and the log for each member, the principal, and the clipboard.

Third Meeting

1. Attend to logistics:

☐ Acknowledge the leader and recorder of today's meeting.

☐ Acknowledge any feedback from the principal on the log from last meeting.

☐ Share reflections about the last meeting.

2. Revisit the study group action plan:

☐ Discuss any new thoughts, perspectives, and suggestions.

☐ Discuss any adjustments needed as a result of feedback from the principal.

3. Take action:

☐ Do what the group decided to do at the last meeting.

4. Bring closure to meeting:

☐ Have at least one member respond to the question on the log, "What major implication does what we did today have on our classroom practice?"

☐ Confirm what actions will be taken at the next meeting.

☐ Confirm what members need to bring and be prepared to do at the next meeting.

☐ Confirm the leader, the recorder, the date, the time, and the location of the next meeting.

☐ Confirm that copies will be made and distributed of today's log.

Checklist for Implementation of the Procedural or Process Guidelines

Date:

Study Group Members:

Directions: As a group, rate your study group using the following symbols:

* = We're there!

+ = We're developing; almost there!

X = We're struggling; still not close!

_____ All group members actively participate (e.g., bring agreed-on items, share classroom experiences related to the action plan, read assignments).

_____ We have established a regular meeting time and begin our meetings on time.

_____ We adhere to our established group norms, which are as follows

_____ We have established a rotation of leadership schedule.

_____ We have an action plan.

_____ We have received feedback on the plan and the plan is posted in a public place.

_____ We complete a log after each meeting and follow procedures for posting it.

_____ We have adequate resources and have contacted or obtained the person or material that will serve as the "expert voice" on the student needs we are addressing.

_____ We maintain an instructional focus during all of our meetings.

_____ We routinely examine student work using a protocol.

_____ We are or we are planning for observing each other's students as a data-collecting strategy.

_____ Our group works well together and shares responsibilities.

_____ We are sharing our work with other study groups.

For those items that the groups rated "developing" or "struggling," what do you need to do to be able to mark those items "We're there!" by the end of the next month? (Use back if necessary.)

Checklist for Substantive Content

School _____ Study Group # _____

Directions: As a study group, reach consensus on the responses to the following statements. Write "Yes" or "No" or "?" in each blank. If the group response is "No" or "?" on three or more of the statements, the group should have a specialist in the study group's content area meet with the study group and help it further clarify its work.

Your content is what you listed on the action plan that you will do when the study group meets and the resources that you listed.

_____ 1. The content requires us to examine student work to see evidence of the impact we are having on the student need we are addressing.

_____ 2. The content is aligned with the student needs that we are addressing; what we are doing will affect the needs our students have.

_____ 3. The content has potential for closing the gap between the current status of student achievement and the desired level of student achievement in the area of student need that we are addressing.

_____ 4. The content requires us to carefully examine our practices.

_____ 5. The content will deepen our understanding of what we teach. *How?*

_____ 6. The content will deepen our knowledge of what we teach. *How?*

_____ 7. The content is not a review or a rehashing of what we already know.

_____ 8. The content will push us beyond the level of skill we currently have in how we present information to students and how students are organized for learning.

_____ 9. The content has been researched and shown to be effective in meeting the student need we are addressing.

_____ 10. The content has resulted in higher levels of student learning in other classrooms and schools.

_____ 11. The content can be supported with resources here at this school.

_____ 12. The content is complex, rigorous, and substantive enough to keep all members of the group engaged and immersed in the learning process.

What Has Changed
as a Result of
Your Study Group Work?

1. Do you have more knowledge and a deeper understanding of subject matter content (e.g., math, science, writing, reading, language development, history)? ＿＿ Y ＿＿ N

2. Do you use materials and resources in new and different ways? ＿＿ Y ＿＿ N

3. Are you modifying and using teaching strategies in your repertoire in new and different ways? ＿＿ Y ＿＿ N

4. Are you now using teaching strategies and practices that you have not used in the classroom? ＿＿ Y ＿＿ N

5. Have you modified how you plan and organize for instruction? ＿＿ Y ＿＿ N

6. Have you modified how you assess student learning, or are you using new assessment practices? ＿＿ Y ＿＿ N

7. Are student needs more prominent? ＿＿ Y ＿＿ N

8. Have teacher-to-teacher relationships changed ＿＿ Y ＿＿ N

9. What changes have you made that have had the greatest impact on students? ＿＿ Y ＿＿ N

The Study Group Takes a Status Check:

Do We See Eye-to-Eye?

Going around the table, one member completes the first sentence (orally). Without discussion, the second member completes the same sentence. Repeat until each member has shared their ending of the first sentence. Was there consensus? Discuss. Follow the same pattern with all or any four of the following items.

1. In our study group, we started

2. The hardest thing for us to do seems to be

3. As far as student changes, I see

4. Our group seems to be making the most progress in

5. Our greatest challenge is

6. One of my disappointments is

7. It's encouraging to see

Using the Study Group Action Plan
to Assess the Work of the Study Group

School _____   Study Group # _____

Instructions: As a study group, discuss the following items. Each member is to have a copy of the latest version of the group's Study Group Action Plan (SGAP). In the spaces provided, one member records the group's consensus response for each item (except for 2b.). *The SGAP is to be stapled to this questionnaire.*

1. Look at the section on the SGAP titled "Students need to"

    a. What data supported the needs listed?

2. Look at the section on the SGAP titled "Therefore, in this study group, teachers will"

    a. What verbs describe the actions that you took?

    b. *On the SGAP,* beside each statement that states what the group will do, write a number (0 to 5) that indicates the degree to which the study group did what the group said it would do. Use "0" to mean *no action* and "5" to mean *to the fullest.*

    c. What implications can you draw from the discussion you had in doing 2b?

    d. Which action(s) on the SGAP had the most impact on how you taught and what you taught?

    e. Do you think the SGAP is descriptive of the work you did when the study group met? _____   If no, why not?

(continued)

Using the Study Group Action Plan *(continued)*

3. Look at the section on the SGAP where the group listed Student Performance Goals and the Data Sources that would provide evidence the goals are met. Below, indicate what was written on the SGAP and what the data now show.

Data Source	Student Performance Goals when SGAP was written	Actual student performance as of today

4. For each student performance goal that was not attained, tell why you think that goal was not met and what you think *the study group* could have done to meet or to have come closer to meeting the goal.

Performance Goal	Why not met? What could SG have done?

5. What student performance goals did you *not* list that you think would have been more realistic or descriptive?

6. Did you use a protocol for looking at student work? _____ If no, why not?

7. Did everyone in the study group bring student work to the study group meetings? If no, why not?

8. What was the most valuable resource that you used? Why?

9. What will you do differently next year in your study group to increase the effectiveness of the study group's work on student performance?

10. What types of assistance or support did you receive from

    The principal

    District-level staff

Reflection on the Process and Examination of the Inquiry

School _____   Study Group # _____

The focus team, which includes the principal, discusses the following questions. In the spaces provided, one member records the responses.

Reflection on the Process	*Examination of the Inquiry*
How do you feel the following facilitated or impeded the work? ■ Time of the meetings ■ Group size ■ Composition of groups ■ Rotation of leadership ■ Group norms ■ Sense of equality ■ Focus of work ■ Communication among groups	What is the evidence that teaching strategies, attitudes, assessment practices, and materials are changing as a result of the study group's work?
What evidence is there that a sense of community is deeper among the staff (e.g., level of trust, how decisions are made, sense of oneness, norms of collaboration)?	What is the evidence that the student performance goals listed on the action plan were reached?

Resource B

Study Group Action Plans

The study group action plans for the 14 focus areas listed and shown on the following pages are composites of action plans from study groups in several schools.

1. English-Language Arts
2. Mathematics Across the Curriculum
3. Research Skills
4. Student Exhibitions, Communication Skills
5. Project-Based Learning
6. Reading, Writing Across the Curriculum
7. Listening and Following Directions
8. Language Arts
9. Learning Strategies
10. Problem Solving
11. Connecting Learning
12. Reading
13. Integrating English and History
14. Writing

The schools from which ideas were pulled are

- Keeseville Elementary School and Au Sable Forks Elementary School, Au Sable Valley Central School District, New York (an ATLAS Communities site)

- Kimball Elementary School and Mercer Middle School, Seattle Public Schools, Seattle, Washington (an ATLAS Communities site)

- Kingsbury Elementary School and Booker T. Washington High School, Memphis City Schools, Memphis, Tennessee (an ATLAS Communities site)

- All the elementary schools in Strawberry Mansion Cluster, School District of Philadelphia, Philadelphia, Pennsylvania (an ATLAS Communities site)

- Schools in Shoreline School District, Seattle, Washington (an ATLAS Communities site)

- Schools in Hamilton County School District, Jasper, Florida (an ATLAS Communities site)

- Hurst Middle School and Destrehan High School, St. Charles Parish Public Schools, Destrehan, Louisiana

- Jackson Elementary School, Weld County School District, Greeley, Colorado

Study Group Action Plan

School _____ Study Group # _____ Date _____

Group Members _____

What is the general category of student needs the group will address?

_____ Reading _____ Writing _____ Math _____ Other: <u>English-Language Arts (ELA)</u>

Essential Question *(Example: How can we teach students to comprehend what they read?)*:
How do we teach so that students' writing is well organized and thoroughly developed and reflects use of effective language?

We **PLAN** according to data indicating that **students need to** ➤	We **ACT** on the students' needs by agreeing that **when the study group meets** we will ➤
- Use details to support an answer. - Develop a story with a beginning, middle and end. - Use a graphic organizer as a prewriting technique (web, clusters) - Write a paragraph with a topic sentence and 3 or 4 supporting sentences. - Understand figurative language. - Use comparisons and similes. - Identify morals of stories. - Restate questions. - Listen to a passage and respond appropriately.	- Review previous years ELAs (weaknesses and strengths.) - Compile resources and organize in a mutual area for all teachers to use. - Research literature-based materials that reinforce ELA skills; share use of the material and how students respond. - Share samples of student work. - Research what other districts are doing to prepare their students. - Develop rubric for (bi) monthly types of writing that correlates with ELA. - Develop a universal graphic organizer. - Create writing centers to use with students. - Establish and share use of early intervention strategies. - Chart impact of the strategies and materials we use on student performance.

We **REFLECT** on our actions and on our use of the **following resources.** ➤	We **ASSESS** our work according to evidence that **student learning has increased and understanding has deepened.**

	STUDENT PERFORMANCE GOALS	DATA SOURCE
- Literature books - Computer programs - ELA Curriculum Guide - Student work - ELA sample tests	100% of the students will fall into 3 or 4 range.	ELA
	All students write a 3-page story that clearly identifies a beginning, middle, and end.	Student Work
	50% of writings have a graphic organizer.	Student Portfolios
	All students can respond appropriately to a passage that is read to them.	Student Work
	100% will improve by 1 whole indicator from fall to spring semesters.	ELP

Study Group Action Plan

School _____ Study Group # _____ Date _____

Group Members _____

What is the general category of student needs the group will address?

_____ Reading _____ Writing _____ Math _____ Other: <u>Measurement</u>_____

Essential Question *(Example: How can we teach students to comprehend what they read?)*:
How can we teach students to develop measurement skills in all content areas?

We **PLAN** according to data indicating that **students need to** ➡	We **ACT** on the students' needs by agreeing that **when the study group meets** we will ➡
1. Convert various measurements. 2. Understand and communicate time. (vocabulary, digital, analog) 3. Estimate area, distance, perimeter, volume. 4. Calculate area, distance, perimeter, volume. 5. Communicate their thinking of math processes (oral and written). 6. Know specific math vocabulary. 7. Read and interpret word problems. 8. Distinguish between essential and nonessential information in word problems.	1. Examine data to assess strengths and weaknesses. 2. Demonstrate effective strategies <u>WE</u> have learned. 3. Develop and modify lessons which incorporate technology. 4. Examine software to determine usefulness and appropriateness for a variety of instructional levels and group sizes. 5. Investigate and study current practices and mathematical concepts in order to deepen our knowledge and understanding of the content. 6. Examine resultant student work.

We **REFLECT** on our actions and on our use of the **following resources.** ➡	We **ASSESS** our work according to evidence that **student learning has increased and understanding has deepened.**

1. NCTM 2. Teacher's manual 3. Internet 4. SDE consultants 5. Courses, workshops, conferences 6. Software 7. InClass material 8. Professional journals	STUDENT PERFORMANCE GOALS	DATA SOURCE
	100% of the students score a minimum of 80%.	End of unit test
	Using age and grade appropriate content, measure correctly in standard units.	Performance observation
	Show a 20% increase in the number of students scoring above the 80th percentile.	ITBS

Study Group Action Plan

School _____ Study Group # _____ Date _____

Group Members _____

What is the general category of student needs the group will address?

_____ Reading _____ Writing __X__ Math _____ Other: _____

Essential Question *(Example: How can we teach students to comprehend what they read?)*:
How can we teach math skills in all content areas?

We **PLAN** according to data indicating that **students need to**	We **ACT** on the students' needs by agreeing that **when the study group meets** we will
- Increase computation skills (basic facts). - Communicate their thinking of math processes (oral and written). - Understand math processes/concepts. - Know strategies to solve problems. - Know specific math vocabulary. - Know how to sequence events. - Connect math processes/concepts to all content areas.	- Design lessons based on Burns' book. - Practice strategies from the book and share outcomes of use. - Examine student work. - Create vocabulary quizzes and context sentences. - Examine and develop rubric. - Examine a variety of sample tests to determine skills necessary for success. - Design activities that are aligned with multiple standards and share results. - Determine how we can feature the role of mathematics in all content areas, including art, music, and physical education. - Plan a math fair that features "across the curriculum" math projects.

We **REFLECT** on our actions and on our use of the **following resources.**

We **ASSESS** our work according to evidence that **student learning has increased and understanding has deepened.**

- District math and other content area specialists
- Marilyn Burns' <u>Writing in Math Class</u>
- WASL sample test
- State and district standards
- Curriculum guides
- Student text books

STUDENT PERFORMANCE GOALS	DATA SOURCE
25% or more students will meet standard in math.	WASL
All students can explain how they solve problems.	Student Work
All students are focused on the task and responding.	Observation Records
90% of students pass.	End of course exam
80% of students will earn C or higher average	Report cards

Study Group Action Plan

School _____ Study Group # _____ Date _____

Group Members _____

What is the general category of student needs the group will address?

_____ Reading _____ Writing _____ Math _____ Other: Research Skills

Essential Question *(Example: How can we teach students to comprehend what they read?)*:

How can we teach students basic research skillswhile helping develop a deeper understanding and appreciation of historical events?

We **PLAN** according to data indicating that **students need to**	We **ACT** on the students' needs by agreeing that **when the study group meets** we will
- Develop deeper understanding of local history. - Take notes. - Develop research skills. - Plan, conduct and preserve oral interviews. - Video and audio tape interviews using various technologies. - Comprehend what they read and hear. - Synthesize information. - Evaluate sources. - Write for purpose/audience. - Distinguish between essential and nonessential information. - Be self-directed. - Understand the importance of preserving historical information.	- Design a survey to determine what students already know about conducting various types of research. - Develop checklist for students to use when conducting research. - Be trained in all aspects of oral interviewing. - Be trained in how to conduct and teach students to conduct video and audio interviews. - Be trained in using digital images and compiling these images on the school's website. - Interview students about their experiences. - Develop resource guide for preparing for, conducting, and reporting on interviews. - Demonstrate how we teach students to do written summaries of their findings. - Role play challenging interview situations and plan for using these simulations in our classrooms.

We **REFLECT** on our actions and on our use of the **following resources.** We **ASSESS** our work according to evidence that **student learning has increased and understanding has deepened.**

	STUDENT PERFORMANCE GOALS	DATA SOURCE
- Books and transcripts. - Local and state museums - University professors - Interview information - Questionnaire responses - Public library - Foxfire books and magazines - Internet	100% show an increase in knowledge and appreciation of topic.	Student surveys
	100% of students use computers and AV equipment proficiently.	Equipment records
	Students connect what they learned to their lives.	Student interviews
	All students conduct at least 5 interviews.	Student work
	Students have approved plan for preserving historical information.	Student work

Study Group Action Plan

School _____ Study Group # _____ Date _____

Group Members _____

What is the general category of student needs the group will address?

___X___ Reading __X__ Writing __X__ Math _____ Other: Student Exhibition _____

Essential Question (*Example: How can we teach students to comprehend what they read?*):

How can we teach students to demonstrate what they know about a specific topic or subject?

We **PLAN** according to data indicating that **students need to** ➤	We **ACT** on the students' needs by agreeing that **when the study group meets** we will ➤
- Communicate what they know in a variety of ways. - Improve clarity and quality of how they exhibit in a public way what they have learned. - Improve presentation skills. - Use a variety of media to express understanding. - Speak clearly and correctly. - Know how to conduct an I-Search. - Synthesize information from a variety of sources. - Demonstrate/apply what they understand. - Select best work for showcase portfolio. - Solve real-life problems through integrating and connecting what they have learned in various subject areas and the real world. - Know how to participate in the design and evaluation of performances of understanding.	- Establish procedures for student exhibitions in our classrooms and an ongoing evaluation system of those procedures. - Demonstrate to each other what we expect from students. - Research and establish our role as exhi. coaches. - Develop and keep updated rubrics for the exhibitions. - Identify specific skills for high quality exhibitions and develop strategies/materials for teaching those skills. - Develop and demonstrate lessons that require students to apply/demonstrate what they know. - Interview students, teachers, and parents and summarize that information. - Identify the Communication Standards that are addressed through student exhibitions.

We **REFLECT** on our actions and on our use of the **following resources.** ➤	We **ASSESS** our work according to evidence that **student learning has increased and understanding has deepened.**

	STUDENT PERFORMANCE GOALS	DATA SOURCE
- I-Search materials - Rubrics other schools and districts use - Teachers from other ATLAS schools - Projects from former exhibitions - Teacher questionnaire - Information from interviews of students and teachers who have participated in past exhibitions	All students conduct an I-Search.	Student work
	Student projects will show - appropriate oral presentation - use of a variety of info. sources - visual attractiveness - application/demonstration of learning - self-evaluation	Student work
	75% attain passing level.	Exhibition rubric
	All students meet or exceed standards.	District standards

Study Group Action Plan

School _____ Study Group # _____ Date _____

Group Members _____

What is the general category of student needs the group will address?

_____ Reading _____ Writing _____ Math _____ Other: Project-Based Learning _____

Essential Question *(Example: How can we teach students to comprehend what they read?)*:
What do students need to know to successfully complete projects that demonstrate their understanding of the selected or assigned content?

We **PLAN** according to data indicating that **students need to**	We **ACT** on the students' needs by agreeing that **when the study group meets** we will
- Explore a subject in depth. - Learn skills for doing high-quality projects. - Practice and demonstrate higher-order thinking skills. - Use time and resources effectively. - Develop skills needed for self-reflection. - Produce finished products. - Use a variety of media. - Understand cause-and-effect relationships. - Know how to evaluate their own work. - Be engaged in quality research-based learning. - Incorporate technology in gathering and evaluating information. - Demonstrate leadership skills while engaging in collaborative activities.	- Identify necessary skills for high-quality projects. - Investigate startegies for teaching skills for project-based learning. - Look at examples of projects. - Design projects that incorporate technology and share how we use these ideas in our classrooms. - Design projects that provide for different learning styles and multiple intelligences. - Develop rubrics for assessing projects. - Reflect on the process, new knowledge, and student responses. - Investigate a range of media that would enhance student projects (i.e., art, music, models, video, photography). - Examine student projects from our classrooms.

We **REFLECT** on our actions and on our use of the **following resources.** We **ASSESS** our work according to evidence that **student learning has increased and understanding has deepened.**

- WASL
- Curriculum framework
- I-Earn projects
- Big Six
- Student work
- Museum
- Science teachers
- Books and articles
- District content specialists

STUDENT PERFORMANCE GOALS	DATA SOURCE
Students will produce a finished product that will - show cause and effect relationship - show evidence of research-based learning - use a variety of media - include self-evaluation	Student work
60% of students read at grade level.	Distrct standards
At least 20% more will meet standards in math, reading, and writing.	WASL
50 more students than last year will enter academic competitions.	Teacher records

Study Group Action Plan

School _____ Study Group # _____ Date _____

Group Members _____

What is the general category of student needs the group will address?

__X__ Reading __X__ Writing __X__ Math _____ Other: Assessment _____

Essential Question *(Example: How can we teach students to comprehend what they read?)*:
How can we assess reading and writing skills in all areas of the curriculum?

We **PLAN** according to data indicating that **students need to**	We **ACT** on the students' needs by agreeing that **when the study group meets** we will
- Improve and enlarge vocabulary. - Improve communication (oral and written) skills. - Increase ability to read a variety of genres. - Apply writing skills in all disciplines. - Organize their writing. - Know how to edit and proofread.	- Analyze ITBS scores and diagnostic scores. - Use data to target needs in designing student instruction and assessment. - Identify a variety of assessment techniques. - Examine student work using assessments we design. - Read, discuss articles and books. - Learn how to use informal reading inventories. - Review the result of the inventories. - Develop vocabulary list, with examples, that can be used in all content areas. - Demonstrate to each other lessons to be taught in our classrooms. - Develop topic sentences to be used in different subject areas. - Share observations of students working in each other's classrooms.

We **REFLECT** on our actions and on our use of the **following resources.**

We **ASSESS** our work according to evidence that **student learning has increased and understanding has deepened.**

Resources	STUDENT PERFORMANCE GOALS	DATA SOURCE
- Rick Stiggin's book on assessment practices - ITBS - Grant Wiggin's articles - Workshop: "Using Multiple Intelligences in Assessment Practices" - Staff members - Computer software - District specialists - <u>Reading for Meaning: Fostering Comprehension in the Middle Grades</u>	95% of 8th graders show at least 1.0 year of growth for one year in school.	ITBS
	75% of students score 2 or higher.	Writing rubric
	75% of students earn C or higher.	Report card
	All students show an increase in vocabulary and appropriate use of vocabulary.	Student portfolios
	All students are focused on the task.	Classroom observation records

Study Group Action Plan

School _____ Study Group # _____ Date _____

Group Members _____

What is the general category of student needs the group will address?
__X__ Reading __X__ Writing __X__ Math _____ Other: Listening _____

Essential Question *(Example: How can we teach students to comprehend what they read?)*:
How can we teach students to listen and follow directions?

We **PLAN** according to data indicating that **students need to**	We **ACT** on the students' needs by agreeing that **when the study group meets** we will

- Demonstrate listening skills and ability to follow oral and written directions so that they can score a 3 or 4 on the ELA and ELP in
  - reading
  - writing
  - listening/speaking
 	
- Understand that listening is a basic skill that must be taught, practiced, and developed.
 	
- Understand that listening is a prerequisite skill for being successful in all curriculum areas and in life.
	- Identify what constitutes good listening.
	- Review materials.
	- Identify resources that teach listening skills.
	- Examine student work.
	- Develop an assessment tool for listening and following directions (a rubric).
	- Practice activities we plan to use with students.
	- Design games that strengthen listening.
	- Compile list of strategies that promote better listening habits based on our use of the strategies.
	- Design assignments that require students to listen to and critique each other.
	- Interview students to determine what facilitates and impedes listening in our classrooms.
	- Discuss possible schoolwide activities to focus on listening and following directions.
	- View videotapes of ourselves giving directions.

We **REFLECT** on our actions and on our use of the **following resources.**

We **ASSESS** our work according to evidence that **student learning has increased and understanding has deepened.**

- DeGaetano's <u>Following Auditory Directions</u>
- <u>Follow Me!</u> (listen and do activities)
- <u>Listen and Learn</u>
- <u>The Direction Book</u> by Weekly Reader
- Musical obstacle course
- Computer software
- Steve & Greg's songs and dances
- <u>Beginning Listening Skills</u>
- <u>Listen Up!</u>
- "Mozart Affects"
- <u>The Complete Handbook of Indoor and Outdoor Games and Activities</u>
- Internet

STUDENT PERFORMANCE GOALS	DATA SOURCE
100% of students will meet promotion criteria.	End of year records
100% will fall into the 3 or 4 range.	ELA
100% will increase Listening score by 1 whole indicator from Fall to Spring or score a 4.	ELP
90% of students will follow directions on daily work.	Student work
100% will score "accomplished" by the end of school year.	Listening rubric

---

Study Group Action Plan

School _____ Study Group # _____ Date _____

Group Members _____

What is the general category of student needs the group will address?

_____ Reading _____ Writing _____ Math _____ Other: Language Arts _____

Essential Question (*Example: How can we teach students to comprehend what they read?*):

How can we teach students to utilize technology to strengthen and deepen language skills?

We **PLAN** according to data indicating that **students need to**	We **ACT** on the students' needs by agreeing that **when the study group meets** we will
- Organize paragraphs. - Write complete sentences. - Use correct spelling. - Proofread finished work. - Read and follow directions. - Improve comprehension.	- Review what we currently do; then, plan for how to use appropriate software that allows us to maximize student data collected for ELP. - Do more in-depth analysis of student data. - Determine what software is appropriate for student writing. - Be trained on appropriate use of software and applications when we meet. - Practice using applications when we meet. - Share our use of the applications. - Keep records (i.e., charts) that indidate student progress based on our work in this group. - Examine student work using a protocol.

We **REFLECT** on our actions and on our use of the **following resources.**

We **ASSESS** our work according to evidence that **student learning has increased and understanding has deepened.**

- NCTRC workshops
- Claris Works for Kids
- Microsoft Works
- Storybook Weaver, Hyperstudio, File Maker Pro
- SDE, Compu Master and NEI workshops
- ELA Curriculum Guides
- Woodrow Wilson Foundation

STUDENT PERFORMANCE GOALS	DATA SOURCE
100% of students proofread and edit their work.	Student writing and portfolios
100% of student will fall into the 3 or 4 range.	ELA
All students use computer at all stages of paper writing.	Computer-assisted student work
All students express desire to increase computer skills.	Student interviews
Students will reach proficiency on at least 1 ELP standard each quarter.	Student portfolios

Study Group Action Plan

School _____ Study Group # _____ Date _____

Group Members _____

What is the general category of student needs the group will address?

_____ Reading _____ Writing _____ Math _____ Other: <u>Learning Strategies</u>

Essential Question *(Example: How can we teach students to comprehend what they read?)*:

How can we use the latest brain research to teach students to use multiple intelligences?

We **PLAN** according to data indicating that **students need to**	We **ACT** on the students' needs by agreeing that **when the study group meets** we will
- Think at higher levels. - Understand how the brain learns and apply this to school and real life experiences. - Experience learning in an environment which is conductive to learning according to the latest research. - Learn the importance of metacognition when solving complex problems.	- Investigate ways to teach students about the brain. - Investigate the impact of emotions and experiences on student learning. - Develop lessons that are congruent with the latest brain research and share how students respond. - Interview students and teachers to determine how and when brain research should be discussed with students. - Examine student work in order to determine the impact of brain based lessons. - Examine a variety of sample tests to determine skills necessary for success. - Identify specific strategies that increase learning and long-term memory and plan lessons that incorporate those strategies. - Demonstrate the strategies to each other. - Chart the effect of the strategies on students.

We **REFLECT** on our actions and on our use of the **following resources.**   We **ASSESS** our work according to evidence that **student learning has increased and understanding has deepened.**

- Books and articles on the latest brain research
- Video on brain research
- Invited experts and district leaders and teachers who have attended conferences and workshops
- Student work and its implications
- Conferences and workshops that we can attend as a study group

STUDENT PERFORMANCE GOALS	DATA SOURCE
Students interpolate and extrapolate from data appropriately.	Student work
Students evaluate and predict results of real or fictional events.	Student work
Students show an increase in overall scores.	ACT scores
Students show an increase in overall scores.	GEE scores
At least 90% indicate increased satisfaction with school and personal work.	Student interviews

Study Group Action Plan

School _____ Study Group # _____ Date _____

Group Members _____

What is the general category of student needs the group will address?

_____ Reading _____ Writing _____ Math _____ Other: <u>Problem solving</u> _____

Essential Question *(Example: How can we teach students to comprehend what they read?)*:

How can we help students to effectively use problem-solving skills and strategies?

We **PLAN** according to data indicating that **students need to**	We **ACT** on the students' needs by agreeing that **when the study group meets** we will
- Use a variety of strategies to solve complex problems. - Persist in their efforts even when problems are hard. - Verify that their solutions actually answer the question asked. - Present their solutions clearly, correctly, and completely.	- Research problem-solving strategies. - Examine resources for good problems and strategies. - Develop a list of the most useful problem-solving strategies, with clear examples and explanations of each from our text book and share their use. - Develop an easy to use, student-friendly rubric for grading problem solving. - Use the rubric to assess student work. - Evaluate the effectiveness of the rubric by sharing assessments of student work. - Interview students about how the strategies and rubric helped or didn't help to improve in problem solving. - Collect problem-solving strategies used in all disciplines. - Create a blended problem-solving strategies list for all disciplines based on common language.

We **REFLECT** on our actions and on our use of the **following resources.**	We **ASSESS** our work according to evidence that **student learning has increased and understanding has deepened.**

	STUDENT PERFORMANCE GOALS	DATA SOURCE
- District content area specialists - Books and articles from NCTM and other publishers - Student text books - Teachers' editions of text books - Conferences, workshops, courses - Curriculum frameworks and guides	Interviews indicate 90% of students are more confident of their problem-solving skills.	Student interviews
	90% use more than one strategy to solve a problem.	Student work
	90% apply problem-solving skills in nonmath courses.	Student questionnaire
	90% are presenting solutions clearly, completely, and correctly.	Portfolios
	More students than last year take ACT and pass.	ACT scores

Study Group Action Plan

School _____ Study Group # _____ Date _____

Group Members _____

What is the general category of student needs the group will address?

_____ Reading _____ Writing _____ Math _____ Other: _Connecting/Intergrating Learning_

Essential Question (*Example: How can we teach students to comprehend what they read?*):
How can we help students to see that all learning is connected?

We **PLAN** according to data indicating that **students need to**	We **ACT** on the students' needs by agreeing that **when the study group meets** we will
- Make connections between the core concepts in their various classes. - Use skills learned in one class in other classes. - Understand that what they are learning is important outside the classroom. - Apply skills learned in school to problems or situations outside school.	- Create a matrix of core learnings in one or more courses. - Identify common skills that cross over between courses taken by the same students. - Study the principles of applied learning and share how we apply those principles in our classrooms. - Develop activities we will teach that promote students making connections. - Research careers tied to course content and develop ways for our students to explore options. - Develop a teacher survey to determine most logical links. - Develop strategy for shadowing several students and sharing our observations. - Interview students. - Provide opportunities for students to apply their knowledge through different media.

We **REFLECT** on our actions and on our use of the **following resources.** We **ASSESS** our work according to evidence that **student learning has increased and understanding has deepened.**

- Course descriptions
- District content area specialists
- Guidance counselors
- Community resource people
- Students: current and graduates
- Books and articles on applied learning
- Postgraduate admission officers

STUDENT PERFORMANCE GOALS	DATA SOURCE
25% of students make A's or B's.	Student work
Students demonstrate course objective by using a vatiety of media: art, models, prose, poetry, projects.	Student work
75% of graduates attend post secondary schools.	Postgraduate records
All students indicate that they are making more deliberate connections.	Student questionaire
90% of students in a classroom are on task.	Observations of students

---

Study Group Action Plan

School _____ Study Group # _____ Date _____

Group Members _____

What is the general category of student needs the group will address?

_____ Reading _____ Writing _____ Math _____ Other: <u>Reading</u>

Essential Question *(Example: How can we teach students to comprehend what they read?)*:

How can we teach students to be successful readers?

We **PLAN** according to data indicating that **students need to**	We **ACT** on the students' needs by agreeing that **when the study group meets** we will
- Demonstrate ability to decode new words by using structural and phonetic clues. - Increase vocabulary and sight words as well as understanding of word meaning. - Apply reading skills in the content areas and real-world experiences. - Read to increase comprehension using multiple strategies. - Increase the amount of reading for pleasure or independent reading.	- Clarify what skills are taught at identified reading skill levels. - Identify the vocabulary and word meanings to be taught in the content areas. - Investigate a variety of materials that enhance life applications of reading. - Research, share, and model strategies for teaching reading. - Share our private and individual analysis of video-taped lessons we teach. - Develop a floorwide individual incentive reading program, such as Book-It. - Be trained in effective strategies. - Share our observations of how students respond to the lessons we design together when we observe in each other's classes.

We **REFLECT** on our actions and on our use of the **following resources.**	We **ASSESS** our work according to evidence that **student learning has increased and understanding has deepened.**	
- Manuals and other materials for Book-It and Accelerated Reader - "How To" books and articles and activities on -Spelling -Vocabulary -Phonetic and structural analysis skills - Resource for motivating readers - Supplementary language arts material in correlation with students' skills - Computer software - Reading specialists at district and university level	**STUDENT PERFORMANCE GOALS**	**DATA SOURCE**
	100% of students use structural and phonetic clues to decode words.	Student work
	All students meet criteria for promotion.	End-of-year records
	75% of students are at or above their grade level placement.	Informational reading inventory
	All read at least 3 books per month and pass comprehension check.	Reading records
	50% or more of students meet all reading standards for grade level.	Memphis standards

Study Group Action Plan

School _____ Study Group # _____ Date _____

Group Members _____

What is the general category of student needs the group will address?

_____ Reading _____ Writing _____ Math _____ Other: <u>Intergrating History and English</u>

Essential Question (*Example: How can we teach students to comprehend what they read?*):

How can we teach students to see the interrelatedness of historical events and the English language?

We **PLAN** according to data indicating that **students need to**	We **ACT** on the students' needs by agreeing that **when the study group meets** we will
- Make connections between literature and historical time periods. - Improve and increase vocabulary. - Meet state standards in both areas. - Learn to communicate more effectively in a variety of settings. - Recognize the common goals and skills in subject areas.	- Design and teach to each other lessons that integrate the two curriculums. - Share and demonstrate how the lessons are related to state standards. - Reflect on new knowledge, experiences, and student responses. - Interview students to give us feedback. - Design activities that are aligned with multiple standards and share the outcomes of those activities. - Design activities that provide students with opportunities to be successful and share how students demonstrated success. - Plan for observing in each other's classrooms those lessons we design together. - Share what we learn about students during those observations.

We **REFLECT** on our actions and on our use of the **following resources.** ➡ We **ASSESS** our work according to evidence that **student learning has increased and understanding has deepened.**

- Course descriptions
- District content area specialists
- Community resource people
- Cross-curriculum workshops
- Other schools' integrated curriculum (successes and failures)
- Computer software
- University personnel
- State Department of Education personnel

STUDENT PERFORMANCE GOALS	DATA SOURCE
80% of students earn A's or B's.	Student work
90% of students will pass both History and Literature exams covering integrated study.	Improved scores
90% of students can explain and give examples of integrated lessons.	New integrated curriculum
90% of students score 2.0 or higher.	Florida Writes scores
Students develop at least one integrated project each reporting period.	Student work

Study Group Action Plan

School _____ Study Group # _____ Date _____

Group Members _____

What is the general category of student needs the group will address?

_____ Reading _____ Writing _____ Math _____ Other: Writing_____

Essential Question (*Example: How can we teach students to comprehend what they read?*)**:**

How can we help students become better writers?

We **PLAN** according to data indicating that **students need to** ➡	We **ACT** on the students' needs by agreeing that **when the study group meets** we will ➡
- Become better writers. - Organize writing into a flowing progression of ideas. - Construct passages with logical sequences. - Create fluent transitions with their ideas. - Identify and evaluate words based on variety and creativity. - Increase knowledge and apply spelling patterns. - Write a nonfiction summary with a topic, main idea, and supporting details. - Express in a variety of ways a nonfiction summary with a topic, main idea, and supporting details.	- Develop plans and strategies to have students write daily, using DOL, journal, creative writing, Writer's Workshop. - Score, using district rubric, the schoolwide monthly practice writing assessments and chart on a grid the monthly progress of each of our classes, as per all study groups. - Explore strategies that help students plan writing. - Plan and share lessons that we teach that help students develop sequential writing, based on the writing rubric. - Create a dictionary of terms. - Design questions for students to use in self and peer editing. - Collect data and search for common spelling errors on monthly writing assessments. - Investigate strategies to teach main idea, supporting details, and summarizing nonfiction text.

We **REFLECT** on our actions and on our use of the **following resources.** ➡ We **ASSESS** our work according to evidence that **student learning has increased and understanding has deepened.**

Resources	STUDENT PERFORMANCE GOALS	DATA SOURCE
- Houghton Mifflin - Read-Write Connection (Maureen Auman) - Student work and its implications - Writer's Express - Scholastic publications and services - List of district frequency words - Write Source 2000 - Pat Hagerty's Writing Process - Write On - Teaching Young Chidren to Draw - Intended Learnings - Books Don't Have To Be Flat, by Kathy Pike - Faculty workshops - Literature books	Students will write a nonfiction summary with appropriate topic, main idea, and supporting details.	Student work
	50% of all students will move to proficiency level.	State standards (CSAP)
	50% of all students will move to proficiency level.	District writing assessment
	Student will use self and peer editing.	Student work

Resource C

Study Group Logs

The Logs From Keeseville Elementary School

- Keeseville Elementary School is one of two elementary schools in Au Sable Valley Central School District. The district is located in the northeast corner of New York state about 50 miles south of the Canadian border. The district also has a middle school and a high school.

- The district is an ATLAS Communities site and the four schools in the district form a PreK-12th grade pathway. As do all ATLAS schools, the four schools have WFSGs in place. The 1999-2000 school year was the first year of implementation of the ATLAS Communities design, which includes WFSGs.

- Keeseville Elementary had seven study groups. The principal gave all the study groups verbal feedback and support through periodic memos. These memos are part of the story.

- The logs were rewritten by one person for consistency. The logs were not written for public view or for publishing purposes. The logs were written for study groups members by the members. Readers will naturally want more information and have questions as outside or onlooking observers. However, what is written was sufficient and appropriate for the members as they made notes that were relevant to them and to their work.

- The districtwide improvement goals were in the areas of Language Arts and Mathematics. All the study groups in the two elementary schools, the middle school, and the high school focused on the district goals of improving instruction and student learning in language arts and mathematics.

- The study group logs that follow were for a study group that chose to address Language Arts and Mathematics through how students listen and follow directions. "Listening" is a skill that is assessed on the New York State English Language Arts Assessment that is administered annually beginning in kindergarten. The logs are reprinted by permission from Keeseville Elementary School.

- Many of the artifacts from the study group, such as the student work the study group examined, cannot be included here. Such artifacts would add more pages to this book than is practical for publishing purposes.

Study Group Action Plan

School _Keeseville_   Study Group # _2_   Date _10-5_

Group Members _Sue, Barb, Jen, Sheree, Diana, Cheryl_

What is the general category of student needs the group will address?

_____ Reading _____ Writing _____ Math _____ Other: _Listening_

Essential Question (*Example: How can we teach students to comprehend what they read?*):
What listening skills do we need to teach students to increase their performance in reading and math?

We **PLAN** according to data indicating that **students need to** ➤	We **ACT** on the students' needs by agreeing that **when the study group meets we will** ➤

- Demonstrate listening skills and ability to follow written + oral directions so they can score a 3 or 4 on the ELA and ELP in
    > reading
    > writing
    > listening
	- Identify what constitutes good listening.
	 - Develop and share use of a listening rubric.
	 - Demonstrate to each other activities we will use with our students
	 - Examine student work
	 - Develop activities that require students to respond appropriately to stories read to them

We **REFLECT** on the results of our actions and on our use of the following resources. ➤

We **ASSESS** our work according to evidence that **student learning has increased and understanding has deepened.**

- ELA + ELP
- Listen and Learn
- Computer software
- Internet
- Listen Up!
- Following Auditory Directions

STUDENT PERFORMANCE GOALS	DATA SOURCE
100% will fall into the 3 or 4 range	ELA
100% will increase listening score by 1 whole indicator from Fall to Spring	ELP
At least 98% will follow directions on daily work	Student work
100% can take notes on what is read to them	Student work

STUDY GROUP LOG

School _Keeseville_ Log# _1_ Date _9-27_

Group Name _Listening & Following Directions_ Today's Leader _Jen_

Members Present _Sue, Barb, Jen, Sheree, Diana, Cheryl_

Members Absent _Roles_ Pre-K teacher, Music teacher, K teacher, 3rd teacher, Sp. Ed. teaching assistant, 1st gr. teaching assistant

What happened Today? Brief summary of discussion and activities.		
Established weekly rotation of leaders:	Jen	
Shared ideas for Action Plan	Sue	will
Established group norms:	Diana	change
- Be prompt	Barb	if needed
- Be prepared	Sheree	
- Stay focused	Cheryl	
- Follow leadership schedule		
- Let someone in group know if you will be absent		

Classroom Application: What are students learning and doing as a result of what you are learning and doing

We spent most of the hour discussing the connection between listening and successfully completing assignments in all curriculum areas. If students do not listen and follow the written or oral directions, low scores will be the result.
 Our focus will be "listening" tied to reading, writing, and math assignments.

Did you look at student work? _No_

General comments, such as: what you are ready to share, IC/Reps meeting.	What concerns or questions do you have For school leaders?

Next Meeting (agenda items, work to prepare) _We will bring ideas for the action plan._

Date _10-5_ Time _2:30_ Leader _Sue_ Location _library_

STUDY GROUP LOG

School *Keesville*   Log# *2*   Date *10-5*

Group Name *Listening & Following Dir.*   Today's Leader *Sue*

Members Present   *all*

Members Absent   *none*

What happened Today? Brief summary of discussion and activities.

We developed our action plan – will review it next week after we've had time to reflect on our decisions.

We are going to bring to the next meeting any materials we have on listening.

Classroom Application: What are students learning and doing as a result of what you are learning and doing

We are going to try to determine what percentage of the work students do is unacceptable work because directions were not followed.

Did you look at student work? *No*

General comments, such as: what you are ready to share, IC/Reps meeting.	What concerns or questions do you have For school leaders?
	We do not know at this time all of the materials we may use. Action plan only has those listed that we currently know.

Next Meeting (agenda items, work to prepare) *Bring materials and examples of student work that is done from oral directions.*

Date *10-19*   Time *2:30*   Leader *Diana*   Location *library*

STUDY GROUP LOG

School _Keesville_ Log# _3_ Date _10-19_

Group Name _Listening & Following Dir._ Today's Leader _Diana_

Members Present _all_

Members Absent _____

What happened Today? Brief summary of discussion and activities.

- We revisited our plan.
- Shared strategies that work for us.
- Reviewed materials that Barb, Sheree, & Diane brought.
- Discussed difference between listening and hearing.
- Shared ideas on what is done in classrooms to get students' attention so they are ready to listen.
- Talked about ways to better prepare children at assemblies to be ready to listen.
- Looked at student work — a math activity that required students to listen to patterns.

Classroom Application: What are students learning and doing as a result of what you are learning and doing

We are all more observant, — and are being more deliberate and conscious of how we give directions to students. We were surprised by the # of students that require individual assistance due to not listening. This week we will do more with giving auditory directions in language development activities.

Did you look at student work? _Yes_

General comments, such as: what you are ready to share, IC/Reps meeting.	What concerns or questions do you have For school leaders?

Next Meeting (agenda items, work to prepare) _Review assembly ideas; bring materials to share_

Date _10-25_ Time _2:30_ Leader _Barb_ Location _library_

STUDY GROUP LOG

School __Keeseville__   Log# __4__   Date __10-25__

Group Name __Listening and Following Dir.__ Today's Leader __Barb__

Members Present __all__

Members Absent _____

What happened Today? Brief summary of discussion and activities.

We discussed specific ways to better prepare children to be ready to listen at assemblies. We discussed having K-2 and the two special ed classes use carpet samples (13X18) to sit on. This would help organize the rows and define each child's space. We discussed activities for students to do as they enter gym to keep them focused and ready to listen.*

We looked at material Sue brought, "Following Auditory Directions" by Jean Gillian De Gaetano

---

Classroom Application: What are students learning and doing as a result of what you are learning and doing

Sue has begun to use a rainstick to tell her students when its time to listen and focus.

Jen has started to use the idea that was shared last week - having her class be quiet enough to hear sounds of the heater (environmental sounds)

Diana is using the Beginning Listening Skills Activities with success! She brought an example with her today.

Did you look at student work? __Yes__

General comments, such as: what you are ready to share, IC/Reps meeting.	What concerns or questions do you have For school leaders?
Jen will attend IC meeting — Action Plans will be reviewed.	*We would like to meet with Pat about our assembly ideas — we think being <u>ready to listen</u> is an important 1st step.

Next Meeting (agenda items, work to prepare) __Jen will bring listening rubric from the web.__

Date __11-2__   Time __2:30__   Leader __Sheree__   Location __library__

STUDY GROUP LOG

School _Keeseville_ Log# _5_ Date _11-2_

Group Name _Listening & Following Dir._ Today's Leader _Sheree_

Members Present _all_

Members Absent _____

What happened Today? Brief summary of discussion and activities.

We reviewed the listening rubric Jen found - we will use it this next week.

Each of us shared an activity we will use to develop listening and following direction skills.

We discussed developing listening skills through music.

Sheree brought in a list of listening skills found on the internet and "The Direction Book" from Weekly Reader that help students learn, practice, & improve following directions.

Classroom Application: What are students learning and doing as a result of what you are learning and doing

Sue is continuing to have success with rainstick

Barb is using environmental sounds to get her music classes quiet and ready to listen (music is a content area!)

Sheree tried activity from book Sue brought last week that she used when reviewing place value in math (see attached)

Did you look at student work? Yes - Sheree

General comments, such as: what you are ready to share, IC/Reps meeting.	What concerns or questions do you have For school leaders?
Jen shared what the other study groups are doing - the reps at the IC meeting want our listening rubric when we get it done.	

Next Meeting (agenda items, work to prepare) _Bring student work from Activity we discussed today._

Date _11-9_ Time _2:30_ Leader _Sue_ Location _library_

STUDY GROUP LOG

School _Keesville_   Log# _6_   Date _11-9_

Group Name _Listening & Following Dir_ Today's Leader _Sue_

Members Present _all_

Members Absent _____

What happened Today? Brief summary of discussion and activities.

Barb shared the student work from students who listened to music and drew what they thought of while listening. The students found it difficult to write what they think and feel. Most found it easier to draw. Sheree suggested that the students be told to write three sentences before they can draw. We discussed the game "Listen Up". We will all try it this next week. Jen brought "Listen Up!" activities.

Classroom Application: What are students learning and doing as a result of what you are learning and doing

Barb used the "SOL LA MI" game having students listen carefully to what she sang. Jen found it works best when she uses "Be My Echo" and does things step by step. Sheree has been giving directions one at a time until everyone does what she instructed — this resulted in all her students demonstrating that they could write three sentences properly sequenced.

Did you look at student work? _Yes_

General comments, such as: what you are ready to share, IC/Reps meeting.	What concerns or questions do you have For school leaders?
We need a time schedule for our meetings so we can get to all we want to do.	

Next Meeting (agenda items, work to prepare) _Student work - bring activities from "Listen Up!" Do a rubric._

Date _11-16_   Time _2:30_   Leader _Jen_   Location _library_

STUDY GROUP LOG

School _Keeseville_ Log# _7_ Date _11-16_

Group Name _Listening & Following Dir._ Today's Leader _Jen_

Members Present _____

Members Absent _Cheryl_

What happened Today? Brief summary of discussion and activities.
Sheree shared the Following Directions sheet that she completed with her 3rd graders. We looked at the student work from the math assignment and saw that many of them had trouble following directions. Jen brought 3 articles from the internet about listening - we will read for next meeting, hoping the articles will help us create our own rubric. We discussed inviting a speaker from Speech Dept. at Plattsburg State.

Classroom Application: What are students learning and doing as a result of what you are learning and doing
Sheree's work that we examined (identifying parts of a whole) Diana is using the Echo Game. Sue finds that singing directions helps her children calm down and follow directions. Barb and Jen are continuing their use of the listening games and activities.

Note: Barb will attend IC meeting. Carlene Murphy will be there.

Did you look at student work? _Yes_

General comments, such as: what you are ready to share, IC/Reps meeting.	What concerns or questions do you have For school leaders?
Our agenda for each meeting will be: 1st 20 min - discuss classroom application / student work 2nd 20 min - Share new information and material 3rd 20 min - Work on and practice classroom activities NOTE: Looking at student work may replace any / all other	

Next Meeting (agenda items, work to prepare) _Read 3 articles and be ready to discuss_

Date _11-16_ Time _2:30_ Leader _Cheryl_ Location _library_

STUDY GROUP LOG

School _Keeseville_ Log# _8_ Date _12-7_

Group Name _Listening & Following Dir._ Today's Leader _Cheryl_

Members Present _all_

Members Absent _____

What happened Today? Brief summary of discussion and activities.

*Barb shared what she learned at the IC meeting. We shared the key points in the articles - one article confirmed what we know: not following directions (auditory and written) is a major factor in low scores on teacher tests and state tests - also ITBS and other standardized tests. Barb shared "Mozart Affects" from a book she is reading that shows that music catches a child's attention and influences mood.

Classroom Application: What are students learning and doing as a result of what you are learning and doing

Barb is using ideas from the article "Mozart Affects."
Diana shared what she is doing with 2 step directions.
Cheryl is using clapping and snapping patterns to get classes' attention.

Did you look at student work? _No_

General comments, such as: what you are ready to share, IC/Reps meeting.	What concerns or questions do you have For school leaders?
We'll put copies of articles in all teachers' boxes. (Carlene complimented us on our logs at IC meeting!)	Is there any procedure we need to follow to invite speaker to our study group?

Next Meeting (agenda items, work to prepare) _Bring student work_

Date _12-14_ Time _2:30_ Leader _Sheree_ Location _library_

STUDY GROUP LOG

School _Keeseville_ Log# _9_ Date _12-14_

Group Name _Listening & Following_ Today's Leader _Sheree_

Members Present _Directions_

Members Absent _Sue_

What happened Today? Brief summary of discussion and activities.

Barb is using a listening and following directions game called "Bop It". Students are required to listen, follow directions, and react in short amounts of time. We looked through a book Barb brought, The Complete Handbook of Indoor and Outdoor Games and Activities for Young Children.

Worked on our rubric.

We continue to use & discuss the rubric Jen got from internet - and as we develop one of our own.

Classroom Application: What are students learning and doing as a result of what you are learning and doing

Jen brought the student work from an activity she used with her kindergarteners. She gave the directions once and asked the students to do the best they could. This was a difficult task! It was exciting for us to see how well they did.

Sheree has begun writing recipe directions.

Jen is using Letter People songs.

Diana's class made number books that required students to follow directions.

Did you look at student work? _Yes_

General comments, such as: what you are ready to share, IC/Reps meeting.	What concerns or questions do you have For school leaders?
We have almost completed the first part of our listening rubric.	We will put the student work we use in our notebooks. If you want to see it, any of us can get you a copy. We don't think putting it on the clip board is appropriate

Next Meeting (agenda items, work to prepare) _We need to finish rubric. Bring any materials you can find._

Date _1-3_ Time _2:30_ Leader _Sue_ Location _library_

STUDY GROUP LOG

School *Keeseville*   Log# *10*   Date *12-21*

Group Name *Listening and Following Dir.*   Today's Leader *Sue*

Members Present _____

Members Absent *Diana*_____

What happened today? Brief summary of discussion and activities.

We reviewed the book *Listen and Learn* (K-3). Stories in the book are read aloud. There are questions and activities to go with each story. (main idea & sequence skills) We continued to work on our listening rubric.

We reviewed our action plan. Made no adjustments. We think we are doing what we need to do to address the needs we identified. Also reviewed our norms.

Classroom Application: What are students learning and doing as a result of what you are learning and doing

Sue has been playing the Dreidel game with her class. Following directions is necessary to play.
Jen played color/shape Bingo. Listening and following directions are really necessary.
Sheree is writing flt charts. "Sequence of how things are done" is stressed and students illustrate each step. She brought one that isn't finished to show us. "Sequence" is on the ELA and covers several standards: Language Arts and math.

Did you look at student work? *Yes*

General comments, such as: what you are ready to share, IC/Reps meeting.	What concerns or questions do you have for school leaders or what do you what them to know?
→	Do you want us to share the part of the rubric that we've done? It is attached.

Next Meeting (agenda items, work to prepare) *Review and critique the part of the rubric that is done. Collect other rubrics.*

Date *1-4-2000* Time *2:30* Leader *Diana* Location *library*

> **AuSable Valley Central School District**
> Keeseville Elementary School
> Patricia W. Atkinson, Principal
> 1825 Route 22
> Keeseville, New York 12944
> 518-834-2839

TO: WFSG / Listening Skills

FR: Pat Atkinson

RE: Current Logs

DT: December 29, 1999

I wanted to share some thoughts and comments with you regarding your current logs:

> I think your logs show that **all of the individuals in your groups are actively participating and working to help the group realize its objectives.**

> I like the way **members** of the group **bring in materials and class experiences to share.**

> I was really pleased to see that you have started bringing student work to your group. I hope Jen can lead you all through the protocol for evaluating student work (Wows & Wonders). **Student performance** will be an important indicator of the success of your group.

> It is reaching the mid-year mark. Your group may want to concentrate on how you will evaluate the success of the group. (**Assessment**).

 Keep up the good work!

STUDY GROUP LOG   (C. Murphy's WFSG Model)

School _Keeseville_   Log# _11_   Date _1-4-2000_
Group Name _Listening and Following Dir._ Today's Leader _Diana_
Members Present _all_
Members Absent _____

What happened today? Brief summary of discussion and activities.

*Barb brought a worksheet about punctuation
and symbols used for punctuation. She
explained how instruments or any sounds
can be used for punctuation. Diana shared
the book, On First Reading for ages 4-7. We
discussed the feedback memo from Pat.
Distributed a protocol we will review for next meeting.
We completed in "Comments" section on the
Study Group Feedback Report.*

Classroom Application: What are students learning and doing as a result of what you are learning and doing

*Sheree used book Jen shared, Listen and
Learn. She said her class was very
attentive and was able to answer
all the questions correctly. The students
are very anxious to go on to more
stories.*

Did you look at student work? _No_

General comments, such as: what you are ready to share, IC/Reps meeting.	What concerns or questions do you have for school leaders or what do you what them to know?
Jen learned how to use a protocol, "WOWS and WONDERS", for looking at student work at the IC meeting just before the holidays.	

Next Meeting (agenda items, work to prepare) _Review the protocol for looking_
at student work

Date _1-11_ Time _2:30_ Leader _Barb_ Location _library_

Study Group Feedback Report

School *Keesville Elem.*   Observer/Participant *WFSG*

Study Group **2**   Date *Jan 4 2000*   Time *2:50 p.m.*

Summary of Study Group Discussion:
(attach agenda if available)

Check all evidence observed:

✓   The study group had established group norms. Group norms were posted.

✓   Group norms were adhered to by group members.

✓   Study group roles were used effectively (i.e., facilitator, recorder, process observer, timekeeper)

___   Student work was shared using a structured protocol.

✓   Classroom implications were discussed (next steps, instructional strategies, assessment, etc.)

✓   An agenda was provided for the meeting.

✓   The study group discussion reflected the goal of the action plan.

Suggestions for Study Group:

___ Use an agenda to guide meetings   ___ Maintain an instructional focus

___ Designate times for each agenda item   *   Receive additional training in study group process

___ Use group roles for study groups   **   Use the protocol when looking at student work

___ Develop norms and post norms   ***   Share with other study groups

___ Have several members bring student   **** Receive training in the content of the
     work to be discussed   study group

___ Complete a log after each meeting   ___ Revise action plan

___ Maintain and update the study group
     portfolio regularly

Comments:

*   As a group, we could accomplish this, if we are given the W.F.S.G. training guide

**   We were given copies of protocal to read and plan to dedicate one meeting on reviewing them to make sure we follow proper procedures.

***   We plan to invite a representative from other study groups to exchange ideas.

****   We have discussed bringing in a guest speaker that could give some new and fresh ideas.

STUDY GROUP LOG

School _Keesville_ Log# _12_ Date _1-11-00_
Group Name or #_Listening & Following Dir._ Today's Leader _Barb_
Members Present _all_
Members Absent _____

What happened today? Brief summary of discussion and activities. Keep artifacts in notebook.

Jen led us through using the "Wows and Wonders" protocol. She had made copies of the attached poem. It was fun! In the debriefing we said
- one person did not do all the talking
- it gives the teacher new insights
- supports/encourages reflection
- wouldn't matter about grade or content

Classroom Application: What are students learning and achieving as a result of what you are learning and doing?

We spent all the time on the protocol. Cheryl shared an idea for working with rhyming words. Sheri did share that her students are writing stories that require listening to the sequence of events in stories that she reads to them. Jen's students are listening to and acting out the theme songs for the letter people - they have to remember the order and the movement.

Did you examine student work today? _Yes_ Who brought? _Jen_

General comments, such as: what you are ready to share, IC/Reps meeting.	What concerns or questions do you have for leaders or what do you want them to know?
Cheryl will attend IC meeting on Jan. 24	We want to meet with a study group at Ausable Forks that is also focusing on listening.

Next Meeting (agenda items, work to prepare) _Share our use of Cheryl's ideas for working with rhyming words._
Date _1-18_ Time _2:30_ Leader _Cheryl_ Location _library_

AuSable Valley Central School District
Keeseville Elementary School
Patricia W. Atkinson, Principal
1825 Route 22
Keeseville, New York 12944
518-834-2839

TO: WFSG / **Listening/Following Directions**

FR: Pat Atkinson

RE: Current log

DT: January 14, 2000

I really liked the work you did on **the listening rubrics!** You seemed to have zeroed in on cues that we use for feedback when we assess whether or not children are listening to us. I think you should share the rubric with the greater faculty at large. **I think everyone could benefit from your work.**

I also thought you did a great job of describing levels of listeners. Your descriptors parallel the ELP assessment, and so they are even more meaningful and useful to classroom teachers.

It's great to see that you are using student work in your group. The success of any group is shown through careful examination of what students are doing as a result of your efforts.

I would like to have a building-wide Instructional Council Meeting on January 24, 2000, at 2:30 in my office. If you could, please send a representative to this meeting who is prepared to share what your group has been doing...**the Wows & the Wonders!** This would also be a good time to present questions that might be troubling your group.

Carlene Murphy will be back at AVCS February 10 & 11. I know she is planning on holding **a district -wide instructional council meeting from 3:00 - 5:00 on the 10th.** Please select a member of your group to attend this meeting. ery Attendance is very important because **your representative will share what Carlene brings to the council with your group.**

I think you are doing great things!

STUDY GROUP LOG

(C. Murphy's WFSG Model)

School _Keeseville_ Log# _13_ Date _1-25_

Group Name _Listening + Following Dir_ Today's Leader _Cheryl_

Members Present _____

Members Absent _Diane_

What happened today? Brief summary of discussion and activities.

2 teachers from the Listening Study Group at AuSable Forks Elem. Sch. met with us. We exchanged ideas and information. We finished the rubric!
Barb led us in an activity she does with the students. She gave directions on folding and cutting paper. We had 3 different results from the same directions. We learned that for listening to improve we should ask questions.

Classroom Application: What are students learning and doing as a result of what you are learning and doing

Barb distributed three items she got off the web. One is the activity we did today (the Listening Assessment Experience)

The activity put us in the students' place and that was really helpful!

Sheree shared how she had used Cheryl's idea (rhyming words).

Did you look at student work? _No_

General comments, such as: what you are ready to share, IC/Reps meeting.	What concerns or questions do you have for school leaders or what do you what them to know?
Cheryl shared how we are looking at student work at the meeting with Pat yesterday	We would like to go to AuSable Forks and meet with the group that had reps meet with us today.

Next Meeting (agenda items, work to prepare) _Encourage students to ask questions if they don't understand directions._

Date _2-1_ Time _2:30_ Leader _Jen_ Location _library_

Listening Skills Rubric

Listener	Poor	Fair	Satisfactory	Excellent
Focuses attention on the speaker				
Communicates appropriately to speaker through body language and other nonverbal responses				
Communicates appropriately to speaker through verbal responses				

	Emerging	Developing	Proficient	Accomplished
After a Listening Activity, a student	Can answer nonsubjective factual questions, such as the names of the characters, the stated setting of the activity, the subject matter of the activity. Examples: 5 W's	Can summarize the listening activity in an organized fashion with a beginning, middle, end.	Can summarize the listening activity in sequential order, including such things as details, dialogue, and characterization.	Demonstrates the ability to retell the listening activity using figurative language and making it relevant to the listener.

STUDY GROUP LOG

(C. Murphy's WFSG Model)

School _Keesville_   Log# _14_   Date _2-1_

Group Name _Listening + Following Dir._   Today's Leader _Jen_

Members Present _all_

Members Absent _____

What happened today? Brief summary of discussion and activities.

We reviewed our rubric and discussed how to determine where various students would be placed on the rubric. We are very pleased with our work and will use it!
Barb shared excerpts from a book of Movements.

Classroom Application: What are students learning and doing as a result of what you are learning and doing

Diana shared Listening Skills, a Frank Schaffer Publication. The activity book focuses K-1 listening skills using crayons and pictures. She is using the activities.
Barb shared a listening/following directions game she uses.
Sue did an art project with specific directions to follow.
Jen played "Around the World" with #'s 1-20. The children had to really listen to rules + follow directions in order

Did you look at student work? _No_ / to play (number skills)

General comments, such as: what you are ready to share, IC/Reps meeting.	What concerns or questions do you have for school leaders or what do you what them to know?
We need to have a schedule for looking at student work to make sure that is a regular, routine Activity.	

Next Meeting (agenda items, work to prepare) _We will create a schedule for bringing in student work._

Date _2-8_   Time _2:30_   Leader _Sue_   Location _library_

AuSable Valley Central School District
Keeseville Elementary School
Patricia W. Atkinson, Principal
1825 Route 22
Keeseville, New York 12944
518-834-2839

MEMORANDUM

TO: Listening & Following Directions Group 1

FR: Pat A. *Pat*

RE: Current logs

DT: February 6, 2000

I am really glad that your group had the opportunity to share with the AFPS W.F.S.G. that is working in the same area you are. You didn't note it in your log, but I'm wondering if your groups have been examining similar issues. **It seems that poor listening skills are pretty universal.**

I enjoyed reading the listening activities that you included with both logs. It seems that you have found a lot of valuable information on the internet. **I was also glad that you tried the Listening Assessment Experience in your group.** I think the results show that we all need to work on our listening skills!

I noted that your last log (14) indicates that you will be creating a schedule for bringing in student work. **I think you will find the examination of student work both interesting and challenging.** I hope you'll include samples in your future logs.

Please remember that **Carlene Murphy will be in AVCS the 9th & 10th of this month.** She will be facilitating an Instructional Council Meeting on Thursday, February 10, at 3:00 PM. Please make sure that your group is represented.

STUDY GROUP LOG

School *Keesville*   Log# *15*   Date *2-8*

Group Name *Listening & Following Dir*   Today's Leader *Sue*

Members Present _____

Members Absent *Sheree*

What happened today? Brief summary of discussion and activities.

Barb brought ideas dealing with Friendship and Prejudice. The activities include the use of books, writing, and rubrics. The Student Participation Rubric would be appropriate for any grade level. Barb also brought activities for choices and consequences. These also had rubrics.

We used the "WOWS and WONDERS" protocol for looking at Barb's 3rd grade music class. The work covered lines, staff, notes, and space notes that involved

Classroom Application: What are students learning and doing as a result of what you are learning and doing

step by step directions. We will use this protocol when student work is brought as scheduled below.

Did you look at student work? *Yes – Barb – Used protocol*

General comments, such as: what you are ready to share, IC/Reps meeting.	What concerns or questions do you have for school leaders or what do you what them to know?
Sue will attend IC meeting. We want feedback on our rubric.	Developed a set schedule for bringing student work: Feb. 29-Diana Mar. 7-Jen Mar. 14-Barb Mar. 27-Sue May 2-Sheree

Next Meeting (agenda items, work to prepare) *Look for software that incorporates listening skills.*

Date *2-15*   Time *2:30*   Leader *Diana*   Location *library*

STUDY GROUP LOG

School _Keesville_   Log# _16_   Date _2-15_

Group Name _Listening & Following Dir_   Today's Leader _Diana_

Members Present _all_

Members Absent _____

What happened today? Brief summary of discussion and activities.
Sue attended the IC meeting on Feb. 10. She shared the following helpful information.   - forms, student work (formats)   - more tips for using Wows & Wonders protocol   - Developmental Stages of Groups   - ideas for videotaping our teaching   - The Final Word protocol   - Synergistic check-list

Classroom Application: What are students learning and doing as a result of what you are learning and doing
Sheree has been giving series of directions for orderly transitions). 75% have routine down. Jen has been using the activity book, Listening Skills. The students enjoy the activities and are doing very good listening. Barb brought a booklet, "Listening Games", that she is using.   We extended our time to meet (40 min) to brainstorm and offer suggestions on classroom problems that some of us are experiencing. It was very productive !!

Did you look at student work? _No_

General comments, such as: what you are ready to share, IC/Reps meeting.	What concerns or questions do you have for school leaders or what do you what them to know?
It will take several meetings for us to use the ideas from the IC meeting.	We have not received any responses to our Rubrics survey. * for this meeting only !

Next Meeting (agenda items, work to prepare) _Diana will bring student work on March 7._

Date _2-29_   Time _2:30_   Leader _Barb_   Location _library_

STUDY GROUP LOG

School _Keeseville_   Log# _17_   Date _2-29_
Group Name _Listening & Following Dir_ Today's Leader _Barb_
Members Present _all_
Members Absent _____

What happened today? Brief summary of discussion and activities.

We shared ideas about different incentive programs and how they work.

Sheree suggested that we create a packet of listening & following directions activities that can be kept in a central place for all teachers to use as resource.

We revisited our action plan and norms.

Classroom Application: What are students learning and doing as a result of what you are learning and doing

Sheree is giving directions only one time and does not repeat them. Students have adjusted and really pay attention now when she gives directions.
Jen & Sue are using The Listening Skills book - they too are only giving directions one time.
Jen is using a clap pattern for attention.
Barb is trying a new technique for refocusing the students: the students watch her while saying "s" to see when she slows down, speeds up, or changes pattern. It's working great!

Did you look at student work? _No_

General comments, such as: what you are ready to share, IC/Reps meeting.	What concerns or questions do you have for school leaders or what do you what them to know?

Next Meeting (agenda items, work to prepare) _Diana is going to bring student work._
Date _3-7_   Time _2:30_   Leader _Sue_   Location _library_

```
┌─────────────────────────────────────────────┐
│  AuSable  Valley  Central  School  District   │
│        Keeseville  Elementary . School        │
│      Patricia  W.  Atkinson,  Principal       │
│               1825  Route  22                 │
│       Keeseville,  New  York   12944          │
│             5 1 8 - 8 3 4 - 2 8 3 9           │
└─────────────────────────────────────────────┘
```

MEMORANDUM

TO: WFSG / LISTENING & FOLLOWING DIRECTIONS # 1

FR: Pat Atkinson

RE: LOGS #15, 16, & 17

DT: MARCH 5, 2000

WOW!   I read Log #15, and I was very impressed with the progress you have made. You are the only group that has constructed a schedule for examining student work (at least the only group that has shared that information with me!).

When you examined the student work that Jean brought in, I wonder if you came to any conclusions as to why one third of the children did not follow the directions. Do you use group time to suggest how the success of the same assignment might be improved if it were to be tried a second time?

I really like the games that Barb brought into the group at the February 15, 2000 meeting. **I hope you will share these games with the recess monitors.** They have been looking for games that can be used at indoor recess. The games that Barb copied look like they would work wonderfully in our primary classrooms.

I was glad to see that you extended your meeting time 40 minutes to discuss problems that are occurring in the classroom related to listening & following directions.   Diana sound very enthusiastic. I think she felt that even though the group went over time, some worthwhile discussion resulted.

Your classroom applications look as though everyone is incorporating activities that build listening skills on a daily basis. I liked Sheree's approach. I sometimes believe that we don't really listen the first time because we know the speaker will repeat what he/she has said. I'll bet her students were frustrated the first few times she tried this!

Let me know what you decide when you revisit your action plan.

Keep up the great work! Our children will be the better for your efforts!

STUDY GROUP LOG

School _Keeseville_ Log# _18_ Date _3-7_

Group Name _Listening & Following Dir_ Today's Leader _Sue_

Members Present _All_

Members Absent _____

What happened today? Brief summary of discussion and activities.

Diana brought student work and we used the "Wows & Wonders" protocol. The work was on the placement of a shape. The students did a good job overall. Some had difficulty with the directions that asked them to draw a spaceship behind the creature. Some students turned their paper over to draw the ship on the back. We wondered what would happen if the class did the activity again and colors added to the directions. We also wondered about separating

---

Classroom Application: What are students learning and doing as a result of what you are learning and doing

students during the activity, to reduce copying and influences of other students. We discussed possible reasons why students missed or didn't follow directions

Diana's activity stressed skills on shapes; spacial relationships; up-down-under-over-above-beneath-right-left

---

Did you look at student work? _Yes - Diana - used protocol_

General comments, such as: what you are ready to share, IC/Reps meeting.	What concerns or questions do you have for school leaders or what do you what them to know?
It took us longer than we expected to follow the protocol — but we did a great job!	

Next Meeting (agenda items, work to prepare) _Jen will bring student work._

Date _3-14_ Time _2:30_ Leader _Diana_ Location _library_

AuSable Valley Central School District
Keeseville Elementary School
Patricia W. Atkinson, Principal
1825 Route 22
Keeseville, New York   12944
518-834-2839

MEMORANDUM

TO: W.F.S.G. / Listening and Following Directions (#1)

FR: Pat Atkinson

RE: Log 1 8

DT: March 14, 2000

Hurray! I was really pleased to see that your group spent its meeting time discussing a student listening-based project. It looks like you had some really good input concerning the students' work on that particular project.

Diana's comment that i t appeared that the students had a hard time understanding the direction that asked them to put the spaceship behind the alien (some went on the back of the paper), showed the power that examining a task can give to a teacher. Both Diana and Barb realized that based on the apparent confusion there might be a need to review the terms in front of, behind, below, and between.

Dialogs about student work like the one your group had point out why WFSG examination of student work can be so beneficial. Your examination of this activity actually helped redirect instruction (or at least create a climate to question why instruction was not successful)! That is the goal of W.F.S.G.! Remember, "What's happening differently in your classroom as a result of what you're doing and learning in your W.F.S.G."

Congratulations!   You've got it!!!!!

PS Thanks for all the materials you have shared with me and the other WFSG that is working in the area of listening skills

STUDY GROUP LOG

School *Keeseville*　　Log# *19*　　　　Date *3-14*

Group Name *Listening & Following Dir*　Today's Leader *Diana*

Members Present　*All*

Members Absent

What happened today? Brief summary of discussion and activities.

Jen brought student work that required the students to follow 5 instructions when making a leprechaun. She did not repeat the instructions. Students didn't really know what a leprechaun is but did associate them with St. Patrick's Day. We agreed that some of the instructions needed to be changed to give the children a clearer understanding. Found that the protocol works with art work. (See attached leprechaun)

Classroom Application: What are students learning and doing as a result of what you are learning and doing

Barb's classes are making music posters according to specific directions. She brought the posters for us to see. Barb used "Coyote and Crow" with the 2nd grade, using music with punctuation. She is stressing language arts skills.
Sheree sent home, with progress reports, a list of activities for parents to help their children to listen.

Did you look at student work?　*Yes - Jen - used protocol*

General comments, such as: what you are ready to share, IC/Reps meeting.	What concerns or questions do you have for school leaders or what do you what them to know?
Materials members brought: ① *Listening and Following Directions from Educational Insight* ② *Following Directions B by Joy Evans + Jo Ellen Moore* ③ *Near and Far (a listening game)*	*We are inviting study group #3 to meet with us on March 27.*

Next Meeting (agenda items, work to prepare) *Bring any new materials we have found.*

Date *3-21*　Time *2:30*　Leader *Sue*　Location *library*

STUDY GROUP LOG

School _Keesville_ Log# _20_ Date _3-21_
Group Name _Listening and Following Di_ Today's Leader _Sue_
Members Present _all_
Members Absent _____

What happened today? Brief summary of discussion and activities.

Barb and Sheree shared several articles and activities that they copied for us. We looked over the materials and decided what we would read for later discussion.

We went back to our action plan to see if we need to add or delete - its OK! We think we have kept the Content (Language Arts) in focus - even though we are doing it through "listening"

Classroom Application: What are students learning and doing as a result of what you are learning and doing

Sheree is dictating sentences with spelling words. She reads the sentences twice. They are listening carefully but having trouble spelling the words. Barb is using "Music Bear" with Kindergarten to stress listening & following directions. Sheree also shared an activity with 3rd graders. The students were given a sheet with specific directions to draw the Chinese flag. The students had to read the directions on their own and then check their work on the computer. Most could do it!

Did you look at student work? _No_

General comments, such as: what you are ready to share, IC/Reps meeting.	What concerns or questions do you have for school leaders or what do you what them to know?

Next Meeting (agenda items, work to prepare) _Sue will bring student_
Work.
Date _3-27_ Time _2:30_ Leader _Sheree_ Location _library_

AuSable Valley Central School District
Keeseville Elementary School
Patricia W. Atkinson, Principal
1825 Route 22
Keeseville, New York 12944
518-834-2839

MEMORANDUM

TO: WFSG / Listening and Following Directions #1

FR: Pat Atkinson

RE: Logs #'s 19 & 20

DT: March 25, 2000

Your group has been the most prolific group in terms of sharing materials! I want to thank you for all the copies of activities and research that you have given me. **I'm also glad to see that members of the group are using materials that other group members bring in.** WFSG's are a way to build your files and share materials with your colleagues.

I hope you will try to use the reaction sheet that I gave Jen when you look at students' work. If you do, please attach a copy of it with your weekly log.

I'm glad that you took the time to revisit your Action Plan. I think that's pretty important just to make sure that the group is still on track! **How have you decided to evaluate your group's success?**

You might want to think about RE-ADMINISTERING an activity to the same group of children that you had given it to previously. If you compare their work it might give you some sense of whether or not classroom instruction has been improving.

I think it's neat that you are meeting with the other Listening Skills group. Is your Spring Fling a celebration?

I've scheduled an Instructional Council Meeting for Thursday, April 6, at 2:30 PM in my office. Please send a representative to share what your group has been doing.

KEEP UP THE GREAT WORK!!!

STUDY GROUP LOG

School _Keeseville_   Log# _21_   Date _3-27_

Group Name _Listening and Following Di_ Today's Leader _Sheree_

Members Present _all_

Members Absent _____

What happened today? Brief summary of discussion and activities.

Sue brought student work from her kindergarten class. The activity is attached. It took longer to follow the protocol because we extended the time for each part. Having 10 people here instead of 5 made a difference.

Classroom Application: What are students learning and doing as a result of what you are learning and doing

Sue has started a second booklet on following auditory directions (a little more difficult than the 1st booklet). Students must process more information before they begin.

Sheree will begin a new listening comprehension activity, "The Tale of the Lazy Gardener". Students must take notes.

Did you look at student work? _Yes - Sue - used protocol_

General comments, such as: what you are ready to share, IC/Reps meeting.	What concerns or questions do you have for school leaders or what do you what them to know?
Study group #3 met with us and participated in using the W&W protocol when looking at the student work.	Sue will attend Apr. 6 meeting - will we discuss how to assess our progress?

Next Meeting (agenda items, work to prepare) _Be thinking about the whole faculty sharing._

Date _4-4_   Time _2:30_   Leader _Diana_   Location _library_

STUDY GROUP LOG

School _Keeseville_ Log# _22_ Date _4-4_

Group Name _Listening & Following Dir_ Today's Leader _Diana_

Members Present _all_

Members Absent _____

What happened today? Brief summary of discussion and activities.

We discussed parts of the articles we received two weeks ago. We really enjoyed the conversation — very professional!

We started planning what we will do with the whole faculty to share our work.

Classroom Application: What are students learning and doing as a result of what you are learning and doing

We are all continuing to stress how important it is that students listen & follow directions — all are using activities from the materials we have shared and discussed in this study group.

Increases in ELA scores MAY be a result of listening and following directions!

Did you look at student work?

General comments, such as: what you are ready to share, IC/Reps meeting.	What concerns or questions do you have for school leaders or what do you what them to know?
Spring vacation and a meeting at AuSable Forks Elem. will mean we won't meet again here until May 2.	Barb will attend IC meeting on Apr. 24.

Next Meeting (agenda items, work to prepare) _Sheree will bring_ _student work._

Date _5-2_ Time _2:30_ Leader _Barb_ Location _library_

```
┌─────────────────────────────────────────┐
│   AuSable Valley Central School District  │
│        Keeseville Elementary School        │
│      Patricia W. Atkinson, Principal       │
│              1825 Route 22                 │
│       Keeseville, New York    12944        │
│              518-834-2839                  │
└─────────────────────────────────────────┘
```

MEMORANDUM

TO: WFSG / Listening & Following Directions # 1

FR: Pat Atkinson *Pat A.*

RE: Current logs (#21 & 22)

DT: April 19, 2000

Your group has been BUSY! I noted from log 21 that you met with the other group that is working on listening skills. I was glad to see that you arranged the meeting independently. **One of the outcomes of Whole Faculty Study Groups is an increased amount of sharing with colleagues.** It's wonderful to be able to sit down with colleagues who have a shared interest and discuss what you have been doing to bring about student improvement in that area.

Speaking about student improvement, THANK YOU for sharing copies of Sue's class's work. I was really amazed with the quality of work the children were able to acheive! One of the most important skills our children need is LISTENING. I think we have all become accomplished at tuning out the voices and sounds we don't wish to hear. Our students have also become adept selective listeners. **To be successful in school (NOT TO MENTION LIFE!) we need to teach children to focus and listen critically.** I think your group has found some interesting activities that help children practice and develop those skills. When you looked at the student work, did you use your listening rubric, or is that used for in-class assessment?

Keep up the great work!

REMINDER-Carlene Murphy will be leading an Instructional Council Meeting on April 24th, at 3:00 PM in the MHS Library. Please make sure someone is there to represent your group.

Replaces Log #23

Instructional Team Meeting Report *

Looking at Student Work

* Completed each time a P.G. at looked at S.W. & used protocol

Date: May 2, 2000

Team: Listening & following Directions

Attendance: Sue ▓▓▓▓   Jean ▓▓▓

Jen ▓▓▓   Barb ▓▓▓

Sheree ▓▓▓   Diana ▓▓▓

Pieces of Work Looked at: Sheree ▓▓▓ 3rd grade group (7 students) → Listening and Following Directions Activities

Standards Used: Paper and pencil, the story "The Boy who Hated to Wash" and the question sheet. Everything was read to the students.

What we discovered about student *LEARNING*	What we discovered about *INSTRUCTION*
- Students reacted negatively to the activity from the start. - Most of the students answered the questions correctly, showing that they were comprehending the story. - The students are starting to use complete sentences to answer the questions. (about ½ of the students did).	- Students have a hard time doing activities without talking and asking questions during it. - Students do better when they are allowed to take notes during the story. (they are use to this process).

- the environment & students' attitudes effect the outcome of the work.

What will we do now to IMPROVE LEARNING? What help do we need to do that better?

- She will be trying this same activity with another group of students to see how they do.
- Allow the students to take notes during the story.
- Remove any distractive students from the group.
- Try to improve the environment (find a quieter place to work) and minimize the distractions.
- Read another story to the same group, about not liking to wash and have them compare the two stories.

Use back for additional comments

Adapted from Ruth Mitchell, Front-End Alignment: Using Standards to Steer Educational Change, 1996, p. 39.

⊛ Overall, Sheree was not real pleased with the outcomes.

> **AuSable Valley Central School District**
> Keeseville Elementary School
> Patricia W. Atkinson, Principal
> 1825 Route 22
> Keeseville, New York 12944
> 518-834-2839

MEMORANDUM

TO: WFSG / Listening and Following Directions # 1

FR: Pat A.

RE: Log # 23

DT: May 6, 2000

 STUDENTS' NEEDS

Thank you for sharing Sheree's student work. I wonder why her students "reacted negatively" to this activity from the start. I liked the format of the assignment. Listening is a key component of the new learning standards, and also, a key component of a successful learner.

I am sorry that neither of the listening groups responded to your rubric. **I hope you bring copies of it to the sharing and celebration scheduled for May 15, at the MHS cafeteria.** I know there is a group concerned with study skills in the MHS. I am sure they -- and all groups interested in effective teaching practices -- would benefit from looking at and using your listening rubric.

I am enclosing a form that Karl Clauset has suggested we use to evaluate the progress of our WFSG's. If your group could take some time and thought to complete this form before May 22, I would appreciate it. I would like a representative from each group to bring the completed evaluation form to an Instructional Council Meeting I have scheduled for May 22, at 2:30 in the office.

Thanks for the time and effort you have given for the benefit of our students.

STUDY GROUP LOG

School *Keesville* Log# *24* Date *5-9*

Group Name *Listening + Following Dir* Today's Leader *Jen*

Members Present *all*

Members Absent _____

What happened today? Brief summary of discussion and activities.

What we will do with whole faculty on May 21:
We are going to read an adult poem to them — give them an activity to do to check their listening — and use a rubric to score their papers!

Classroom Application: What are students learning and doing as a result of what you are learning and doing

---

Did you look at student work?

General comments, such as: what you are ready to share, IC/Reps meeting.	What concerns or questions do you have for school leaders or what do you what them to know?

Next Meeting (agenda items, work to prepare) *May 15ᵗʰ District Celebration!*

Date _____ Time _____ Leader _____ Location _____

Study Group Action Plan

School __RRHS__   Study Group # _Opening Doors_ Date __8-5__

Group Members _Barnes, Cameron, Steinberg, Cubberley, Graf_

What is the general category of student needs the group will address?

___✔___Reading _____ Writing _____ Math _____ Other: _____

Essential Question (*Example: How can we teach students to comprehend what they read?*):

How can we teach students to comprehend literature with unfamiliar themes, vocabulary, and language?

We **PLAN** according to data indicating that **students need to** ➡	We **ACT** on the students' needs by agreeing that **when the study group meets** we will ➡
- Improve comprehension skills - Appreciate the underlying cultures found in texts	- Develop a deeper understanding of the literature we teach - Explore a variety of multicultural texts through reading and discussion. - Examine multiple intelligence media. - Research, read, discuss journals and books. - Demonstrate strategies and materials we use in our classrooms.

We **REFLECT** on the results of our actions and on our use of the following resources. ➡	We **ASSESS** our work according to evidence that **student learning has increased and understanding has deepened.**

	STUDENT PERFORMANCE GOALS	DATA SOURCE
- Using Literature Circles in Classrooms - The English Journal - TAAS - Teaching a Multicultural Classroom - Songs, poems, movies, videos - Books from our Curriculum	95% will pass	Course exit exam
	Increase in daily attendance	Attendance records
	100% indicate more understanding of cultural differences	Student questionnaire
	90% earn a C or higher final grade	Report cards

"The test of literature is, I suppose, whether we ourselves live more intensely for the reading of it." Elizabeth Drew

Opening Doors

Volume 1, Issue 1

September 16, 1998

Items Addressed

• Discussed ordering multi-cultural anthologies from NCTE. Can order member copies for $15.00 Jessica will order copies for all of us.

• Lessons for *Night*/Holocaust. Can order free material from the Holocaust Museum in Washington D.C. They also have a web page on the Net. Jessica, Carrie, and Rachelle brought information on Holocaust and provided copies. Discussed using poetry and artwork from *I Never Saw Another Butterfly*. Everyone needs to send letter home to parents concerning *Night*.

• Reviewed material on Native Americans. Historical background and statistics: Rachelle. Music, poetry, short stories: Rachelle and Kelly. "A Man Called Horse" will lead into the Hero's Journey, "Dances With Wolves" and *The Odyssey*.

Implementation: News from the Classroom

♦ Jessica and Michelle are working on using artwork and music in their classroom with "Pictures at an Exhibition," a composition written solely for artwork.

♦ Kelly and Rachelle have just finished their trip to South Africa with the freshman and report that everything is going well. Next on the itinerary: Mexico. They've located art-

work, music, a video clip, poetry, and short stories. Now they're looking for background information on the Hispanic culture. Possible solution for next year: assign groups of students to research the different countries and let them be the flight crew for the day.

"The world is your exercise book, the pages on which you do your sums."
Richard Bach

♦ Michelle and Jessica will be beginning the descriptive paper with their freshmen. This year they're trying a restaurant review.

Plans for Next Meeting

♦ Michelle: Bring copy of "The Elf King" lyrics and song.

♦ Kelly: Talk to Toastmasters and find a Holocaust survivor that we could use as a guest speaker.

♦ Jessica: order books from NCTE.

♦ Rachelle: Copy list of connections and books for each culture.

NEXT MEETING:
October 7, 1998
Room 722
2:00
Staff Development

Group Members

Jessica Barnes	**Carrie Cubberley**
Rachelle Cameron	**Michelle Graf**
Kelly Steinberg	

1

The Logs from Round Rock High School (RRHS)

■ RRHS is in Round Rock, Texas, which is a suburb of Austin. The 1998-1999 school year, the school's fourth year to have WFSGs in place, was the year in which the following work was done. At this time, the school had over 3,000 students enrolled and a faculty of 226 (professionally certified). The study groups continued during the 1999-2000 school year.

■ The faculty refers to the study groups as *target groups*.

■ One study group (Opening Doors) chose to use a newsletter format for reporting its work instead of the standard log form.

■ The following materials cover the work of the Opening Doors study group.

■ The action plan and one log from August is included in the following set of documents.

■ No documents are included for September. The Newsletter logs begin in October.

■ Because the study group log did not include a space for describing student work the group examined, the study group did not specifically address looking at study work in the newsletters. The study group did bring student work to the meetings.

■ This set of logs was chosen because they indicate substantive and rigorous teacher work. The logs are also an example of how one study group kept a very large faculty informed of its work. They are reprinted with the permission of Round Rock High School.

Round Rock High School's
Whole-Faculty Study Groups

At RRHS, the study groups are called "target" groups. The 1999-2000 school year was the fourth year the school had used WFSGs as its professional development model.

The Focus Team used the Campus Improvement Plan to identify the student needs the study groups addressed. The Focus Team confirmed with the whole faculty that the identified instructional student needs were the needs that all study groups would address. For the 1998-1999 school year, it was determined that students at RRHS needed to

- Integrate math and science

- Use correct grammar and punctuation in all content areas

- Increase vocabulary

- Improve reading comprehension

- Demonstrate respect and responsibility for assignments

- Read more, both in class and out of class

- Write for audience or purpose

- Be successful 9th graders

The faculty chose not to categorize the student needs or to prioritize the needs. It was the consensus of the faculty that all of the needs were generic to all curriculum areas and could be combined in many different ways. With such a large faculty, this approach would give the 40+ groups the flexibility to address the needs from many perspectives. Teachers formed their own groups, keeping to the guideline: no less than 3, no more than 6. Groups had the freedom to pursue any aspect of the identified student needs and any combination of the student needs. Each study group gave themselves a name that was an indicator of the composition of the group or the student need addressed by the group.

Study Group Focus	*Number of Teachers in Group*
1. Integrating calculus	6
2. Personal fitness	4
3. Critical thinking in biology	6
4. Physical Science: Using Dell Computers	4
5. Technology	7

(continued)

Study Group Focus	Number of Teachers in Group
6. Work ethics in business	5
7. Graphing lab	4
8. Higher expectations	6
9. Relationship between math and science	4
10. Respectful communication with students, parents, faculty	7
11. Incorporating L/D students with band rehearsals	5
12. Computer technology	6
13. Multicultural literature in the classroom	5 ("Opening Doors")
14. Respect, responsibility with Life Skills Studies	7
15. Communication with parents and students	6
16. Communication with parents and students	5
17. Responsibility and character	5
18. Responsibility and character	6
19. Integration of software into regular lesson plans	6
20. Working with athletes for academic improvement	6
21. Integration of math and science	5
22. Internet, websites for students and teachers	6
23. Study skills	5
24. Using games to enhance oral skills	6
25. Parent-teacher-student communication	4
26. Writing for publication	3
27. Vocabulary acquisition and reinforcement	5
28. Improving reading comprehension	3
29. Pre-AP	3
30. Respect and responsibility	7
31. C++	3
32. Vocabulary development	5
33. Vocabulary development	4
34. Writing for audience	6
35. Student theater production work	4

Study Group Focus	*Number of Teachers in Group*
36. Encouraging students to read	5
37. Integrating chemistry and math	3
38. Academic support for athletes	4
39. Social Studies standards	5
40. Internet potential for reference materials	6
41. Use of community resources	5
42. Work study programs	5
43. Special education inclusion	4
44. Nontraditional teaching techniques	5
45. Administrators as instructional leaders	6
Certificated* personnel in study groups	226

* Certificated:

- Regular classroom teachers
- Special education teachers
- Resource teachers (i.e., remedial)
- Vocational, technical teachers
- Coaches
- Guidance counselors
- Administrators
- Media specialists

Approximately one third of the study groups were homogeneous (same department or grade). The other two thirds were heterogeneous (across departments and grades).

"The test of literature is. I suppose. whether we ourselves live more intensely for the reading of it."
—Elizabeth Drew

Opening Doors

Volume 1, Issue 2

October 1998

Target Group Focus:

- Improve student compre-hension skills and abilities through multicultural litera-ture.

- Aid in students' appreciation of the underlying cultures found in the texts.

Target Group Members will:

- Explore a variety of multicultural texts through reading and discussion.

- Collect multiple intelligence media: music. dance. art. costume. flags. etc.

- Research profes-sional journals and software for teach-ing strategies and Ideas.

- Develop a list of appropriate connec-tions and resources

Items Addressed

- Holocaust Material: Jes-sica brought the informa-tion she received for free from the Holocaust Mu-seum in Washington, D.C. We plan on making photo-copies of victims of the Holocaust to assign to each student. We also discussed *I Never Saw Another Butterfly*. Rachelle, Kelly, and Jes-sica will each get a color overhead made of one poem and one picture. Schreck has additional poetry from Holocaust.
- Concern: Teaching cul-tures we know little about. What immediate re-sources do we have for cultural background? Suggestion: Jessica and Michelle contact Barbara Baker for information on South Africa, Mexico, Ger-many, Italy, Greece, and Russia. Suggestion: "Pre" discovery learning with students.
- Concern: Need to start correlating TEKS with in-dividual lesson plans and create objectives to why we're teaching each les-son.
- Elf King: Michelle brought lyrics and music. Dis-cussed possible uses in classroom: mood, igno-rance, Holocaust, Ger-many.

Implementation: News from the Classroom

- Carrie and Michelle will be teaching *Animal Farm* next. Their focus will be not only on the satirical work as it relates to the Russian Revolution but also how the idea of tyranny and persecu-tion could relate to many different cul-tures and time peri-ods.
- Kelly and Rachelle are winding up their Mexico Unit. Some activities they used: man-goes (using Imagery in writing), Latino Artwork (creative writing using art), freewriting us-ing video clips and music from the Hispanic culture, and reading poetry in Spanish.
- Jessica, Kelly, and Rachelle will begin *Night* at the end of October. Currently looking for: mu-sic, food, flag, cultural info., and artwork.
- The search goes on for a copy of "Romeo and Juliet in Sarejevo." Not available through Amazon...maybe PBS? We're also still looking for a Holocaust survivor to be a guest speaker.

"The world is your exercise book, the pages on which you do your sums."
Richard Bach

Plans for Next Meeting

- Michelle: Bring background info on Elf King, Nazi coins.
- Jessica: Bring overhead from *Butterflies* and order book from NCTE
- Kelly: Bring overhead from *Butterflies* and call about Holocaust speaker
- Carrie: Bring copy of lesson plan format.
- Rachelle: Bring copies of 25 people from Holocaust, over-head from *Butterflies*, tape of Animal Farm songs
- EVERYONE: Objectives/Ra-tionale for teaching units.

NEXT MEETING
October 26th
2:30, Room 722
Staff Development

Group Members

Jessica Barnes	Carrie Cubberley
Rachelle Cameron	Michelle Graf
Kelly Steinberg	

1

"The test of literature is. I suppose. whether we ourselves live more intensely for the reading of it."
~Elizabeth Drew

Opening Doors
October 26, 1998
Volume 1, Issue 3

Target Group Focus:

- Improve student comprehension skills and abilities through multicultural literature.

- Aid in students' appreciation of the underlying cultures found in the texts.

Target Group Members will:

- Explore a variety of multicultural texts through reading and discussion.

- Collect multiple intelligence media; music, dance, art, costume, flags, etc,

- Research professional journals and software for teaching strategies and ideas.

- Develop a list of appropriate connections and resources

Items Addressed

- **Concerns:** Group members discussed the actual goal of the Target Group. There is a concern that instead of coming up with teaching strategies that are universal, we're focusing on specific pieces of literature. The group has decided that one member will be designated at each meeting to bring an article concerning multiculturalism in the classroom. The article will be distributed ahead of time so that members will have time to read it and be prepared for the discussion that follows: how to implement the concept in our own classroom.

- **Target Group Portfolio:** Group members will work together to create a Target Group Portfolio that will be copied and distributed at the end of the year to group members and the appropriate administrators.

- **Materials:** Members shared copies of music, children's books, magazine articles and reference materials.

- **Correlating Skills:** Group members compiled a list of skills taught in English I, the piece of literature they're covered in, and the assessment techniques used.

Implementation: News from the Classroom

Basic Skills of English I
The Odyssey
- **Personal Narrative:** visual and written
- **Research Skills:** Writing Letter (Carrie)
- **Supporting Opinions with Facts/Evidence:** Trial, Debate, Persuasive Writing
- **Unique Stylistic Qualities of the genre:** Epic form, Homeric simile, oral tradition, epigraph
- **Theme/Journey**
- **Cultural Literacy:** intertextuality, allusions, ancient Greek culture, mythology, heroic tradition
- **Archetypes**
- **Character Education:** responsibility, compassion, etc.

"The world is your exercise book, the pages on which you do your sums."
Richard Bach

Romeo and Juliet
- **Research Skills:** letters, projects, Renaissance Faire
- **Persuasive Essay**
- **Performance/Interpretation of Text:** both physically and orally. Masks (symbolism), drama, dance
- **Cultural Literacy:** Shakespearean England, Gangs, Societal connections, familial connections
- **Unique Stylistic Qualities:** meter, rhyme scheme, sonnet, couplet, Elizabethan English (word attack skills)
- **Paraphrasing and Comprehension**
- **Character Education**

Plans for Next Meeting

- Michelle: Bring copies of character education questions: "Ignorance leads to oppression."
- Jessica: Get copy of Becky Lowe's archetype information
- Kelly: Still trying to get a hold of Lucy Katz.
- Carrie: Bring copy of multicultural article and copy of

"Ignorance leads to oppression" questions.
Rachelle: Start putting portfolio together for group. type up newsletter.

NEXT MEETING
November 11th
1:00   Room 722
Staff Development

Group Members

Jessica Barnes	**Carrie Cubberley**
Rachelle Cameron	**Michelle Graf**
Kelly Steinberg	

1

> "The test of literature is, I suppose, whether we our-
> selves live more intensely for the reading of it."
> ~Elizabeth Drew

Opening Doors
November 11, 1998
Volume 1, Issue 4

Target Group Focus:

• Improve student comprehension skills and abilities through multicultural literature.

• Aid in students' appreciation of the underlying cultures found in the texts.

Target Group Members will:

• Explore a variety of multicultural texts through reading and discussion.

• Collect multiple intelligence media: music, dance, art, costume, flags, etc.

• Research professional journals and software for teaching strategies and ideas.

• Develop a list of appropriate connections and resources

Items Addressed

• **Betty Moss Packet:** Group members discussed the multicultural packet provided by Marsha. One concern is that the AP-level strategies need to be modified in some way for regular freshmen. Marsha has a modification packet somewhere in her room. General consensus: Major themes and cultural information provided in the packet will be useful in the classroom.

• **Developing Student Voices Article:** Carrie provided a copy of an article from the *English Journal*. This seems to be focusing the group and therefore we will continue with this idea. See "Implementation" section for more details.

• **Materials:** Group members discussed the book we ordered from NCTE and decided to send it back since it did not include copies of the literature pieces. Rachelle will bring a book from home about teaching multicultural short stories.

• **Literature Circles:** Group members briefly discussed using Literature Circles in the classroom. We will begin compiling a list of books that deal with personal journeys and different cultures.

Implementation: News from the Classroom

Developing Student Voices with Multicultural Literature
by Linda Blair

• **Hero's Journey:** Article discusses the idea that students must become acquainted with their own voices and learn to mold them into various forms. We offer this already in our classrooms with journals, writer's logs, the personal odyssey, writing poetry, etc. It's the whole idea behind our Hero's Journey/Odyssey Unit: You have to know who you are before you know where you're going.

• **Personal Odyssey:** Must tap into student experience and prior knowledge of their own personal culture, but what is culture? What is American culture? We have many students who belong to a very specific culture, but what about the other 75 percent of our students? Can we use this with the Personal Odyssey by offering a choice in the narrative writing to incorporate cultural/ethnic experiences?

• **SSR Books:** Reader's experiences of alienation, assimilation, and acculturation is a universal theme, so let's compile a list of SSR books that incorporate that theme, specifically non-fiction works.

> "The world is your exercise book, the pages on which you do your sums."
> Richard Bach

Plans for Next Meeting

♦ Michelle: Bring copies of character education questions: "Ignorance leads to oppression." Also bring copies of high school poem "I am..." example.

♦ Jessica: Get copy of Becky Lowe's archetype information. Also, bring copy of next article.

♦ Carrie: Bring copy of "Ignorance leads to oppression" questions.
Rachelle: Bring copy of multicultural book. Start putting portfolio together for group, type up newsletter.

EVERYONE: Bring list of books dealing with personal journey/cultures for SSR list.

NEXT MEETING
December 12th
4:15   Room 739

Group Members

Jessica Barnes	Carrie Cubberley
Rachelle Cameron	Michelle Graf
Kelly Steinberg	

1

"The test of literature is. I suppose. whether we ourselves live more intensely for the reading of it."
~Elizabeth Drew

Opening Doors

December 12, 1998

Volume 1, Issue 5

Target Group Focus:

• Improve student compre-hension skills and abilities through multicultural litera-ture.

• Aid in students' appreciation of the underlying cultures found in the texts.

Target Group Members will:

• Explore a variety of multicultural texts through reading and discussion.

• Collect multiple intelligence media; music. dance. art. costume. flags. etc.

• Research profes-sional journals and software for teach-ing strategies and ideas.

• Develop a list of appropriate connec-tions and resources

Items Addressed

• **Bringing "Women" into the classroom:** Group members discussed the possibility of adding quite a bit more female influ-ence into the curriculum via music and poetry. Members also discussed switching paradigms: Is Penelope the real hero? Is she actually stronger than Odysseus? See notes in Implementation section for further details on incorporating women into the classroom.

• **Night Movie Connection:** Kelly suggested using "Shawshank Redemption" next year as the in-flight movie to Germany. Some ideas in the movie which we've discussed in class are: "Hope": whether hope kills you or keeps you alive in desperate situations and "Prison": whether or not a person can still be in prison but be free in the mind.

• **Materials:** Group mem-bers discussed ordering copies of a new book called *Teaching a Multi-cultural Classroom*, but decided it wasn't exactly what we're looking for.

Implementation: News from the Classroom

• **Women Characters in the Odyssey:** Since we are all in agreement that "women" in litera-ture can be considered multicul-tural, we have decided to try and incorporate more women into our studies. And although The Odyssey is arguably "male," we have found connections to the text through Suzanne Vega's "Calypso" song (which the students insist they hate but they sing for the rest of the year), and poetry from both Margaret Atwood and Eleanor Wilner. In addition to being written by females, all three of these pieces can be used quite successfully for Point of View. We have decided that

"The world is your exercise book, the pages on which you do your sums."
Richard Bach

the best way for students to appreciate other cultures is to understand their point of view as best as they can and in turn see themselves within that understanding. Members report focusing in the classroom on the fe-male characters' portrayal...that they're evil mon-sters or witches, etc. How to switch paradigms? Who was the real hero? WHY do the female charac-ters act the way they do? Who are the strongest char-acters? What are the stereo-types?

Plans for Next Meeting

♦ **Michelle:** Bring copies of "Myths from Around the World"

♦ **Jessica:** Bring copies of "Sirens Song" and Penelope poem. Also, see if you can download the music from the Internet.

♦ **Carrie:** Bring copies of "Afterwards" and "Cyclops" to use with Odyssey.

♦ **Rachelle:** Newsletter, copy all Target group info and give to Mr.

Perez.

♦ **Kelly:** Bring information on Greek culture/beliefs, etc.

EVERYONE: Try and find any art-work for the Odyssey

NEXT MEETING
February 15th
4:15 Room 722

Group Members

Jessica Barnes	Carrie Cubberley
Rachelle Cameron	Michelle Graf
Kelly Steinberg	

1

> "Ignorance is the curse of God.
> Knowledge the wind
> wherewith we fly to heaven."
> ~ William Shakespeare

Opening Doors

February 15, 1999

Volume 1, Issue 6

Target Group Focus:

• Improve student comprehension skills and abilities through multicultural literature.

• Aid in students' appreciation of the underlying cultures found in the texts.

Target Group Members will:

• Explore a variety of multicultural texts through reading and discussion.

• Collect multiple intelligence media: music, dance, art, costume, flags, etc.

• Research professional journals and software for teaching strategies and ideas.

• Develop a list of appropriate connections and resources

Items Addressed

• **Point of View with the Odyssey:** Group members discussed several different pieces of literature that would expose students to and help them view the world from different points of view. "*Ancient Gesture*" (poem) to be used at end of the *Odyssey* with Penelope's point of view. "*Polyphemus Moth:*" An Annie Dillard short story that connects to the Cyclop's point of view. Kate Chopin's short story (Jessica) that connects to Penelope's point of view. "*Siren Song*" by Margaret Atwood (poem) for Siren's point of view.
• **Nonfiction Pieces:** Group is concerned about providing an adequate number of non-fiction companion pieces for the *Odyssey* and *Romeo and Juliet*. There is a documentary from PBS entitled "Romeo and Juliet in Sarejevo," but we have not been able to find a copy of it. Some suggestions were to contact Reed (through Chris) and/or Region XIII media center.
• **Romeo and Juliet material:** Group members began discussing information for the Shakespeare unit. Some companion pieces mentioned include Purgatory by Maxine Kumin, Dreams by Gwendolyn Brooks, and We Wear the Mask by Langston Hughes.

Implementation: News from the Classroom

• "*Cyclops*" by Margaret Atwood: This poem provoked insightful discussions of the importance of point of view and of "re-visioning" literature. Some topics covered in class were: man versus nature and who is to blame when "nature" is provoked, how we fear things we don't understand, how we can all be the Cyclops and what we can do to avoid it. Students enjoyed this poem and it worked well with the Cyclops artwork.
• "*Shelter from The Storm*" by Bob Dylan: Using this song as a connection to Odysseus' time on Circe's island is a good way to lead students to seeing how a theme can be universal and timeless. Although this song was not specifically about the Odyssey, it fits well and the students are amazed to hear it's about the Vietnam War.
• "*Afterwards*" by Eleanor Wilner: This poem was easy for the students to following and understand, and it also encouraged discussion of seeing things from another point of view (Odysseus's men), and ultimately led to writing a poem from Circe's point of view.
• **Land of the Dead Dialogue:** Group consensus was that we needed to spend more time preparing the students with dialogue practice. One suggestion was to have the students put Odysseus' conversation into modern English and have them mark with the correct punctuation (would also act as a summary).

> "The world is your exercise book, the pages on which you do your sums."
> Richard Bach

Plans for Next Meeting

◆ Michelle: Have Chris call Reese and find out if he has a copy of "R&J in Sarejevo."
◆ Jessica: Bring a copy of "Dream" poem by Gwendolyn Brooks.
Carrie: Bring copies of "Purgatory" by Kumin, poem from list (also "We Wear the Mask by Hughes). Also bring a audiotape of R&J from Shakespeare Festival
Rachelle: Bring copies of artwork for the Odyssey, newsletter., Romeo and Juliet rap tape (copies for everyone)

EVERYONE: Bring suggestions for nonfiction connections.

**NEXT MEETING
February 24th
4:15   Room 722**

Group Members

Jessica Barnes	Carrie Cubberley
Rachelle Cameron	Michelle Graf
Kelly Steinberg	

1

" Ignorance is the curse of God.
Knowledge the wind
wherewith we fly to heaven."
-- William Shakespeare

Opening Doors

Volume 1, Issue 7

February 24, 1999

Target Group Focus:

- Improve student comprehension skills and abilities through multicultural literature.

- Aid in students' appreciation of the underlying cultures found in the texts.

Target Group Members will:

- Explore a variety of multicultural texts through reading and discussion.

- Collect multiple intelligence media: music. dance. art. costume. flags. etc.

- Research professional journals and software for teaching strategies and ideas.

- Develop a list of appropriate connections and resources

Items Addressed

- **Odyssey Connections:** Group members discussed several different companion pieces to the Odyssey. "The Story of an Hour" works well with Penelope's Dream poem and could lead into a comparison essay about husband/wife relationships. "Penelope's Despair" (Poem)
- **Romeo and Juliet:** Kelly shared her R&J unit and lesson plans with the group. Members will integrate new ideas with lessons from last year that proved to be successful. Focus during the first two days of instruction will be on the prologue, background, literary elements such as iambic pentameter and sonnet, and comprehension skills. Carrie brought a copy of the children's version of Romeo and Juliet. Rachelle brought information on the Renaissance Faire that she used last year. Group discussed "Purgatory" connection as a possible culminating activity in conjunction with viewing the two different versions of the movie. Also, members discussed using "Moody Musician Metaphors" with the Italian music played during the flight to Italy. Students would write two separate poems in first person based on the mood of the musical pieces.

Implementation: News from the Classroom

- **The Odyssey Trial:** Kelly and Michelle are both using the trial with great success. Following the actual trial presentations, students are required to write a persuasive essay which includes citations from the book that support their opinion as to whether or not Odysseus is a hero.
- **The Class Odyssey:** Carrie and Rachelle are using the Class Odyssey this year as their research project. Still in the early stage, two significant concerns have been time constraints and library availability. We have discovered that students are not receiving (or retaining??) information from lower grades concerning research skills. Mr. Hammerly provided a handout on the Big Six that might prove useful next year if revamped.
- **Concerns/Recommendations:** Perhaps all of the "extra" activities and connections to the Odyssey are interfering with the skills that the students should be developing. What are we trying to teach them? Are we assessing them appropriately? Are we rushing too quickly in order to fit everything in? Do we need to slow down and spend more quality time on major skills?

"The world is your exercise book, the pages on which you do your sums."
Richard Bach

Plans for Next Meeting

- Michelle: Have Chris call Reed for "Romeo and Juliet in Sarejevo" video.
- Jessica: Bring copy of "Dreams" by Gwendalyn Brooks (along with quote from Marcia that ties in). Also, make copies of the Jotting Sheet and the Renaissance Faire information.
- Carrie: Bring a copy of "We Wear the Mask" by Langston Hughes.

- Rachelle: Retype the Mask worksheet and put on disk for everyone, type the newsletter, and make copies of the R&J Rap song.

EVERYONE: Music for Italy

NEXT MEETING
March 10th
4:15 Room 722

Group Members

Jessica Barnes	Carrie Cubberley
Rachelle Cameron	Michelle Graf
Kelly Steinberg	

1

> "Ignorance is the curse of God.
> Knowledge the wind
> wherewith we fly to heaven."
> ~ William Shakespeare

Opening Doors

Volume 1, Issue 8

March 10, 1999

Target Group Focus:

- Improve student comprehension skills and abilities through multicultural literature.

- Aid in students' appreciation of the underlying cultures found in the texts.

Target Group Members will:

- Explore a variety of multicultural texts through reading and discussion.

- Collect multiple Intelligence media: music, dance, art, costume, flags, etc.

- Research professional journals and software for teaching strategies and ideas.

- Develop a list of appropriate connections and resources

Items Addressed

- **Romeo and Juliet Connections:** Group members discussed several different companion pieces to "Romeo and Juliet." Jessica brought the poem "Kitchenette Building" by G. Brooks which is written in loose Petrarchan sonnet format and addresses the issue of whether a dream can survive in a hostile or stifling environment. Also included in the packet was an overview of G. Brooks. This poem would be ideal to use with Mercutio's "Queen Mab" speech. Carrie brought copies of Langston Hughes's dream poems to use with the same scene; a copy of "Passing Love" to use with Act II, Scene I; and also a copy of "We Wear the Mask" by Dunbar to use with the ballroom scene.
- **Quotation Book:** Group members decided to start compiling a book of quotations that supplement the readings. Carrie suggested an on-line source that is searchable by subject.
- **Technology:** Members will begin using on-line resources, such as websites that allow multicultural information to be downloaded, to supplement teaching strategies. Also, members discussed ways to electronically share information and stay in touch over Spring Break.
- **Jessica:** jbarnes@mail.utexas.edu
- **Carrie:** carriecubb@mail.utexas.edu
- **Michelle:** misha@austin.rr.com
- **Kelly:** kelfit@aol.com
- **Rachelle:** ryancy@ix.netcom.com

Implementation: News from the Classroom

- **Research Projects:** Carrie and Rachelle have started their class research with the *Odyssey* and have suggested that we teach research skills during the first semester next year. The students are still "fresh" and the library is still open. Students would be able to use the skills they've acquired throughout the remainder of the year, and they will have learned persuasive writing *before* the TAAS practice. *Night* and "Flight Crew" projects lend themselves well to research, both of which are in the first semester.
- **New Curriculum Standards:** Group members support Mrs. Blackett's new curriculum plan and are eager to get started. Grade level teachers will need to get together to set goals and standards.
- **"Story of an Hour":** While most members "ran out of time" to implement the poetry we discussed at the last meeting, Jessica is using "Story of an Hour" as a culminating activity for the *Odyssey*. She reports that the students especially enjoy the ending of the story and not only catch the irony, but seem to be discovering interesting connections to the *Odyssey*. Her only suggestion would be to change the assessment from an essay to a class discussion with a short Quickwrite instead.

> "The world is your exercise book, the pages on which you do your sums."
> Richard Bach

Plans for Next Meeting

◆ Michelle: Have Chris call Reed for "Romeo and Juliet in Sarejevo" video. Bring copy of multicultural article for discussion. Talk to Massey about setting up a day for curriculum planning.
◆ Jessica: Get quote from Marcia that ties in with Brooks poem.
◆ Carrie: Bring website address for quotes and list of children's books that teach literary elements.
◆ Kelly: Bring web address for the site where we can download multicultural information.
◆ Rachelle: Make copies of R&J rap and Dream soundtrack, bring copies of "creating own culture," type the newsletter, examples of Renaissance Faire exhibits.
EVERYBODY: Review copy of article Jessica brought for discussion. Bring copies of quotes for book.

NEXT MEETING
March 21st
4:15 Room 722

Group Members

Jessica Barnes	**Carrie Cubberley**
Rachelle Cameron	**Michelle Graf**
Kelly Steinberg	

"Ignorance is the curse of God.
Knowledge the wind
wherewith we fly to heaven.
~ William Shakespeare

Opening Doors

March 24, 1999

Volume 1, Issue 9

Items Addressed

- **Multicultural Children's Books:** Carrie brought a great list of multicultural children's books that can be used to teach different literary devices that she discovered in the English Journal. Though the list is extensive, as a group we only had copies of a couple of them. We have agreed to add them to our "Wish Lists" and try to acquire copies to use next year.
- **Romeo and Juliet Characterization:** Kelly and Rachelle each provided copies of different worksheets that aid in students' comprehension of character differences in Romeo and Juliet.
- **Quotes and Technology:** Jessica brought a list of Odyssey quotes and Internet addresses to add to our new "Quote Book." Members discussed the possibility of getting together over the summer to put together our resources so that it is manageable and easily accessible.
- **Music/ Multimedia:** Rachelle provided copies of about 15 songs and their lyrics that deal with the idea of "dreams." She used this last year with Mercutio's Queen Mab speech with great success. Students love this lesson and tend to bring more copies of songs each year. Also, copies were provided of the Romeo and Juliet rap to use with the prologue.

Implementation: News from the Classroom

- **Poetry/Masks/Romeo and Juliet:** Group members report using Langston Hughes' poem, "Dreams" and Paul Dunbar's poem "We Wear the Mask" with great success. "Mask" is especially effective in discussing acceptance, individuality, and different cultures. It ended up being a wonderful piece to finish up the year because it relates so well to nearly all of the pieces we have read. It also works extremely well with the ballroom scene performance and the "mask assignment." This year we've changed the assignment so that each student must express their own duality with their indivual masks. This ties in with their very first assignment...the mandala.

- **Concerns and Recommendations:** Group members are concerned that we do not have enough time to incorporate all of the multicultural resources that we have acquired this year. The consensus is that we need to focus on the skills we're teaching as opposed to classroom activity. Group has agreed that we need to categorize everything that we do under specific TEKS in order to better assess what areas need to be developed.

"The world is your exercise book, the pages on which you do your sums."
Richard Bach

- **Renaissance Faire:** Teacher info and student examples were shared. Kelly, Michelle and Jess will be using the Faire as their research project this year.

Plans for Next Meeting

◆ Michelle: Bring copy of an article to share with group.
◆ Jessica:
◆ Carrie:
◆ Kelly: Notes to Mr. Perez
◆ Rachelle: Newsletter

EVERYBODY: Review copy of article Jessica brought for discussion. Bring copies of quotes for book.

This will be our last meeting for the year!!!
NEXT MEETING
April 7th
4:15 Room 722

Group Members

Jessica Barnes	Carrie Cubberley
Rachelle Cameron	Michelle Graf
Kelly Steinberg	

Resource D

Examples of Instructional Council Meetings

- Jackson Elementary School
  Minutes for October 20

- Jackson Elementary School
  Minutes for January 19

- Jackson Elementary School
  Minutes for February 23

- Maynard Elementary School
  Minutes for September 24

- Webster County Elementary-Middle School
  Minutes for December 7

NOTE: These documents are reprinted by permission from Jackson Elementary School, Maynard Elementary School, and Webster County Elementary-Middle School, respectively.

Jackson Elementary School
Instructional Council Minutes: October 20

Representatives present were Kyle, Jennifer, Maggie, Pam, Jennifer, Jane, and Teresa. Barry Shelofsky, principal, facilitated the meeting. Linda is taking notes (Linda is Focus Team member). Barry read the purpose of the Instructional Council from Murphy & Lick's book, page 60. Each representative is to share their study group's Action Plan and its connection with students. We will also share our concerns and our causes for applause. Barry reminded the representatives that ALL study groups will share their work on Monday, December 14.

Review of Action Plans

SG #1:

- Focusing on spelling and increasing accurate spelling of high frequency words

- Looking at Houghton-Mifflin (H-M) series for spelling structure and to correlate words from H-M with high frequency words

- Looking for common spelling errors and using a No Excuses list. This list was brought to the group by a member who had visited a teacher from Loveland.

- Looking at ways to apply spelling knowledge by looking at research on spelling and using the H-M series

SG #2:

- Focusing on revising within the writing process, identify and evaluate words based on variety and creativity, need to include details which consistently support the topic

SG #3:

- Focusing on secondary trait of grammar and mechanics
- Sharing strategies for spelling
- Looking at grids for student documentation of progress
- Surveying all teachers

SG #4:

- Starting with a focus on expository writing but narrowed the topic down to writing summaries

- Looking at H-M which does a lot with oral summaries but doesn't do as much with written summaries

- Looking at Read-Write Connection
- Developing story maps to use with H-M

SG #5:

- Looking at summarizing, identifying topic and main ideas to support topic
- Looking at summaries for nonfiction and have shared strategies
- Realizing that using strategies may not be the problem, but lack of modeling could be

SG #6:

- Started talking about spelling but problems with handwriting kept surfacing
- Researching D'Nealian handwriting and will receive a teachers edition and student workbook from Scott-Foresman to preview
- Enlisting the help of a 2nd and 4th grade teacher so that one teacher from grades K-5 will use the D'Nealian Program for handwriting during this school year
- Developing an Action Research design for users and nonusers of the D'Nealian Program
- Developing a letter to give to all parents about the handwriting program at conference time. Parents of students not involved in the research will be notified of the action research project in the Jackson Newsletter

SG #7:

- Experiencing frustration because only two classroom teachers are in this study group—should assistants be doing something else to help students?
- Using the Internet to look for information on planning writing
- Looking at weekly writing tasks because we have noticed that students are having trouble with order in their stories
- Researching how to provide consistency across grade levels

SG #8:

- Barry invited a group of administrators to form a study group
- Reading and discussing WFSG book
- Reflecting on study groups as a process; how can the concept be taken to the district level?
- Spelling and handwriting issues could have implications for district

Concerns

SG #1: No concerns. Kristine will attend a spelling conference. Master spelling list from H-M was received.

SG #2: One study group member (part-time person) is not always available.

SG #3: One study group member is not always available. Maggie would like for us to share more often. **Response:** Barry will contact the staff members. Carlene stresses consistent attendance. The situation necessitates a give and take to resolve attendance issue.

SG #4: This group has good cross-grade-level representation. How can we share more with grade-level members in other study groups? **Response:** Study group members will need to schedule these meetings on their own. Study groups involved in similar research/activities could hold a joint meeting to share information. Both study groups might want to invite a resource person to address the groups on the topic they are pursuing.

SG #5: Questions—Does the study group have to have an end product? Do other teachers at the same level have other great ideas that we could use in our study group? **Response:** 1) Study groups have created action plans. Each action plan has a section that speaks to intended results of the work of the study group. While an end product is not required, at the December and April sharing, study groups should be able to share how their work in study groups have made it into the classroom with children. Carlene states that the desired end result of these collegial relationships is increased success for all students. 2) We are going to have two all-faculty sharing sessions on Monday, December 14, and on Monday, April 26.

SG #6: Study group is sending a letter to parents about the students learning D'Nealian.

SG #7: Only two classroom teachers in the study group. Could assistants be using their time in another way? **Response:** Instructional Assistants that work directly with children are an integral part of the study group/ schoolwide project process. Study groups are urged to look for ways all group members work toward the goals of each action plan. Carlene states that individual study group members must "take responsibility for their own learning and for seeking resources for the study group." Also, since IAs are not paid for staying at school when the children are released early, we are paying them for study group time.

Each representative is reminded to take part of the next study group meeting to share with all members what we have discussed today.

Jackson Elementary School
Instructional Council Meeting: January 19, 7:00 A.M.

Representatives present were Dorothy, Caryn, Darlene, Ken, Elisa, and Lloyd. Jo is sick and unable to attend. Kris facilitated the meeting. Roslyn is taking notes. Barry is out of town (Kris and Roz are Focus Team members).

Kris read the purpose of the IC from WFSG book on page 60. Kris reviewed the whole-faculty sharing session that was held on December 14. Each study group had made a poster. All groups used the same format for doing the posters. On each study group's poster, they were to share

- Purpose/goal of study group, as per action plan

- Topic of study

- Things we've tried, ideas to share

- Questions we still have

- Where we are going

The posters were due to Barry on the morning of Dec. 14. Posters were hung in the Gym and the whole faculty met in the Gym at 2:00. Groups were formed, having one person from each study group in a group. The "mixed" groups moved from poster to poster at 10-minute intervals. Upon arriving at each poster, the person in the "mixed" group that is in that study group explained the information on the poster.

Representatives were asked to share their experience with making the poster and sharing the information on the poster. **One poster is attached to these minutes.**

SG #1: After reviewing the group's action plan as we were preparing to do the poster, the group was concerned that some of us are not able to apply the work in the classroom. Julia brought a phonics game she is using. The group is going to make the materials for the game in our meetings. Ken will attempt to use the game during PE time with students who are unable to participate. If it works, we are considering purchasing the game, although it is expensive. Jane is coming to talk to the group about spelling.

SG #2: When making the poster, we realized how hard it had been for us to agree on a focus. We need to revise our action plan to better meet the classroom application part.

SG #3: Our group is working on spelling and writing strategies. The group is very focused. We are continuing to look for more spelling strategies to use. We are currently using Sharon's program and strategies from Lynette and Pat. We are working toward using consistent vocabulary in all grades. The group would also like to see D'Nealian Handwriting used consistently.

SG #4: The poster was not difficult to complete for our group. Sharon did artwork for the poster so the group did not see the completed poster until the sharing day. Having Sharon in our group is great because she has wonderful ideas, but the consistency of her schedule is difficult. The study group has a new member, Pat XXX. We are excited to have her and may need to consider updating our action plan to incorporate what Pat has to offer the group.

SG #5: The poster that we completed seemed to be reflective of how the group functions with each person taking a part and putting it all together and seeing it all work out. We work well together. A concern that we have is that we need to change or update our action plan. We have been working of penmanship and we have noticed students being more careful when writing. The next part of our action plan needs to be for us to work on punctuation. We noticed some overlap of our work with other study groups.

SG #6: The poster was fun to complete. Our study group feels as though we are focused and know what we are working on. The group is struggling with only having 2 out of 5 members who teach in the regular classroom. This leads us to sometimes wonder if what we are doing is really making an impact. The study group will continue to use more materials.

Other Questions or Concerns

Dorothy wondered how Barry's study group is doing. We would like to hear more about what the group of administrators is doing.

Elisa said she felt that the groups are going well. The study groups are discussing and working on important things.

The meeting adjourned at 8:10 A.M.

Remember: Take back to your study group what you learned today!!

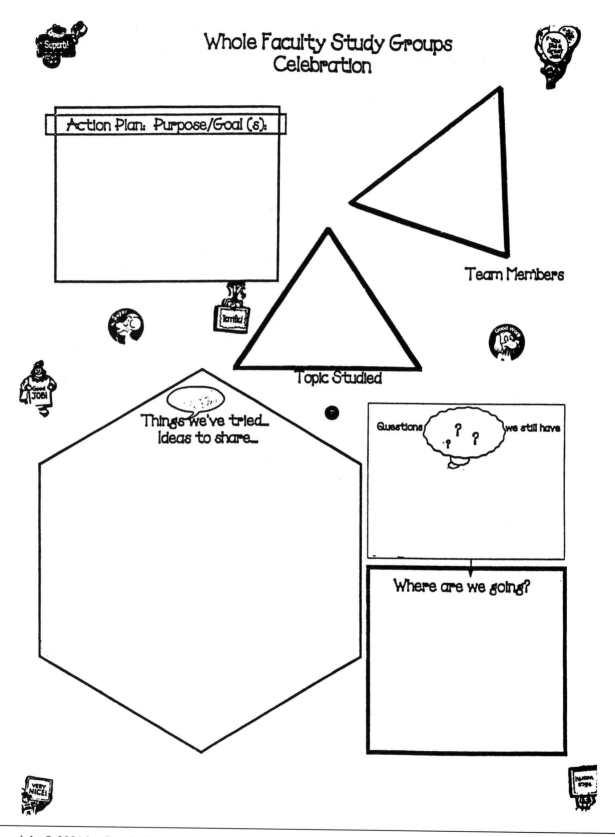

Whole Faculty Study Groups
Celebration

Action Plan: Purpose/Goal (s):

Team Members

Topic Studied

Things we've tried...
Ideas to share...

Questions we still have

Where are we going?

Jackson Elementary School
Instructional Council Meeting: February 23, 7:45 A.M.

Representatives present were Kyle, Audrey, Lynnette, Elisa, Kelly, Beth, and Tracey. Roz facilitated the meeting. Linda is taking notes (Roz and Linda are Focus Team members).

Each representative was asked to share the work the groups are doing every Monday afternoon.

SG #1: We have been working on spelling. We have narrowed our study to phonetic spelling. Julia has taught the group how to play the Phonics Game and now the group is making classroom sets of cards to use with all of our students. Even coach will make a set for kids who need to sit out of gym activities!

SG #2: We have been working on developing a revising checklist students can use to help them revise their papers. We have watched demonstrations on tape of second and fifth graders peer editing. (Second graders with second graders and fifth graders with second graders). The purpose of this was to listen for words they use with each other in hopes the words would help us make the checklists student friendly. Jennifer has a checklist she uses with her students. We will look closer at that list and develop a parallel one for second grade that will be developmentally appropriate. We may also look at the one Jennifer is using to see if it is exactly what we want students to use or if in fact is should undergo changes.

SG #3: We have been developing a dictionary for primary and intermediate grades to go along with our spelling focus. The primary dictionary will have 119 words and the intermediate, 500 words. We are also looking at resources dealing with spelling.

SG #4: We are also using Maureen Auman's summarizing resources to apply in our classrooms. Roe Ann is teaching summarizing by having the students orally sum up the activities of each day. She has also shared her activity with parents in her newsletter and has received good feedback. Kristine has used summarizing activities for CSAP [Colorado Student Assessment Program] preparation and in math with the problem of the day. Jennifer and Kelly have worked on narrative summarization using picture books. The students have described a strong character and then summarized the book, dressed as the character. We have videotaped the summaries. Pam has helped her students write strong summaries in the fewest amount of words to align with CSAP expectations.

SG #5: We have been using strategies to help students with summarizing. After looking at some of Maureen Auman's work, the dash outline was adapted to grade levels and used in classrooms, as was the jot story plan. Peggy and Caryn shared how the activities worked in their classrooms. Sharon's student teacher is participating in our study group and he has shared how he has adapted a plan in art.

SG #6: We are researching handwriting curriculums. We are working on questions like, Is there a need to teach handwriting? Will the district adopt a handwriting curriculum? How many students do not pass the writing assessment because of handwriting? Why do students use nice handwriting during handwriting and then not carry it over in other areas? We talked to teachers in other schools in our district about handwriting and to teachers in other districts. We are continuing the application of D'Nealian in classrooms.

SG #7: We are focusing on sequencing. We have used Maureen Auman's materials and have shared application of the materials in our classrooms. Audrey has used familiar rhymes and had her students illustrate the rhymes. Teresa has used comic strips and as the students manipulate the strips into correct sequence, organizational skills are improved. Audrey and Tracey have made centers with sentence strips, using first, next, and last to reinforce the beginning, middle, and end of a story as well as transition words. We are planning to look through the CSAP modules geared at organization and adapt those to our specific classroom needs.

Concerns

Lynnette's group (#5) expressed a concern about study groups next year being homogeneous.

Kelly's group (#4) is questioning the accountability of students concerning the CSAP. Right now, teachers are held accountable but not students.

Audrey's group (#7) is concerned about whether instructional assistants should be compensated for attending Instructional Council meetings.

Beth's group (#2) is having a problem with two study group members that are not able to attend Instructional Council meetings because of the conflicts with special education meetings.

Representatives were reminded to take time at the next study group meeting to discuss the work of all the study groups.

Instructional Council Meeting

Maynard PK—6 School
An ATLAS Communities' School
September 24, 1:00 P.M.

This is the first Instructional Council meeting. Of the seven study groups, all have met twice except one group. Representatives from six of the seven study groups were present. Mr. Dancy, the principal, served as the facilitator of the meeting. Carlene Murphy was present.

Mr. Dancy began the meeting by reviewing the WFSG status. The whole faculty was trained in the procedures of WFSG on August 30 and 31. Seven study groups were formed. There are two study groups focusing on writing, three study groups focusing on reading, one math study group, and one science study group. The study groups met for the first time during the week of September 13. The study groups were asked to accomplish four tasks by the end of the groups' second meetings. The study groups met a second time on September 21. The tasks to be accomplished during the first two meetings were

- Establish group norms. Write in log.
- Establish the leadership rotation schedule. Write in log.
- Establish the dates and times the study group will meet for the school year, totaling at least 20 hours. Write in log.
- To develop the Study Group Action Plan.

Mr. Dancy asked the representatives from each group to bring the action plans with them. It is assumed that after the Instructional Council meeting, the representatives will have suggestions to take back to the study groups that will cause the groups to revisit past decisions.

The purpose of today's meeting is for each representative to share each study group's action plan and any problems that the group is having in making decisions about what the group will do. Carlene will respond to those points that she feels will emphasize aspects of WFSGs that will be helpful for all the representatives to hear discussed.

- *SG #1:* The representative reported that her study group had decided to use the norms that the whole school had approved last school year. Carlene asked the teacher to share with her what those norms were. The teachers did not have a copy of the norms and could not remember what all of the norms were. Carlene suggested that the norms for a group of four people might be different than the norms for a group of 30 people. Since all of the study group members did not have a copy of the faculty's norms when the study group made the decision to adopt that set of norms, a copy should be given to each study group member at the next meeting. If revisions are made, this would be recorded in the Study Group Log. The representatives from the other study groups were asked to share one or two norms that their groups had established. Carlene emphasized that the norms should be revisited at every other study group meeting. The notation to do so should be recorded on the logs in the space titled "For next meeting, we need to." This will remind the leader of the next study group meeting to ask if the norms are supporting the learning of all group members.

■ *SG #2:* The representative shared that she thought that her study group had selected a student need that was too general. Carlene asked her to state that need, and she said, "Students need to read more books at home." When the teacher was asked to share what the teachers will do when the study group meets to address that need, she read what the teachers wanted the students to do. Carlene then asked, "If that is what you want your students to do at home and in the classroom, what will **you** do when the study group meets?" The teacher responded that in October when the students do the book reports, the study group will examine the book reports. Carlene said, "What will you do between now and then?" The teacher replied, "Oh, I see." The teacher was led to a clearer understanding that the study group needs to state what the study group members will do at the study group meeting to cause the students to "read more books at home." These actions become the group's body of work. Other study group representatives joined in the conversation and began to make suggestions. The study group could design a letter to be sent to parents. The study group could meet in the media center and identify appropriate books in each content area for the students to check out. The study group could design a rubric or other type of rating system for the books. The representative saw that it wasn't that the student need was too general but that the study group had not put the emphasis on what the teachers had to do to bring about the change in student behavior.

■ *SG #3:* The representative spoke directly to two concerns. First, is there money available to buy a book for the study group? The principal said that there is and if the teacher would supply the information, the book would be ordered. The other concern that the teacher expressed related to the participation of each study group member. She indicated that even though it was stressed in the study group that the Action Plan was to reflect the opinions of all members, one or two members did not talk, and the teacher is afraid that those teachers will not feel ownership in the Action Plan. She also indicated that she and another member are so excited about what the group is going to do that she may have talked too much. She wondered if this dynamic continued, if someone could observe the group to give the group feedback on "talk time." Mr. Dancy said that there are individuals that he could ask to be process observers.

■ *SG #4:* The representative reported that her study group is going to compile a list of all the software and other resources available to teachers at the school and to give that list to the faculty. Carlene cautioned the teacher about taking this path. Carlene said that the group should be doing what the members themselves need, not what they think other teachers need. If the study group needs to know what is available, then not only would they do an inventory, but they would use the materials with their students. At some point, the group would probably want to share the results of their usage. The representative indicated that this was very helpful information and that it would certainly make a difference in what the group would now do. The group had completed its Action Plan but will now revise it to reflect today's discussion.

- *SG #5:* The representative shared that her study group of three teachers had met with only two members present. Even though the two had a good discussion, the presence of the third member at the next meeting would be important. The third member serves more than one school, so the group may have to adjust when it meets to make sure all three members will be present at the meetings. The group is still working on its action plan.

- *SG #6:* The representative shared that the group has a long list of what they want to do in the study group meetings and that they are having difficulty deciding what they will actually have time to do. Carlene asked her to share the specific student needs the study group is addressing. The teacher just looked at Carlene and smiled. Carlene's question told her what the group had not done. The study group selected the general category, reading, but had not specified the specific student needs in reading that the study group will address. Once the study group is specific about which reading needs the group will address, it will be clearer as to which of the actions on their list the group should take. The representatives were reminded that student needs drive the work of the study groups.

- It was reported by the principal that one group had not met and is not represented today. Mr. Dancy will meet with members of the group to determine the status.

Other items discussed:

- All of the groups that have met have group norms and have established the rotation of leadership schedule. There is a general feeling of appreciation that no one member felt the pressure of being THE leader.

- All the representatives expressed the opinion that more work needs to be done on the action plans.

- The representatives wanted to know what to do if the group needed resources that are not available at the school, such as a textbook in how to teach reading. Mr. Dancy said to let him know and he will do what he can to secure the needed items.

- The representative had questions about the route Study Group Logs should take. Whoever is the leader for a meeting will make copies for each study group member, plus two. One extra copy will be given to the principal. The other extra copy will be put on the study group's clipboard. All of the study groups should expect Mr. Dancy to give the groups feedback on what the groups are doing. This feedback will be verbal, a Post-it note on the log from the last meeting, or another form of written feedback. Mr. Dancy stated that his main concern is seeing that the study groups have the resources needed.

- The representatives were reminded to share what was discussed today at the next study group meetings.

- The next IC meeting will be in four weeks.

INSTRUCTIONAL COUNCIL MEETING

Webster County Elementary School
An ATLAS Communities' School
December 7

Background: Webster County Elementary School is a PreK-8th-grade school. There are 31 classroom teachers and 15 teaching assistants. The 31 teachers are in six study groups. There are three study groups composed of teaching assistants. All of the study groups are focused on language development skills, including reading comprehension, vocabulary development, and written expression. A five-member Focus Team, which included the principal, received instruction from Carlene Murphy on the WFSG approach on September 8, 9, and 10. Within 2 weeks of that time, the study groups had formed. All of the groups are heterogeneous. By the last week in September, the principal had faxed the Action Plans for each study group to Carlene. By way of the FAX, Carlene gave feedback to each study group on its Action Plan. The plans were revised and by the second study group meeting, the groups were taking action on the planned activities. At the end of each week, the principal mailed to Carlene an envelope that contained a study group log for each study group. The study groups meet 1 hour after school each Tuesday. Pat Turner visited the school every other Tuesday and observed in the classrooms and offered content instruction to the study groups that requested her services. All teachers kept looseleaf notebooks of the work of their study groups. The notebook contained the study group's Action Plan, the log from each meeting, work that has been generated by the study group (i.e., lesson plans), and articles the members read.

On December 7, 1999, Carlene met for the day with one person from each of the nine study groups. This was a day-long Instructional Council meeting. This was the school's second IC meeting, which is usually a 1-hour meeting every 6 weeks. Carlene had requested prior to her arrival that each person bring their study group notebook and examples of student work. By this day, each study group had nine study group logs representing the nine times the study groups had met. The minutes from the meeting follow and are reprinted with permission from Webster County Elementary School.

The Instructional Council is meeting all day today. A representative from each of the nine study groups and the principal are present. The representatives have substitutes in their classrooms. The purpose of the meeting is for Carlene Murphy (hereafter, "Carlene," as she insists that we call her) to provide more instruction and clarification on the procedural guidelines and to introduce the representatives to a protocol for looking at student work. Each representative is to take the next study group meeting to go over what Carlene does with us today.

Agenda:

- Establishing norms
- Reviewing action plans for resources groups are using

- Reviewing logs to diagnose types of actions the groups are taking
- Learning to use a protocol to look at student work

I. RESOURCES as listed on the Action Plans

Each person was given copies of the Action Plans from all of the nine study groups. The plans were examined to determine what internal and external resources had been identified or were needed. Carlene stressed the importance of the "expert voice," either by way of the written word, the physical presence of an individual, or through video/audio transmission. The group collectively made the following list of possibilities and recorded the items on chart paper.

1. **Teachers' manuals.** The group decided that this is the most underused resource that the teachers have. The manuals that go with the textbooks have a wealth of information about how to teach the content. The group agreed that every teacher would bring the teachers' manuals to future study group meeting to explore how the basic skills are introduced at each grade level. Supplementary materials and textbooks need to be examined.

2. **Student textbooks.** Since developing vocabulary is one student need being addressed, it was suggested that if the study groups examine the textbooks in one content area (e.g., math), the teachers would be more consistent with the vocabulary they use when teaching. Even though publishers have published vocabulary lists, actually manipulating the students' texts would give the teachers a greater feel for what the students experience. Some of the teachers present had not looked at the student texts at other grade levels. Some of the upper grade teachers that teach one subject area had not reviewed student texts in another subject area.

3. **People** (real live). Persons from RESA (regional agency), Georgia Southwestern University, Troy State University (Alabama), GLRS (learning resource lab), state department, textbook representatives, independent consultants, and other school districts could be rich sources of information. Pat Turner was listed, as were teachers within the building that were known to have specific expertise.

4. **Books.** Sources might include textbooks from courses previously taken (e.g., reading courses), college bookstores, publishers' lists, ASCD, and other professional organizations. Several groups are interested in using a book to give their study more structure. The group developed a cycle for such a study: read a chapter or section of the book, discuss and reflect on the reading (1 meeting), try ideas in classroom, share results of actions in classrooms and demonstrate lessons taught (1 or 2 meetings), reflect on outcomes, examine student work (1 meeting), go to the next chapter, repeat process. The cycle (plan, act, reflect) for one reading could take up to 4 study group meetings.

5. **Articles.** The school library subscribes to *The Reading Teacher, The Journal of Reading, The Journal of Educational Research, Educational Leadership,* and others. However, within the context of the focus at this school, the ones listed might generate

this most information. It was decided that if an article is to be used to generate ideas for actual classroom trials, the article should be copied for everyone in the group.

6. **The Internet and computer software.** Several groups had already copied information from the internet.

7. **Public television.** The Georgia Department of Education has courses and other professional opportunities offered via television. The media specialist copied the schedule for everyone.

8. **Workshops, conferences.** One person from the study group may attend workshops and conferences and bring the information to the study group.

9. **Commercial sources.** The following companies have materials that stress the importance of reading: Georgia Power Co., Pizza Hut, Atlanta Braves, Six Flags Over Georgia.

10. **Pat Turner.** ATLAS' site developer has a graduate degree in Reading and she has served on several state and regional committees and commissions focused on the language arts curriculum. Several groups expressed how helpful Pat has been in delivering instruction to the study groups.

11. **Student work.** Carlene had to pretty much pull this out of the group. However, once the group started the discussion, they immediately began giving examples. Since student work was to be a major part of the day's work, we decided to save the elaboration of this resource for a later time in the day.

II. STUDY GROUP ACTIONS as noted in the Study Group Logs

Since all of the representatives had copies of all of their study group's logs, each person took time to diagnose the most common actions their study group is taking. Carlene asked the representatives to skim the logs and to highlight the verbs. They found that the most common verbs were: looked, discussed, shared. The group explored what "shared" looked like in actual practice. Members discovered that "demonstrated" and "practiced" were more descriptive of what the groups were actually doing. One teacher described a phonics lesson that was taught in its entirety to the study group by another teacher and how much they had all learned from the lesson. Phonics is coming back real strong in all the reading programs, and many teachers have not been taught how to teach phonics. The discussion also underscored the shift that the representatives are beginning to see in the roll-out of the study group process. They started from an investigative perspective, taking a more passive role. Now they are ready to "act," such as developing lessons together, teaching each other, demonstrating actions taken in the classroom, looking at student work.

III. LOOKING AT STUDENT WORK

Prior to Carlene's arrival, she had requested that each representative bring with them to the meeting examples of student work. Her instructions were

"Bring one student's work from one class assignment and four copies of that same piece of student work. If the work is too large to copy, just bring the original work. Also, from another assignment, bring the work of four students that represent a range of performance."

Before the group began the process of looking at the work the teachers brought with them, members brainstormed on chart paper:

1. Types of student work:

    - Written work on 8½" × 11" paper
    - Projects involving manipulatives (e.g., science, math, social studies)
    - Exhibits (e.g., posters, tri-boards, cutouts)
    - Performance (e.g., videos, audiocassettes)
    - Art
    - Portfolios

2. Types of assignments that generate student work

    - Creative stories, poems
    - Descriptions of experiences
    - Answering questions
    - Research reports
    - Multiple choice
    - Open-ended responses
    - Illustrations
    - Data analysis and collections of information
    - Experiments
    - Problem solving
    - Interviews
    - E-mail and other correspondence

After a very rich discussion, the nine representatives were divided into two groups. They used the Wows and Wonders protocol on two pieces of work when everyone was looking at the same piece of work, and they used the protocol when looking at the work from different students. After spending about 2 hours looking at the work they brought, Carlene asked them what they saw as the advantages of using a protocol. The responses that we recorded on chart paper were

- One person does not do all the talking
- It gives teachers new insights into the work
- It does not matter what grade the work comes from, we can see common problems across grade levels

- We gain knowledge about what and how content is taught in other grades
- Causes self-reflection
- It is the teacher who brings the work that is the learner (we had thought that it was just the opposite)

IV. REFLECTION on the day

Each representative outlined a plan for how he or she would take the information we covered to their study group. Each representative stated that he or she would bring student work to the next study group meeting and teach the group the protocol.

The next Instructional Council meeting will be on January 25, 2000, from 2:00 to 3:00 p.m. Classes will be covered for the representatives who attend the meeting.

Resource E

The Decision-Making Cycle

Examples are given in this section of how faculties experience the steps on the decision-making cycle (DMC), as shown in Figure 6.1.

- A Plan for Working With the Whole Faculty
- A Script for Leading the Faculty Through the DMC
- Example 1: Using Strategy 1 for Completing Step 2 and Step 3 on the DMC
- Example 2: Using Strategy 2 for Completing Step 2 and Step 3 on the DMC
- Example 3: Using Strategy 3 for Completing Step 2 and Step 3 on the DMC
- Example 4: Using Strategy 4 for Completing Step 2 and Step 3 on the DMC

A Plan for Working With the Whole Faculty

I. Dates and Times

    1. When will the focus team meet to continue planning?

    2. The date for Session 1 (Orientation)

    3. The date and time for Session 2 (DMC)

    4. Target date for first round of study group meetings

    5. Target date for when study group action plans are due

    6. Target dates for Instructional Council meetings

II. What data will need to be gathered for Session 2?

III. Agenda for Session 1

    1. What will be the content?

    2. Who will present what?

    3. What materials will be needed? (Hint: looseleaf notebooks)

IV. Agenda for Session 2

    1. Who will be responsible for Steps 1 through 4 on the DMC?

    2. What will be in the data folder on each table?

    3. Who will "set up" the room?

    4. How will be faculty be organized into table groups?

    5. Who will have a laptop computer to record the groups' work?

    6. What option will you use for categorizing the specific needs?

    7. What materials will you need to have copied for everyone?

IV. Who will you invite from outside the school?

A Script for Leading the Faculty
Through the Decision-Making Cycle

Session 1 With the Whole Faculty

Prior to leading the faculty through the DMC, the focus team has provided a general orientation to the WFSG process. This can be done in a 2-hour block of time or in two 1-hour blocks and usually on a day prior to the day faculty experiences the DMC. For the general orientation, focus teams that have attended a WFSG institute would select from materials and activities used during Day 1 of the institute. For planning teams that have not attended a WFSG institute, the team would use materials from Chapters 1 through 6 in this book. Focus teams that attend an institute are asked to read Chapters 1 through 4 prior to the institute, and likewise, the teams give the faculties material to read prior to the whole-faculty orientation. Key materials to cover in the orientation are most of Chapter 3, research from Chapter 5, and guidelines from Chapter 6. Teams are encouraged to use novel ways to introduce faculties to this material. Cooperative learning strategies work best.

Between Sessions 1 and 2

After the orientation and preferably on another day, the focus team leads the whole faculty through the DMC. This should be scheduled on a day and at a time when the faculty can concentrate on this most important task.

Prior to this session, the focus team identifies and collects data the faculty will use in the decision-making process. In Chapter 7, there is a list of data. The key to quality, meaningful study group content is the quality and appropriateness of the data the faculty reviews. Teams want the faculty to focus on the instructional or academic needs of students. Therefore, the data collected for the faculty to review should show evidence of instructional needs.

Session 2 With the Whole Faculty

The whole faculty convenes in one place. The faculty will remain together for the entire exercise, or the faculty will be divided into groups and assigned to classrooms to work. If the whole faculty stays in one room, individuals would sit at tables with not more than 6 at a table. It is important to use some technique to ensure that the 6 people represent different grade levels or different departments. A technique often used is to have a sheet of paper taped to the table that has written on it, for example, Pre-K Teacher, First Grade Teacher, Third Grade Teacher, Fifth Grade Teacher, Special Needs Teacher, Librarian. Don't use names, just positions. This will facilitate the analysis of the data. For example, first grade teachers can explain tests that are administered at the primary levels, and fifth grade teachers can explain tests that are administered at the upper grade levels. A focus team member would be at each table, or the team would circulate among the tables.

If the whole faculty is divided into working groups that will go to different class-rooms to do the work, the groups should be mixed by grade or department. The faculty would be given a sheet of paper that lists the names of individuals in the groups, in which classrooms the groups will meet, and any special instructions. Focus team members would be assigned to each of the classrooms to facilitate the work of the groups. The groups would also be told when everyone is to report back to the large meeting area.

At each table in the large meeting room or in each classroom, there would be a chart stand with chart paper and markers. Also, appropriate forms and checklists (see Resource A) and samples of action plans (see Resource B) will need to have been copied and ready to distribute at the appropriate time. Suggested materials are as follows:

- The form "Stating Specific Student Needs After Analyzing Data"
- The form "Study Group Action Plan"
- Checklist for Writing an Action Plan
- Samples of action plans
- Figure 6.2 in WFSG textbook
- Figure 6.4 in WFSG textbook

Step 1

Each table group in the large meeting room or table groups in the classrooms should have a set of data in a folder in the middle of the table (each table group has the same set of data) or the school improvement plan. Each working group distributes the data among those at the table so that each person has data to review. The groups spend about 30 minutes reviewing and discussing data.

Step 2

After analyzing and reviewing the data, each individual in each working group uses the form "Stating Specific Student Needs After Analyzing Data" to write specific student needs that are apparent from the data that that individual is reviewing. Individuals may also include academic needs that they know students have even if there is no evidence of the needs in the current data. Before writing a student need, the need should fit within the following parameters:

- The need is evident in the work that the students produce; therefore, examining student work will be an activity of the study group.

- The need can be addressed through how and what teachers teach.

- The need is an enabling need, meaning it is a need that enables the student to be academically successful, such as reading and writing; or you could say it is a terminal need, meaning at some point, the need will no longer exist or will end. This is unlike a perennial need, a need that is always there, such as the need to attend school, the need to feel good about self, the need to cooperate. Teachers have direct control of or influence on instructional needs.

Each working group in the large meeting room or in the classrooms brainstorms specific student needs, using the three needs that each person wrote. The group's recorder writes the student needs on chart paper as individuals call out the needs. The chart paper is titled "Students need to _____." Needs are numbered. Every need should begin with a verb! Step 2 usually takes about 30 minutes.

Step 3

There are at least four strategies for categorizing and prioritizing student needs, briefly described in the following discussion. Later in this section, there are examples of the four strategies.

Strategy 1 (see example on page 283)

- The whole faculty remains together and completes Steps 1 through 4 together.

- Groups of teachers work at tables, and each table group completes Steps 1 and 2.

- The leader surveys the student need lists generated by all the table groups. The leader selects what appears to be the most comprehensive list. This list becomes the master list and is taped to a wall. (A break may be called at this time and the master list quickly typed, printed, and copied for everyone.)

- When everyone can view the master list, student needs from other groups that are not on this master list are added and numbered sequentially.

- The leader asks everyone to look at the master list and on a sheet of paper, working alone, put the student needs into categories.

- The leader asks for volunteers to share one of their categories and the numbers of the student needs that fit in that category. A volunteer shares one category he or she has, giving the numbers of the student needs and the name of the category. This is repeated until all categories or similar categories that individuals formed have been listed.

- The leader then asks everyone to work alone and prioritize categories and for priorities #1 and #2 to write a rationale justifying each priority. Individuals share at their table. Focus team members scan tables to check the level of consensus.

- Note: Prioritizing the categories may not be necessary. One category of student need may be so outstanding that it is obvious that the category must be confronted immediately by all teachers. Also, some faculties may not want to prioritize categorizes because they want all categories to remain as choices.

Strategy 2 (see example on page 285)

- The whole faculty is divided into subfaculty or work groups and are assigned to different classrooms to complete Steps 1 through 3. Groups are cross-grade or department. Each group is to

  1. Analyze the data

  2. List the student needs

3. Categorize the needs

4. Prioritize the needs

■ Each working group writes a rationale for the prioritizing. (A break may be called at this time, giving each group time to type, print, and copy for the whole faculty the group's work.)

■ The whole faculty reconvenes, and each small group shares its work. Because all the working groups are working with the same data, there is usually a high level of consensus among the groups; groups may not have used the same names for the categories, but the names will be synonymous.

Strategy 3 (see example on page 290)

■ The whole faculty is divided into subfaculty or work groups. The groups are cross-grade or department. The work groups may stay in one room, or the groups may be assigned to classrooms. The groups are instructed to only complete Step 1 and Step 2, meaning that the groups are to

1. Analyze the data

2. State and list the student needs

■ The focus team collects all lists (on chart paper) of student needs from all the tables in the large meeting room or from all the groups in the classrooms. If working groups are in classrooms, everyone returns to the large meeting room.

■ All the lists are taped to the walls in one line (list to list) in the large meeting room, or the lists have been entered into a computer, printed, and copied for everyone.

■ Lists are renumbered so that they are sequentially numbered. For example, if the first list on the wall ends with number 12, then the first number on the second list becomes 13, and so on.

■ The whole faculty views the lists, and individuals put the needs in categories. Some individuals may need to stand or move to read the lists if the lists have not been entered into a computer, printed, and copied for everyone.

■ The leader asks for categories and the numbers of the student needs that make up the categories until there is general agreement that all the student needs have been put in a category.

■ If the faculty wants to prioritize, then the leader facilitates this discussion. Refer back to last bulleted item in Strategy 1.

Strategy 4 (see example on page 295)

■ This strategy is basically the same as Strategy 1. The difference is in the decisions that are made when the faculty is asked to prioritize the categories.

■ If it is clear to the faculty that one category of student needs outweighs all the other categories, the faculty will need to do an analysis of that category. The faculty will need to examine all the student needs that form the category and categorize those needs into subcategories. The subcategories become the basis for organizing the study groups.

Step 4

If there is little or no consensus regarding what the priority needs are, this is an indicator that the faculty wants to accept all or most of the categories as options for study groups. If there is a clear consensus as to the priority need, this is an indicator that the whole faculty will address one student need in all the study groups. The leaders now have direction for how to organize the groups.

Practice Writing Action Plans

Before study groups are formed, everyone needs to know how to write a SGAP. Each person is given a handout that includes a blank SGAP form, Checklist for Writing a Study Group Action Plan, and samples of action plans that are in Resources A and B. This is the time for every individual to practice writing an action plan. This is not to be group work; each person works alone.

The leader directs the faculty through this practice, by saying

- Select the category you want to address in a study group. Write it. (Leader waits until everyone has done this!)

- List specific student needs in the category that you want to address, going back to specific needs on brainstormed lists. (Leader waits until everyone has done this!)

- List what you want to do when your study group meets to address the student needs you listed. (Leader checks lists!)

After everyone has written an action plan, plans are rotated around the table so that everyone at a table reads all plans developed at the table. The leader will have everyone pass his or her plan to the person on the right. After about 1 minute, the leader says "Pass." This is repeated until each person's plan is returned to him or her. Plans are not discussed nor questions asked when plans are being passed. Individuals can make notes on a piece of paper about the plans they would like more information or clarification about. After all plans have been rotated around the table, groups have a 10- to 15-minute discussion.

Forming Study Groups

The leader states, "Those who wrote an action plan for Reading, stand." If 6 or less stand, the leader will say "You are a study group." If more than 6 people stand, the leader will say "Go to Room ___ and form groups of 6 or less. Write the names by groups on a piece of paper, and bring me the paper."

The leader repeats the foregoing procedure for every general category that the faculty wanted to leave as choices for study groups.

At the first study group meeting, the members share the individual plans that were written. This sharing will provide ideas that will go into the one action plan for that study group.

Step 5

By the end of the second study group meeting, groups should have

- Established the rotation of leadership
- Established group norms

- Completed the group's SGAP
- Established a meeting schedule (if there are options for meeting dates and times)

At the third study group meeting, or as soon as the action plan has been completed, select one of the actions on the plan and do it! As soon as the action plan is finished, do what is on the plan.

- Ready!
- Set!
- Go!

Step 6

Once the group begins carrying out the actions listed on the right side of the action plan, there will be an ongoing cycle of

- Taking action
- Collecting data
- Reflecting on action
- Adjusting plan

Step 7

Assess progress by looking at the evidence reflected in the data that were originally used to identify the student need.

Example 1:
Using Strategy 1 for Completing Step 2
and Step 3 on the DMC

A faculty used part of a preplanning day for the focus team to give the faculty an orientation to the WFSG process. On an afternoon during the second week of school, the team led the faculty through Steps 1 through 4 of the DMC. The teachers understood that by the end of the 2-hour session, as a whole faculty, they would determine what the study groups would do and how the groups would be organized. For the 2 hours, the 30 teachers remained in the same room, with 5 people at each table. At each of the six tables, a cross section of grades was represented.

The faculty was given the following instructions:

1. Review the student data in the folder on the tables.

2. Discuss the data.

3. Individually, complete the "Stating Specific Student Needs After Analyzing Data" form.

4. On chart paper, with each person using his or her list, make one composite list that represents all the individuals at the table.

5. *Do not categorize or prioritize the list.*

6. Tape the list to the wall. (At the end of this activity, six lists were taped to the walls.)

When all the six table groups had taped the lists to the walls, the leader instructed everyone to look at all the lists and to read each list carefully. Individuals were encouraged to move closer to the lists if they could not see from where they were sitting.

The leader stood next to the list that seemed to be the most comprehensive and stated that this list would be the master list. The leader then asked,

■ Are there student needs on the other lists that are not on this one? If so, let's add those needs to the master list.

■ Are there student needs that are not within the parameters of instructional needs that are on the list? If so, we need to determine who will be the appropriate person or what committee or other unit at the school should address that need. Once that assignment is made, we will scratch the need off the master list. (The chart will be saved so that the needs scratched off the list can be given to the appropriate person or committee.)

The leader renumbered the master list as needed.

Everyone was asked to use a piece of paper to categorize the needs, working alone. The student needs listed on the master list were separated into "like" groups (similar to separating dirty clothes for washing—the whites in one pile, the darker colors in one pile, the heavy items in one pile, the delicate in one pile, the heavily soiled in one pile). The leader told the teachers to give a name to each group or category and, beside each name, to list the numbers in front of the student needs on the master list that fit in that category. Teachers were reminded that a student need may fit in more than one category. Almost everyone had to stand or move closer to the master list.

After about 15 minutes, the leader, using a clean piece of chart paper, asked for a volunteer to share one of his or her categories. The volunteer called out "Reading: 2, 4, 5, 7, 10, 11, 12, 13, 16."

The leader asked if anyone else had that same category and had additional numbers to add. Several teachers raised their hands, and the leader called on each, adding numbers, until there was general satisfaction among the faculty. The leader also asked if individuals had the same category but had given it a different name. If so, synonyms should be written for the category name. *The leader very wisely took all responses and did not evaluate any as right or wrong.* (Don't waste time debating opinions!)

The leader asked for a volunteer to share another category. One teacher called out "Writing: 2, 3, 7, 9, 11, 12."

The leader repeated the process, adding categories, until there was general satisfaction that the categories listed represented the student needs.

Before prioritizing, the leader told the teachers that the reason for prioritizing is to establish the number of choices teachers will have when organizing the study groups.

The leader then asked everyone to list the categories on a piece of paper and to put a "1" after the category they felt is the #1 student need at the school. The leader continued until the top three were identified. (This leader said "three" because of the size of the school. She could have said "five" or any other number. In large schools, the faculty may not want to prioritize so that teachers have a wide range of choices.)

A discussion followed around the question: Is the # 1 need so great that it must be addressed by everyone before the other needs can be addressed? The consensus was "No." Due to new state standards, the faculty felt that reading, writing, and mathematics needed to be addressed. The study groups then formed around those three categories.

Note: If the answer had been "Yes," the leader would have done what the leader did in Example 4 at the end of this section.

Example 2:
Using Strategy 2 for Completing Step 2
and Step 3 on the DMC

A whole faculty began its instruction for implementing WFSGs 2 days prior to the students arriving for the beginning of school. The whole faculty in the PK-6 school met for 2 days. The faculty did not have a focus team because arrangements had been made for the whole faculty to participate in the 2-day training at the school. The size of the faculty and the time of the year made that arrangement feasible. The faculty included 11 regular classroom teachers, 6 teaching assistants, 9 support specialists, the librarian, the counselor, and the principal. Also present were two parents and three district-level staff developers. Carlene Murphy was the leader of the institute. As the leader, Murphy did exactly what a focus team would have done in leading the faculty through the DMC in making decisions about what study groups would do and how study groups would be organized.

During the first day, the faculty learned about the functions and procedures of WFSGs, as well as the research that supports collaborative work in schools. This is what a focus team would have done at an orientation session with the whole faculty. On the second day of the training, the faculty participated in Steps 1 through 4 of the DMC. If the school had had a focus team, the team would have done the orientation during a 1- or 2-hour session. On another day, probably a week or so later, the team would have led the faculty through the DMC.

To make the decisions about what study groups would do and how the study groups would be organized, every faculty member was given a folder that contained the following:

- Early Literacy Assessment, Grades K-2

- Iowa Tests of Basic Skills, Grade 3

- Massachusetts Comprehensive Assessment System, Grade 4

- California Achievement Tests, Grade 5

The teachers began the day in a large meeting room where the faculty was given a general overview of the decision-making process. The faculty was given a handout that had on it how the faculty was to be divided into three groups. Each group had about 10 teachers in the group, and each group represented a cross section of the faculty. For example, in one group, there were 4 classroom teachers, 2 paraprofessionals, 3 support specialists, and 1 parent. Each group was assigned to a classroom. On the handout, written instructions told the groups what to do. Also on the handout was a reminder that the student needs to be identified were to be needs that teachers could address through how they teach and what they teach.

The directions given to the three subgroups were to do the following activities in a 2-hour block of time:

1. Review the student data.

2. Discuss the data, with the primary teachers explaining the information on the Early Literacy Assessment and sharing how they use the information to plan

their instruction, and the intermediate and upper-grade teachers explaining the Iowa tests, the Massachusetts system, and the California tests and how they use the test data to make decisions about their students.

3. After the analysis and discussion (30 minutes), as individuals, write at least five specific student needs on the "Stating Specific Student Needs After Analyzing the Data" form.

4. Giving individuals 10 or 15 minutes to finish, a recorder lists on chart paper the needs that individuals have identified as the individuals call out the needs. The group will have one list. Discussions may occur during the making of the composite list, stressing the data that validate the needs. Some needs may need to be assigned to an administrator or a committee.

5. *Categorize the specific student needs.*

6. *Prioritize the categories.*

7. Return to the central meeting room with the charts that display the group's work.

The groups worked from 10:00 a.m. to noon. At noon, the charts were given to the principal, and the teachers went to lunch. They were to report back to the large meeting room at 1:00. In the meantime, the principal had the information on the three charts entered into a computer, printed, and copied for each teacher. When the teachers returned to the general meeting room, they were given a copy of the work from the three groups. The work of the three groups was very similar and repetitious, which was expected because all three had the same data. The results from each group were as follows:

Group 1

Students need to

1. Be more skillful in expressive writing

2. Write across the curriculum

3. Spend more time with science curriculum

4. Increase independent reading in and outside the classroom

5. Increase reading comprehension across the curriculum

6. Interpret data

7. Develop oral expression skills

8. Increase critical thinking skills

9. Increase vocabulary

10. Increase ability to respond to open-ended questions (oral/written)

11. Improve basic math skills

Category	Number of Student Need	Priority
Reading	1, 2, 4, 5, 6, 7, 8, 9, 10	2
Writing	1, 2, 8, 10	3
Science	3, 5, 6, 7, 8, 9, 10	4
Math	2, 5, 6, 7, 8, 9, 11	1

Group 2

Students need to

1. Develop and improve on writing skills

2. Improve writing across the curriculum

3. Improve reading with greater comprehension

4. Improve math skills, both computation and conceptualization

5. Improve use of portfolio assessment

6. Develop proficiency in handwriting skills

7. Gain competency in gross motor skills

8. Improve use of technology

9. Improve subject area vocabulary

10. Develop oral presentation skills

11. Develop visual perception functions

Category	Number of Student Need	Priority
Communication	1-11	1
Math	1-11	2
Science	1-11	3

Group 3

Students need to

1. Become proficient readers

2. Improve writing skills and mechanics

3. Improve listening skills

4. Write across the curriculum

5. Demonstrate study skills (maps, charts, graphs, reference materials)

6. Improve writing skills
   - Content (all content areas)
   - Organization and mechanics

7. Comprehend what they read in all content areas

8. Improve early literacy skills

9. Improve spelling

10. Exhibit uniform writing standards

11. Increase vocabulary in all content areas

12. Follow instructions

13. Use computers in all content areas

14. Increase independent reading

15. Demonstrate knowledge of social studies concepts

16. Make oral presentations

17. Increase skill in computation, problem solving, and geometry in Grades K-6

Category	Number of Student Need	Priority
Math	1, 3, 4, 5, 7, 8, 11, 12, 13, 16, 17	3
Writing	1, 2, 3, 4, 6, 8, 10, 12, 13	1
Reading	1, 2, 3, 4, 5, 7, 8, 11, 13, 14, 15, 17	2
Science	1, 3, 4, 5, 7, 11, 12, 13, 16	4
Social Studies	1, 3, 4, 5, 7, 11, 12, 14, 15, 16	5

Each group presented its work to the whole faculty. After viewing all the information, the faculty concluded that the study groups would focus on four categories of student needs: Reading, Writing, Math, and Science. Each faculty member could choose one of the four. The faculty also agreed that because most of the needs fit into any of the four categories, all groups would be basically addressing the same needs but through different content.

Every faculty member was given a blank SGAP form. Each member was asked to make a personal choice: Which of the four categories would you choose to address in a study group? On the blank form, as the leader led the faculty through each step, individuals wrote

- Their category of choice

- The specific student needs in that category (going back to the brainstormed lists) they would want to address in a study group

- What they would want to do, when the study group meets, to address those specific student needs

At each table, each faculty member shared what he or she had written on the SGAP form. During the next 15 minutes, the study groups were formed. The leader asked those individuals who had chosen "Reading" as the category they wanted to address in a study group to stand; 13 individuals stood. The leader asked those 13 people to go to one area of the room. The leader did the same with "Writing," and 11 individuals stood. When "Math" was called out, 4 faculty members stood, and 3 stood to indicate their interest in "Science." The "Reading" group was asked to subdivide into three groups. They did this after a brief discussion, with 5 in one group (Reading Group 1), 4 in another group (Reading Group 2), and 4 in the third reading group (Reading Group 3). The "Writing" group formed one group of 5 people (Writing Group 1) and one group of 6 (Writing Group 2). There was one Math study group and one Science study group.

The possible dates and times for study groups to meet had already been determined by the faculty. The institute leader asked the seven newly formed study groups to do the following by the end of the second meeting of the study groups:

- Establish group norms.

- Establish the leadership rotation schedule.

- Establish the exact meeting schedule for the school year, totaling 20 hours.

- Share the individual SGAPs and reach consensus on one action plan to represent the group's proposed work.

Example 3:
Using Strategy 3 for Completing Step 2
and Step 3 on the DMC

A high school faculty of about 100 met during a staff development day when the students were not present. Previously, the faculty had attended an orientation to WFSGs led by the school's focus team. The orientation was held on the afternoon of an early release day in September. The orientation included a general overview of the meaning and functions of the WFSG approach and the procedural guidelines. The previous spring the faculty had voted to implement WFSGs in the fall. The focus team attended a 3-day training institute in August and then spent time planning for the orientation in September and today's meeting.

The study groups were to meet twice a month. In accordance with the union contract, the teachers may stay 2 hours a month beyond the school day. Traditionally, that has been used for two faculty meetings, on the first and third Tuesdays. The district had approved a plan for students to be released 2 hours early on the second Tuesday of each month. Study groups would meet during the 2 hours of early release on the second Tuesday, and the principal would give up the faculty meeting on the third Tuesday, scheduling the second meeting for the study groups on the fourth Tuesday. In this way, the study groups would meet for a total of 3 hours on 2 days a month.

For today's meeting, the focus team divided the faculty into four groups that would meet in four different classrooms, with about 25 teachers in each group. The focus team paired themselves so that two focus team members would be in each classroom to meet with the 25 teachers in that room. The teachers were given a sheet of paper that told them in which group they were and in which classroom they would meet. The focus team had deliberately mixed the groups so that all departments were represented in each of the four groups. In each of the classrooms, the focus team members had arranged chairs around five tables. On the tables were copies of the school improvement plan, chart paper, and pens. In each room, in a box, was a collection of data from a variety of sources.

As the faculty began its work, there were 25 teachers in four classrooms, and in each classroom, there was five small groups at tables. Two focus team members were the leaders in each of the classrooms. The groups were given *1 hour* to complete the work. After 1 hour, there was a 15-minute break, and after the break, everyone reported back to the library (they were dismissed at 9:15, due back at 10:30).

In each classroom, the teachers had been told that they could sit at any table, if no other person from their department was already at the table. On each wall in the classrooms was a large poster that had the parameters for identifying student needs:

- The need can be evidenced in student work.

- The need can be addressed by how and what teachers teach.

- The need can be met, meaning the specific need will no longer exist as it does now. Teachers have direct control over or influence on terminating the need.

On the walls of the classrooms were the directions for what the subgroups of the faculty were to do. The focus team member assigned to each room went over the directions that each subfaculty group (the 25 teachers in a classroom) was to follow:

1. Review the school improvement plan.

2. Review other data in the folders on each table.

3. Have a general discussion about the data as each piece of information is being reviewed.

4. *After about 30 minutes,* each person is to use the "Stating Specific Student Needs After Analyzing Data" form and write the student needs that can be addressed through instruction and are within the given parameters.

5. *After about 10 minutes,* individuals at each table are to share their lists and combine the student needs, making one list on chart paper that represents all the individuals at the table.

6. *After 15 minutes,* each table reports. After all the tables have shared, *one list* will represent all the individuals in the room.

7. *DO NOT CATEGORIZE the composite list of student needs.*

8. The focus team member will take the one list representing the 25 people in the room to the general meeting area.

After the work was done, the classroom groups were dismissed and reminded to report to the library in 15 minutes.

During the break, the focus team members met. One member of the focus team entered the four lists of student needs in a laptop computer. The four lists were printed on one sheet of paper exactly like the lists on the chart paper so that each group would recognize its list and see that nothing had been changed. After the list was printed, a focus team member used a pen to renumber the student needs so that the student needs were numbered sequentially. For example, the first list ended with #9, so #1 on the second list was changed to #10. The list was copied for each faculty member and distributed when the teachers returned to the library:

Group 1

Students need to

1. Follow written instructions

2. Locate information using a variety of resources

3. Identify stated cause-effect

4. Students will use five-step process in writing persuasive and expository papers

5. Have more writing opportunity in all curriculum areas

6. Be responsible for assigned work

7. Use real-life application in math

8. Identify work-related skills

9. Transition more successfully from elementary to middle to high school

Group 2

Students need to

10. Demonstrate responsibility for assigned tasks

11. Be successful 9th graders

12. Write for an audience or purpose

13. Improve reading comprehension and math skills

14. Be more successful at solving word problems

15. Proofread and edit work

16. Increase vocabulary

Group 3

Students need to

17. Increase reading skills

18. Increase leisure reading time

19. Use technology across the curriculum

20. Demonstrate competency in the five-step writing process

21. Develop portfolios and exhibitions

22. Develop study skills

23. Develop career plan and goals

24. Demonstrate understanding of math concepts

25. Communicate mastered content through a variety of performance assessments

26. Apply reading skills in the content areas

27. Know what is expected for success in the "real" world

Group 4

Students need to

28. Demonstrate proper usage of correct grammar and punctuation in all curriculum areas

29. Identify Web sites that support the curriculum

30. Acquire second-language proficiency

31. Increase reading comprehension skills

32. Increase readiness for college in the basic skill areas of reading, writing, and math

33. Improve and develop study skills

34. Master the basic skills to pass standardized tests

35. Focus on career goals to prepare for the workforce

The teachers were asked to review the printed list of all the student needs listed by the four subgroups of the faculty. The renumbering was explained. The teachers were asked to use the space at the bottom of the paper to put all the student needs into categories or like groups, using the numbers in front of the student needs, and to give each category or group a name. Because teachers were sitting at tables, the teachers were told to first do the categorizing as individuals, to share their work, and to reach consensus on the categories and the needs placed in each category.

After about 20 minutes, a focus team member went to the overhead projector and asked for a volunteer to call out one set of numbers and the name given to the set. The first category was Reading. After the numbers and name were written on a transparency, the leader asked if anyone else had that category and had additional numbers. Some did, and those numbers were added. The leader asked if a table group had used the same numbers but given the category a different name. The process was continued until no one else had another category to suggest.

Name of Category	*Number of Student Need*
1. Reading	1, 2, 3, 14, 15, 16, 17, 18, 19, 27, 31, 32, 33, 35
2. Writing	4, 5, 13, 16, 21, 29, 31, 33, 35
3. Math	1, 8, 15, 17, 25, 33, 35
4. Assessment	22, 26
5. Technology	20
6. Career, School-to-Work	6, 9, 11, 16, 22, 24, 28, 29, 36
7. Study Skills	6, 11, 16, 17, 23, 34
8. 9th Grade, Transition	10, 11, 12, 17, 23

The faculty was asked to prioritize the categories. After some discussion, the faculty did not want to prioritize. They wanted to leave all the categories as options.

Blank action plans were distributed. The teachers were asked to select one of the eight categories they would want to pursue in a study group and to write that category at the top of the action plan. They were then asked to refer to the list of student needs within that category and select 2 or 3 of the needs they would like to target in a study group, writing those needs on the action plan. Next, the teachers were asked to write the actions they would want to take when their study group met. The teachers were given copies of Figure 6.2 (List of Student Needs) and Figure 6.4 (What Teachers Do When Study Groups Meet) from Chapter 6 in the WFSG textbook.

Members of the focus team walked around the library as the teachers were working, answering questions and making suggestions to teachers.

A focus team member called out the name of a category and the teachers who had selected that category were told to go to a specific classroom. Each category was handled in the same way. For example, all the teachers who chose Reading went to Room 206. A focus team member went to each of the designated rooms to serve as facilitator for the teachers in that room.

After all the teachers were in one of the eight rooms (eight categories, eight rooms), the teachers in each room shared what they had written on the action plan. The facilitator in each room told the teachers to form groups with from 3 to 6 members. The teachers could do this in any way they wanted. Once a group formed, the names were written on a sheet of paper, the papers were given to the facilitators, and the groups were official study groups.

The following Tuesday was to be the first study group meetings. Prior to Tuesday, the teachers received a list indicating the members of all the groups and each group's assigned place to meet for the first meeting. The teachers were also given instructions as to what was to be accomplished at the first meeting.

Example 4:
Using Strategy 4 for Completing Step 2
and Step 3 on the DMC

An elementary school (Grades PreK-5) with 40 faculty members contracted with a consultant (Carlene Murphy) to get WFSGs started at the school. On part of a staff development day in late September, Murphy conducted a 2-hour orientation, sharing the purposes, research base, and procedural guidelines. On a day in mid-October, the consultant returned to lead the faculty through the DMC. On this day, substitutes were hired to cover the classes of every classroom teacher. The teachers met in a large faculty meeting room at the school, and lunch was served. The teachers were warned by the principal not to go near their classrooms, or they may never return to the meeting. Amazingly, everything went great—no emergencies in the classrooms. Even the principal managed to stay in the room most of the day. The school had a grant to cover the cost of the substitutes.

Prior to the meeting, the principal had prepared folders that contained all the standardized test data from all the grades and other information that she thought would be helpful in making decisions about what the study groups would do and how the groups would be organized. Tables had been arranged so that at least one teacher from each grade level was at each table. A folder was on each table containing the student data. The teachers were given a written set of instructions and told that they would have an hour and a half to complete the assignment. The instructions were as follows:

1. Distribute the items in the folder among those at the table, making sure that everyone has at least one item to study.

2. Allow time for each person to study his or her assignment.

3. Have a general discussion about all of the items, asking questions and stating implications.

4. At the end of 45 minutes, the consultant will signal that all the table groups should be ready for each person to write the instructional needs that are evident in the item that person was assigned.

5. After everyone at the table has written down the student needs they see in the data, the table group is to combine individual lists onto chart paper. Make sure that if a need is questioned by another table group, you can point to the evidence. (All the tables have the same data.)

6. After the lists are complete, tape each table's list to the wall.

The consultant had the seven lists from the seven tables put side by side on one wall. After the lists were up, the consultant led a debriefing of the activity. What were you surprised about? What were the disagreements? What were the areas of immediate agreement? How did you feel about the data from other grade levels? Were you comfortable with the data? What did you learn about your colleagues? The activity and the debriefing took a full 2 hours.

The consultant went to the chart that seemed to be the most comprehensive. She said that it would be the master list. The teachers were asked to look at the other six lists and see if there were needs on those lists not on the master list. Several needs were added. There were discussions about whether or not several of the other needs were instructional. After there was clear consensus that the master list was acceptable to everyone, the consultant asked the teachers to put all the needs on the master list into groups or categories. This was to be done first as individuals, then as a table.

As the table groups worked, there was a lot of frustration expressed with the categorizing. The teachers felt that most, if not all, of the needs were in the area of reading. *After a general discussion, the faculty decided that reading was obviously a schoolwide need, the #1 priority, and should be the focus of all the study groups.*

Because Reading would be the category that all study groups would address, the faculty wanted to do an analysis of the reading needs.

The consultant then asked the table groups to use the master list and any information in the folders to put the reading needs into *reading categories*. This created a very interesting discussion about how reading is taught at the school. Several teachers left the room to go get their teacher's manuals. The teachers did finally reach a general agreement. The reading categories were as follows:

- Vocabulary
- Word identification
- Comprehension strategies
- Classroom management of the reading program

In previous discussions, the one concern that kept coming to the surface was the lack of consistency across the grades in how skills are taught and the vocabulary that teachers use to teach the same skill. The teachers raised several questions:

1. Should all the study groups target all four reading categories?
2. If so, would all the study groups move along at the same rate with the same category? Meaning, would all the study groups begin with vocabulary and focus on vocabulary for 2 months, then word recognition for 2 months, then comprehension for 2 months, ending with management?
3. How often should everyone meet together to share the work?

The teachers want to *survey* everyone to find out in which of the four reading categories teachers feel less confident. Four teachers volunteered to develop the survey and it was to be distributed as soon as possible. Also, the reading specialist for the district would be contacted for assistance.

Because each study group would decide when it would meet and there would be no common time for all groups to meet, it seemed like time would be the variable for forming study groups. Who wanted to meet before school, after school, during school? Teachers would log the hours for comp time on staff development days later in the school year. Also, on every Wednesday, teachers stayed 1 hour later for faculty meetings. The principal has said that she would only use two Wednesdays a month for faculty meetings. The teachers agreed to meet in study groups for 4 hours a month. It was up to each study group to determine the dates and times. Each study group would put that group's schedule in its first log.

The principal announced that at the faculty meeting the following week the results of the survey would be shared and study groups formed. Everyone was asked to be thinking about what would best meet the needs of their students.

A survey similar to the one the committee developed follows on the next page.

Reading Survey for WFSGs

This is a two-part survey.

Part 1: Circle the number that indicates your comfort level of *understanding* the concept or skill listed (4 = *most comfortable*).

Part 2: Number the concepts in order of *priority* in each major category to implement in all classrooms (1 = *most important*). Use only 1, 2, or 3.

	Understanding	*Priority*
Vocabulary Strategies		
Am I comfortable with		
Contextual analysis as a way to use vocabulary words in all areas (i.e., social studies, science)?	4 3 2 1	_____
Content-specific vocabulary, including MSPAP vocabulary, in all aspects of instruction?	4 3 2 1	_____
Semantic analysis to develop word meaning?	4 3 2 1	_____
Word Identification		
Am I comfortable with		
My list of sight words for my grade level?	4 3 2 1	_____
Using sight words in the classroom in a meaningful ways and not just with flash cards (i.e., identifying in LEA stories, word boxes)?	4 3 2 1	_____
Teaching phonics?	4 3 2 1	_____
Teaching the CTBS skills involving structural analysis (i.e., root words, prefixes, suffixes, syllabication)?	4 3 2 1	_____
Comprehension Strategies		
Am I comfortable with		
Questioning skills?	4 3 2 1	_____
Reciprocal teaching?	4 3 2 1	_____
Response logs?	4 3 2 1	_____
Semantic feature analysis?	4 3 2 1	_____
Visualization?	4 3 2 1	_____
Comprehension 8?	4 3 2 1	_____
QAR?	4 3 2 1	_____
Classroom Management Skills		
Am I comfortable with		
My students' independent skills?	4 3 2 1	_____
Implementing the scope and sequence in my grade?	4 3 2 1	_____
Grade-level standards of assessment of mastery of skills?	4 3 2 1	_____

Resource F

Team Training Activities

The activities on the following pages may be used during a WFSG institute (initial training for a school team).

The activities are also options for focus teams to use with their faculties.

At least a few of the activities are appropriate for individual study groups to do.

Study Group Action Plans: Option 1

1. At each table, number off 1 to 5. This is home base.

2. Regroup table membership so that each table has 5 people with the same number (for example, tables with 5 #1s, 5 #2s, etc.) These table groups become the "expert" groups.

3. The tables with #1s will analyze Action Plans 1, 5, and 9. The tables with #2s will analyze Action Plans 2, 6, and 10. The tables with #3s will analyze Action Plans 3, 7, and 11. The tables with #4s will analyze Action Plans 4, 8, and 12. The tables with #5s will analyze Action Plans 13, 14, and 15.

4. "Expert" groups should

   a. Focus on one plan at a time.

   b. Read the plan.

   c. Discuss each element of the plan.

   d. Determine what individuals think are that plan's strong points.

   e. Determine if it is clear that there will be student work for the study group to examine.

   f. Determine what questions individuals would ask the study group.

   g. Repeat b through f for another assigned plan.

   Time: About 10 minutes per plan (30 minutes)

5. Everyone return to their home bases and share specific information about their assigned plans.

6. Each person shares the one action plan that impressed him or her the most.

   Time: About 5 minutes per person (25 minutes)

   Total time for activity: 1 hour

Study Group Action Plans: Option 2

1. Form pairs. It does not matter if the two are from the same school or not.

2. Turn to Resource B: Sample Study Group Action Plans

3. Each pair selects a SGAP in Resource B that the pair thinks will best meet the needs of their students.

4. Each pair is to take *15 minutes* to plan how they will convince another pair that the action plan they have chosen is *the* best action plan for students at their school. Each pair is to prepare arguments to persuade the other pair that the selected action plan is the best one. What documentation (real or imagined) of student need can each bring to the other's attention? Pairs may use visuals or any presentation technique that would advance their argument. The arguments may be based on fact or fiction.

5. Pairs pair up. Pairs are to present their arguments as if they are from the same school, whether they actually are or not.

6. Each pair has *10 minutes* or less to persuade the other pair that their action plan will get the best results (20 minutes total).

7. After the pairs have presented to each other, each pair writes what impressed them about the other pair's presentation (5 minutes).

8. Each pair takes no more than *5 minutes* to share their impressions of the other pair's arguments (10 minutes total).

Total time for activity: 1 hour

Study Group Action Plans: Option 3

1. Review all the action plans in Resource B.

2. In groups of 5, number off from 1 to 5.

3. 1s: Take "Mathematics"

   2s: Take "Project-Based Learning"

   3s: Take "Assessment"

   4s: Take "Problem Solving"

   5s: Take "Connecting and Integrating Learning"

4. For your assigned plan,

   a. Highlight the student needs that are listed that you believe the students at _____ (your school) have.

   b. Add to the list any needs in this category that are not on the list that you believe students at _____ (your school) have.

   c. Highlight the actions the group will take that you think would be meaningful to you if you were in this group.

   d. Add to the list any actions not on the list that you would want added to the list if you were in this group.

   e. Add resources that you know about that this group could have used and were not listed.

   f. Highlight the student performance goals that you think are realistic and could be achieved at _____ (your school). In any empty space, tell why.

   Time for doing steps a through f: 15 minutes

5. After everyone has finished doing steps a through f, beginning with #1, share your responses for the plan you examined. It is important that everyone at the table looks at the plan that is being discussed! After the examiner of a plan is finished sharing his or her responses, individuals at the table may express their agreement or disagreement.

   Time for doing Step 5: 10 minutes per plan

6. Debrief activity.

   Total time: 50 minutes

Study Group Action Plans:
Option 4

1. Form groups of 4 or 5 at tables and pretend that you are a study group.

2. Using a piece of chart paper, reproduce the format of the study group action plan (in other words, draw the action plan format on chart paper).

3. Using the chart paper, develop an action plan for the group. Write the following on the chart paper:

   - Names of group members
   - General category
   - Essential or guiding questions
   - Specific student needs
   - Actions the study group will take when it meets
   - Resources the group will use
   - Student performance goals

4. All groups tape action plans to walls.

   Steps 1 through 4: 1 hour

5. One person from each group will stand by their action plan taped to the wall.

6. At the signal from the activity leader, all participants will read the plans on the walls and may ask the person representing a plan any question pertaining to that plan. Individuals may want to take notes in case they want to have more in-depth conversations with designers of plans later.

   Steps 4 through 6: 20 minutes

7. At the signal from the activity leader, all participants will return to their home base (the foursome that developed a plan). Participants will *not* have time to read all the action plans.

8. The persons representing the groups will share questions that participants asked about the action plans.

   Steps 7 and 8: 15 minutes

9. All participants take 10 minutes to write the following:

   - Five things that are clearer about how to write a study group action plan.
   - What you will do as a team member to communicate the importance of and the process for writing strong action plans.

   Total time: 2 hours

Chapter 1:
Paying Attention to What Has Been Learned

Of the four lessons,

■ Which was the most expected? Why?

■ Which was the most surprising? Why?

■ Which gives the most direction for making current decisions? How?

■ Three years from now, which of the four lessons do you think you will be telling others that they should pay more attention to?

School teams have 40 minutes to discuss each item—about 10 minutes per bulleted item.

Chapter 2:
Knowing Why

- ■ Why initiate WFSGs?

- ■ Why create turbulence? (Schools do have climates.)

- ■ Why change the way the school does business?

There are at least seven reasons. (See functions of WFSGs in Chapter 2.)

Form groups of 5, and count off, 1 through 5.

Number 1s take the first function, 2s take the second function, 3s take the third function, 4s take the fifth function, and 5s take the seventh function.

Select a timekeeper.

- ■ Person #1 takes 2 minutes to tell "What struck me the most about Function 1 was _____" (everyone turns to the narrative in the book). Moving around the table, each person takes no more than 1 minute to respond to what #1 said.

   Total time: 10 minutes

- ■ Person #2 takes 2 minutes to tell "What struck me the most about Function 2 was _____" (everyone turns to the narrative in the book). Moving around the table, each person takes no more than 1 minute to respond to what #2 said.

   Total time: 10 minutes

- ■ Person #3 takes 2 minutes to tell "What struck me most about Function 3 was _____." Continue as with #1 and #2.

- ■ Person #4 takes 2 minutes to tell "What struck me most about Function 5 was _____." Continue . . .

- ■ Person #5 takes 2 minutes to tell "What struck me most about Function 7 was _____." Continue . . .

Debrief.

   Total time for activity: 50 minutes

Chapter 3:
The Context of Schools

This is a focus team activity.

- Review the 13 factors that seem to have the greatest impact on the contextual features of a school.

- Write a narrative description of the context of your school. (Allow 15 minutes.)

- Form pairs.

- Read the narratives to each other.

- Do not discuss the narratives until both individuals have read what they wrote.

- Discuss the similarities in the narratives.

Chapter 3:
Five Confusing Questions
Near the End of Chapter 3

In groups, use the following questions to have a general discussion around the five questions near the end of Chapter 3.

- Why does the wording seem awkward?

- Why might the questions make teachers feel defensive?

- Why might the questions be objectionable?

- Do you think the questions make sense within the context of this book?

- Do you think these questions give too much power to the student voice?

- How would you defend the wording of the questions?

Chapter 4:
Working With the Louis, Marks, and
Kruse Quote That Opens Chapter 4

■ Write in your own words what the quote means to you in relation to the purpose of WFSGs.

■ Pair up with someone in the room that you do not know and read to each other what you wrote.

Chapter 4:
Research Connects Collaboration
to Student Learning

As a focus team, complete the following chart:

Researcher(s)	Pages	Would you use with faculty? If so, how?	Summarize (Use the back of the page if more room is needed for your answers.)
Louis, Marks, and Kruse	Top 43 Top 46		
Louis, Marks, and Kruse	Bottom 43 Top 44		
Rosenholtz	Bottom 44 Top 45		
McLaughlin and Talbert	Middle and Bottom 45		
Darling-Hammond and McLaughlin	Bottom 27 Bottom 46		
Saphier and King	Middle 46		
Murphy et al.	166-171		
HSTW	42		

Chapter 4:
The Instructional Council

Refer to Figure 4.1 in Chapter 4; then,

1. Form groups of 6.

2. Within the group of 6, form three pairs. If possible, work with someone with whom you have not worked.

3. Pair 1: Read the three sets of minutes from Jackson Elementary School's Instructional Council in Resource D.

4. Pair 2: Read minutes from Maynard Elementary School's Instructional Council in Resource D.

5. Pair 3: Read minutes from Webster County Elementary School's Instructional Council in Resource D.

6. Each pair writes four statements that express how the school's instructional council fulfilled the functions of an instructional or representative council.

7. Share your impressions.

Time limit: 1 hour

Chapter 5:
Process or Procedural Guidelines

Select a partner, and complete the following chart. (You may leave the room and find a quiet place to work. Spend about 5 minutes on each guideline.)

Guideline	Key Points in the Rationale (Chapter 5)	What I Like About the Guideline
1		
2		
3		
4		
5		
6		
7		
8		
9		
10		
11		

Guideline	Key Points in the Rationale (Chapter 5)	What I Like About the Guideline
12		
13		
14		
15		

Which of the 15 guidelines do you think will be the most troublesome at your school? _____ Why?

How do you plan to keep it from being a problem?

Time for activity: Completing chart—1 hour, 15 minutes

When the school's focus team reconvenes, discuss how the key points may be used to orient the whole faculty on the procedural guidelines.

Resource C:
Study Group Logs

1. Read the Keeseville Elementary School set of logs.

2. In the space below, write five statements about how the study group functioned.

3. What was the most outstanding aspect of the work of the group?

4. What one question would you ask the group if you could meet with it today?

5. Do you think the student performance goals were adequate? Why?

6. What do you think was the value in the principal's participation in the study group's work?

7. Do you think the principal's input had an impact on the quality of the group's work?

Chapter 5:
Strategies Study Groups Use

(End of Chapter 5 and Resource C)

Strategy	Used (Y or N)	Log Number	How could the strategy have been used more effectively?
Sharing observations of students			
Comentoring			
Examining student work			
Listening to students			
Videotaping			
Shadowing students			
Action research			
Case-based learning			
Curriculum development			
Immersion			
Portfolios			
Protocols			
Training			

Chapter 6:
Resources Study Groups Use

(Resource C)

	On a scale of 0 (none) to 10 (high), to what degree of effectiveness did the study group in Resource C use the following resources?	Give each type of resource a number from 1 to 13, using a number only once, to indicate how usable the team feels the resource is.
Student work		
Teachers' manuals		
Students' textbooks and materials		
Other teachers not in study group		
District leaders, staff		
Books		
Articles		
Internet		
Computer software		
Public television		
Workshops, conferences		
Businesses, community agencies, higher education		
Students (current and past)		
Instructional program materials		
District or state sources		

The Final Word

On pages _____ to _____, what passage struck you the most?

■ First choice:
Page # _____, paragraph # _____
Why?

■ Second choice:
Page # _____, paragraph # _____
Why?

Directions for the activity:

1. One person begins by giving the page number and paragraph number and reads what struck them the most.

2. The others turn to the page and follow the reading.

3. The person tells why that passage struck them the most *in less than 3 minutes.*

4. Proceeding around the table, each person briefly responds—*in less than 1 minute each.*

5. The person that began has the final word—*no more than 1 minute* to respond to what has been said by the others.

6. The person next to the one who started now shares what struck them the most . . .

7. Repeat the cycle.

Caution: At no time is there any dialogue between or among individuals at the table!

If there are 5 people at the table, one round will take 8 minutes.

Adapted from ATLAS Communities material.

Differences in Types of Meetings

Part 1: Information to consider:

Department meetings, grade-level meetings, and team meetings *generally*

- Focus on managerial or logistical directives, issues, or needs
- Have an agenda that is usually determined by directives from the school, district, or state
- Are leader driven by a grade chair, team leader, or department chair
- Have a "talk to" format, meaning the leader presents information, and the participants primarily respond to topics generated by the leader

Study group meetings *generally*

- Are aimed at the professional development of the members
- Focus on "what I need to do and learn in order to change how I teach and what I teach"
- Have an action plan that is the group's agenda
- Are driven by member needs that are generated from student needs
- Rotate leaders-facilitators, with the leader-facilitator not being responsible for the content of the meeting or what the group will do
- Recognize all members as being equal in status and responsibility

Part 2: As a table group, do the following:

Suppose it has been decided at your school that the study groups will be organized so that teachers that teach the same grade level or are in the same department will be in the same study groups. Pretend this is true. A teacher or someone with recent experience with department or grade-level meetings is to use his or her experience as the basis for the table group doing the following four steps:

1. Discuss an agenda at a grade-level meeting (elementary), team meeting (middle school), or department meeting (middle or high school).

2. Write that agenda so others at the table can see it.

3. Discuss how the agenda for a study group would be different.

4. Determine what items would be deleted from the department or grade-level meeting agenda to make it an agenda for a study group. Now, add items to the agenda that would give it more of a "what I teach and how I teach" flavor.

Recommended Reading

Branson, R. (1987). Why the schools can't improve: The upper limit hypothesis. *Journal of Instructional Development, 10*(l), 7-12.

Calhoun, E. (1993). Action research: Three approaches. *Educational Leadership, 5*(2), 62-65.

Charles, L., Clark, R., Roudebush, J., Budnick, S., Brown, M., & Turner, P. (1995). Study groups in practice. *Journal of Staff Development, 16*(3), 49-53.

Joyce, B. (1991). The doors to school improvement. *Educational Leadership, 48* (8), 59-62.

Joyce, B. (1992). Cooperative learning and staff development: Teaching the method with the method. *Cooperative Learning, 12*(2), 10-13.

Joyce, B., & Murphy, C. (1990). Epilogue. In B. R. Joyce (Ed.), *ASCD yearbook: Changing school culture through staff development.* Alexandria, VA: Association for Supervision and Curriculum Development.

Joyce, B., Wolf, J., & Calhoun, E. (1993). *The self-renewing school.* Alexandria, VA: Association for Supervision and Curriculum Development.

LaBonte, K., Leighty, C., Mills, S., & True, M. (1993). Whole faculty study groups: Building the capacity of change through interagency collaboration. *Journal of Staff Development, 16*(3), 45-47.

Little, J. (1981). *School success and staff development in urban desegregated schools: A summary of recently published research.* Boulder, CO: Center for Action Research.

Little, J. (1990). The persistence of privacy: Autonomy and initiative in teachers' professional relations. *Teachers College Record, 9*(4), 509-536.

Louis, K. S., & Miles, M. (1990). *Improving the urban high school: What works and why.* New York: Teachers College Press.

Lucas, B. (2000). *Whole-faculty study groups' impact on the professional community of schools.* Unpublished dissertation, University of Minnesota.

Miles, M., & Huberman, M. (1981). *Innovation up close: A field study.* Andover, MA: The Network.

Murphy, C. (1990, October 16). *The role of the central office staff in restructuring.* Keynote address at the International Society for Educational Planning, Atlanta, GA.

Murphy, C. (1991). The development of a training cadre. *Journal of Staff Development, 12*(3), 21-24.

Murphy, C. (1993). Long-range planning for individual and organizational development. *Journal of Staff Development, 14*(2), 2-4.

Murphy, C. (1997). Finding time for faculties to study together. *Journal of Staff Development, 18*(3), 29-32.

Murphy, J., Murphy, C., Joyce, B., & Showers, B. (1988). The Richmond County School improvement program: Preparation and initial phase. *Journal of Staff Development, 9*(2), 36-41.

National Staff Development Council. (1994). Powerful designs. *Journal of Staff Development, 20*(3), 22-55.

Raywid, M. (1993). Finding time for collaboration. *Education Leadership, 51*(l), 30-34.

Showers, B., Murphy, C., & Joyce, B. (1996). The River City program: Staff development becomes school improvement. In B. R. Joyce & E. Calhoun (Eds.), *Learning experiences in school renewal: An exploration of five successful programs.* Eugene: University of Oregon Press. (ERIC Document Reproduction Service No. EA 026696)

Wieman, H. (1990). *Man's ultimate commitment.* Denton, TX: Foundation for the Philosophy of Creativity.

References

Barnett, C. (1999). Cases. *The Journal of Staff Development, 20*(30), 26-27.

Blanchard, K., Carew, D., & Parisi-Carew, E. (2000). *The one-minute manager builds high performance teams.* Escondido, CA: Blanchard Training and Development.

Birmbaum, R. (1988). *How colleges work: The cybernetics of academic organization and leadership.* San Francisco: Jossey-Bass.

Blythe, T. (1998). *The teaching for understanding handbook.* San Francisco: Jossey-Bass.

Bradley, A. (1993, March 31). By asking teachers about "context" of work, center moves to the cutting edge of research. *Education Week, 12*(27), 6.

Bryk, A., Rollow, S., & Pinnel, G. (1996). Urban school development: Literacy as a lever for change. *Educational Policy, 10*(2), 172-201.

Conner, D. (1993). *Managing at the speed of change.* New York: Villard.

Covey, S. (1990). *The Seven habits of highly effective people.* New York: Fireside.

Cronan-Hillix, T., Gensheimer, L., Cronan-Hillix, W. A., Cronan-Hillix, W. S., & Davidson, W. S. (1986). Students' views of mentoring in psychology graduate training. *Teaching of Psychology, 13,* 123-127.

Darling-Hammond, L., & McLaughlin, M. (1995, April). Policies that support professional development in an era of reform. *Phi Delta Kappan, 76,* 597-604.

Fullan, M., & Steigelbauer, S. (1991). *The new meaning of educational change.* New York: Teachers College Press.

Glasglow, N. (1997). *New curriculum for new times: A guide to student-centered, problem-based learning.* Thousand Oaks, CA: Corwin.

Graff, L. (1996). Committed to growth through a learning organization. *On the horizon, 4*(2), 5-6.

Guralnik, D. B. (Ed.). (1986). *Webster's new world dictionary* (2nd ed.). New York: Prentice Hall.

Guskey, T. (1990). Integrating innovations. *Educational Leadership, 47*(5), 11-15.

Hord, S., Rutherford, W., Huling-Austin, L., & Hall, G. (1987). *Taking charge of change.* Alexandria, VA: Association for Supervision and Curriculum Development.

Joyce, B., & Calhoun, E. (1996). *Learning experiences in school renewal: An exploration of five successful programs.* Eugene: University of Oregon Press. (ERIC Document Reproduction Service No. EA 026 696)

Joyce, B., Murphy, C., Showers, B., & Murphy, J. (1989). School renewal as cultural change. *Educational Leadership, 47*(3), 70-77.

Joyce, B., & Showers, B. (1982). The coaching of teaching. *Educational Leadership, 40*(1), 4-16.

Joyce, B., & Showers, B. (1995). *Student achievement through staff development.* New York: Longman.

Joyce, B., & Weil, M. (1999). *Models of teaching.* Boston: Allyn & Bacon.

Joyce, B., Weil, M., & Showers, B. (1992). *Models of teaching.* Boston: Allyn & Bacon.

Kaufman, R., Herman, J., & Watters, K. (1996). *Educational planning: Strategic, tactical and operational.* Lancaster, PA: Technomic.

Killion, J. (1999). Journaling. *Journal of Staff Development, 20*(3), 36-37.

Levine, D., & Eubanks, E. (1989). *Site-based management: Engine for reform or pipe dream?* Manuscript submitted for publication.

Lewis, A. (1997, May/June). A new consensus emerges on the characteristics of good professional development. *The Harvard Letter, 13*(3), 3.

Lick, D. W. (1998). Proactive comentoring relationships: Enhancing effectiveness through synergy. In C. A. Mullen & D. W. Lick (Eds.), *New directions in mentoring: Creating a culture of synergy.* London: Falmer.

Lick, D. W. (Winter 2000). Whole-faculty study groups: Facilitating mentoring for school-wide change. *Theory Into Practice, 39*(1), 43-48.

Little, J. (1993, Summer). Teachers' professional development in a climate of educational reform. *Educational Evaluation and Policy Analysis,* pp. 129-151.

Loucks-Horsley, S. (1998a). *Ideas that work: Mathematics professional development.* Washington, DC: Eisenhower National Clearinghouse for Mathematics and Science Education and USDE.

Loucks-Horsley, S. (1998b, Summer). *JSD* forum. *Journal of Staff Development* [pamphlet].

Louis, K. S., Marks, K., & Kruse, S. (1996). Teachers professional community in restructuring schools. *American Research Journal, 33*(4), 757-798.

Louis, K. S., Kruse, S. D., & Marks, H. M. (1996). Schoolwide professional community. In F. M. Newmann (Ed.), *Authentic achievement: Restructuring schools for intellectual quality.* San Francisco: Jossey-Bass.

Lucas, B. A. (2000). *Whole-faculty study groups' impact on the professional community of schools.* Unpublished doctoral dissertation, University of Minnesota.

Mullen, C. A., & Lick, D. W. (1999). *New directions in mentoring: Creating a culture of synergy.* London: Falmer.

Murphy, C. (1991a, October). Changing organizational culture through administrative study groups. *Newsletter of the National Staff Development Council,* 1, 4.

Murphy, C. U. (1991b). Lessons from a journey into change. *Educational Leadership, 48*(8), 63-67.

Journal of Staff Development, 16(3), 37-44.

Murphy, C. U. (1992). Study groups foster school-wide learning. *Educational Leadership, 50*(3), 71-74.

Murphy, C. U. (1995). Whole-faculty study groups: Doing the seemingly undoable. Murphy, C. U., & Lick, D. W. (1998). *Whole-faculty study groups: A powerful way to change schools and enhance learning.* Thousand Oaks: Corwin.

Murphy, C. U. (1999). Study groups. *Journal of Staff Development, 20*(3), 49-51.

National Staff Development Council (2000). *Standards for staff development.* Oxford, OH. Author.

Newmann, G., & Wehlage, G. (1995). *Successful school restructuring: A report to the public and educators by the center on organization and restructuring of schools.* Madison: Wisconsin Center for Education Research.

Richardson, J. (1996, October). School culture: A key to improved student learning. *The School Team Innovator,* I, 4.

Riley, P. (1994). *The winner within.* Encino, CA: Berkeley Books.

Rosenholtz, S. (1989). *Teacher's workplace: The social organization of schools.* New York: Longman.

Saphier, J., & Gower, R. (1997). *The skillful teacher: Building your teaching skills.* Acton, MA: Research for Better Teaching.

Saphier, J., & King, M. (1985, March). Good seeds grow in strong cultures. *Educational Leadership, 42*(6), 67-74.

Sarason, S. B. (1990). *The predictable failure of educational reform: Can we change schools before it's too late?* San Francisco: Jossey-Bass.

Schlechty, P. C. (1993). On the frontier of school reform with trailbrazers, pioneers, and settlers. *Journal of Staff Development, 14*(4), 46-51.

Sebring, P., & Bryk, A. (2000). School leadership and the bottom line in Chicago. *Phi Delta Kappan, 81,* 440-443.

Senge, P. (1990). *The fifth discipline: The art and practice of the learning organization.* New York: Currency.

Shelofsky, B. S. (1999, July). *A summative report on the whole-faculty study group process at the Jackson Elementary School, 1995-99.* Greeley, CO: Jackson Elementary School.

Sizer, T., & Sizer, N. (1999). *The students are watching: Schools and the moral contract.* Boston: Beacon.

Southern Regional Education Board. (1998). *High schools that work: 1998 secondary school teacher survey.* Atlanta, GA: Author.

Vanzant, L. (1980). *Achievement motivation, sex-role acceptance, and mentor relationships of professional females.* Unpublished doctoral dissertation, East Texas State University.

Webster's new world dictionary (2nd ed.). (1986). New York: Prentice Hall.

Zemelman, S., Daniels, H., & Hyde, A. (1993). *Best practice: New standards for teaching and learning in America's schools.* Portsmouth, NH: Heinemann.

Index

CORWIN
PRESS